The New
Cold-Molded
Boatbuilding

The New Cold-Molded Boatbuilding

From Lofting to Launching

Reuel B. Parker

International Marine
Camden, Maine

First Hardbound Printing 1990
First McGraw-Hill Paperback Edition 1992

Published by International Marine
10 9 8 7 6 5

Library of Congress Cataloging-in-Publication Number 89-24572

Questions regarding the content of this book should be addressed to:

International Marine
P.O. Box 220
Camden, ME 04843

Questions regarding the ordering of this book should be addressed to:

The McGraw-Hill Companies
Customer Service Department
P.O. Box 547
Blacklick, OH 43004
Retail customers: 1-800-262-4729
Bookstores: 1-800-722-4726

Printed by Arcata Graphics, Fairfield, PA
Design by Faith Hague/Watermark Design, Rockport, Maine
Imagesetting by High Resolution, Camden, Maine
Production by Janet Robbins
Edited by J.R. Babb, Heidi Brugger, Jonathan Eaton, Laura Tringali
Photo page 272 by Sandy Wolf
Photo page 292 top right by Elizabeth Stevens
All other photos by the author

ACKNOWLEDGMENTS

I would like to thank the people who helped, in the lessons of life, make this book possible: my mother, who taught me to write; my dad, who taught me to look at the world with a discerning eye; Ed Pladdys, who taught me about boats and the water; A.J. Dixon, who taught me how small boats are put together; Patrick Cotten, who taught me how big boats are put together; George Loucks, who taught me rigging; Bob Henderson, who taught me how sails are made.

And those who helped in the more immediate sense: Jon Eaton and Jim Babb at International Marine, who guided me gently through the alien experience of being published; Laura Tringali, who patiently edited the jungle of manuscript; and Beth Stevens, who in the last scramble helped me put the whole thing together. Finally, I must thank Faith Hague, Heidi Brugger and Janet Robbins, who took the raw materials and transformed them, through many hours of meticulous work, into the viable tool you now hold in your hands.

Many of the wonderful books which contain invaluable knowledge that shaped my learning about boatbuilding are listed, insofar as I can remember them, at the end of this book.

CONTENTS

INTRODUCTION

It is the purpose of this book to present a pragmatic methodology for laminated wood/epoxy/fabric boat construction to the amateur and low-profile professional who must work with limited time, resources (both material and financial), tools, space and skilled labor. This methodology will consist of design, design adaption, and construction techniques aimed at ultimate hull strength, integrity, durability, simplicity, safety, economy, and low maintenance. The work methods themselves have been developed with the deliberate intention of streamlining construction processes and conserving both labor and materials. I have tried to incorporate the best from all technologies and ages into new and better ways of doing things.

Even with the wonderful artsy-craftsy renaissance of the last 20 years, the wooden boat is an endangered species and may well go the way of the dinosaur. Right at the critical time when the traditional wooden boat was in decline, and before new uses of wood could take over, fiberglass came on the scene and stole the show. As glues, resins, fabrics, and techniques became available to the wooden boatbuilding industry, the old guard resisted and the new guard was in infancy. Only a handful of artisans developed the new wood technologies, hence they developed slowly. Cold-molded boatbuilding was limited to an adventurous few, usually seeking ways to create one-off custom boats without the elaborate molds typically demanded in fiberglass construction. As the high strength-to-weight ratios of cold-molding became known, the ball shifted into the court of the multihull and light/ultralight racing groups, where it developed in a somewhat exotic and limited direction. And there it has largely remained. As far as the boatbuilding *industry* is concerned, wooden boats are a long-dead issue. The financially successful Americans and Europeans who make up the vast bulk of the pleasure boat market have neither the time, skill, patience, nor inclination to buy, build, maintain or own a traditional wooden boat. Many of them no longer even have time to sail, which is one major contributing factor to the demise of the big-sailboat market.

We now live in a time of dwindling resources, changing values, and a highly accelerated pace involving transportation, communication, and lifestyles. More knowledge and information are available to us than ever before. We have greater opportunities, yet we have less time to do the things we want to do. Every freedom has its price. We need ways to enjoy our maritime environment that are sensible, practical, economical, and that allow our diminishing sense of individuality to remain intact.

There is another consideration. I have a great fear that in the not-too-distant future, all those mass-produced fiberglass boats are going to become embrittled and break up into sharp-edged glass and plastic fragments with an awesome half-life. They can't last forever. While it is true that modern cold-molded boats take advantage of much of the same technology, they also use it to a much smaller degree, and even that can be improved, most notably by eliminating the use of fiberglass cloth. Would you want it in your lungs, skin, and internal organs? Do you want your great-grandchildren to ingest it from the flesh of the seafood they eat in the future? Wouldn't it make more sense to build biodegradable boats? This book humbly presents an alternative.

My personal hope is that humankind will soon find cold-molded wooden boats superior to those built of any other material. The average boat owner is growing sick of the ubiquitous blisters on his fiberglass bottom, and the Environmental Protection Agency has banned the use of tin-based antifouling paints, which are almost vital for steel and aluminum boats.

Many books on boat construction deal only with certain aspects of the project, leaving the amateur to look elsewhere for techniques to finish his boat, or even start it. This can result in mixed technologies or styles, often detracting from the harmony of the finished product. I have no intention of doing this to you. Because I am a long-distance, long-time cruising sailor as well as a shipwright and designer, I have had to repair and maintain vessels, often in obscure places with limited resources. It is, therefore, the honest intention of this book to help the reader through the entire process of finding the right design, organizing his or her life to meet the challenges ahead, building the entire vessel in all aspects, and properly outfitting her for her intended purpose. Because a thorough presentation of these subjects could fill volumes, I will be pretty specific about many things, recommending what I have found to be practical, economical, and complementary to the construction techniques described. In other cases, I will refer the reader to sources I have come to respect over the years. I will try to be as brief and concise as possible. The goal is to build your boat and go sailing—or deliver her to your clients on time, exceeding their expectations.

I, for one, happen to think that wood, used in conjunction with the right resins and fabrics in efficient and sensible ways, can produce the best all-around boats that have ever been available on earth.

Reuel B. Parker
Rockport, Maine, 1988—
Islamorada, Florida, 1989

CHAPTER 1
CONSTRUCTION

A Brief History of Cold-Molding/
A Simplified Method for Cold-Molding

There are as many ways to build boats as there are people building them. Opinions are plentiful, as are prejudices. Keep in mind that there is no one way to do anything. The ways described herein are simply those that I have found to work, and I present them in the spirit that they may work for you, too.

A BRIEF HISTORY OF
COLD-MOLDING

All cold-molded wooden boat hulls, like those built of fiberglass, steel, aluminum, and ferrocement, are of "monocoque" construction. ("Unibody" is an analogous term.) This simply means they comprise one structural unit. There are no individual parts with seams between them that can move or flex independently, as in traditional wooden plank-on-frame hulls. The term "cold-molded" is somewhat ambiguous; it refers indirectly to a nearly obsolete system in which laminates were joined with glue that had to be heated. "Cold-molding" superseded "hot-molding" with the advent of urea-formaldehyde and

plastic-resin glues. The most dramatic and universal application of cold-molding is manufactured plywood. Monocoque structures must possess both tensile (stretch) and compressive (push) strengths in all directions across their inner and outer surfaces to have structural integrity. The presence of both forces in balance provides stiffness and impenetrability.

Cold-molded construction acquires its tensile and compressive strengths from wood fiber. But because tensile strength is mostly unidirectional with the grain, wood must be laminated in different directions. If an adequate glue holds the laminates together, and if the wood is not deformed beyond its natural "spring constant" (which would break its tensile continuity), structures made of two or more multidirectional wood laminates have extremely high strength-to-weight ratios, stiffness and durability. Wood rates very highly in the spring-constant department; trees flex back and forth their whole lives. They suffer very little fatigue—a great deteriorating factor among many other materials.

An example of a long-lasting wooden spring is the longbow, which works even better when laminated.

In boat construction, cold-molding introduced large-scale lamination techniques previously not practical. Three modes of construction first became popular: strip planking, with or without diagonal veneer coverings; laminated diagonal veneers (sometimes with fore-and-aft veneers incorporated); and tortured plywood. In most early cases, all three modes included permanent sawn or laminated frames. Dinghies appeared, made of laminated veneers and no frames, and large powerboats were built having longitudinal stringers with or without frames. The latter were typically double or triple diagonal planked. The Huckins Yacht Corporation pioneered this construction for PT boats during World War II.

Many of the early plywood boats eventually developed chronic problems involving glue delamination and rot, which consequently gave plywood a bad name. I have repaired numerous early cold-molded powerboats and sailboats which suffered from such problems; the glues that were used typically failed in planking-to-keel joints, and paint systems (especially inside) were inadequate for preventing rot. The hull exteriors often held up well enough, but suffered from weathering, erosion, abrasion and worm damage.

Epoxy revolutionized cold-molding because it is waterproof and has controlled pot-life and gap-filling properties. It also allowed the lamination of a wide range of materials—including protective fabrics, metals, and plastics—previously unavailable for cold-molding. Polyester resin, which is so compatible with glass fiber, is nearly useless as a universal glue, and will not adequately bond fabric to wood without mechanical fasteners. The early cold-molded hulls either had no fabric covering or had fiberglass bonded with polyester resin, which eventually delaminated from the wood. The advent of epoxy permitted a long-lasting sheathing of fabric, initially fiberglass, over vulnerable wood surfaces, as well as the use of fabrics for structural purposes (providing tensile strength) over joints.

Wood is vulnerable to infestation by plants and animals, and that's where epoxy and fabric really come to the rescue. Coverings of epoxy-impregnated fabrics are ideal for exteriors and abrasion areas, and coatings of reduced (thinned) epoxy resins followed by epoxy or polyurethane paint systems protect interior surfaces. Epoxy-impregnated fabrics also greatly limit the effects of erosion, corrosion and hydrostasis, the latter being the big problem for fiberglass and ferrocement. Water gets into the pores of the material by osmosis, then expands to form blisters on the exterior surface. Cold-molded wood does not seem to suffer from this phenomenon, even when skin punctures allow water to soak into the wood for long periods of time. I suspect this has to do with its softness; fiberglass and ferrocement are hard, brittle materials in which there is no place for expanding water to go but to push the surface out. Incidentally, I have seen cracks in fiberglass applied over wood, and I believe this is because fiberglass is too brittle and inflexible to yield as the wood absorbs moisture and expands. I have never, however, seen this happen to epoxy-impregnated Xynole-polyester fabric applied over wood. The greater flexibility and higher tensile strength of polyester cloth seem dramatically more compatible with wood.

Epoxy used as glue holds wood laminates together in ways previously not possible. Its gap-filling and grain-sealing properties allow joining of end-grain to side-grain, and decrease the problems previously caused by voids in joints.

To take advantage of the high strength-to-weight ratio and durability of wood/epoxy/fabric lamination, most hulls are built with relatively thin planking over frames, longitudinal stringers, or both. Perhaps the most extreme application has been to ultralight racing multihulls. The resultant hull is incredibly strong when confronted with evenly distributed forces such as water pressure, but markedly vulnerable to "point-load-impact" forces such as those generated by collision with a rock, coral head, dock, another boat, a partially submerged oil drum or log. When this technology is applied to ballasted monohulls, the weight of the finished boat increases its inertia (mass times velocity) well beyond that of an unballasted multihull, altering dramatically the forces that can be placed upon the hull planking in the moment of impact.

Many beautiful boats have been created with these and similar methods. But I feel that too much attention has been paid to light weight and speed at the expense of safety and longevity.

Much of cold-molded technology in the last decade has centered around the West System, or Wood Epoxy Saturation Technique. This system frequently involves construction of the kind just described, including strip-planked hulls with or without diagonal outer laminates. But can epoxy really saturate wood? Even greatly reduced (thinned) epoxy will soak into side-grain softwoods only a tiny fraction of an inch. In order to achieve "wood epoxy saturation," the wood veneers have to be 1/16 inch thick or less. To achieve a hull thickness of any consequence, many layers are needed, with fantastic quantities of epoxy resin. The expense is dramatic, both in materials and labor. Because of this, the methods described in this book will make no attempt at wood epoxy saturation! Instead, we will use epoxy resins as glues, fillers, bedding compounds, fillets, sealants, and in

paint systems. As developers of the West System, however, the Gougeon Brothers must be credited with making great pioneering strides in epoxy technology. Their products are excellent, though expensive and hyperallergenic. Because of the latter problems, I confine my use of West products primarily to the lamination of high-performance spars.

A SIMPLIFIED METHOD FOR COLD-MOLDING

The American Bureau of Shipping, which promulgates guidelines for hull construction (among other things), favors thicker-skin/lower-frequency-of-frame construction techniques. A thicker, stronger skin (planking layer) is safer because it is harder to puncture. One might think this gain in strength will be paid for with added weight, but this is not necessarily true in all cases, as we shall see. When it is true, the increase may be small or confined to the bottom of the hull where its effect is least deleterious to the performance of the vessel.

The construction methods shown in this book will produce frameless hulls with relatively thick bottom sections incorporating watertight bulkheads. The component layers of the skin will also be thicker, fewer and simpler than those generally used in cold-molded construction, saving much time and money (veneers are very expensive, as are milling and epoxy resin). Hulls built with these methods frequently cost less than half in materials and labor what similar hulls built with other cold-molded or traditional methods cost. And it is my sincere belief that they are generally stronger and safer. Figure 1-1 shows a cutaway drawing of a frameless cold-molded boat of the type discussed throughout this book.

The elimination of frames and stringers in the hull provides an increase in the internal

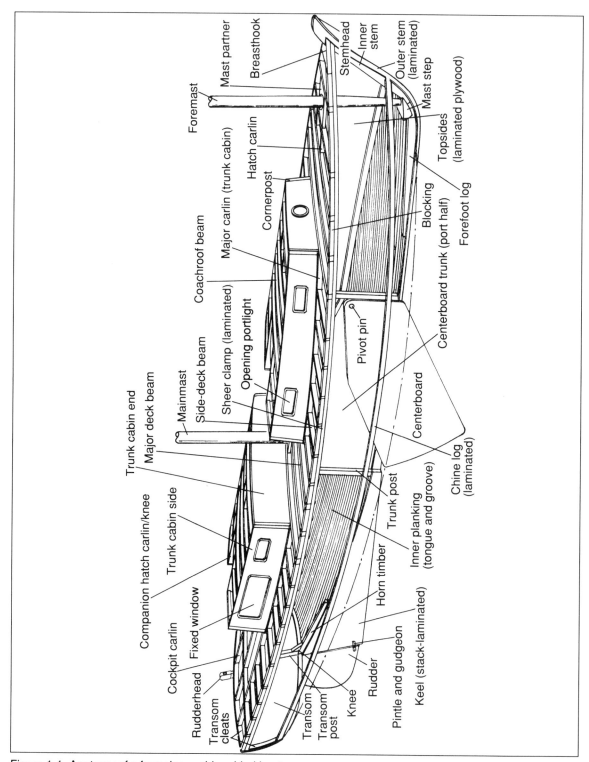

Figure 1-1. Anatomy of a frameless cold-molded boat.

volume of the vessel and greatly simplifies interior construction; cabinetry won't have to be fitted around internal structure, and there will be no need for ceiling planking. The absence of frames, stringers, ceiling planking and, frequently, floors largely compensates for the weight of a thicker skin. The simpler, cleaner hull interior also greatly reduces the costs of finishing and maintenance. Dirt, insects, molds, fungi and rodents will find an inhospitable environment in these vessels.

The methods to be described can be adapted to most hull shapes of any size, with a lower practical limit of around 20 feet depending on hull shape. The cornerstone is the use of tongue-and-groove lumber, either soft or hardwood, available from large lumber suppliers, as a primary self-fairing hull layer. The tongue-and-groove material, usually around 3/4 inch thick by $3\frac{1}{4}$ inches wide,

is laid fore and aft over temporary mold frames established at the hull design stations (the hulls are built upside down). In the case of "canoe"-type hull forms, a centerplank, wide in the middle and tapered at both ends with tongues routed on each edge, is laid first. In the case of V-bottomed or wineglass hulls, the tongue-and-groove planking overlaps a backbone structure. Two diagonal planking layers, each laid in a different direction, are then laminated with epoxy over the tongue-and-groove layer and fastened with staples, screws or small nails. The diagonal planks may be either solid lumber or plywood, of a thickness to conform to the maximum curve of the bilge without breaking. I prefer plywood because it is less expensive, more readily available, and has higher grain-crushing, impact, and abrasion resistance. It also can be bought in a wide range of thick-

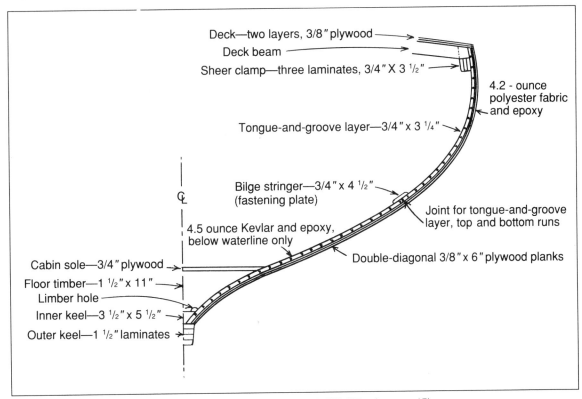

Figure 1-2. Midship section for a cold-molded wineglass hull (PILOT schooner 45).

nesses; plank stock almost always has to be resawn and/or surfaced to the required dimension with attendant expense and waste. A final advantage of plywood is that, in the unlikely event of worm infestation, damage is almost always limited to the outermost plywood veneer. Worms rarely cross a glue joint.

Topsides that are flat may be planked with full sheets of plywood in one or more layers (I usually use two) joined to the bottom at a "chine log." This reduces weight above the waterline, where it counts, and further simplifies construction. The longitudinal chine log is employed to provide fastening surfaces and reinforce the bottom-to-topsides joint. The various planking layers are overlapped and interlocked at the chine log to create an extremely strong integral joint. Conic sections may be incorporated in the ends of such vessels' topsides to develop curved flare or tumblehome. This involves forcing or "torturing" the plywood into a curve at the stem or stern.

In hulls with compound curves in their topsides, the multiple lamination of diagonal layers over tongue-and-groove planking is carried right to the sheer, or even higher to form integral bulwarks. In these cases, there may still be a longitudinal stringer at the turn of the bilge, acting like a fore-and-aft butt block or fastening plate for the tongue-and-groove layer. Because there is no spiling or tapering of planks in this construction method, the natural shape of any hull forces more and more edge curve in the tongue-and-groove planking as more planks are added. To prevent this from getting too severe, planking is applied from the keel toward the turn of the bilge as well as from the sheer toward the turn of the bilge. The two operations meet and join at the longitudinal bilge stringer (see Fig. 1-2). Boats are often planked this way in the Caribbean islands, where a lack of power tools prohibits plank tapering.

It is my opinion that much of the lamina-tion employed in cold-molded construction is unnecessary. The attraction of lamination has often exceeded its benefit; I have seen nearly straight stems laminated—these could have been made from solid stock at tremendous savings in material and labor. Wherever possible I will indicate the use of solid timber to save time and money. Lamination should be reserved for areas where extra strength, a real need to save weight, or difficult shapes require its use. Inner stems, forefoot logs, keel planks or backbones, sternposts, horn timbers, transom posts, deck beams and carlins on all but very large craft should be made of solid timber. Outer stems and keels, on the other hand, are usually laminated.

Sheer clamps are laminated in place in slots cut into the mold frames before planking. Deck beams are fastened over the clamps before the deck is laid. Decks are generally made from two layers of plywood, with seams staggered over sawn beams. An alternative method for insulated decks with internal beams is also described, as is a method for teak overlay.

I strongly recommend that all external wood above and below the water be covered with an epoxy-saturated fabric and painted with epoxy or polyurethane paint systems. The exceptions are bulwarks, trunk cabin sides, coamings, rubrails, trim, and spars, which can be oiled, varnished or painted. Remember that epoxy deteriorates in sunlight and must be protected, and that unsealed wood will expand and contract much more than sealed wood, placing unequal forces on glue joints. I have found that 4.2-ounce Xynole-polyester cloth is the best covering fabric for cold-molded construction because of its high tensile strength, peel strength, flexibility, compatibility with wood and epoxy, fast wet-out, abrasion resistance, user friendliness and low toxicity—it does not itch!

Hull interiors need not be fabric covered in

most cases (exceptions will be explained later), but are sanded, sealed thoroughly with reduced (thinned) epoxy resin and painted with epoxy paints. If you want to see the wood grain, apply clear polyurethane over the epoxy resin.

I will also present a highly simplified technique I refer to as Quick-molded construction—a double-diagonal planking method appropriate for simple sharpie and batteau (V-bottom) hulls. The hull bottoms are slightly arced for strength, and the planking is laid up over several stringers, some of which are later removed. This is an extremely fast, strong, simple, and economical construction. I have designed a series of boats (the TERRA-PIN schooners) that can be built with the method; these may be seen in Appendix A.

CHAPTER 2
DESIGNS

Choosing a Design/ Adapting Designs/
The EXUMA Series

CHOOSING A DESIGN

No one boat can do everything, so the prospective boatbuilder must carefully establish his or her intentions for it. Considerations should include: size; accommodations; general use (yacht, charter, cargo, fishing, etc.); area of use (coastal, local, island, shoal water, deep water, protected water, world cruising, etc.); cost; maintenance; crew size; performance (sail and power); bridge clearance heights; and so on. All boats are compromises—you must choose and balance the qualities you most need.

A major consideration is the scope of the project. A 40-foot sailboat built as economically and simply as possible can still cost $30,000 in materials and require over 5,000 hours of efficient labor. A 40-foot powerboat will often cost much more. If you are working alone on weekends, evenings, holidays and vacations, this project could take years. To build a boat of any size, you will need help and/or lots of time. An alternative is to buy a bare hull and finish the boat; but keep in mind that a hull represents only about 15

percent of a finished boat; the decks, trunk cabins and cockpit are another 10 percent.

Whether you are interested in building large boats for personal use or as a profession, I suggest that you thoroughly research the subject by reading, talking to experienced boatbuilders and studying boats by simply looking at them and sailing on them; then try some repair work. For some of us boatbuilding's promise of romance is emphatically worth the challenge of eternal hard, dirty work; for others it is not. First-timers will benefit from choosing a simple, practical design, well within their means and skills.

My designs, several of which are included in Appendix A, are intended for the construction methods described herein.

ADAPTING DESIGNS

Most hulls can be built using the methods in this book. (Possible exceptions are hulls with extremely hard bilges or other small-radius sections, and hulls with duck-tail sterns.) Existing designs can be adapted with-

Table 2-A. Finished Hull Thicknesses for Light to Moderate Displacement Hulls.

Length on Deck (feet)	Bottom Thickness (inches)	Topsides Thickness (inches)	Deck Thickness (inches)
25	1	1/2	1/2
35	1 1/8	5/8	1/2
45	1 1/2	3/4	5/8
55	2	1	3/4
65	2 1/2	1 1/4	7/8
75	3	1 1/2	1

scantlings (component dimensions), planking-layer thickness, location of chine log, use of plywood in topsides and type of backbone structure:

1. *Length and Displacement* These two factors determine finished hull thickness. In general, light to moderate displacement hulls will have the bottom and plywood topsides (if utilized) dimensions that appear in Table 2-A. Moderate to heavy displacement hulls should be 1/8 inch to 3/4 inch thicker in bottom dimensions, varying with size increase. Plywood topsides should be the same to 1/4 inch thicker; decks, the same to 1/8 inch thicker.

2. *Hull Shape* Hulls with flat midship bottom sections, such as those in the EXUMA series, may incorporate a "centerplank" in place of an inner keel. These canoe-shaped hulls can take advantage of their flat inner hulls by eliminating inner keel, floors and cabin sole—you can walk right

out changing their exterior shapes or by making slight modifications, usually in the topsides or keel-garboard area, to simplify construction. This can be done by me, other marine architects, by the builder or perhaps by yourself. Any adaptations, however, should be checked by someone with some engineering abilities to confirm scantling strengths and proportions.

The following considerations determine

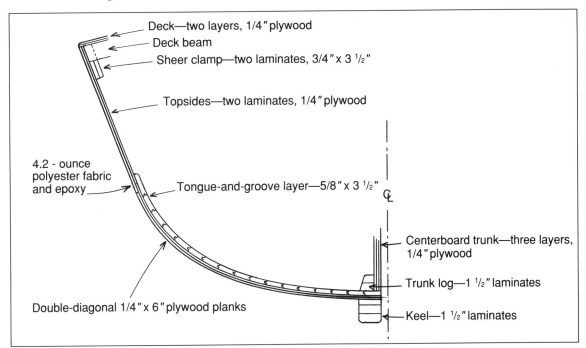

Deck—two layers, 1/4" plywood

Deck beam

Sheer clamp—two laminates, 3/4" x 3 1/2"

Topsides—two laminates, 1/4" plywood

4.2 - ounce polyester fabric and epoxy

Tongue-and-groove layer—5/8" x 3 1/2"

₵

Centerboard trunk—three layers, 1/4" plywood

Trunk log—1 1/2" laminates

Double-diagonal 1/4" x 6" plywood planks

Keel—1 1/2" laminates

Figure 2-1. Midship section for an EXUMA 36.

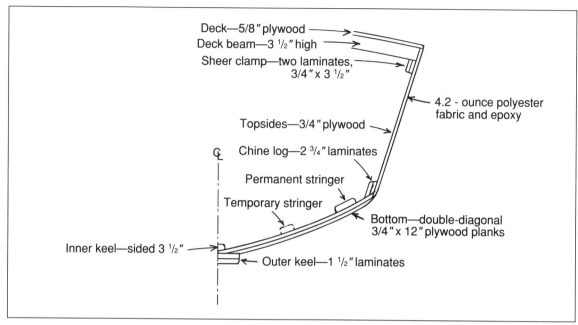

Deck—5/8″ plywood
Deck beam—3 ½″ high
Sheer clamp—two laminates, 3/4″ x 3 ½″
4.2 - ounce polyester fabric and epoxy
Topsides—3/4″ plywood
Chine log—2 ¾″ laminates
Permanent stringer
Temporary stringer
Bottom—double-diagonal 3/4″ x 12″ plywood planks
Inner keel—sided 3 ½″
Outer keel—1 ½″ laminates

Figure 2-2. Bow section of a TERRAPIN 45.

on the inside of the hull. This gives more space, lower cabin heights, and saves the expense of the above-named components.

Hulls with flat topsides sections can make use of plywood sheets joined to the bottom planking by chine log or bilge stringer to simplify construction. Figure 2-1 shows an EXUMA 36 midship section employing plywood topsides in a canoe-type hull. The vessel is a cold-molded adaption of Commodore Ralph Munroe's famous *Presto*, popular in the late 19th century.

Wineglass hulls—or planked, full-keel hulls, incorporate an inner keel, to which the planking layers is attached. An outer keel is laminated in place over the inner keel and planking edges, forming the vessel's finished backbone. In Chapter 1, Figure 1-2 shows the midship section of a PILOT schooner 45, adapted from Isaac Webb's early 19th century yacht *Dream*.

V-bottom hulls, such as batteaux, simple powerboats and skipjacks, can make use of the simplified Quick-molded system, as can flat-bottom sharpies, scows, and barges. A moderate arc (athwartships curve) is incorporated into the bottoms of these vessels to provide greater strength. Figure 2-2 shows a bow section of a TERRAPIN 45 schooner. This batteau-type hull was popular in the Chesapeake Bay throughout the 19th century.

3. *Other Factors* When employing plywood sheets in topsides planking, the thickness must increase with the vertical span.

Very long distances between structural bulkheads would indicate heavier bottom sections. Deck thickness is determined by frequency of beams. In the preceding examples, deck beam spacing ranges from 12 inches on center to 24 inches on center and beam size varies from 1½ inch by 2 inches to 5½ inches by 3¾ inches for Douglas fir or yellow pine.

Light and ultralight displacement hulls require more careful consideration. While the

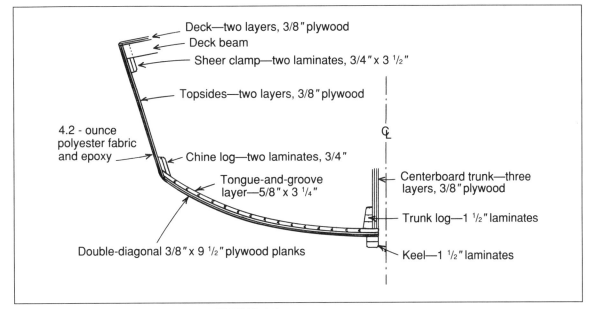

Figure 2-3. Midship section for *Teresa* (EXUMA 44).

penalties for underbuilding and overbuilding are different, both practices should be avoided. Very light displacement vessels should be designed or adapted by a qualified marine architect or engineer.

The dimensions in Table 2-A are for total lumber and/or plywood layers. Finished dimensions are increased by epoxy glue joints and outer cloth/epoxy skin as much as 1/4 inch. Obviously scantling determination demands care and attention; the table gives approximations only.

THE EXUMA SERIES

As previously stated, cold-molded vessels with a flat hull section amidships (canoe-type hulls) need have no internal structure at all (other than chine logs and sheer clamps), allowing the inner surface of the hull to become the cabin sole. This creates a tremendous savings in material and labor, as well as increased headroom and lower trunk cabin and decks. The result is less windage and topside weight, and a lower center of gravity,

all of which improve the performance of the vessel. Vessels with ballasted fin keels make use of shallow floor timbers above their keels; floors can be wood, aluminum, galvanized steel or preferably stainless steel, and are covered by a small cabin sole in their vicinity only. The floors are determined by hull size, weight, shape and keel-induced forces. They will distribute loads imposed by keel and ballast over a larger area of the hull planking. The EXUMA Series hulls, including *Sarah* (EXUMA 52) and *Teresa* (EXUMA 44) which are used as construction examples throughout this book, have large centerboards with integral ballast boxes on either side (see Fig. 2-3). Each EXUMA hull also incorporates several watertight bulkheads for strength, safety and privacy.

Where the inside of the hull serves as the cabin sole, engine compartments are totally isolated from living compartments by watertight bulkheads, and have their own bilge and pump system. Cold-molded hulls don't leak (the shaft stuffing box is isolated in the engine compartment); the only water entering cabins is from spray or rain. In conventional vessels, this water is minimal and typically is sponged up. In these unconventional hulls, large, manual bilge pumps have as their sump the lowest portion of each hull compartment. Bilge pumps are for emergency only, and their strum boxes should be placed high enough to easily slip a sponge under them. The concept of "no bilges" seems alarming at first, but after three years of living with it on board *Teresa*, I will now have it no other way!

CHAPTER 3
GETTING ORGANIZED

Time and Money/ Workspace/ Tools/ Materials/
Safety and Approach

Building a boat is a unique experience. Boat anatomy is so organic that building a boat gives us the eerie sense of creating an animal—indeed, boats seem to be alive. I believe the experience of boatbuilding is separate from other endeavors; unique work creates unique demands.

As with any endeavor, good organization makes work go more smoothly, efficiently and economically. People who plan to build a boat, especially a large cruising sailboat on which they intend to live and travel, should "center" themselves—organize their personal life and align their attitudes and goals for success insofar as possible. The importance of positive attitudes toward the project and work in general cannot be overemphasized.

Potential builders first should examine what roles building, owning and using a boat will play in their lives. They should then evaluate their skill levels and resources; the goal is to develop a sense of the quantities and qualities of skills, time, tools, money, help and workspace that the project will re-

quire. Good research is vital—I have listed some helpful books in a "Suggested Reading List" at the end of the book. Have books and magazine articles that contain pertinent information close at hand. Keeping a notebook is very helpful; research and list sources for materials and information, and record your ideas, problems, successes and failures.

TIME AND MONEY

Boats always cost more and take longer than anyone thinks. I would rather give you the most efficient and practical access to a boat that I know of and have you understand what it will demand, than lure you with false figures that will lead to your future souring on the project.

It is important to create a projected schedule of completion and a budget; this is true even for the first-time builder who does not have enough experience to make accurate time and cost estimates. Try to be as realistic as possible, keeping in mind the old axiom that it will cost twice as much and take twice as long! I will explain how much time the different stages of construction take and what they cost, when possible. I have included labor time and materials costs for the EXUMA 44 *Teresa*, which is used as an example throughout the text, in Appendix C.

Keep it simple. Complication seems a natural tendency without human intervention. A great rule to keep in mind is: You can't screw up when you clean up. In the throes of complication and confusion, clean up and reorganize. It can't hurt and it may provide the time you need to calm down, clear your mind, and return to the task successfully.

Following are some examples of labor hours and materials costs for different boat projects. The labor hours are projected for moderately skilled amateurs with some, but not extensive, experience to complete the boat in entirety. The materials costs are approximately 10 percent less than retail prices; amateur builders can obtain discounts by purchasing materials from discount houses, catalogues, boatbuilders' clubs and by talking to the managers of their major sources of lumber and plywood. All figures given are approximations.

12-foot plywood skiff— 60 hours/ $150 materials

20-foot plywood open sharpie—220 hours/ $1,300 materials

28-foot cold-molded cowhorn—1,800 hours/ $8,500 materials

32-foot cold-molded sloop EXUMA 32—2,750 hours/ $18,000 materials

34-foot Quick-molded TERRAPIN schooner—2,500 hours/ $20,000 materials

36-foot cold-molded cutter EXUMA 36— 3,500 hours/ $23,000 materials

40-foot cold-molded cutter BLUE WATER 40—6,000 hours/ $33,000 materials

44-foot cold-molded cat schooner EXUMA 44—5,500 hours/ $30,000 materials

45-foot Quick-molded TERRAPIN schooner—4,500 hours/ $27,000 materials

45-foot cold-molded PILOT schooner 45— 6,500 hours/ $35,000 materials

52-foot cold-molded schooner EXUMA 52— 6,250 hours/ $36,000 materials

WORKSPACE

The construction site must be carefully chosen and organized. I prefer to live where I work; others prefer to isolate their workspace from their residence. Whichever you choose, the site should be close to your home to minimize commuting time, especially if you will work in your spare time. Make sure your lease or rental agreement, zoning laws, neighbors and boat moving plans will all work in harmony with your chosen construction site.

Considerations for the work site should include the following:

• *Shelter*—You will need to prepare an on-site shop area whether you are working outside, in an existing building or intending to construct a temporary building. Most of the boatbuilding books I have read include the author's concept of a temporary building. Because this subject has been covered elsewhere and conditions vary with each project, I will just add a reminder: Provide lots of light, air and space. An example of the temporary buildings I use in the benevolent climate of south Florida is shown in Appendix B.

• *Adequate room*—Work space will quickly become scarce, so it is important to organize your work and storage areas carefully before starting. (You may find yourself changing things from time to time as the project evolves.) The basic site will be divided into spaces for the hull; large tools; hand tools; workbenches; storage for lumber, plywood, hardware, epoxy, paints, solvents, fabric rolls, scrap and trash. Where you station these spaces will affect your working efficiency, so keep relationships between spaces in mind as you set up. Bench tools such as the table saw, planer, jointer, radial arm saw and bandsaw will need working area around them. For example, a planer may need as much as 20 feet on each end when planing mast lumber. Usually it is impractical to always have this much room, so bench tools and surrounding items should be moveable. Doors in the shelter, or removable panels, will be helpful when you need to pass long lengths of lumber across bench tools.

Lumber racks should be strong and away from both extreme moisture and direct sunlight; they can be near the roof if you plan to dry some of your own lumber. Planks should be stored flat, separated with lath, and air circulation should be good. Plywood should be elevated off the ground and likewise stored flat (but without lath); plywood stored vertically may eventually warp.

Paints and solvents ideally should be stored in a metal cabinet or shed away from lumber and other flammables. At the least, store them in a specific part of the shop (or even a separate work area) where there is excellent ventilation, to prevent the accumulation of fumes. Storage could even be outdoors on shelves under a roof. Solvent-soaked rags are a fire hazard; they should be burned, dried out or stored in a tightly-sealed metal container.

Outdoor work areas should be flat and clear of obstructions such as tree roots and rocks. Inside, provide as much light and air as possible—plan the cross-ventilation so that it takes advantage of prevailing winds. A dark, stuffy shop is an unhealthy environment.

Other space considerations are room to turn the hull over, which may involve being able to get a boom truck or small crane next to it, and room to unload and move materials when they are delivered.

- *Electricity and Water*—Check your power tools to find out whether you need a 220-volt line. (Large table saws and air compressors frequently require 220 volts.) Safety is critical—the main panel should be clean, properly wired and grounded. Locate it out of the way of truck and unloading areas, and protect it from weather. Carefully plan the number and location of outlets, so that you don't rely on extension cords, which are inconvenient and hazardous. If you must use them, use heavy-duty industrial-quality cords with a minimum #12 wire size. Starving your tools for electricity (voltage drop due to inadequate wire size, called I.R. drop) will damage tool motors. Circuit breakers or fuses should be the right size, dry and clean.

  While water isn't essential, it's inconvenient to be without it and safer to be with it. The ability to rinse eyes or wounds and flush chemical burns is invaluable. An onsite shower is wonderful; work dirt does not leave the workplace.

- *Time*—Anticipate construction delays and plan so that delays don't scuttle your project. Make sure your lease or rental agreement gives you time to finish your boat. Work in an orderly fashion so that you can easily stabilize your projects and leave them for a time. Numerous incomplete projects in vulnerable stages, scattered around the shop, will be more difficult to leave abruptly than they should be.

- *Access*—Trucks with lumber or other materials need to get into your site, deliver their loads and get out. A trailer or truck will have to load your boat and move it when the time comes, too. Avoid steep sites, blind driveways and sharp turns.

TOOLS

The construction methods described in this book use commonly available materials, particularly lumber, as much as possible. This minimizes millwork and enables the builder to use standard-sized lumber available from local lumberyards. As a result even very large vessels can be built without a planer or jointer, greatly reducing tool expense. You can even get by without a table saw, although this would be inconvenient, particularly in terms of interior cabinet work.

Required Power Tools

To build a medium to large power or sail vessel, you will need the following power tools and accessories:

a right-angle (gear-drive) circular saw with carbide-tipped blades;

two drill motors—one 1/2-inch variable speed reversing and one 3/8-inch;

a large, complete drill index of good quality;

a full set of spade bits;

a set of Fuller counterbore bits from #8 to #16;

several tempered screwdriver bits (slot and Phillips heads) for use in the 1/2-inch drill motor;

various good-quality hole saws ranging in size from $1^1/_8$-inches up to 3 inches (these can be purchased as you need them for installing pipe and through-hull fittings);

a hand-held jig or scroll saw;

a router with 3/8-inch and 1/2-inch quarter-round (bullnose) bits with roller bearings and a 1/2-inch flute bit;

a low-speed body grinder (polisher) with a 7-inch hard rubber pad for discs and an 8-inch soft pad for paper;

an orbital sander (pneumatic jitterbugs are the best);

a 3-inch by 21-inch belt sander (this size is best for working in tight spots or overhead) of the type that you can turn upside down and clamp to a workbench for use as a stationary platform sander;

a $3^1/_2$-inch power plane with two extra sets of blades (you will need them);

Optional, highly desirable power tools include the table saw, bandsaw, planer, jointer and bench grinder with fine and coarse wheels. For an economical, good-quality table saw, I recommend the Rockwell 10-inch contracter's saw with a larger motor than the one supplied (such as a $2^1/_2$ h.p. 220-v Granger) and a carbide-tipped combination blade. A 12-inch bandsaw is about the smallest useful size, and is helpful during interior joinery and trim work. A thickness planer and long-bed jointer are wonderful but expensive. I use a Hitachi combination planer-jointer with drop-down end tables that runs on 120 volts and cuts very smooth surfaces.

An air compressor capable of driving air tools, a staple or nail gun and spray-paint equipment is also very desirable. It will pay for itself many times over in labor savings. In warm climates, epoxy cures so rapidly that a staple or nail gun is essential. The alternative is to have a crew large enough to drive several hundred thousand nails by hand! Air is great for cleanup, too. Air-powered tools stay cool and are often lighter, more powerful, more compact and less expensive than electric tools. They have become a common flea market item and can often be bought cheaply. They and the compressor, however, require more maintenance than electric tools. Beware of buying a compressor that is too small; it is a terrible nuisance if the compressor cannot keep up with a jitterbug sander, dual-axis grinder, or at least a siphon-feed paint-sprayer. A 3 h.p. 220-volt single-phase compressor is just adequate.

A 1/2-inch drill press is a great help, especially if you plan to fabricate a lot of your own hardware.

The following hand tools are essential:

a 20-ounce straight-claw hammer;

a wooden mallet;

a good 16-point crosscut handsaw;

a backsaw;

several different-size screwdrivers (slot and Phillips heads);

pliers and Vise-Grips;

cutters, diagonal and end-nose;

a bevel square;

large and small carpenter's roofing squares;

a sliding-pin contour gauge;

a try square;

an adjustable protractor square;

levels (2-foot, 4-foot and line);

a basic set of wrenches (crescent, box, open end, monkey, sockets and ratchets). I use a cut-off 3/8-inch drive extension as a socket drive in my 1/2-inch drill motor to save time;

channel-lock pliers, medium and large;

two 20-foot by 1-inch tape measures;

soft carpenter's pencils (flat), soft round pencils, felt-tip pens and indelible markers;

a full set of wood chisels (some of these should be expendable since they will be used in wood that may be embedded with fasteners);

a block plane, jack plane and rabbet plane;

several files and rasps, both flat and rounded;

a good collection of putty knives of varying width and thickness;

several matt knives and plenty of blades;

sailmaker's shears, kept sharp and clean;

an 8-inch wallboard-taping knife and stainless-steel tray;

an 18-inch stainless-steel fairing knife with a plastic handle the length of the knife;

strip-rubber Squeegee material of the kind used by the automotive industry;

sturdy 9-inch roller frames, wooden extension handles and plastic paint trays;

bubble rollers (chasers) for eliminating air trapped under fabric during epoxy wet-out;

a sharpening stone (a two-sided synthetic stone used with a very light oil—I buy WD-40 by the gallon—works well; a fairly coarse, soft Arkansas stone is also good; and the new diamond stones are perhaps the best, though very expensive);

a sharpening jig, such as that made by General, with a clamp for chisels and plane blades, and an adjustable roller wheel;

at least four pipe or bar clamps (48 inches);

many assorted C-clamps between 4 inches and 8 inches (smaller ones will rarely be needed);

two or more wooden carpenter's clamps;

a medium-size crowbar and a flat pry bar;

chalk line and box and a roll of stranded nylon twine for layout work;

exhaust fans;

an industrial wet/dry vacuum cleaner.

The last two items are vital to boatbuilding

as far as I am concerned; I would be crippled without them.

Other Required Tools

Other tools include a sturdy bench-mounted vise (many people prefer two—one for machine work and one for wood), several jacks (hydraulic and/or house-type), and paint-spraying equipment suitable for poly-urethanes (external mix/siphon feed). At least two big, sturdy workbenches or tables are essential, as are numerous sawhorses and staging planks. I prefer four to eight horses 24 inches high and 36 inches wide, two to four horses 30 inches high and two horses 36 inches high.

MATERIALS

I recommend obtaining lumber and materials for one project ahead of the one in progress. This prevents delays, allows me to organize materials and helps stabilize lumber moisture content. Ordering materials so they arrive in time for each project, but not so early that they create a storage problem, is a real art. It calls for an accurate materials list and carefully planned storage areas. You will need to research availability of your materials and lead times for delivery. Many times I have been in the situation where the lack of one item shut down a whole work crew.

Wood—In America, the most common lumbers used in construction are Douglas fir, southern yellow pine, hem-fir (hemlock or fir) and spruce. The first two are excellent for all structural members in cold-molded boat construction, but "bright" yellow pine (not pressure treated) is sometimes hard to get and must be ordered. Hem-fir is inferior, but can be used in laminations where strength is not too critical, such as in keel deadwood (the outer or bottom lamination should be

something harder), and rudder and center-board core laminations. Spruce meets requirements for hem-fir end uses and can also be used for internal (hidden) deckbeams for foam-core decks, coach roofs and hatches. Spar-quality spruce is hard to come by; I strongly prefer Douglas fir for all spars, laminated or solid.

Other serviceable softwoods include hackmatack, red and white cedars, and cyprus. Base your choices on local knowledge of the woods indigenous to your region.

Good-quality Douglas fir can be expensive, but it is the all-around best for laminating sheer clamps, chine logs, planking, bulwarks, masts, deck beams, frames, stems and so on. If you use yellow pine for these structures, it must be *untreated* and dry. Pressure-treated wood cannot be used in cold-molded boatbuilding because nothing will stick to it. Large structural members (stem, keel, horn timber, sternpost, floors, carlins and deck beams), will have to be either Douglas fir or yellow pine in most cases. Often, the best way to buy this lumber is to look through the beam stock at one or more lumberyards for pieces that have been in stock long enough to dry out. Don't be afraid of a weathered gray color or drying checks; these are signs that you are seeing dry, stable timber. Do beware rot spoors, warpage and large loose knots. Lumber in large sizes (3 x 10, 3 x 12, 4 x 10, 4 x 12 and 6 x 6) may be of number-two quality and should cost around half the price of number-one clear plank stock (3/4-inch surfaced). Select-structural and clear-heart lumber will rarely be required for anything except mast construction. From timbers, structural members are laid out carefully on both sides (to avoid serious flaws such as cracks or large knots), then cut out from each side with a circular saw. This saves a fortune over laminating the same structures from small stock, and the waste is used in blocking later.

I frequently buy timbers that have severe checks along the heart-line, twists and badly-weathered surfaces for reduced prices because they are not suitable in the construction trade. These timbers are air-dried and have stabilized moisture content, and I re-saw and surface them.

Because the hull materials are laminated and encased in epoxy, standards of allowable wood quality in cold-molded boatbuilding are less rigorous than in traditional wooden boat construction. Hulls, keels, decks and coach roofs are covered with fabric and epoxy outside, and epoxy-sealed and painted inside. Rot-resistance and strength of the wood are still important, but to nowhere near the degree that they used to be. Rot-resistance is of primary concern in cabin trunks and corner posts, masts, mast partners and steps, bitts and their partners and steps, hatches and hatch coamings, and bulwarks. Masts must be carefully made of the best materials available, as explained in Chapter 30.

Hardwoods are largely limited to furniture and trim in cold-molded boats. Exceptions might include rubrails, caps, handrails, deck overlays, belaying pins, bitts, boom and gaff jaws, cleats and chocks. Below decks I particularly like using cherry, English walnut, ash, white oak, red oak, birch and maple. Above deck I use white oak and teak. I find the use of teak below decks an ostentatious extravagance.

Plywood—Plywood in America is virtually always made with Douglas fir and exterior glue. The main considerations are number of laminates, core quality (voids and laps) and face quality. Marine plywood is best but it is very expensive. ACX, which has an inferior core and one bad side, is acceptable for boat construction where the C faces can be laminated together, leaving A faces on both sides of the finished product. Look through stocks of plywood from different mills until you find the best quality you can afford, be it marine or ACX. Yellow pine form-ply (for casting concrete) can be used in building Quick-molded boats, boats with nearly flat hull sections and very large boats; it can also be used for bulkheads. The cement-release coating is compatible with epoxy and epoxy paint, the plywood has two good faces, and it is made with exterior glue. However, it varies in quality and should be chosen carefully. It is available only in 5/8-inch and 3/4-inch thicknesses. The exotic imported plywoods are extremely expensive but usually of excellent quality. The exceptions are some of the inexpensive, imported plywoods, particularly those from South America. Often the wood and lamination quality is excellent, but the glue is not water-resistant.

I personally believe that we are all responsible for the welfare of our planet, and so must pay attention to the sources of our materials, particularly wood. We need to be aware of the disastrous deforestation taking place in South America and Africa, not to mention our own national forests. These trees create the air that we breathe! This global depletion of precious forest resources carries several drastic penalties, and this is why I have come to prefer using woods that are common to America and Canada and are being replaced by active re-forestation programs. One advantage of cold-molded construction is that we don't really need the quality wood that our ancestors found in abundance—second-growth timber is adequate for everything, with the possible exception of masts.

Epoxies—Epoxies vary greatly in quality, utility and cost. Avoid 1-to-1 mix epoxies except for non-critical gluing, filling and glazing. (To achieve 1-to-1 ratios, the hardener must be bulked up in volume, thereby diluting the epoxy and weakening its tensile strength.) You will need large quantities of epoxy to build a boat—drumfuls. Stick with one kind throughout a project; this ensures chemical compatibility and allows you to get used to its properties. Two-to-1 mixes are convenient; mixes using other proportions require special measuring methods. Because heat and moisture are major factors in curing time and quality, different climates require different epoxies. A pot life of at least one-half hour for large batches (one or more quarts) is minimal. But overnight cure is also essential. This will take local research and consultation—the epoxy we use in Florida might never cure in Maine! More information on epoxies may be found in Appendix D. I don't recommend using West epoxy because it is very expensive and many people seem to develop severe allergies to it. In Florida, we have to refrigerate West epoxy to achieve even 10 or 15 minutes of pot life when using their slow catalyst! I occasionally use it in mast lamination where I want maximum glue strength, but other epoxies can serve this purpose as well.

Thixogens are the fillers used to thicken epoxy. These include Cabosil, microballoons, talc, fibers and dry, sifted sawdust. Cabosil is used most often. Because it is hard to sand, it is used for making glues, fillets and fillers that require little sanding. Microballoons are easier to sand but tend to sag if applied too thickly. Talc is great for fairing compound and skim coats (glazing) prior to paint layers. It is also used to thicken paint (including epoxy paint) for high-build priming, but it must be mixed very thoroughly. Chopped fibers (glass, asbestos and polyester) are for glue joints where high tensile strength is required. (Most fibers are toxic and I rarely need them, so I avoid their use.) Sawdust is limited to fillers, especially where a wood color is desired.

Reducers or thinners must be properly matched to specific epoxies and paints; follow manufacturers' recommendations. The generic reducer for most epoxy is half methyl ethyl ketone and half toluol or toluene. This reducer will dissolve uncured epoxy, but must not be used to clean epoxy off skin (see "Safety and Approach" later in this chapter). Other reducers commonly used are mineral spirits (for oil-based paints, varnishes and oils), acetone (multi-purpose), Xylol and Xylene (for vinyl anti-fouling paints) and denatured alcohol.

Fabric—I am a firm believer in covering all major exterior wood surfaces with epoxy-impregnated cloth. The wood surfaces I don't cover are teak deck overlays, caps and sometimes small bulwarks or log rails, some cabin trunks, gaffs, booms, bowsprits, some solid masts, rubrails, handrails, companionway doors, fiferails, pin rails and trim. The fabric I prefer above all others is polyester—especially Xynole-polyester, which is a 4.2-ounce, open-weave cloth, much like a scrim or backing material. It comes in a 60-inch width, and is similar to the Japanese acrylic Dynel. Xynole-polyester conforms to curved surfaces, wets out very quickly, has high peel strength, high abrasion resistance, high flexibility, good tensile strength, a light weight for its thickness (roughly equivalent to 8-ounce fiberglass cloth) and moderate cost. It is extraordinarily user-friendly.

I restrict my use of fiberglass to tapes for fastening plywood bulkheads and covering seams in small craft. I use Kevlar to reinforce the inner surfaces of concave hull sections on large hulls. Appendix F has more information on fabrics.

Fasteners—Throughout this book, I primarily specify steel fasteners. The staples used by pneumatic staple guns are cement-coated zinc-electroplated steel; anything else is prohibitively expensive and unnecessary. Remember that all fasteners will be isolated, embedded and sealed in epoxy. For screws and bolts, I specify series 304 18-8 stainless steel. Large bolts, lag bolts and eyebolts are frequently hot-dipped galvanized steel. Nails may be hot-dipped galvanized box nails or stainless-steel ring-shank nails. In rare cases, bronze ring-shank nails are specified. In some instances, finishing nails are used during interior trim work; these should be hot-dipped galvanized steel or brass. Galvanized wallboard screws are finding their way into boatbuilding at an increasing rate. While they are useful for temporary construction such as supporting and bracing mold frames, they are ineffective for some fastening applications because they push the members apart when the screw-tips break through between layers, even when the layers are clamped. They are, however, useful for some planking operations.

Hardware—Deck hardware and portlights may be of various materials; I prefer cast bronze, stainless steel or hot-dipped galvanized steel. Most fabricated hardware (especially that which is welded) is stainless steel. Davits are fabricated of galvanized steel pipe, cold-galvanized over welds and painted. Aluminum, which I use occasionally for above-deck structures, has a relatively short life.

SAFETY AND APPROACH

Safety equipment should include all-rated fire extinguishers; a good first aid kit; professional face masks (particle and fume filters); paper face masks for cutting, grinding and sanding; safety glasses and goggles; hearing protection; protective clothing for epoxy and paint work; good lights and natural lighting; exhaust fans. I have mixed feelings about many tool-guards, because I feel they impede access, vision and control of the tool and material. Real safety is a state of mind; know your limitations and abilities, and use the right tools in the right ways.

Wear appropriate protective clothing and eye and ear protection. Latex gloves (often called examination gloves) can be purchased by the box from most drug stores. Chemical-resistant gloves can be purchased from hardware and automotive stores. I frequently wear two pair of latex gloves and keep changing them as necessary. (Dust your hands liberally with talc before putting on gloves.)

Avoid getting epoxy, paint, varnish and oil on your body, and wash them from your skin and hair with mechanics' liquid or paste soaps (the ones with grit added work best) and lots of warm water. Cured epoxy will wear off skin but must be cut from hair. Rinse chemicals from eyes and mucous membranes with large quantities of fresh water and if necessary, call a hospital emergency room or poison control facility for information. Powerful detergents—and chemicals—damage skin and hair, so use skin moisturizers and hair conditioners frequently.

Many of the wonderful chemicals that enable us to build better things cheaper and faster are also poisonous. Basic safety and health practices greatly reduce the hazards of these products. Because we wear protective clothing, and avoid breathing the fumes and using solvents to wash epoxy or paint off our skin, neither I nor any of my associates have ever experienced a serious health problem from our work. None of us has become sensitized to epoxy either. It is not that difficult or inconvenient to protect yourself. When you have that occasional accident, remember that the important thing is to learn from it and improve because of it.

Rapid disposal of waste becomes a consideration when building boats. Wood scraps can often be burned, if local zoning and fire marshal rules allow this. Sometimes a permit is required. Do not breath fumes from wood that has been coated or painted. Paint and epoxy waste can be obnoxious as well as toxic—uncured epoxy is particularly offensive. Think about where your waste materials will end up, and dispose of them thoughtfully.

Take care of yourself! Remember to eat well, drink water, rest and stretch out once in a while. Boatbuilding is physically demanding, often in unexpected ways. I find that practicing a few simple yoga exercises each morning (and after a hard day) works miracles—I don't have back problems.

It is important to enjoy the *process* as well as its result. Being organized, centered and prepared will have a lot to do with making that enjoyment—and success—possible. Keep this in mind as we make our step-by-step journey through the procedure of building cold-molded boats.

BASIC SAFETY AND HEALTH PRACTICES

Don't breathe epoxy or paint fumes; wear a fume-filtering mask such as a Binks double-filter paint spray respirator.

Don't get reducers, solvents, epoxies or paint on skin, eyes or hair.

Have and maintain a thoroughly equipped first aid kit.

Have fresh water and soap available; have an eye cup in the first aid kit.

Know where the nearest hospital emergency room is and have two emergency routes to it.

Post a list of emergency phone numbers for fire department, rescue squad, hospital and poison-control center.

Don't breathe dust of any kind, even pure wood; wear a particle mask.

Use the right tool in a proper manner; know where your hands are.

Always wear safety glasses, and wear goggles or a face mask when required.

Wear hearing protectors when using loud tools.

Keep proper fire extinguishers within reach and charged. Make sure everyone knows where they are.

Disconnect power to tools and extension cords when not in use.

Keep a clean, orderly construction site. This will maintain a healthy state of mind as well as protect you from accidents, complaints and possible lawsuits.

CHAPTER 4
BEGINNING

The Strongback/ Lofting/ Building Frames/
Erecting, Fairing, Adjusting and Cross-Bracing Frames

THE STRONGBACK

The strongback, upon which the hull is built upside down, must be strong and stiff and true. It will support many forces: the weight of the hull and workers; tools pushing, pulling, and shaking; braces; and the resistance of wood being formed into compound curves.

The components of the strongback are the two rows of legs used to support it; two girders, each of which consists of paired planks fastened to each side of each row of legs; and upright stanchions that fit between the girder plank pairs and support the mold frames.

The strongback should be considerably shorter than the length of the hull, and around half the beam (see Fig. 4-1). In my designs, the strongback girders are usually located at the quarter-beam buttock lines; this simplifies the location of the frames on the upright stanchions used to support them. The stem and sometimes the stern will need to be supported independently; hence the floor of the shop must be strong and stable. I prefer to build right on the ground.

I usually dig one-cubic-foot holes and set 2 x 4 or 2 x 6 legs in concrete. Legs should be no more than 12 feet apart when 2 x 12s are used for the strongback girders, and closer when the girders are smaller. Use stakes and string lines, and lay out the legs accurately. During layout, locate the legs in such a way

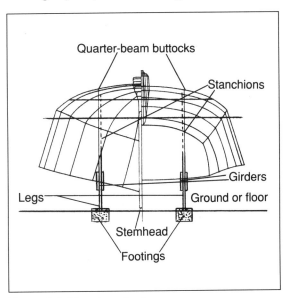

Figure 4-1. The strongback.

Photo 4-1. Set up the strongback legs using stakes and nylon twine. The legs are set in holes approximately 12 inches by 12 inches by 12 inches and filled with concrete.

Photo 4-2. After the first strongback girder plank is in place, it is planed true. The other girder planks are installed true to it.

Photo 4-3. A level taped to a straight 2 x 4 is used to true the second strongback girder to the first one.

that they will not end up within 12 inches of the hull design stations, where support stanchions will be located. Use a level to plumb the legs to the strings; it is not as critical for the posts to be vertical fore and aft as from side to side. Pour concrete around the legs, keeping them plumb and aligned to the strings. Keep the concrete wet for several days to cure it. If the legs are too tall, they can be cut off later, but it is important that the girders be level, flat, and parallel for their length. Watch for a slope to your site and leave the legs tall enough to compensate for it. (See Photo 4-1.)

Nail the girder planks to the legs with stage nails temporarily. Use a line level to true the first girder half through its length, and cut off any legs that protrude. The legs should end just below the girder surface so as not to interfere with planing the tops. Use a long-bed plane to level the top surface (see Photo 4-2). Assemble the other girder half level to the first, and use a straight 2 x 4 with a four-foot level taped onto it to true the second girder as you assemble it (see Photo 4-3). Double-check everything. Now bolt the girders firmly to the legs, and attach plywood butt blocks firmly to the girders (see Photos 4-4, 4-5). In Photo 4-5 the butt block is glued and pneumatically stapled.

Design stations are laid out along the length of the strongback. Care must be taken when laying out the second side that station alignment is exactly perpendicular to the strongback by measuring across diagonally twice at the start (making an "X") and double-checking at the ends the same way. The upright stanchions (2 x 4s) are placed at the stations to support the mold frames. To avoid beveling the mold frames, offset them from the design stations toward the widest beam of the hull (usually around station 7). Thus frames toward the bow will be set on the aft side of the station, and frames toward the

Photo 4-4. The girder planks are bolted to the legs.

Photo 4-5. Plywood butt blocks are epoxy-glued and stapled to join girder planks.

stern will be set on the forward side. This way the "high" edge of the frame will lie at the design station. To achieve this, the stanchions are placed "outside" the design stations from the midsection fore and aft, so that the frames end up "inside" the design stations. Cut notches into the stanchions at the level of the frame cross-bracing, which is the same for all frames for alignment purposes. (See Photo 4-6.) Stanchion height and cross-brace location are determined from the lofting or body plan design. From it, you must also determine how the hull will be positioned on the strongback: where fore and aft, and how high. The

Photo 4-6. Stanchions to support the mold frames, pre-notched for the frame crossbars, are installed between the girder planks.

frame cross-braces are determined by starting with the design section having the lowest sheer part (usually frame eight) and drawing a line across the lofting (or body plan) so as not to interfere with the sheer clamp notches. For an EXUMA 44, for example, the notches are seven inches below the sheer; the frame cross-brace would be set between $7^1/_2$ inches and 11 inches. Keep in mind that the hull gets narrower and lower (upside down) at the ends, and must clear both the strongback and shop floor. The stemhead should be just at or near ground level; you want the whole boat to be as low as possible. Don't worry about getting under it; you will rarely need to except to look.

The stanchions must be plumb (vertical) both fore and aft and side to side (which will be determined by the strongback), and hence must be made from straight stock. They can be held in place by #16 staging nails or through-bolted (essential for large vessels).

LOFTING

Lofting is reproducing the body plan of the hull full size. Most designs have 11 stations; if yours does not, it may need to be redrawn. If it has somewhere around 20 or 30 stations (some older designs have stations for every

Photo 4-7. Lofting points, taken from the designer's table of offsets, are located by using two tape measures. Every point has a "height from base line" and "half breadth from centerline."

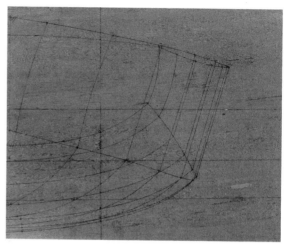

Photo 4-8. Shown is the lofting table for *Teresa* (EXUMA 44).

frame, and some computer-generated designs have many stations), you may be able to loft every second or third one. In the case of very large vessels, more than 11 stations are an advantage. Small craft may have as few as three stations; often no more are needed. Mold frames, around which the hull is built, are made from the lofted design stations.

Hulls utilizing a tongue-and-groove primary planking layer generally don't need frames closer than three feet apart, and can accurately span distances of around 5 feet. Therefore the lofted design stations should be within these distances, as mold frames will be made from them.

Station one is usually at the bow waterline and is almost never made into a frame. Station 11 is usually at the stern waterline and is always made.

A loft floor is set up, either as a temporary table or overlaid on a permanent surface. I usually loft onto plywood that will be used in some later aspect of construction (after the hull is built, the lofting is of little or no use and is often dismantled). The loft surface dimensions are a little more than the total height of the hull (usually from the top of the stemhead to the bottom of the keel), by a little

more than half the maximum beam. Two sheets of ACX plywood will suffice for vessels up to almost 16-foot beam and about 3-foot draft (most small and medium-sized centerboard sailboats and power boats). I loft both ends of the vessel together (on one side of the vertical centerline); if you loft them separately you will need twice the surface. The plywood surface must be flat, smooth and sturdy, and the edges must be straight and perpendicular to each other.

Lofting methods vary and can be researched in many books. I am only going to describe the method I use in relation to my designs and adaptions, because I have simplified this often tedious process down to a few hours.

Assuming the loft floor to be 8 feet by 8 feet (as for the EXUMA 44 *Teresa*, shown in Photos 4-7, 4-8), we arbitrarily assign the left edge to be the centerline of the hull and the bottom edge to be the baseline. The centerline divides the hull in half vertically fore and aft, and the baseline represents a waterline plane originating from the lowest point of the keel. Next, lay out the waterlines parallel to the baseline and draw the buttock line(s) parallel to the centerline. Use an 8-foot straightedge to draw these lines; chalk lines are not accurate enough.

The actual points on the hull defined by the table of offsets are located on the lofting by using two tape measures simultaneously. One measures out from the centerline, the other measures up from the baseline. These two dimensions for each point are called half-breadths and heights. Care must be taken that the tapes are kept perpendicular to the edge from which they measure; this sometimes requires taking duplicate measurements along the edges for large hulls (use a helper with a third tape). Photo 4-7 shows a third tape along the base line for this purpose. Figure 4-2 shows *Teresa's* body plan (EXUMA 44), from which the lofting is made (Photo 4-8).

After all table-of-offsets points are plotted on the lofting, the design stations are drawn, one at a time, to avoid confusion. In most of my designs, a plywood master curve is reproduced from the plans: It appears separately in a grid. This "giant French curve" will be used to draw most or all of the hull design stations by orienting it on the lofting such that the curve intersects the points from the table of offsets. A line is then drawn through the

points along the master curve. (See Photo 4-9.) As each curved section is drawn, mark one or more reference points on the master curve, such as the centerline, waterline, chine, bilge stringer center (for wineglass hulls with curved topsides) and sheer, and number them for the station you are drawing. This will help you reorient the curve when making mold frames and bulkheads. Without a master curve, the table of offsets must contain many more points, which must then be intersected by a flexible batten, along which a line is drawn.

There is no need to draw the whole hull

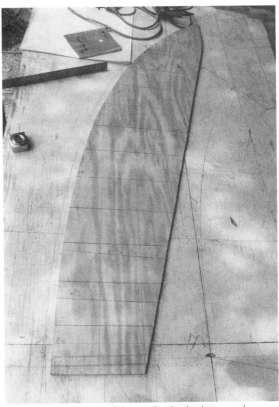

Photo 4-9. In most of the author's designs and adaptations of designs, a master curve is used to simplify lofting, framing and construction. This one is for *Sarah* (EXUMA 52). The master curve is gridded on the blueprints and is used to draw most or all of the lines in the body plan. It is also used as a template to trace and cut out mold frames and bulkheads.

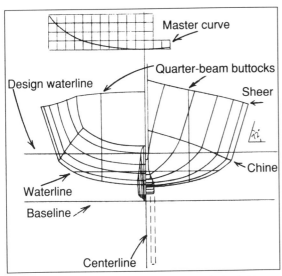

Figure 4-2. *Teresa's* body plan, the basis for lofting.

profile in the lofting, but the transom, sheer-line and chine should be drawn in the body plan with a flexible batten to make sure they are fair. Corrections and adjustments can be made during lofting—and to the frames even after they are set up. It is not uncommon to shim out longitudinal stringers if you see a flat spot where they cross a frame. Remember that your eye is your most important tool. The width of a pencil line from a design can be magnified to equal a quarter-inch or more on a lofting. The backbone components of some hulls will need to be lofted to lay out those timbers. In the centerboard hulls used as examples throughout this book, the stem/forefoot assembly and the horn-timber/transom-post assembly are lofted. These procedures are described in Chapter 5. Keel hulls with inner keels or keel planks often have these structures laminated in place across their mold frames; hence their keels are not lofted. However, their stems and stern-post/horn-timber areas are lofted, and these assemblies are laid up on the lofting table.

The fore-and-aft longitudinals (sheer clamp and chine log—exemplary sections are shown in Chapter 6: Figs. 6-1, 6-2) are laid out on the lofting to visualize their location and makeup in the mold frames. I usually draw them onto frame seven. Figure the thickness of the hull skin when establishing their location. The sheer clamp laminations are set a constant distance below the sheer (the same for every frame). This distance is determined by the deck thickness and the height of the deck beams. The chine log or bilge stringer joining topsides to bottom may be a little harder to figure because it changes in shape fore and aft. My plans will show this in detail; if you are adapting a plan, you will have to design this in. Chine logs have four faces: The outer face is parallel to the hull topsides; the inner face is parallel to the outer face (the plank laminations of the log are also parallel to these faces); the lower face is parallel to the hull bottom; and the top face is beveled several degrees from horizontal to shed water. In V-bottom and wineglass keel hulls, the keel plank or backbone likewise will have to be figured for each frame.

BUILDING FRAMES

Mold frames should be made of average lumberyard wood—3/4-inch or 1½-inches stock, pine, hem-fir or spruce—but the stock should be dry and stable. Hulls less than 40 feet long can use the lighter stock unless they are heavy displacement. *Teresa* was framed with 1 x 12 and 1 x 4 #2 common white pine, and we found the sides to be too light. Had the sides been 1 x 6 they would have been fine.

Plywood gussets join the frame sections together. I use yellow carpenter's glue and staples to fasten the gussets to both sides of the frames, and set them away from the outer frame edges about 1/2 inch so as not to interfere with longitudinals or planking. (See Photo 4-10.)

Because the design body plan (and consequently the lofting) is usually drawn to the outside surface of the hull planking, the frames must be made by subtracting the thickness of the hull. This is simple, but keep in mind that in the ends of the vessel the planking is crossing the frames at a slight angle, hence the subtracted distance to get to the inside surface of the hull is slightly more than the planking thickness. This additional amount is typically less than 1/8 inch and can almost be ignored, except in very curvaceous hulls (i.e., those with ducktail sterns or bulbous bows). Different standards of accuracy apply in the construction of cruising boats than in the construction of America's Cup defenders. Fair curves are more important than extreme technical accuracy.

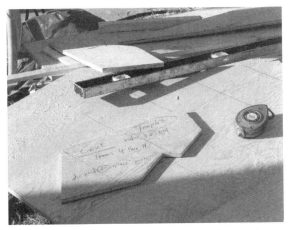

Photo 4-10. Plywood frame gussets can be made identically by using the first one as a template for many others; as frames approach the bow (and sometimes the stern), their shape will change, requiring gussets of different shapes. The gusset shown here, for an EXUMA 44, will provide gussets for frames 4 through 11.

Photo 4-11. Among the tools shown for lofting is the plywood angel or set-back gauge, used to determine frame location. Turning the angel around allows it to be used for both topsides and bottom planking.

An "angel" or marking gauge is made to transfer from the lofted outside hull surface to the frame edge. (See Photo 4-11.) The angel is a piece of 1/2-inch plywood about one foot long by two or more times the thickness of the frame material. In this case, the angel has one end notched for the topside's thickness (7/8 inch) and the other end notched to the bottom thickness ($1^1/_2$ inches). The notches are as high as the thickness of the frame stock. The frame sides are simply laid in place over the lofting, set back by the angel to represent the planking thickness and carefully marked for the sheer, sheer clamp notch, cross-brace, waterline and at the intersection to the bottom frame plank. This intersection is determined by dividing the angle made by the hull-bottom and topsides in chine hulls, and by deciding the easiest way to join the planks along a curved hull. Usually, when figuring the angle for a joint between frame planks, a line is drawn perpendicular to a tangent to the hull curve at the point where the joint will start. The bottom frame plank, or any frame plank for a curved hull section, is determined by placing the master curve just above the bottom frame lofting (or inside the lofted curve), and moving it around until the angel verifies that it is inside the lofted curve by the thickness of the hull planking. You should be able to locate the master curve approximately by lining up the reference marks you made on it during lofting. Note that when you have it lined up in the new position (set-in for planking thickness), the master curve will be shifted slightly to the smaller-radius end. This is because the inside of the hull has a slightly smaller radius than the outside of the hull. Conversely, the inside of a concave hull section (such as that for the lower-aft stations of a wineglass hull) will have a slightly larger radius, shifting the master curve in the opposite direction. Make new reference marks at the same places as before, and label them for the station number, location (centerline, chine, etc.) and the letter "I" for inner hull surface. These new reference marks determine master curve location inside the hull and are used both to scribe frame planks for cutting and during bulkhead layout later. One of the marks you make will locate the joint at the cut between frame planks (where they will be joined). A bevel square is set to the angle of the frame intersection. Planks are laid over the lofting, positioned so that the section of the hull curve you are framing will comfortably fit on the plank and enough wood will remain for the gussets to be attached to it, and the ends are scribed. Very curvaceous hulls will need wider frame stock or more sections. The centerline is usually scribed by placing a straightedge on the plank above the centerline, lining it up to the parts of the lofted centerline exposed and tracing it. The other joints are scribed using the bevel square. The plank ends are then cut to the scribed lines and the plank is laid back on the lofting, aligning the cut ends carefully. The curve is then drawn

Photo 4-12. Mold frames are cut out with a circular saw after marking them with the master curve.

by placing the master curve in place on the frame plank and aligning it to the reference points. Some portion of the lofted curve should still be exposed, allowing use of the angel in helping to locate the master curve. The notched portion of the angel will extend over the frame plank to touch the master curve, while the bottom of the notch touches the lofted curve. The topside frame sections are placed to start at the hull sheer and are cut at the intersect angle for the next lower frame section. They are notched for the sheer clamp and (frequently) the chine log or bilge stringer. The chine log notch will usually cut partway into the bottom frame section too, and care must be taken to position it correctly.

After these sections are cut (see Photo 4-12) and laid back out on the lofting to confirm their correctness (use the angel), they are used as templates to duplicate the other half of the frame (for the other side of the hull). At this point the frame sections are gusseted together in place on the lofting, and turned over and gusseted on their other sides. The frame halves are joined by gussets at the bottom and cross-braces at the determined marks from the lofting, which correspond to the notches in the stanchions (remember the stanchions?). Care must be taken to position the halves correctly by measuring the half-beam of each frame at the sheer (remember to subtract topside hull thickness), multiplying this by two, and measuring across the frame heads. It doesn't matter which side you attach the cross-brace to as you can turn the frame around. (See Fig. 4-3.) Sometimes a gusset will interfere with a stanchion and the stanchion will have to be notched to position the frame correctly.

ERECTING FRAMES

Even though the frame cross-braces should

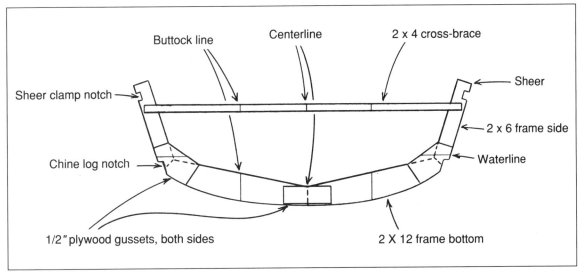

Figure 4-3. Joining the frame halves with gussets and cross-braces.

be straight stock (usually 2 x 4 for hulls over 30 feet) some adjustments are usually necessary to true the frames. To allow for this the notches in the stanchions are cut slightly oversize and shim-shingles are used to jack up the frames if necessary. In positioning the stanchions, the bottoms of the notches should be in line, of a uniform height above the strongback girders. It can be seen why the strongback must be true. Frame adjustments are usually made "up" only. If everything were perfect the frames would only need to be aligned athwartships to the hull centerline.

Every frame must have accurate waterlines, buttocks, cross-brace lines and centerlines (one usually where the hull bottom frame halves are joined and the other marked in the center of the cross-brace) scribed on it on both sides from the lofting before assembly. These reference lines must be carefully aligned during frame assembly and double-checked after assembly. Mark buttock lines on the frame cross-braces by measuring out from the centerlines.

The frames are hung in place on the stanchions as already described; forward frames on the aft side of stanchions and aft frames on

the forward side. Cross-braces fit into the notches and frames are centered side to side. Clamps are used at the stanchion tops to hold frames; none are fastened until all are in place and aligned. Start in the center with frames six and seven and work fore and aft simultaneously, one frame in each direction. You will need at least 20 5-inch or larger clamps. (See Photo 4-13.) Initial centering consists of lining up buttock marks on the cross-braces to the stanchions. After all 10 frames are in place, final alignment is performed by eye, standing at each end of the hull and sighting the centerlines, buttocks and waterlines. All should visually form a straight line. If frames have to be jacked up on one side with shim shingles, the centerline will be shifted and the frame will need to be re-centered. Strings may be set up fore and aft to help alignment, but they must be set up very taut so there is no sag. I prefer the eye. A surveyor's sight level (transit) on a tripod is very helpful in alignment, especially for larger hulls.

After the frames are hung and aligned, they are fastened in place and cross-braced. In vessels below 45 feet and of light to moderate displacement, staging nails are adequate for

Photo 4-13. All the mold frames are set in place with clamps during alignment.

fastening and very little cross-bracing is necessary. "Zigzag" 2 x 4 bracing should run from stanchion across to the next stanchion both fore and aft. This will prevent strongback deformation and provide something to stand on while planking with tongue and groove. Longer spans or heavy workers will require 2 x 6s for zigzag bracing. In large or heavy or deep-bodied vessels, cross-bracing is installed diagonally across each frame and

Photo 4-14. Mold frames for larger hulls are braced with diagonal struts.

sometimes fore and aft between frames. Tremendous forces will be exerted on the frames, sometimes unequally, and they must be stiff and strong. (See Photo 4-14.) For larger and heavier vessels, the frames are through-bolted to stanchions.

Fairing is done with long battens as a double check to expose any errors. A straight 20-foot 1 x 2 with no large knots or grain irregularities is best for this. It should be sprung in place all over the frames and should describe a smooth curve. Hard spots and flat spots may indicate a problem. A high frame will lift the batten off each adjacent frame; a low frame may not touch the batten. Refer to the lofting and the hull lines drawing if you suspect a problem. Some curve changes are designed in, especially near the bow. True flaws may be resolved by shifting a frame, planing a little off a frame or using shim shingles. This is particularly true through the sheer clamp and chine log notches, where sometimes the notch may have to be altered to allow a fair curve.

CHAPTER 5
BACKBONE

*Stem and Stern Assemblies/ The Transom/
The Centerplank/ The Inner Keel or Keel Plank*

The backbone varies with different hull types. By definition, the backbone of a hull is the fore-and-aft centerline structure to which the hull halves are attached. This structure may be internal, external, or both. In addition to providing fastener and gluing planes for the hull halves, the backbone stiffens and reinforces the hull along its centerline. It is, traditionally, the largest and strongest structural hull component. In modern cold-molded construction, much strength and integrity comes from the monocoque or unibody nature of the whole hull; the role (and dimensions) of the traditional backbone is diminished.

V-bottom hulls, wineglass hulls and planked-keel hulls typically have both inner and outer keels, which function together as a backbone. If the dimensions of an inner keel are wider than they are high, the timber is often called a keel plank. In cold-molded construction, the inner keel (or keel plank) can be a relatively light structure because it essentially acts as a cleat to join the laminated hull halves together, and does not perform

the rigorous structural functions of a keel in traditional plank-on-frame construction. Rather than rabbet the keel for planking, the planking laminates simply overlap the beveled inner keel. An outer keel is laminated in place after the planking is trimmed off flush to the surface of the inner keel (refer back to Fig. 5-1).

In triple-laminate canoe-type hulls with either fin keels or centerboards, there may be little or no backbone structure other than a stem. In canoe-hulls with full-length skeg-type keels, the skeg keel is the backbone. The EXUMA series canoe hulls, used as construction examples throughout this book, have internal backbone structures in their bows and sterns, but none in the cabin areas of the hull. The bow and stern structures combine with the tapering full-length skeg keel to form the backbone (see Fig. 5-2).

I use Douglas fir or southern yellow pine for all backbone structure. Red oak, white oak or mahogany is also suitable but usually more expensive and harder to find in large sizes.

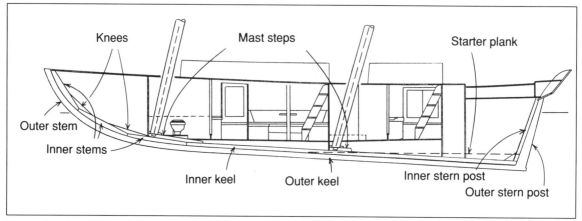

Figure 5-1. Backbone structure for 45-foot keel schooner.

STEM AND STERN ASSEMBLIES

The stem assembly acts as a large cleat to join the bow halves. It must be strong, stiff, stable and able to hold many fasteners. It need not be laminated except in extremely curvaceous bows. For vessels of moderate displacement between 35 feet and 60 feet I use stock sided $3^1/2$ inches. The stem should be at least as deep as it is wide, hence it is usually cut out of a 4 x 6. Vessels under 35 feet can use $2^1/2$-inch stock; vessels over 60 feet will require $4^1/2$-inch and larger stock. The planking overlaps the beveled stem and is trimmed off, and an outer stem is laminated over all, analogous to how the planking is finished when using an inner and outer keel.

The net effect of this construction is similar to that of traditional construction in that the planking terminates in what looks and acts like a rabbet, but all the components are laminated in place and consequently should never work and leak as garboard planks and hood ends eventually do in traditional construction.

The stem assembly typically requires two or three pieces. These are joined by knees, epoxy glued and fastened with large screws, lag bolts, or through-bolts. The stem assembly must be lofted from the hull lines drawing. In canoe hulls, the forefoot log, or lower stem, must extend aft as far as the bow V-sections go. Once the hull bottom flattens out

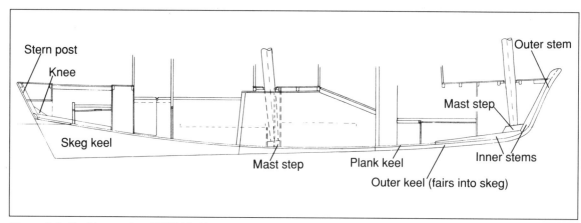

Figure 5-2. Backbone of an EXUMA 44.

and can be cross-planked without breaks at the centerline, the forefoot log ends. In some hulls this may extend quite far into the cabin and may have to be covered with a small cabin sole or incorporated into the furniture.

As previously mentioned, all backbone structure must be made of dry, stable wood. Eventually it will be totally sealed with epoxy resin and epoxy paint, and should have a stabilized moisture content.

Photo 5-1 shows the stem for *Sarah* (EXUMA 52) being laid out and cut; it was cut from both sides because the sawblade was not large enough to cut it all the way through from one side. This is actually an advantage: The smaller the sawblade, the smaller the

Photo 5-1. The stem and forefoot log are lofted and a simple template is used to transfer the lofting onto timbers which are then cut with a circular saw from both sides. They are trimmed up until they match the lofting.

radius of the curve it can cut. Shown is a Skil #367 saw, which uses a 6½-inch blade. As you can see, it has cut a tight curve to a depth of 2 inches. Photo 5-2 shows the stem and stern assemblies being laid up for *Teresa* (EXUMA 44).

The horn timber in these examples helps support the transom during planking and stiffens the hull between the outboard wells. The transom is hung from the post joined to the horn timber after it is in place. In wineglass keel hulls there is a sternpost-horntimber-transom post structure. In double-ended hulls, there is only a sternpost, which resembles a long stem.

Both stem and stern assemblies are notched into two or more frames at each end of the vessel. It is easiest to cut the notches (make them oversize) when making the frame halves, but I often do it in place. Use shims to adjust the position of the forefoot log and horn timber in the frame notches (see Photo 5-3). Anchor the stemhead and transom post firmly to the shop floor or earth and align them to the frame structure. This is simplified by drawing centerlines on both the inner and outer faces of the stem and transom post. Sight under the frame centerline joints and across the marked centerlines on the

Photo 5-2. Here the stem and forefoot assembly and the transom post and horn timber assembly are being fastened and glued together right on their loftings.

Photo 5-3. Shim shingles are used to center and adjust backbone assemblies. Note the tapering, rolling bevel on the forefoot log.

frame cross-braces and have a helper align the stem and transom post. Braces are added between them, the strongback, and the first and last frames. (See Photo 5-4.)

Once in place, the stem is beveled to receive the planking. I plan my planked stem width to equal the stem-stock thickness—3½ inches in this case. Lay out lines on each side of the centerline on the front of the stem where the inside of the planking will lie—this will be the front of the bevel. To locate these lines, subtract the planking thickness from each side of the stem, mark it, and draw the bevel lines through those points. (See Photos 5-4, 5-5.) In hulls with plywood topsides, the bevel line is not as deep (close to the center-

Photo 5-5. This shows the stemhead and layout on the face. Diagonal lines on the side show the hull sheer line. The short-handle (one-handed) adze is a handy tool for hogging off large quantities of wood.

Photo 5-4. One-by-two braces to the strongback, as well as stakes driven into the ground, help secure the stem. The author is starting to plane the stem bevel to the marks laid out on the stem's outer face.

Photo 5-6. The inner edge of the stem and keel bevel is called the bearding line. It is shown roughly sketched in on the stem and forefoot log. During shaping, this bevel is continuously checked by springing battens around the forward frames until they lie flat across the bevel. The diagonal lines show where the chine log will join the stem, and the step in the stem bevels between the lines is where the tapered chine log rabbet starts; this compensates for the different planking thicknesses of the triple-laminated bottom and double-laminated topsides.

line) as for the thicker bottom lamination (see Photo 5-6). The location of this break in depths is at the center of the chine log. Ascertain the proper bevel with a batten placed across the stem and first few frames. The bevel can be cut with an axe, adze or power plane, but it must be finished carefully to the proper depth and angle. This is probably one of the more difficult tasks in the construction of the hull in terms of skill level—and it's not that hard! Keep double-checking with the batten as you cut, orienting the batten in the same direction as the planking will lie. When working from an adaption of a traditional design, the outer edge of this bevel is the rabbet line, and the inner edge is the bearding line. Note that the bevel "rolls"—because the planking meets the stem at a different angle at the bottom than the top, the bevel angle changes, causing a wider gluing/fastening plane at the bottom than the top.

THE TRANSOM

Transom layout comes from the "expanded transom" on the lines drawing. Transoms are expanded by the designer to show their actual size and shape before they are curved in place on the hull. This is a mechanical drawing that extends at right angles from the transom (see Fig. 5-3). It is drawn full size right on the first plywood layer. Cut out the plywood layers oversize and trim them down only after the transom is in place. You can take away wood more easily than add it back on. The layers are staggered or offset to create top and bottom bevels for decking and bottom planking. Transoms wider than 8 feet expanded width will have seams, as will transoms higher than 4 feet. Very curved transoms, such as *Teresa*'s, will require the plywood to be oriented vertically, causing seams every 4 feet. These seams need not be scarfed, but must be offset between layers.

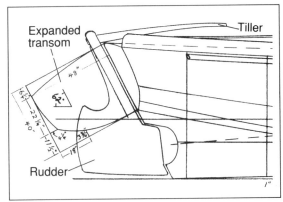

Figure 5-3. Expanded transom of an EXUMA 44.

The transom must be stiff and strong. The flatter it is, the thicker it must be, as curved forms are inherently stronger. Curved transoms should be half-again thicker than the topsides; flat transoms twice as thick. I usually laminate them from three layers of the same plywood we are using for the topsides, and then add two or three more layers cut into curved strips for cleats to broaden the glue surface for planking.

I lay up all three transom layers at once on two or three curved concave jigs using large screws to sandwich the layers to the jigs and smaller screws to pull the layers together between the jigs if necessary. The cleats are glued and screwed in place at the same time. (See Photos 5-7, 5-8.) Clamps may help on the perimeter.

The transom cleats are notched at the center for the transom post, in the lower corners for the chine logs and on the sides for the sheer clamps. Make the sheer clamp notches oversize to allow adjustment during their installation. Try to keep fasteners away from areas that are likely to be cut or planed.

The transom is fastened to the transom post with epoxy and large screws—be careful to align it properly. Brace it to the strongback and to the ground or floor.

Power-plane the raw transom edges after the transom is hung using the eye and battens

Photo 5-7. Curved transoms are laminated on a simple jig by fastening plywood layers to the jig. After curing, the fasteners are removed. Clamps are used on the perimeter where needed.

Photo 5-8. Transom cleats, made of plywood for curved transoms, are laminated right to the transom while it is still on the jig. Note the bevel, set to the angle at which the planking overlaps the transom edges. A gap is left at the center of the bottom cleats for the transom post.

to true it up. Make sure both sides are symmetrical. Use the original layout lines, which should still be on the outer or inner face of the transom as guides; if all is well you should trim almost exactly to them or end up parallel to them. Rely on your eye.

THE CENTERPLANK

The centerplank exists only in those hulls which are nearly flat in section at the centerline. This includes the EXUMA Series vessels, canoe hulls, barges and scows in which the hull will be the cabin sole. The centerplank is a long, wide, double-ended plank with tongues routed or cut on each edge. It helps reduce runoff, or reverse curving and outward angling of the plank ends as the tongue-and-groove planking approaches the chine log, and helps the planks lay up tightly to each other. Without a centerplank, the planks would gradually curve outboard, requiring many more clamps to hold them tight at the middle. The centerplank should be of the same material and thickness as the tongue-and-groove planking; it extends between the forefoot log and horn timber. Large vessels may require two planks scarfed together to achieve the necessary length. For *Sarah* and *Teresa*, the centerplanks were made from 1 x 12s.

Shape is determined by using a batten to draw a long, fair curve along the centerplank's length from the center of each end to the edge at the middle. Cut the curve with a circular saw and use the scrap as a template to scribe and cut the other edge and the other end. The centerplank must be symmetrical side to side and end to end. Rout rabbets on the edges of both sides using a flute bit and edge guide, or cut rabbets on both sides with a table saw to create the tongues. The tongues must fit neatly into the grooves of the planking lumber.

The centerplank is fastened with epoxy and staples, nails, or screws at each end, and with stage nails to every frame it crosses. (See Photo 5-9.)

THE INNER KEEL OR KEEL PLANK

V-bottom hulls, wineglass hulls and planked-keel hulls do not have centerplanks. They have a complete inner keel from one end to the other as if the forefoot log and horn timber continued until they joined. Inner keel width may remain the same or become wider near the middle of the hull in some cases. Solid timber is typically used, joined with knees or scarfs when necessary. As previously mentioned, the planking overlaps the inner keel, is trimmed off, and an outer keel is laminated over all on the outside (see Fig. 5-1 again).

The inner keel is set into notches in the frames, and its sides are beveled for the overlapping planking. The first planks starting at the bottom of the keel (the starter planks) perform a function similar to that of the cen-

Photo 5-9. Here the double-tapered centerplank is being laid up. It is glued and fastened to the forefoot log near the bow, and to the horn timber near the stern. Stage nails hold it to the mold frames. Each edge has a routed tongue to receive the tongue-and-groove planking.

terplank in the canoe hull. They should be wide at the aft end, tapered to a point at the forward end and curved along the top. Tongues are similarly routed or cut along their upper edges. This helps the tongue-and-groove planks lay up tight to each other.

CHAPTER 6
THE LONGITUDINALS

The Sheer Clamps/ The Chine Logs/ Bilge Stringers

Longitudinals are the fore and aft structural hull members. They are called stringers, battens, logs or clamps, depending on their function. Figure 6-1 shows a typical section of the sheer clamp and chine log for *Sarah* (EXUMA 52).

THE SHEER CLAMPS

In all but small vessels (usually under 20 feet) it is best and easiest to laminate the sheer clamp from 3/4-inch stock. Nominal 1 x 4 material is adequate for vessels up to about 60 feet. Vessels of light to moderate displacement under 45 feet will typically have two laminates; longer than that size, three laminates should be used.

The sheer clamps must be strong, as the deck beams will rest on them and be screwed, lag-bolted or through-bolted to them. The space above the clamps and between the beam-ends will be blocked in solid, providing a large gluing and fastening plane for the deck.

I typically use Douglas fir or yellow pine

of good quality (tight grain, no sapwood, no large or loose knots), but other woods may be used. I prefer using the same wood throughout the hull structure as much as possible, because this gives all parts of the hull similar properties of flexibility, expansion and contraction, moisture content, strength, gluing ability and fastener-holding ability.

In hulls with both strong sheer and tumblehome, the sheer clamp laminates may need to be sawn from stock that is wider than the height of the finished clamp in order to make the required compound curve. (In large vessels the sheer clamps are laminated from 1 x 6s.) This is rare, and usually involves the stern only. In the EXUMA series hulls, the sheer clamp laminates will virtually lay into place. In any case, edge setting (bending planks across their flat plane) is not as harmful in cold-molding as it is in planking a traditional vessel, because the subsequent laminations hold the curves in place.

Scarf the sheer clamp laminates by making a one-foot long cut with a circular saw diagonally across the ends. Use the scrap to scribe and cut the mating ends. Lay up all the sheer clamp laminates and place C-clamps vertically at the scarfs. Make sure scarfs are at least four feet away from scarfs in adjacent laminates and that all scarfs lie only in the flattest, least stressed parts of the curve. The laminating epoxy is slightly thickened with Cabosil and applied to all gluing surfaces with a 4-inch roller (3/8-inch nap). Clamp and screw

Photo 6-1. The sheer clamp laminates are epoxied and screwed to the sides of the stem for *Sarah* (EXUMA 52).

Photo 6-2. The sheer clamp laminates are screwed together after being clamped in place. Scarfs are two to one diagonal saw cuts, as seen in the foreground.

the laminates together until the epoxy cures. The screws may be left in or removed. Lay up the sheer clamps for both sides of the hull on the same day to equalize the forces on the frame. The clamp laminates should be let into notches in the transom cleats, but only the outermost laminate need be let into the stem, to avoid weakening it. In many instances, the bow end of the outer laminate is simply cut to a compound bevel and fastened to the side of the stem immediately aft of the stem bevel. The inner laminates should butt flat and true to the after face of the stem and be well-bedded in thickened epoxy. (See Photos 6-1, 6-2, 6-3.)

After mixing medium and large batches of

Photo 6-3. Two drill motors are used for screw-fastening. The 3/8-inch motor (on the ground) drills the holes using a Fuller bit; the 1/2-inch variable-speed reversing motor contains a hardened slot-head screwdriver bit for installing the screws.

epoxy (more than two pints), pour the material into plastic paint trays instead of leaving it in the mixing bucket. Spreading out the material increases its pot life. Reuse the tray without cleaning it until 1/8 inch or more of cured epoxy accumulates, then break it out by twisting the tray back and forth as you would a plastic ice cube tray.

After layup, gluing and fastening, the inner faces of the clamps are toenailed to the mold frames to prevent shifting during subsequent construction. Take care that the sheer clamp doesn't roll out of parallel alignment to the adjacent hull inner skin by checking that the outer surface is in line with the outer surface of each frame.

THE CHINE LOGS

The chine logs are also laminated in place from 3/4-inch stock of the same kind and quality as the sheer clamps, but they are often wider and will typically have only two laminations. If the sheer clamp laminates consist of nominal 1 x 4s, the chine log may consist of one 1 x 4 and one 1 x 6. In practice, because of the beveled lower edge, both chine log laminates might be cut from a 1 x 10, for example, so that only one saw rip need be made to provide both beveled edges. This reduces labor and material waste. In vessels with a hard or semi-hard chine, such as the larger EXUMA Series hulls, the chine log is laid up parallel to the topsides' plywood layers. The top edge is beveled to shed water (two or three degrees) and the bottom edge is beveled for the tongue-and-groove planking, which will overlap it. (See Figs. 6-1, 6-2.) (Hulls without a hard or semi-hard chine will not have chine logs.)

The inner laminate must necessarily be wider than the outer. Both are cut oversize to the bevel that occurs a little aft of amidships. Use an adjustable carpenter's protractor

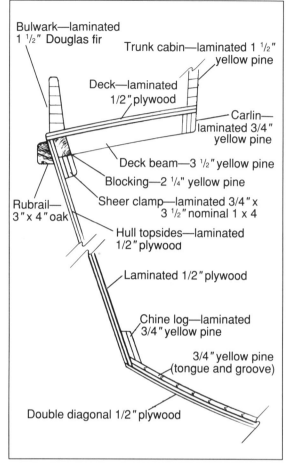

Figure 6-1. Hull and deck section of an EXUMA 52 at design station 6.

square or bevel square to pick up this angle from the lofting.

Near the bow, the chine vanishes as the hull topsides and bottom planking roll into the same plane. To join the two different planking planes, a tapering rabbet must be cut into the outer chine log laminate. This can be formed in part by using a narrower outer laminate of about the same thickness as the tongue-and-groove planking that will fit into the rabbet. (See Photo 6-4.) The gap that will occur at the aft end of this rabbet is filled by thickened epoxy. Another way to make the rabbet is to just continue the outer laminate forward, remove the fasteners after curing

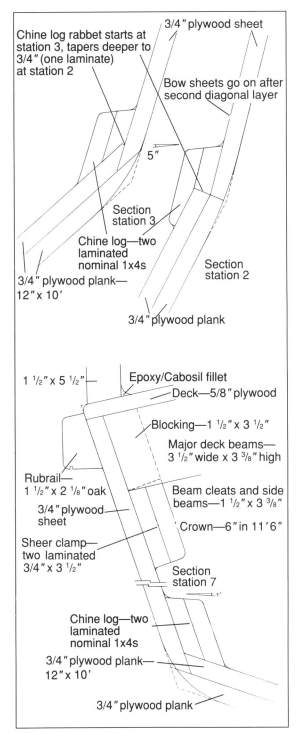

Chine log rabbet starts at
station 3, tapers deeper to
3/4" (one laminate)
at station 2

3/4" plywood sheet

Bow sheets go on after
second diagonal layer

5"

Section
station 3

Chine log—two
laminated
nominal 1x4s

Section
station 2

3/4" plywood plank—
12" x 10'

3/4" plywood plank

1 1/2" x 5 1/2"

Epoxy/Cabosil fillet

Deck—5/8" plywood

Blocking—1 1/2" x 3 1/2"

Major deck beams—
3 1/2" wide x 3 3/8" high

Rubrail—
1 1/2" x 2 1/8" oak

Beam cleats and side
beams—1 1/2" x 3 3/8"

3/4" plywood
sheet

Crown—6" in 11'6"

Sheer clamp—
two laminated
3/4" x 3 1/2"

Section
station 7

Chine log—two
laminated
nominal 1x4s

3/4" plywood plank—
12" x 10'

3/4" plywood plank

Figure 6-2. Hull and deck sections of a Quick-
molded TERRAPIN 45 at stations 7, 3 and 2—
showing chine log bevel and taper

Photo 6-4. The chine log rabbet for the thicker
bottom planking is started by using a narrower plank
in the outer chine log lamination between frame two
and the stem.

and cut the rabbet in with a power plane and
chisels so that it becomes progressively
deeper forward until it is the same depth
as the thickness of the tongue-and-groove
material.

The rabbet and planking bevels are finished with a power plane or hand plane and
rabbet plane. (See Photos 6-5, 6-6.) Figure 6-2
shows hull stations for a Quick-molded TER-
RAPIN 45; the tapered rabbet develops between stations three and two.

The aft ends of the chine logs end in

Photo 6-5. A power plane is used to finish the bevel
on the chine logs.

Photo 6-6. Both a power plane and a hand rabbet plane are used to cut the tapered rabbet and bevel at the forward ends of the chine logs.

Photo 6-7. The sheer clamp and chine log are fastened and glued to the transom in notches in the transom cleats.

Photo 6-8. Here the stem bevels are finished and ready for planking, as are the chine log rabbets and bevels.

notches in the transom clamps (see Photo 6-7) and the forward ends are cut to compound bevels and fastened to the sides of the stem (see Photo 6-8) with thickened epoxy and screws. Photo 6-9 shows *Teresa*'s completed frame ready for planking.

The finished chine logs must be securely fastened to the mold frames or the spring-back of the diagonal planking will lift them off the frames. In smaller vessels, carefully placed toenails will suffice; in larger hulls, angle stock will be required, held in place with screws inside the logs to each frame.

BILGE STRINGERS

A common way to build cold-molded hulls is by laminating several layers of diagonal planking over numerous bilge stringers or longitudinal battens. The disadvantages to this method are a typically thinner skin (more vulnerable to point-load impact), having to build around the stringers inside (requiring many bulkhead notches), and their propensity for catching water and dirt, which leads to fungus, mold, insect habitation and, ultimately, rot. In topside areas the upper surfaces can be beveled to shed water (but they

Photo 6-9. *Teresa*'s frame is ready for planking.

rarely are); at and below the turn of the bilges, weep holes, limber holes or channels must be cut or drilled through the stringers adjacent to the hull skin to allow water to drain to the bilges. These eventually clog with dirt and, if the holes are not carefully sealed during construction, rot starts. I have seen this time and time again in many hulls.

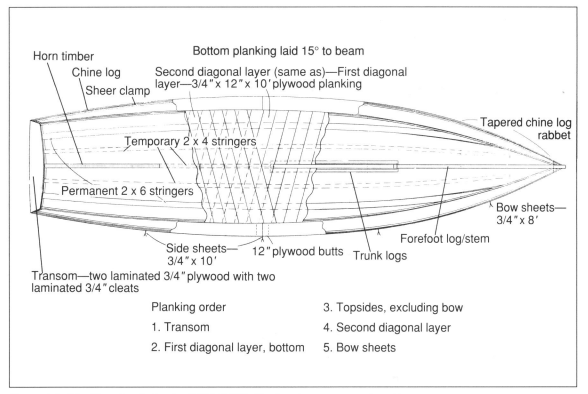

Figure 6-3. Planking details for the TERRAPIN 45, showing permanent and temporary (dotted lines) bilge stringers.

This is why I am basically against this mode of construction, except in the one application of bilge stringers in Quick-molded hulls. In these sharpie or batteau hulls, flat-plank stringers are laid just outboard of where the faces of the fore and aft cabin furniture will lie. The stringers must have large, accessible limber holes cut through them right to the hull inner skin at their lowest points so that water cannot be trapped. These limber holes, or, more properly, channels, must be carefully epoxy-sealed and painted to prevent rot.

They will not weaken the hull. Temporary stringers used during hull-bottom layup are covered with plastic to prevent planks sticking to them and are removed after the frames are pulled out after turning the hull over. An example of this construction is shown in Figure 6-3 (TERRAPIN 45). In this example, 10-foot plywood planks are used to span the hull bottom.

CHAPTER 7
PLANKING

Tongue-and-Groove Planking/ The First Diagonal Layer/ Topsides Layers/ The Second Diagonal Layer and the Final Bow Sheets

Planking is easy and it goes fast. Our three-person crew planks a 44-footer in 11 days. It takes us about 10 days to prepare the work site, build the strongback, loft, set up the frame and build the backbone and longitudinals. We complete the hull and turn it over in another 19 days, for a total of about 40 days. This translates to seven weeks, working five-and-a-half or six days a week. It's intense but rewarding work.

Working alone will, of course, take a lot longer. I strongly advise that you find a helper to see you through the construction of a hull over 32 feet. The mechanics of building a large hull are very awkward for one person alone. During planking, a helper is almost essential: Epoxy must be mixed and applied to both the hull and plywood planks during diagonal planking; then the wet planks must be positioned and fastened to the hull before the epoxy kicks off (cures).

Helpers don't need to be skilled. Older children can be a great help here, but remember to keep epoxy and solvents off them. I keep one person mixing epoxy, carrying it, filling trays, and cleaning up and replacing trays and rollers in which epoxy is starting to kick off. This alone is a real fire drill of a job, but it can be done by almost anyone.

TONGUE-AND-GROOVE PLANKING

After the work of Chapter 6 is completed, the whole hull frame must be checked for fairness by studying the curves and gluing planes (surfaces), and using your by-now-familiar batten. The edges of the mold frames should be coated with wax (rub them with old candles) to prevent glue adhesion, but be careful not to get this on your gluing surfaces.

Figure 7-1 shows planking details for *Teresa* (EXUMA 44). The tongue-and-groove layer is self-fairing from plank to plank because of its interlocking nature. Set aside deformed planks and those with bad breaks in the tongues or grooves. No scarfing is necessary, but the butts must be bedded in thickened epoxy (not so much to join them as to seal them), and the tongues and grooves

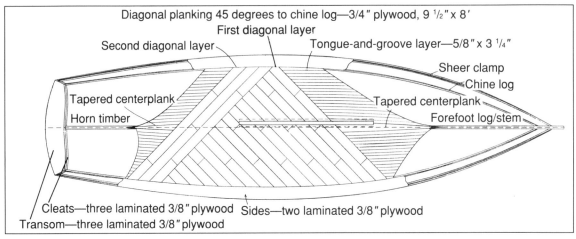

Diagonal planking 45 degrees to chine log—3/4" plywood, 9 ½" x 8'
First diagonal layer
Second diagonal layer
Tongue-and-groove layer—5/8" x 3 ¼"
Sheer clamp
Chine log
Tapered centerplank
Horn timber
Tapered centerplank
Forefoot log/stem
Cleats—three laminated 3/8" plywood
Sides—two laminated 3/8" plywood
Transom—three laminated 3/8" plywood

Figure 7-1. Planking detail for *Teresa*, EXUMA 44.

must be epoxy-coated. Use a throw-away brush or a 4-inch by 3/8-inch nap roller to glue each to the other.

The planks are stage-nailed to each mold frame after being drawn up tightly to the adjacent plank with pipe or bar clamps. (See Photos 7-1, 7-2.). The extreme ends are screwed to the stem and the transom. The first few planks must be trimmed off parallel to the hull centerline; position each plank dry (no glue), scribe it with a batten and pencil or chalkline, take it off and cut it, then install it. These tapered ends are glued and screwed into the lower stem, horn timber, keel plank, or, in the case of a wineglass-shaped hull, the backbone.

Let the plank ends run wild and trim them after the epoxy has cured. The epoxy used here should be thickened slightly with Cabosil. It must still be liquid and quite runny—about the consistency of heavy cream. If you thicken epoxy too much, it loses both tensile strength and penetration and becomes a lousy glue. Thickening it to a

Photo 7-1. The tongue-and-groove planks are epoxy-glued to each other, held in place by bar clamps, stage-nailed at the mold frames, and glued and screwed into the stem and transom. Since the mold frames will be removed, coat the edges with candle wax or beeswax to keep epoxy from sticking to them. When the chine logs are reached, the planks are glued and fastened to them.

Photo 7-2. Beyond the double-tapered center plank, the first pair of tongue-and-groove planks are joined at the centerline by long tapered cuts. The plank ends are glued and screwed to the horn timber and transom, as well as to each other.

nonsagging paste will be good for filling, bedding and filleting, but not gluing. Don't worry about the mess inside the hull; let it drip, unless you have a surplus of help and can send someone inside to wipe it up. If so, cover him or her with protective clothing. Don't neglect hair and eyes. Epoxy in the hair must be cut out unless washed with warm water and shampoo before it cures.

As planking proceeds outboard, screw blocks of wood to the previous day's planking to create purchase for your pipe clamps. Remember that hulls are curved, and there will be a gap between planks on the outside curve. It is a waste to bevel your plank edges except in extremely sharp bilge-turns, as these 1/16-inch or less gaps are filled by epoxy. I mention this now so that you won't try to close these gaps by cranking the dickens out of your bar clamps!

The first few bow planks are often difficult and may require clamping at the stem. Don't be dismayed if you break one or two. In extremely curvaceous hulls, you may need to steam the plank end, fasten it dry, and remove and install it permanently the next day. (See Photo 7-3.)

After completing this first layer (see Photos

Photo 7-4. Here is the completed tongue-and-groove layer for *Teresa* (EXUMA 44). The stage nails are removed during fairing and sanding, then some are reinstalled to hold the plank layer from shifting during subsequent planking.

Photo 7-3. Hulls with sharp bows may require a short, severe twist in the first few bow planks. Here clamps and many fasteners were used to force the plank ends into conformity. Splits are epoxy-filled before the next planking layer.

Photo 7-5. The edges of the tongue-and-groove layer are trimmed flush to the chine logs, first with a broad axe (or circular saw), then with a power plane.

7-4, 7-6), the edges are trimmed (see Photo 7-5), staging nails are pulled (leave or reinstall enough to hold the skin to the frames), holes and gaps are filled, and the whole surface is faired and sanded. (See Photos 7-7, 7-8, 7-9.)

Photo 7-6. The tongue-and-groove layer lays up in the chine log rabbet at the bow, creating a flush surface. Each plank end is trimmed to the right angle, then driven forward into place and fastened, hence all tongue-and-groove planking starts at the bow end.

Photo 7-7. After removing the stage nails and grinding off any globs of cured epoxy, any open seams (caused by the curvature of the hull) and nail holes are filled with thickened epoxy.

THE FIRST DIAGONAL LAYER

In the photographic examples, the diagonal layers consist mostly of 9½-inch by 8-foot planks. For *Teresa* (EXUMA 44), the planks are of 3/8-inch marine plywood; for *Sarah* (EXUMA 52), they are 1/2-inch ACX plywood. (The 9½-inch width is ideal because it divides evenly into the 48-inch width of plywood sheets and matches the common roller-applicator size of 9 inches.) Diagonal layers may also be solid lumber; plywood is simply my preference, for the following reasons: It is more economical, faster to apply because greater widths may be used, and very strong. Because plywood is laminated of veneers running at right angles to each other, it has much higher penetration resistance than solid lumber of similar dimensions, greater tensile strength in all directions, higher grain-crush resistance, greater abrasion and gouging resistance, and superior resistance to marine borers, which will rarely eat through a glue layer. In the bow, planks will often need to be ripped in half because the wide planks either can't take the curve or can't lay flat to the hull. In very extreme cases, such as the upper stern sections of traditional hulls having dramatic tumblehome, sometimes it

Photo 7-8. The whole surface is faired with plane and sander prior to the next layer.

becomes necessary to use plywood layers of half thickness. (For example, four layers of 3/16-inch plywood instead of the usual two layers of 3/8-inch material.) Ducktail sterns might also be planked similarly, using narrower and thinner plywood planks in that one portion of the hull.

No spiling (tapering of width) is necessary. The gap generated between planks is usually no greater than 3/16 inch and is filled with the epoxy that oozes up during fastening or is filled before the next layer goes on. On some wineglass hulls, the planks may need to be thinner and/or narrower to take the curves, and some spiling may be required. Usually numerous planks are laid until the curve across-plank becomes too much. (Fighting the planks into place is called "edge-setting.") At this point a double-tapered plank (both edges of both ends) is made and installed. The first few subsequent planks will require edge-setting in the opposite direction, followed by several planks that will lay up easily before the planks again require edge-setting in the first direction. Often a number of these double-tapered planks can be made up ahead of time and installed between every four to six uniform planks.

Photo 7-9. *Teresa*'s tongue-and-groove layer is now ready for the first layer of diagonal planking. Note that several stage nails have been replaced; these will be removed and their holes puttied as planking advances.

As I've mentioned before, both the hull surface and plank surface must be epoxy-coated. (Coating only one surface of a glue joint is bad practice.) Any small air voids trapped between layers are sealed in epoxy and rendered harmless. Large air voids that are not completely sealed can be harmful if water were ever to get into them. The epoxy, which is slightly thickened with Cabosil to about the consistency of heavy cream, is applied with rollers.

Use a pneumatic staple gun to fasten the planks. Carefully force all air bubbles out of the glue joint by stapling one end of the plank and then walking around on it while stapling the rest. You are going to trash your shoes—keep a sacrificial pair of sneakers on the job. A small nail gun could also be used, but often the nail heads don't have the hold-down strength of a staple. Staples (or nails) should be a little longer than twice the thickness of the plank, but not long enough to penetrate the inner layer. I use cement-coated, electroplated steel roofing/sheathing staples of 7/16-inch crown in 3/4-inch, 7/8-inch, 1-inch and 1^1/$_4$-inch lengths. Remember that air tools need oil periodically during use, but not so much that it sprays out all over your work. (See Photo 7-10.)

Start diagonal planking at the center of the hull. Determine planking angle or bias by laying a plank from the centerline to the chine at the maximum beam. The plank should be around 45 degrees from the centerline, but 10 degrees on either side of that is acceptable. A lot of overhang will be wasteful; if the plank doesn't reach, there will be many butts. Butts must be staggered—planks alternately join at the centerline and span the centerline. (See Photos 7-11, 7-12, 7-13.)

Upon completion, the edges are trimmed, protruding staples are countersunk (if you have many of these your air pressure may be too low), gaps and staple holes are filled, and the surface is faired and sanded. A 1/2-inch cold chisel can be modified to countersink staples by first grinding the tip flat, and then grinding a groove in the flat tip. (See Photos 7-14, 7-15, 7-16, 7-17.)

Photo 7-10. A pneumatic staple gun is used to fasten the diagonal plywood planks. The hammer is used to seat the planks tightly to the layer beneath. This isn't often necessary with planking thinner than 1/2 inch. The sawcuts in the plank centers at the right allow the planking to spring closer together at the chines in the bow section of *Sarah*'s (EXUMA 52) hull. These cuts have the effect of tapering the planks slightly as well as allowing them to curve more easily.

Photo 7-11. Diagonal planking starts at the center of the hull and proceeds both fore and aft. In *Teresa* (EXUMA 44), the planks are 9¹/₂ inches wide by 8 feet long 3/8-inch marine plywood laid 45 degrees from the hull centerline. Planks are epoxy-glued and pneumatically stapled in place; ends run wild and are trimmed after curing.

Photo 7-12. In the bow, planks are ripped narrower to lay up on the tighter curves. Hulls with extremely curvaceous sections sometimes require using plywood planks half the thickness used elsewhere; seams are staggered for greater strength.

Photo 7-13. *Teresa*'s bow planks required many staples and some rather narrow strips. It is important that planks lay up tightly to the layer beneath and that no air bubbles are trapped.

Photo 7-14. In this detail of the bottom planking edge, the layers seen are (from the bottom up) the chine log, the tongue-and-groove layer and the first diagonal layer. As each progressive planking layer goes on, the edge is trimmed flush to the chine log. The surface shown here is ready for the topsides planking, the two laminations of which are laid prior to the final bottom diagonal layer. This forms an interlocking joint, as in Figure 6-1.

Photo 7-15. In the bow, the first diagonal layer is trimmed with a circular saw for butt-fitting the first bow plywood sheets. The hull is now ready for topsides planking.

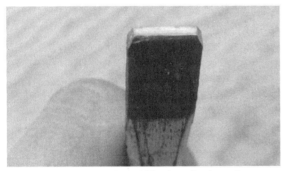

Photo 7-16. A chisel is modified on the bench grinder for countersinking staples.

Photo 7-17. After the staples are countersunk (usually most of the staples are already adequately countersunk by the staple gun—increasing air pressure sinks the staples deeper), they are filled with epoxy putty made using Cabosil.

TOPSIDES LAYERS

Plywood topsides layers go on fast. I usually butt the vertical edges and offset the butts of the next layer, but if there is a large span between the chine log and the sheer clamp, it is best to scarf the joints. This is most easily accomplished by stacking all the topsides sheets so that each is offset from the one below by four to six times the thickness of the plywood. Use clamps to hold the stack together. Then power-plane the end of the stack (go downhill away from the edges or the plywood will shred) until the vertical end grain of each bottom laminate just disappears. With thin plywood, this can be done with a body grinder. Turn the sheets over and do the opposite ends. An alternative to scarfing is to butt the sheets as above, grind out shallow grooves centered on the outside butts 2 inches wide by 1/16 inch deep and epoxy 2-inch wide fabric tape (typically 8-ounce fiberglass) over the butts.

Set the sheets in place, making sure there is enough overlap to reach the sheer line described by the frame ends. Remember that the sheer clamp does not define the hull's sheer line, which will be several inches above it when finished. (See Photo 7-18.) Trace

Photo 7-18. Topsides sheets are butt-fitted. They are hung in place, scribed from behind, removed, cut, then glued and stapled in place. A second layer follows, in which the vertical seams are staggered several feet away from the seams of the first layer.

sheets from the hull bottom, remove them and cut outside the trace line. Trim the sheer line after the sheets are attached: Spring a batten along the sheer line (transfer the framehead locations by measuring up from the sheet edges), trace it and cut outside it. Final trimming of the sheer won't be done until the hull is turned over, the deck beams are installed and the blocking is in place, so don't cut it short.

Epoxy-glue and staple the sheets in place. It may be necessary to use screws, or even a Spanish windlass, to hold tumblehome in the stern. (See Photo 7-19.) If the bow has hollow flare, use screws to pull the sheets into the hollow frame areas. These may remain in place during subsequent construction and be dug out from the inside later.

The second topsides layer goes over the first, its seams staggered. It will be necessary to staple or screw into the mold frames to pull the two layers together, as well as placing staples or screws in the field. These will damage the inner surface (which must be patched later), and must be removed after the epoxy cures. It is important that no large air voids remain between layers, and that a good glue joint results.

The final bow sheets are left off, as they must butt the final bottom diagonal layer, and it's easier to trim a full sheet than each diagonal plank end. (See Photo 7-20.)

Photo 7-20. Here the second topsides layer is on except for the final bow sheets, which go on after the final diagonal bottom layer. The edges of the topsides plywood are planed flush to the angle of the bottom planking and will be overlapped by the final bottom layer up to where the bow sheets will butt it; there it will be trimmed with a circular saw as before.

Photo 7-19. In hull ends employing conic sections for tumblehome or hollow flare, the plywood is tortured into the desired shape. Here 2 x 4s are clamped along the sheer and a Spanish windlass pulls the curve into the sheets. The transom is much handsomer with curved sides than flat ones. Hollow bow sections are incorporated by pulling the bow sheets in with large screws fastened through the sheets into the mold frames and sometimes additional hollow-cut planks placed between frames. The screws may be left in place while the second layer is laid, and dug out from inside when the mold frames are removed.

Photo 7-21. The rough power-planed edges are belt-sanded to a smooth, fair surface for the final diagonal layer.

The topsides edges at the chines are trimmed and faired to receive the final bottom diagonal layer. (See Photo 7-21.)

Vessels with no chines will either be triple-planked right to the sheer, or, if they incorporate plywood topsides, will have overlapping joints like the bow section of the examples shown in the photographs. These overlapping joints will each butt the adjacent bottom diagonal layer. Refer to the detail drawings for this construction type in Appendix A (EXUMA 36), and back to Figure 2-1.

THE SECOND DIAGONAL LAYER AND THE FINAL BOW SHEETS

The second diagonal layer is essentially identical to the first. Reestablish the hull centerline with a chalkline. A carpenter's protractor square duplicates the planking bias or angle, but for the opposite diagonal. (See Photo 7-22.) Planking also starts near the middle of the hull.

After completion, the layer is trimmed, filled, faired and sanded, but in the bow the plank edges are carefully trimmed with a circular saw to butt to the final bow sheets. (See Photo 7-23.)

After the bow sheets are cut to butt this bottom edge, they are installed, taking care to pull them tightly to the layer below, especially if the bows have hollow flare. The butt joint is filled, faired and sanded. (See Photo 7-24.) This completes the planking.

Even with the use of marine plywood, a careful inspection must be made for voids and delaminations. Photos 9-3 and 9-4 in Chapter 9 show voids and the patches made from 1/4-inch marine plywood used to repair them.

Photo 7-23. The trim cut for the final bow sheets has been made here, and the author is checking the location of the cut with a piece of scrap to see if the depth is right so that the planking will come out flush. The rest of the final diagonal layer is on and trimmed off, but hasn't been planed smooth yet.

Photo 7-24. The final bow sheets are now in place and the hull is ready to be sanded, filled and faired. In the bow the rough plywood edges will be trimmed flush to the inner stem and forefoot log in preparation for keel and stem laminations.

Photo 7-22. A carpenter's protractor is used to determine the angle of the diagonal planks, starting at the center of the hull. The angle for the EXUMA 52 is 40 degrees from the beam (50 degrees from the centerline). The angle for the EXUMA 44 is 45 degrees.

CHAPTER 8
THE KEEL

Keel Layout and Lamination/ Outer Stem Lamination

For our purposes, I define three general keel types. The skeg type is usually long, straight and shallow, and added onto the hull. Rowboats and most powerboats have skeg-type keels; the photos in this book all show skeg-type keels. The fin keel is also added onto the hull, but it is short, deep and shapely. Most contemporary sailboats have fin keels, and they almost always include ballast placed as low as possible. The third keel type is the planked keel, often called planked deadwood. This includes very deep V-shapes and wineglass keels, in which the hull planking forms the upper keel portion. The keel is thereby integrated into the hull rather than being added onto it (although in cold-molded construction the final lower extremities are stack-laminated in place as are skeg-type keels; see below). Examples of these types are shown in Appendix A.

The skeg keel is laid up in place on the hull using a process called stack lamination—just like stacking slices of bread. Deep fin keels that include ballast need sheathing over both sides of the stack lamination. This may con-sist of marine plywood or an epoxy-impreg-nated fabric such as Kevlar. The purpose of this sheathing is to provide vertical tensile strength. Such sheathing is unnecessary for skegs and planked keels. The fin keel can be made similarly, but is added to the hull after it is completed and turned over. All keel types may have outside ballast made of cast lead or iron which is added after the hull is right side up. There are variations in keel configuration which are neither skegs nor fin keels, but a blending of the two. Examples may be seen in the designs in Appendix A.

Ballasted fin keels are attached to the hull with long, large, stainless-steel bolts that start in the ballast in countersunk holes (which are eventually plugged) and end in the floors, which distribute the keel-imposed forces over a large portion of the hull. I prefer to make these floors of welded stainless steel and extend them athwartships as far as is practical. Ideally, these floors are tapered I-beams. Their size and shape must be engi-neered, for dimensions depend on vessel dis-placement, ballast weight, depth of keel, hull thickness and bulkhead location. An example may be seen in the BLUE WATER 40 in Appendix A. These floors can also be either laminated or solid timber, especially in smaller vessels or those with shallower keels. Examples of these different types of floor timbers may be seen in Figure 15-4 in Chapter 15.

Planked keels have already been discussed in Chapter 5; refer to Appendix A for another example. The planking layers, which cover the inner keel or backbone structure, are trimmed off much the way the stem will be finished later in this chapter. This edge containing the sandwich of all the hull planking layers is then covered over by one or more solid planks, which form the outer keel. (See Fig. 8-1.) In traditional hulls, the ballast is placed inside on the hull planking adjacent to the keelson, but because there is much more room in the hollow keel created by the type of cold-molded construction I use, a lower center of ballast can be achieved by placing the ballast right on the inner keel. Since the hull is considerably lighter than its traditional ancestor, a higher ballast ratio will also be realized. Both factors improve the performance and safety of the vessel.

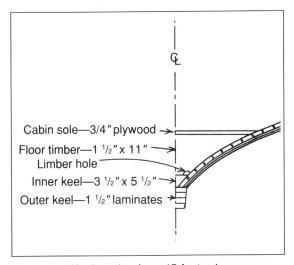

Cabin sole—3/4" plywood →
Floor timber—1 1/2" x 11" →
Limber hole
Inner keel—3 1/2" x 5 1/2" →
Outer keel—1 1/2" laminates →

Figure 8-1. Keel section for a 45-foot schooner.

KEEL LAYOUT AND LAMINATION

First reestablish an accurate centerline on the hull with a chalkline or batten and pencil. Also establish the design stations, or at least several key ones. If the vessel is to have a centerboard, lay out and cut the slot now. Find station locations by drilling small holes from the inside through the hull on the correct side of the mold frames. (These will also help locate or confirm the centerline.)

During the cutting of the centerboard slot, the hull may spring away from the frame. Use pipe or bar clamps to pull it back into place during keel lamination. If need be, fasten small pieces of steel angle stock to the frame and hull from inside. A small amount of springback often occurs along the hull centerline and at the chine log, if the chine log wasn't carefully toenailed into the frames. If 1/8 inch or less, this is acceptable. Don't deform the hull shape by clamping the centerboard slot to the frames when the rest of the hull doesn't touch; make them match.

The keels of most vessels are sculpted shapes, and the shape of the top of the keel is usually very different from the bottom. Take these shapes from the hull lines drawing, and lay them out on two separate planks. One plank will form the keel top and be laminated directly to the hull; the other plank will be the bottom, or final lamination, of the keel. In the case of long keels, use several planks joined by short scarfs. These can simply be 45-degree circular-saw crosscuts. Lay out design stations on the planks. (Remember that the keel top isn't parallel to the waterline, nor is the keel bottom in most designs, so that the stations will be very slightly farther apart.) Keel widths from the designer's table of offsets are then laid out on each station. You may have to take these off the plan yourself with dividers and scale.

Most keels taper both aft and down. Sometimes the circular saw may be set to a slight

Photo 8-1. The keel is stack-laminated in place using 1¹/₂-inch thick stock. It is glued and fastened with screws or nails (the first layer must be screwed to the hull). Scarfs are 45-degree sawcuts. A string is used here to determine the angle of the surface cuts and a 2 x 4 determines the end of the keel. After lamination, a cap covers the bottom and all that exposed end grain. A sternpost caps the end grain at the keel after end (it will be let in 1¹/₂ inches, hence the sloppy end cuts). Note how thick the bottom of the hull is at the transom (1¹/₂ inches when finished). Combined with the compound curves, you can begin to sense the incredible strength of this construction system. Frames, floors, stringers and keelsons are totally redundant. A gentle curve has been planed at the chine.

Photo 8-2. The keel of this EXUMA 52 ends in an elliptical section and is typical of propeller aperture construction. The plywood template has been cut to the desired shape. The other structure is temporary except for the flat cap or shoe at the keel bottom, which is being used as a guide.

Photo 8-3. Here *Teresa*'s keel is being puttied prior to capping and planing.

bevel and each plank used as a template for the next. This is how I do it. However, you must pay attention to changes in the keel shape by frequently referring to the design. The more accurately the laminates are cut, the less planing and grinding will be needed later. Either a taut string or straight plank (the final bottom plank we previously laid out) may be used to determine the keel bottom. This last plank caps the exposed tapered ends of the laminates. (See Photos 8-1, 8-2, 8-3, 8-4, 8-5.)

Determine the tapered ends of the laminates by setting them in place off to one side of the bottom plank or string. Then scribe, remove and cut them from each side with a circular saw. Finish the cut with a sharp handsaw.

Fastening is done with slightly thickened epoxy and screws, at least between the first laminate and the hull. After that, nails may be used if desired. Never stack-laminate with screws longer than 1/4 inch less than twice the thickness of the laminates. Doing so will force the second layer down away from the third layer as the screw points break through. Use 2¹/₂-inch #12 or #14 flat-head wood screws (don't use self-tapping screws) for stack-laminating 1¹/₂-inch wood laminates. When fastening the first layer, do not use screws that break through and damage the inside of the hull. Power-plane the surface after all the laminates are in place. The bot-

Photo 8-4. The cap has been cut and laid out to the left of the keel. The surface of the stack lamination has been planed and is ready for the cap. The small holes in the surface are from ring-shank nails used to pin down the tapered ends of the lamination layers. Note the offset centerboard slot.

Photo 8-5. *Sarah*'s elliptical keel end is finished, and the cap is on. The end will eventually be cut off and a stainless-steel rudder gudgeon fitted.

tom plank then caps and finishes the lamination.

Keels that end straight aft, such as *Teresa*'s, are trimmed off and capped vertically. *Sarah*'s keel, or any with curvature (as with many prop apertures), must be sculpted and sanded. The finished keel is eventually covered with fabric and epoxy. (See Photo 8-5.)

Keels that have shaft logs through them may be precut, layer-to-layer, or drilled after lamination. If you choose to precut, lay out a template alongside the keel larger than the diameter of the shaft log to be used. As each laminate is laid out, make parallel circular sawcuts slightly more than the log width apart in the place where the log will penetrate (usually at a very shallow angle) and chisel the material out. If you choose to drill later

with a shaft bore, take care to keep fasteners away from the central area of the laminates where the log will be located.

OUTER STEM LAMINATION

Extremely curved shapes such as most lower stems are best laminated. This provides great strength where it is needed, and covers all that vulnerable planking end grain with wood and epoxy. Laminates must be thin enough to take the sharpest curve without breaking. Outer laminates may be narrower if the stem is tapered. Because *Teresa*'s stem is traditionally square at the head, we used full-width laminates and planed them down. Consider that the fasteners may be in the way during shaping, and place them closer to the

Photo 8-6. The stem and forefoot surfaces have been planed prior to stem lamination. The flat surface is about 3½ inches wide.

Photo 8-7. The stem lamination layers must be milled thin enough to make the curve at the bottom of the stem. Bronze ring-shank nails are used to fasten the glued strips, because they are easier on the power plane during stem shaping. Of course you should make an effort to locate the fasteners of each subsequent layer closer to the center to avoid hitting them with the plane, but inevitably a few seem to end up in the way.

centerline in each subsequent laminate. I often use bronze ring-shank nails in this one instance to minimize damage to the power plane or hand planes. This problem recurs throughout hull construction, and is another reason to use staples instead of nails or screws during hull planking. The latter really trash planer blades. Plastic staples can be used in small boats to reduce this problem.

The stem should join the keel in two or more steps. (See Photos 8-6, 8-7, 8-8.) These act as a scarf and provide some structural continuity.

Photo 8-8. The stem laminations are step-scarfed into the keel as shown here.

Photo 8-9. This photo shows how the stem blends back into the keel, which flares gradually to its full width. The trailer in the upper left corner contains hand tools, a band saw, air compressor, bench grinder, vise, drill press and other equipment. The sides fold down and lock, simplifying tool storage on the construction site. The tarp to the right of the trailer covers the table saw and planer-jointer.

Upon completion of the stem and the keel, both are filled, faired and sanded. (See Photos 8-9, 8-10, 8-11.)

Photo 8-10. The stem has been power-planed to rough shape.

Photo 8-11. After shaping, the edges of the stem and keel are routed with a 1/2-inch quarter-round bit. The joint between the stem and hull is then faired in with thickened epoxy.

CHAPTER 9
FABRIC AND EPOXY

Shaping the Chines, Keel, Stem and Transom/
Countersinking, Repairing and Filling/
Fairing and Sanding/ Applying the Fabric

There are currently many types of fabric available for covering cold-molded construction: Fiberglass, Dynel, polypropylene, Kevlar and Xynole-polyester are the most common. I use the last almost exclusively because I believe it is the best overall. In certain instances I specify Kevlar inside a hull, particularly to reinforce concave hull surfaces. This is because structurally the inside of a concave hull needs tensile strength athwartships and gets very little from the tongue-and-groove layer. A transverse layer of planking would do the same thing, but Kevlar, with its extremely high tensile, tear and peel strengths, does the job better and more cleanly. A discussion of these cloths is included in Appendix F.

SHAPING THE CHINES, KEEL, STEM AND TRANSOM

Before applying the fabric and epoxy, the hull must be shaped and prepared. Much initial shaping is done with a power plane because it can shear off so much material rap-idly. But care must be taken not to remove too much material or to create uneven or unfair surfaces. When power-planing plywood, "hills" and "valleys" show up as wiggly lines in the exposed laminates—fair planing will show up as even, gently curving or straight, parallel lines. The effect is that of a topographical map in the sense that the plywood laminates become altitude relief planes. This is particularly helpful in cutting scarfs and in shaping the chines.

Because the chines have so much inherent strength and structural mass, they can be softened, or cut away to a large-radius curve, to reduce or eliminate that hard-chine boxiness that people often find visually jarring. A plywood template can be used as a guide for uniformity along the chine, but the most important tool here is the eye. The joining of bottom to topsides will flatten out going forward from amidships until it disappears at the stem. Care should be taken to match both sides of the hull.

After the initial power-planing, the finish-shaping and fairing are done with a belt sander or a low-speed grinder and softpad. The foam softpad must be soft enough so that the grinder can be rolled over the curves of the chine without digging in. Use templates, battens and your eye to check for fairness and uniformity. Pay particular attention to the stern and how it flows into the transom, as this is a dramatic visual area.

The keel should mostly just need cleaning up at this stage. The sides are power-planed fair to remove epoxy and to smooth rough sawcuts. They are then sanded with the grinder and softpad. Sand detailing at the end of the keel fair. Bullnose the bottom of the keel, either with a router or plane and sander—a hard edge here will be vulnerable during groundings. Fillet the keel-to-hull joint with thickened epoxy. (I do this again after the fabric is applied.) The larger the radius of this fillet the better, keeping in mind that epoxy is expensive. I use enough Cabosil to keep the epoxy from sagging, and shape the fillet with a short piece of large diameter (2 inches or more) PVC pipe.

The stem has great visual importance and demands careful shaping. A plywood template may be helpful, but it usually will fit only a limited section. Avoid knife-edge entries; they do not improve hull performance and are fragile besides. The hull surfaces should flow smoothly into the stem unless the design calls for the stem to break at the rabbet, as with clipper-headed bows or squared-off stemheads such as *Teresa*'s.

The edges of the transom are rounded uniformly to make them less vulnerable to damage, or are left hard if a plank overlay is to be added. A plank overlay is used where the effect of bright-finished (varnish or oil) natural wood is desired. I prefer to bed this outer layer in cloth soaked with epoxy. The overlay can be quite thin (1/4 inch), but not so thin that fastener heads will be so close to the surface that they will have to be removed and

their holes plugged. It is stronger to leave fasteners in and epoxy bungs over them, but keep in mind that many years of sanding and refinishing will eventually expose the heads. (See Photos 9-1, 9-2.) After curing, trim the overlay edges to the hull as the fabric covering will overlap and seal their end grain.

COUNTERSINKING, REPAIRING AND FILLING

All fasteners, including screws, nails and staples, must be isolated below the surface of the hull skin and covered with a protective filling of epoxy. Countersink screws with a Fuller bit. If any screwheads have been exposed during shaping, pull, countersink and reinstall them. Countersink nails with a roundhead punch, and staples with the modified chisel shown in Photo 7-16 in Chapter 7.

Also repair any damaged surfaces. Carefully remove any areas of loose or shredded plywood veneer. Examine the entire hull surface for flaws, such as core voids that have been exposed in shaping and core voids one ply below the surface (these are sometimes

Photo 9-1. Teak planks 3/8 inch by 6 inches are laid in epoxy-saturated Xynole-polyester cloth and fastened with countersunk stainless-steel screws (3/4-inch #8 flathead wood screws). The whole process is done at once to achieve a chemical bond among transom, cloth and teak planking. To ensure good glue adhesion, first wash the teak thoroughly with acetone or toluol to remove the natural waxy oils that fill its pores.

Photo 9-2. The countersunk fasteners are bunged with 3/8-inch teak plugs and epoxy. Remember to align the plug grain with the planks. After curing, the edges are trimmed flush to the hull sides and the transom surface is sanded. Later it is either oiled or varnished. The end grain is covered by the fabric and epoxy layers that cover the hull.

Photo 9-3. Prior to covering the hull with fabric and epoxy, examine the entire surface for flaws. Here there are voids in the marine plywood.

visible as a depression or flat spot, and can be felt by pushing on the area with your thumbs). Delaminations may feel soft and spongy or appear as a bubble, particularly after sanding. Even in marine plywood, I have had to rout out delaminated areas measuring several square feet. Use a large flute bit, and inlay a plug of plywood, usually 1/4 inch thick. (See Photos 9-3, 9-4.)

Fill the entire hull surface wherever there are damaged veneers, countersunk holes, cracks, seams or voids with epoxy thickened with Cabosil and/or talc. Large holes may have to be filled twice to bring them flush to the surface. Extreme overfilling or sloppy work will require more sanding, so neatness counts.

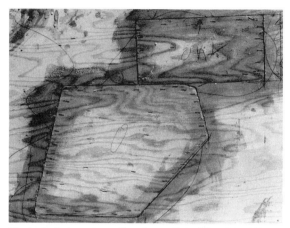

Photo 9-4. A router with a large flute bit set to 1/4-inch depth cleans out the damage, and plugs of 1/4-inch marine plywood are inlaid with epoxy and stapled in place.

FAIRING AND SANDING

Now sand the entire hull in preparation for the fabric covering. Use several battens of different thickness to check for fairness. The fairer the hull is now, the less glazing and filling will be necessary later. The plywood topsides already should be fair and need only a quick sanding, but use a stiff batten to check all the butt joints. Sand any that stand proud until the curve from sheet to sheet is totally uniform. The diagonal bottom planking will be slightly faceted at the seams and will need to be sanded fair. Be careful not to dish out the wood between joints; epoxy is harder than wood and takes longer to sand. Use battens and your eye. The hull shape should flow together in a symphony of planes and curves. (See Photos 9-5, 9-6.) All surfaces should be smooth to the hand and eye, and there should be no voids or openings in the surface.

APPLYING THE FABRIC

The fabric covering is started from the keel. The standard 60-inch width of the Xynole-polyester allows large surfaces to be covered at one time, reducing the number of seams. The fabric is slightly stretchy and pliable, and covers compound curves beautifully. It has excellent wet-out ability and hence is usually applied dry, held in place with masking tape. Where a thicker skin is required, such as on the keel bottom, stem and chines, several layers are overlapped. Long, narrow tapes of cloth may be cut and used where needed. Unravelling of the unselvaged cut can be retarded by coating it lightly with uncatalyzed resin just before application. Use this technique only where you

really need it, as when applying cloth tape over keel and stem areas and rudder and centerboard bottoms. I have found that two layers are adequate for chines, achieved by lapping the topsides cloth over the bottom cloth. (See Photos 9-7, 9-8.) I use three or four layers on high-abrasion areas like the stem and the keel bottom. More layers than this start to become bulky as each layer of cloth is saturated to around 3/64 inch thick, creating more feathering and fairing work later.

Full-strength epoxy resin—neither diluted nor thickened—is applied with heavy-duty 9-inch cage roller frames using good quality covers having 3/8-inch nap. Use roller extension handles to extend your reach. Saturation of the cloth usually takes three coats. A bubble-chaser is essential to ensure that no air is trapped under the fabric. The worker on the left in Photo 9-7 is using a bubble-chaser, or ribbed roller, to remove air bubbles from the wet epoxy-impregnated cloth. We have at times applied the third resin coat on the following day, but it is always best to apply all required epoxy coats at once to achieve proper bonding. In general, fresh epoxy does not adhere well to cured epoxy. Never resin-coat a surface which is to be laminated over or covered with epoxy and cloth. It is essential that the epoxy bond the cloth to the wood by soaking as far as possible into both materials simultaneously. People continually make a tragic mistake by assuming that epoxy will bond to cured epoxy. It will not. Cured epoxy must be coarsely sanded to provide tooth for subsequent epoxy coatings, but this will provide only a mechanical bond, which is greatly inferior to a chemical bond. Sometimes a chemical bond can be achieved between fresh epoxy and partially cured epoxy by using slow catalysts and working fast. Otherwise, coarse sanding is essential.

During epoxy application, remove the masking tape used to hold the cloth in place

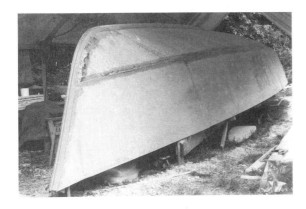

Photos 9-5 and 9-6. Here *Sarah* has been faired and puttied. After a final sanding, her hull will be sheathed in fabric saturated with epoxy. Stem, keel and chine areas will receive two or more cloth layers to provide additional abrasion resistance.

Photos 9-7 and 9-8. Xynole-polyester cloth (4.2 oz.) is applied dry and held in place with masking tape, which is removed as wet-out progresses. Solvent-resistant 3/8-inch by 9-inch roller covers are used to apply full-strength epoxy resin. The bubble-chaser being used by the worker on the left (top) is essential for rolling out air trapped under the wet fabric.

to facilitate cloth saturation. In those instances where staples are used to hold fabric in place, such as when working overhead, they may cause fabric deformation and air bubbles may form around them. It is therefore best to remove staples during epoxy application after the fabric is wet enough to insure that it will remain in place. Use the bubble-chaser to smooth out wrinkles and bubbles. There are situations where staples must remain and be removed later; this is best done while the epoxy is "rubbery," and care must be taken not to cause local delamination. Fully driven staples are almost impossible to remove from fully cured cloth/resin without damage. When staples must be left in, use monel staples.

Wherever the fabric layers overlap (at joints and reinforced areas) feather the edge of the lower layer lightly when possible. Xynole-polyester fuzzes slightly if ground too deeply, especially at reinforced (selvage) edges. The fuzz will lay down and virtually not recur after another resin coat and subsequent sanding. Lightly feathering the lower edge softens the bump to the overlapping next layer, which will largely fair itself out. A light sanding over the finished seam and subsequent fairing will eliminate any hard spot or bump.

CHAPTER 10
PREFINISHING THE FABRIC AND EPOXY SKIN

Fairing, Glazing and Sanding/
Primers and the Waterline

Even though finish coats and bottom paint won't be applied for some time, it is best to prefinish the fabric and epoxy hull skin now. It is far easier to work on the hull while it is upside down than to fight gravity later.

FAIRING, GLAZING AND SANDING

Fairing often challenges the beginner, because it requires practice and skill. The process of fairing a hard surface, like the fabric-and epoxy-covered hull, involves building up low areas rather than the by-now-familiar process of grinding down high ones. Fairing major defects requires applying thick fill coats in especially deep areas or around especially high ones. Glazing consists of troweling on a less thick epoxy coating over large areas to fill pin holes, scratches, gouges, grinder marks, trowel marks, very slight shallow depressions called divots, and coarse textures caused either by inadequate saturation of the fabric or by the roller applicator.

The cold-molded hulls described in this book usually require very little fairing, three or four glazing passes often being all that is necessary. High or low areas more than 1/32 inch from the surrounding plane, as revealed by a batten laid across the hull, are considered severe enough to require fairing.

On cruising and working craft, it is common to fair the topsides to a greater degree than the bottom—unless the vessel is intended to be a highly competitive racing machine, the bottom need not be glazed at all. Most bottom paints are applied by roller and are not extremely smooth anyway, rendering glazing redundant. Rough textures left by rollers or fabric will be faired adequately by the use of high-build epoxy primers which will be described later in this chapter. In any case, barring severe flaws, the fish aren't too critical. By contrast, the topsides will be finished with high-gloss paint systems, and every flaw will show.

The first step in fairing is to carefully examine the hull using both eye and batten. Beaming a flashlight along the hull at night will dramatically reveal even slight defects. Use a pencil or felt tip pen to define the perimeters of areas that will need to be filled prior to general glazing. Lightly sand subtle high areas, being careful not to break through the epoxy into the fabric more than several hundredths of an inch, because this would weaken it.

I use wallboard-finishing tools for fairing and glazing; all three operations have much in common. Use an 8-inch flexible steel taping knife to apply the thickened epoxy, whether for fairing or glazing, working from a steel trough. Fair the applied compound with an 18-inch stainless-steel flexible finishing trowel, the kind that has a full-length plastic handle. It is vital to keep dirt out of the compound; even a grain of sand will leave a surface gouge the length of your fairing pass.

The consistency of the compound is critical to your success. In general, make the compound thicker and stiffer for deeper or thicker application, and thinner and creamier for long, shallow glazing passes. If the compound is too thick, it will drag the flexible finishing trowel and exhaust you. If too thin, it will sag. The proper consistency is about that of wallboard joint compound. The thixogens used also affect consistency and sag, as do pot life and temperature. Cabosil typically has the least sag, but is hard to sand. Microballoons are commonly used for fairing, but are expensive, and may sag if applied in either too thin a mix or too thick a buildup, and often gum up sandpaper. I find talc, the same fine-grained mineral used to make baby powder, to be the best. It is inexpensive (less than 10 percent of the cost of microballoons), has little tendency to sag and sands beautifully. Talc can also be used to thicken paints to create sanding primers. I apply it liberally to my hands before putting on latex gloves to reduce sweating and help keep epoxy off my hands and out from under my fingernails when the gloves tear during work. When gloves become sticky with epoxy, a light

dusting of talc solves the problem. Drawbacks of the mineral are that it must be kept dry to prevent caking and introducing moisture into the epoxy; it must be mixed thoroughly when making either fairing compound or sanding primer, and the cured material will be somewhat softer than cured material made with Cabosil or microballoons. My solution is to custom-blend my fairing compounds using varying proportions of all three thixogens, depending on my specific needs. For most fairing and glazing work, I use a blend of around three parts talc to one part Cabosil, avoiding microballoons altogether because of their cost. Add the thixogens gradually to the catalyzed epoxy after it is thoroughly mixed until the desired consistency is reached. Apply the compound with the 8-inch taping knife as evenly as possible over a long area 15 inches or 16 inches wide. Draw the finishing trowel slowly and steadily over the same area. Too much compound will either create a bulge or bunch up in front of the trowel and start to fall; too little will leave skips or holidays. Trowel angle is critical. For flat surfaces, the blade should approach being perpendicular to the surface; curved areas will call for a low blade angle. These techniques must be acquired by practice. Detailing of edges such as the stem or hard chines is best done with a flexible rubber squeegee, the kind used by the autobody industry.

After the first pass, apply compound to the next horizontal run below the first (always work below or down.) Repeat the process until the whole plane has been glazed.

After the glazing has cured, examine it for fairness and sand with #80 paper using a soft pad. There will be overlaps where the finishing trowel passed the run above; these will need to be sanded down or filled by another pass if they are low. Use the finishing trowel as a batten. When held perpendicular, it will show defects in a flat plane; when held almost flat, it will do the same for a curved plane. After one or two horizontal passes and sandings, make a set of vertical passes. This will remove ripples caused by the knife and fair out defects in the horizontal plane. Keep in mind that the actual thickness of these glazes is often only one or two hundredths of an inch. The divots and troughs being filled are usually no more than a few hundredths of an inch. Frequently only these two or three passes are necessary. Small problem areas, like finishing-trowel overlaps that are still a little low (they are usually high and get sanded off), dirt gouges and holidays can be filled with a 3-inch flexible putty knife.

An unsteady hand or compound that is too thick or too heavily applied may cause ripples during the glazing pass with the finishing trowel. Sometimes another pass (clean the trowel first), made at a slightly different angle to the ripples will smooth them out, but this may leave skips. More than two passes usually requires the addition of more compound, as the surface becomes too dry to work; it is best to make only one pass for this reason. Applying too much or too little compound prior to the pass causes problems that are solved by experience. Experiment and practice with your compound mixes (proportions) and application techniques on the keel. There will be long ridges where the built-up protective bottom fabric layers wrap the edges of the keel bottom and end, and under the final cloth layer near the bottom of the keel sides. Learning to fair these smooth will prepare you for the similar ridges along the chines and stem.

Besides the low-speed grinder/polisher with 8-inch soft pad, the most helpful sander during fairing is the pneumatic dual-axis body grinder. The revolving disc is itself revolved, hence the edge of the sandpaper is always oscillating and can't dig in or cause the marks so common to body grinders. A poor man's alternative is to attach a square grinding pad made from a piece of 1/8-inch plywood to a low-speed grinder/polisher. Sandpaper is glued to the pad in square, slightly oversized sheets with sanding-disc contact cement. Don't try this with a high-speed grinder. Initial sandings are made with #80 paper. When the hull is starting to become very fair, #120 paper is used. The orbital sander with #120 paper is used for the final sanding. Don't sand finer than that; we still want plenty of tooth for mechanical bonding to our primers.

The fairing and glazing should extend below the bootstripe whatever amount is convenient, usually about 1 foot. On chine hulls, fair and glaze right to and including the chine.

Because the chines, stem and transom form visual lines, take care to finish them to a high degree. The techniques involved are a little different from those used for large, gently curving planes, as are the tools. The flexible rubber squeegee previously mentioned is bought in long strips and cut into useful lengths with a razor knife. A 12-inch length is handy for glazing soft chines such as those on *Sarah* and *Teresa*; a 4-inch length will get into the joint between topsides and square-finished stems. Sand these areas with a powerful orbital sander (the pneumatic jitterbug is best) using first #80 paper, then finish them with #120 paper.

PRIMERS AND THE WATERLINE

Next, two-part epoxy sanding primer is applied to the topsides and extended a little below the waterline. (Refer to the plans if you have any doubt where this is.) Usually two coats are sufficient, sanding between with #120 or #180 paper. By now the topsides surface should be like liquid satin. When you compare your hull surface to that of the average production fiberglass boat, the latter will look lumpy and wavy by comparison.

Spray painting creates the smoothest surfaces. Rolling or brushing or a combination of the two rarely approaches the quality of a good spray job. Even in primer application, much sanding will have to be done to eliminate brush marks or roller texture, which usually will necessitate a third coat.

There are many paint systems on the market, and those earmarked for the marine industry usually have the greatest price markup. Although there is nothing quite like Awlgrip (U.S. Paints), Sherwin-Williams sells good, alternative paint systems for much less money. I use its Tile-Clad II epoxy paints extensively for primers and interior finishes, and its Polane H.S. polyurethanes for exterior finishing. When ordering these products, specify "Exterior" or "Non Photochemically Reactive" for paints, catalysts and reducers. Failure to do this will result in eventual chalking of the surfaces.

I like to use Sherwin-Williams Tile-Clad II Enamel as a topsides primer, even though it is not a true primer. It's tough and durable and protects the topsides during construction of the rest of the boat, which will take anywhere from several months for a professional crew to several years for the part-time amateur working alone. I add approximately one-half cup of talc to each gallon of catalyzed paint to convert it to a sanding primer. The thickened paint must be very thoroughly mixed. If you spray this primer, reduce it a little more than normal to compensate for the thixogen. (See Photo 10-1.)

After the topsides primer comes the boottop. The designed waterline, or load waterline, on the plans represents where the hull should float under normal load conditions. The bottom paint, or boottop line, must be several inches above the actual waterline, or marine growth will attach itself to the top-

Photo 10-1. Spraying two-part epoxy sanding primer is done after the topsides have been faired with epoxy fairing compound and carefully sanded. It is vital to wear protective clothing, goggles and a fume-filtering mask.

sides paint. Large, heavy cruising and working craft may have boottops 6 inches or more above the waterline; daysailers can get by with 1½ inches. Transfer your designed waterline from the plans to the hull in four places—stem, stern and hull amidships on both sides—by measuring down from the sheerline.

Because your hull was built to its waterlines (check to make sure nothing has settled) the boottop can be established by the "water-bucket and clear plastic hose method." Fill a 5-gallon pail about two-thirds full with water and place it amidship so the water level is approximately at the hull boottop. A length of small-diameter (1/4-inch to 3/8-inch I.D.) clear plastic hose a little longer than half the hull length (so it can reach the bow and stern and both sides of the hull) is submerged in the bucket. One end is weighted so it stays in the bucket and, the other end is carefully pulled out until the hose is on the ground keeping the end higher than the bucket. Hold the end of the hose against the hull amidships at your predetermined mark where the bottom paint is to start. Water is either added to or subtracted from the bucket until the water level in the hose matches your mark. Note that lifting the hose higher doesn't affect the water level, but lowering it will allow water to siphon out. Hence it will be necessary to place your thumb over the end, particularly when crawling under the hull to mark the other side. Check your marks on the stem, stern and other side of the hull amidships. If they disagree with each other by more than a 1/2 inch, double-check your measurements. Some error will be caused by your sheerline, which is not yet trimmed. Find the sheer points by measuring to the marks on the mold frames inside and transferring the amount outside. Walk the hose all around the hull, making marks every 6 inches to 12 inches. Take particular care with overhanging sterns because the hose won't lie vertically against the hull. A small level will help in severe cases.

Mask off the boottop and prime the hull bottom. Do not cut in a waterline. Not only will it damage the hull skin, but waterlines are often changed during the lives of boats. The high-build primers I recommend for the bottom will leave a ridge that stands proud, making the boottop easy to locate.

A high-build (heavily pigmented) primer on the bottom acts like a protective glazing on the topsides without the work. Usually two coats are applied with a roller with only a scuff sanding (#80 paper) between coats. Remember that the last epoxy coating needs

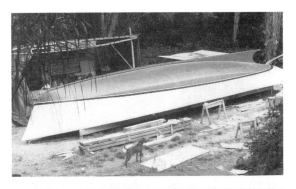

Photos 10-2 and 10-3. *Sarah*'s hull is ready to be turned over. The red bottom is a high-build epoxy primer. This EXUMA 52 hull was built by three workers in eight weeks.

to be sanded before primed. I use Sherwin-Williams Tile-Clad II Hi-Bild Primer for the bottom. This comes in brick red only and has good abrasion resistance, yet sands well. (See Photos 10-2, 10-3.) Do not apply bottom paint until just before launching, as it releases poisonous fumes and deteriorates in the atmosphere.

CHAPTER 11
TURNING THE HULL OVER

Square Wheels/ The Lifting Eye/ Turning Techniques/
Leveling and Cribbing

There are many ways of turning hulls over; these are covered in various books on boatbuilding in the Suggested Reading List. Following is the method I use for cold-molded hulls.

SQUARE WHEELS

Turning wheels must support the entire hull while it is being turned over, hence they must be strong and firmly attached. While the wheels will vary according to hull size, type and weight, those described here will be of similar design and construction. I know of no simpler or less expensive method for turning over large hulls. These "square" wheels were built to turn *Sarah* over, and were modified slightly (mostly the hull supports) to turn *Teresa* over. (See Photos 11-1, 11-2.)

Build the turning wheels from doubled 2 x 10 planks joined at the corners with three pieces of 3/4-inch CDX plywood cut to a 2-foot radius. (See Fig. 11-1.) Fasteners are #16 staging nails and/or bolts in larger wheels. Attach the wheels from the inside to mold

frames 4 and 8 by using plywood gussets to box the frame heads. In hulls with long or heavy sterns, the turning wheels may be shifted one frame aft; they should divide the hull weight as equally as possible. Outside, the wheels brace the hull tightly with additional plywood supports. Old carpet protects the finish. At the initial weight-bearing side, the wheels provide further support by means of 2 x 4 or 2 x 6 braces inside the hull as shown. (See Fig. 11-1 and Photos 11-3, 11-5.) Upright supports on the opposite side of the

Photo 11-1. Sturdy turning wheels are firmly attached to the hull.

hull run parallel to the hull topsides, against which they are tightly fitted.

Hulls under 40 feet and/or of light displacement can use 2 x 8 planks; those below 30 feet can use 2 x 6 planks. Hulls over 55 feet or of moderate to heavy displacement should use 2 x 12 planks. Very large or heavy hulls may require tripled planks with four plywood corners and gussets, or even require three or four wheels. They may also benefit from 4-foot radius corners and need two cranes, one on each wheel, instead of using a single lifting eye. In all cases, the planks and plywood used should be of reasonably good quality.

Photo 11-3. A boom truck from a local lumberyard was used to turn *Teresa*'s hull over. Vertical 2 x 4 braces reinforce the wheel-to-frame connection inside the hull (at the far side of the interior in the photo). Note the lifting hook and rope strops.

Photo 11-4. *Teresa*'s hull is halfway over, presenting a view of the hull rarely seen. From the standpoint of weight distribution, the aft turning wheel should have been better placed at frame 9.

Photo 11-2. Turning wheels are made from 2 x 10 yellow pine planks, joined at the corners with 3/4-inch CDX plywood gussets cut at a 2-foot radius. Carpet padding protects the hull at all exterior contact points. Additional plywood bracing is installed between the wheels and chine area.

Photo 11-5. *Sarah*'s hull at the halfway point reveals several mold frames left in the hull for stiffening. Two-by-six braces can be seen between the turning wheels and the frames. Deformation of the strongback was caused by using it for a winch belay while lowering the hull to the halfway point. The boom truck has been repositioned for the remaining lift-and-lower maneuver.

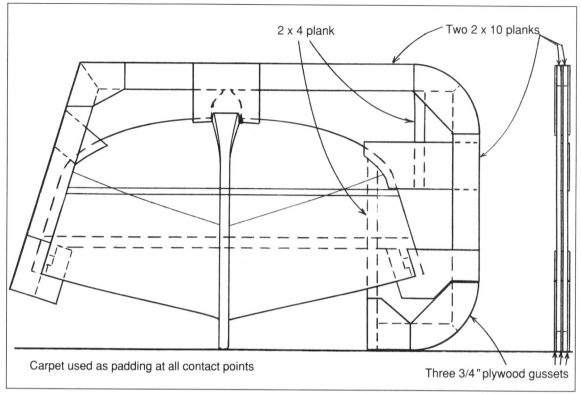

Figure 11-1. Turning wheel for an EXUMA 44.

Avoid spruce planks; use Douglas fir, hem-fir or yellow pine. The planks should not have large knots near their edges.

To lighten the hull, several mold frames are removed before turning. In smaller hulls, all but the frames at the turning wheels and lifting eye may be removed. Remove all supports to the shop floor and all connections to the strongback. Inspect the three remaining frames for strong connections to the hull; in larger hulls you may need to screw steel angles to the joints between the mold frames and the chine logs and sheer clamps. Large C-clamps are also used where needed, shown in several of the photos.

THE LIFTING EYE

The lifting eye is a plywood sandwich attached to the head of a mold frame 6 or 7; it should be as close as possible to the center of gravity (fore and aft) of the bare hull. (See Fig. 11-2.) On heavy hulls, light hulls larger than 50 feet or hulls that are deep of keel, a second cross-brace will be required in addition to the existing frame cross-brace. Heavy hulls may also require the use of wire rope cables between the lifting eye and the lowest opposite point of each wheel to ease the loading on the sheer clamp where the eye is attached. Very large, heavy hulls will need to be lifted, as previously stated, by two cranes stationed at each turning wheel. A heavy rope or cable strop is doubled through holes in the eye sandwich and padded. At the hole there must be solid wood in the plywood sandwich. The hook must be very strong and firmly attached to the hull and frame, because it will support half the hull weight. In hulls over 35 feet, one or more through-bolts (threaded rod) pass through the hook sandwich, the hull skin and the sheer clamp. Large washers or steel plates are placed under the nuts both inside and outside the hull.

TURNING TECHNIQUES

A boom truck, crane or block and tackle rigged to a high tripod can be used to turn the hull. Ratings for any of these should be twice the estimated hull weight, providing a safety factor of four. Your local building material supplier may turn your hull for you for a small fee, but everything must be ready to go so as not to detain truck and driver. The articulated booms of these trucks cannot bear much weight when boomed out, and you will need truck access to both sides of the hull for vessels having over 12-foot beam or of more than light to moderate displacement.

The trickiest, most dangerous part of turning occurs when the hull's center of gravity shifts from one side of the square wheels' pivot points to the other. This happens twice;

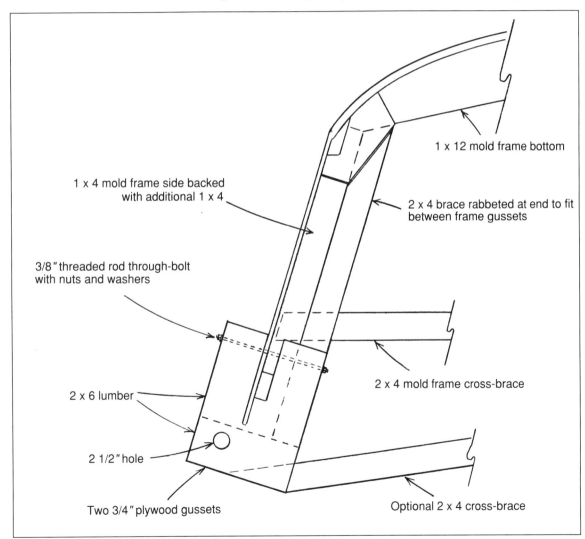

1 x 12 mold frame bottom

1 x 4 mold frame side backed with additional 1 x 4

2 x 4 brace rabbeted at end to fit between frame gussets

3/8" threaded rod through-bolt with nuts and washers

2 x 6 lumber

2 x 4 mold frame cross-brace

2 1/2" hole

Two 3/4" plywood gussets

Optional 2 x 4 cross-brace

Figure 11-2. Lifting eye for an EXUMA 44.

Photo 11-6. The exterior of *Sarah* at the halfway point. Hull-support gusseting can be seen at the chine.

Photo 11-7. The eye is attached to a frame head with gussets and blocking. Because *Teresa*'s frame sides were 1 x 4s, another 1 x 4 doubler was added along with a 2 x 4 to stiffen the frame.

once on the way up and once on the way down. Provide for this by using a second winch or very large block and tackle secured to a tree or other deadman to belay the hull as the weight shifts. Trucks with articulated booms may not need a belay if the boom end is very close to the hull, as in Photo 11-3. The lifting point of a crane, boom truck or tripod should be slightly beyond the point where the weight shift takes place. Obviously, the lifting point will have to be moved after the hull is stabilized at the halfway point so that it will be above and slightly beyond the new weight-shift point as the hull is lowered.

Sarah was turned with a fixed-boom truck using a cable winch; a second cable winch on the front of my Scout truck served as a belay. *Teresa* was turned entirely from the same side using the articulated boom of the local lumberyard's delivery truck. (See Photos 11-3 through 11-11.)

Photo 11-8. In this photo, the 2 x 4 wheel-to-frame braces are seen. One of the strongback girders has been removed to get the boom truck closer to the hull.

LEVELING AND CRIBBING

Level the turned hull by jacking up the bow until the hull is approximately on her waterlines. Use supports, cribbing or even a cradle to firmly hold the hull during remaining construction. Having a level hull greatly simplifies the use of levels during interior construction. The water bucket and clear plastic hose used previously to establish the waterline boottop may now be used to level the hull. In some cases it may be inconvenient to raise the bow high enough to achieve level fore and aft (as in a hull with great drag to the keel). In this case, tape a wood triangle on one side of your level; establish bulkheads and furniture to the wood edge while the level reads true. In any case, the hull should be level athwartships.

The hull will need fewer supports than a plank-on-frame vessel, but the ends should be supported and all structure must be firm and stable to support the increasing weight of construction without settling or deformation. Photo 11-12 shows *Teresa*'s cribbing. Hull supports were spiked to the ground to prevent shifting, and cross-bracing was added to end supports.

During leveling and cribbing, the turning wheels, lifting eye and remaining frames are removed. Care must be taken that the very flexible sheer of the hull is not allowed to deform by placing four or five athwartships cross-braces between the sheer clamps during this process. These temporary cross-braces (1 x 4s or 2 x 4s) are stage-nailed or screwed to the tops of the sheer clamps.

Now, call a turning party to celebrate!

Photo 11-9. As the hull starts its final descent, workers temporarily block the hull when the weight shifts overcenter while we evaluate our lowering system. In general, it is not a good idea to have people under the hull during turning operations.

Photo 11-10. *Teresa*'s hull right side up.

Photo 11-11. *Sarah*'s hull is right side up. The owner, Michael Polvere, stands at the left.

Photo 11-12. Cribbing supports should be simple and strong. The 2 x 4 stacks such as the one under the keel are handy, as are the gusseted supports under the hull amidships. The 2 x 4 posts under the stern will be tied together with 1 x 4 braces that will join under the keel. Carpet padding is used at all contact points.

CHAPTER 12
INSIDE THE HULL

Sanding and Sealing/ Laying Out the Interior Structural Members

SANDING AND SEALING

The inside of the hull will be rough from epoxy glue, nail holes and unfilled voids. It is now cleaned up and rough-sanded to remove splinters and excess glue. Fill any voids with epoxy thickened with Cabosil, talc or a mixture of both. No cracks, holes or voids should remain because these will collect moisture, dirt, fungus, mold or insects. Carefully sand and fair the whole hull interior. Pay particular attention to bottom areas, which may be used as the finished cabin sole in flat-centered and canoe-type hulls.

Sealing the interior of the hull is necessary to protect it and stabilize the moisture content of the wood. Your hull is an open, upright container that will collect dirt and moisture, which must be prevented from damaging it.

Prepare a sealing coat of epoxy by reducing the pure resin mix sufficiently to soak into the wood grain (usually around 15 percent). The generic reducer for most epoxy is equal parts of methyl ethyl ketone and toluene (or toluol), but you should use the reducer recommended by the epoxy manufacturer if it is

different. Apply several coats to the whole hull interior until no more will soak in (rejection). Certain areas will soak up more resin than others, and these should be recoated to rejection. Avoid puddling by re-rolling these areas to redistribute excess epoxy. The goal is

Photo 12-1. Once right side up, several cross-braces are used to hold the hull sheer in place, and remaining frames are removed. The interior surface is filled, sanded and repeatedly coated with reduced epoxy to rejection, after which one last coat is added to completely seal the wood. Note that this is not done above the sheer clamps, where more lamination will take place; the epoxy sealant will have to be ground away wherever bulkheads, cleats and furniture are fastened to the hull.

to achieve a smooth, uniformly sealed surface. Photo 12-1 shows *Teresa*'s sealed interior with temporary cross-bracing to hold the sheer in place. Note that no sealer is applied above the sheer clamps, because deck beams and blocking are yet to be installed.

You probably remember my warning against resin-coating an area that will be laminated over, and you are wondering about bulkhead attachment. When it comes time to attach bulkheads, cleats and furniture, it will be necessary to grind through this coating. This is easy and fast, as this coating penetrates only a few hundredths of an inch.

LAYING OUT THE INTERIOR STRUCTURAL MEMBERS

After the hull is sealed, lay out the bulkheads, deck beams, floors and engine beds where they are to be installed, using a marker or felt tip pen. These are determined by the design and must be very carefully transferred and scaled to the real hull from the plans. When going from drawing to reality, there are occasionally some revelations about placement of bulkheads and hatch/skylight location and size. The time to consider changes is now, not later. It is also critical that your deck beam layout along both sides of the hull be symmetrical. I generally lay out the major bulkheads first, as they define the vessel's interior. Next are the deck beams adjacent to the hatches, skylights, trunk cabins and mast partners; then come the evenly spaced major deck beams and side beams.

Mark both sides of bulkheads and deck beams, and place an 'X' between the marks to avoid confusion. Initial layout is along the sheer clamps. The bottoms of bulkheads are established after the bulkhead-to-deck cleats are installed. These are actually thin (usually 1½-inch) deck beams. After they are in place and leveled vertically (in this sense they are

different from deck beams, which are not leveled but lie perpendicular to the sheer clamp), the bottoms of the bulkheads are located and marked using either a level or plumb line.

Keep in mind the following while laying out bulkheads and beams: which side of the cleat/beams the bulkheads will lie on; and the fact that distances along the sheer clamps, particularly toward the bow, must be longer than the distances between structures fore and aft. I usually get my measurements from the sheer on the plans. Lay them out on the sheer clamps with a pencil, make any necessary adjustments, and mark them in with a felt tip pen. You can erase marking mistakes with alcohol or acetone.

The location of the floor timbers comes from the plans. If the design specifies aligning some of them with the bulkheads, use a level or plumbline from the cleat/beams above to locate them. The plugged nail holes in the hull are useful in locating design stations, from which the remaining floors are laid out. (These are the holes left from the staging nails that held the tongue-and-groove planking to the mold frames, which were, remember, just offset from the design stations.)

Engine beds are similarly located, by using nail holes for orientation and transferring measurements from the plans. The centerline of the hull will be the middle of the centerplank or inner keel in wineglass hulls; from this the athwartships bed location is measured. Make sure the engine beds suit your chosen engine, and that the shaft will line up properly. If the hole for the shaft log was preformed as the keel was being stack-laminated (Chapter 8), use it as an aid to aligning bed angle. Double-check everything, and have a set of engine dimensions and diagrams from the manufacturer on hand to compare to your engine compartment.

CHAPTER 13
DECK STRUCTURE

Deck Beams/ Carlins/ Notching the Sheer Clamp/ Prefitting, Routing and Finishing/ Installing the Main Beams

The interior construction of most boats is not quite as sequential as these next six chapters imply. Rather, different aspects of the work progress more or less simultaneously, with conflicting contingencies often stopping work on one project while something else must be worked on. I have organized the material as sequentially as possible, grouping related projects together to provide clarity.

DECK BEAMS

In large vessels, deck beams need only be laminated when their length and crown make it impractical to saw them from solid timber. In recent decades, amateur builders in particular have been misled into going "lamination crazy." The weight saved by lamination is inconsequential to all but flat-out racing machines; in a 40-foot cruising boat it might amount to 100 pounds or less. Lumber suitable for laminating, glue, labor, the jig and clamps involved, and the extra finishing (cleaning up the sides) will increase the final cost of laminated beams by a factor of between 3 and 10 times over the cost of sawn ones. One-by-four stock, if it can be used, will usually cost between one-and-a-half and two times more than 4 x 12 beam stock, the scraps from which can be used for blocking later. I can cut out all the beams for a 40-footer in two days, the same time it takes to make a double jig and lay up the first two laminated beams. If the laminating stock has to be other than standard lumberyard size (some designs specify 1/2 inch), the second day will be spent in wasteful surfacing.

Deck beam dimensions are determined by the vessel size, beam span, anticipated deck loads and decking material. Scantlings will be on the construction details page of most designs. Note that there are often two or more different sized beams in a boat. For vessels between 40 feet and 60 feet, 4 x 12 stock is usually adequate for the major beams. Vessels below 40 feet can often use 3 x 12 stock. Cleat/beams and side deck beams can generally be cut from $1\frac{1}{2}$-inch stock often simply using 2 x 4 stock for side beams. With careful

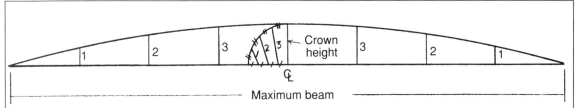

1. Lay out maximum beam on plywood form or plank.

2. Draw perpendicular line at the center for maximum crown (height). This is the centerline (₵).

3. With a compass set to the crown height, swing an arc beside the centerline.

4. Divide the radius along the bottom line into four equal parts, and divide the quarter circle into four equal arcs.

5. Draw lines between the respective radius and arc divisions and number them as shown.

6. Divide the maximum-beam line into eight equal parts, and draw perpendicular lines at each division equal to the lines in the quarter circle.

7. The curve is drawn by springing the batten through the upper points and scribing a line.

8. After the first curve is cut with a circular saw, draw a second curve above it using a sliding marker set to at least 1/8 inch more than the desired deck beam height. Readers who are mathematicians will note that this curve is not truly the arc of a circle; it is parabolic. It is, however, extremely close, the deviation being that the ends of the arc are slightly flattened.

Figure 13-1. Laying out a deck-beam template.

layout, three beams of different lengths can be sawn from a single timber.

First, make a deck beam template to the crown specified in the plans. This plywood form is used to trace the beam shape onto both sides of the timber for cutting. The length of the template is determined by the maximum beam of the boat. Crown is given in inches of height for maximum beam. Lay

Photo 13-1. *Teresa*'s solid Douglas fir deck beams were traced and cut from both sides of 4 x 12 timbers using the template visible to the left of the beams.

out and cut the template as shown in Figure 13-1. It is desirable that the beam-ends flatten out slightly, and this is aided both by the layout method described in Figure 13-1 and by the natural tendency of the batten to straighten at each end. The benefits of this are that the side decks will have less curve and pitch, making them easier to walk on, and that the side deck beams in many vessels can be made from 2 x 4s by slightly curving their tops and leaving their bottoms straight.

In many traditional craft, deck beams are tapered at each end. This practice saves weight without appreciably weakening the beams, assuming it is not overdone. A template for tapered beams can be made by laying out a bottom curve of slightly less crown than the top. Beams that are $3^{1}/_{2}$ inches high at the center might, for example, be $2^{1}/_{2}$ inches high at the ends. When laying out beams with a tapered template, take care to align the centers. In most contemporary boats with large cabins, tapering deck beams just isn't worth the trouble, but it might add a nice touch to taper the coach roof beams.

Photo 13-1 shows the template and beams for *Teresa*. Her main beams are 3½ inches square; cleat/beams and side deck beams are 1½ inches x 3½ inches. Deck crown is 6 inches in 12 feet. The side deck beams were cut from 2 x 4 stock, to which a very slight curve was added to the top edge only. This curve matches that of the last 2 feet at either end of the deck beam template. The finished height of the deck substructure after planing and sanding was about 3⅜ inches. *Sarah's* beams are the same size, but her decking is thicker.

Sawn beams are scribed and cut out from both sides of the timber because an average circular saw can't cut through 3½ inches of lumber—and even a saw that could, might have difficulty following the curve. It is plain that the scribing and cutting should be thoughtfully done or the resulting beams won't match from one side to the other. For this reason, cut the beams a little oversize, and belt-sand them with a #50 belt until smooth and fair. (The beam tops can be planed instead of belt-sanded.) Check the beams for size and fairness with the template. After a little practice, you will probably get good at laying out and cutting things from two sides; you will have already made your

Photo 13-2. After cutting the beams, both top and bottom surfaces are faired and sanded.

stem and stern structures this way by now. Finish-sand the sides and bottom with the belt sander with a #80 belt. (See Photo 13-2.)

Laminated beams are laid up on a jig, (see Fig. 13-2) designed to construct two beams at a time. The sides are cut with 1/2 inch more crown than the plans specify to allow for spring-back of the lamination. I make the jig from two 2 x 12s with 4 x 4 spanners nailed in place between them 1 foot or less on center. These spanners are rabbeted at each end so they will overlap the 2 x 12 sides. Two deck beams are laid up side by side; 2 x 4 blocks are laid across them on edge (working out from the beam centers). These are clamped in place with big C-clamps, bar or pipe clamps,

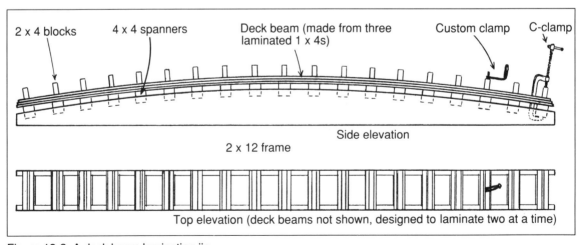

Figure 13-2. A deck beam laminating jig.

or hand-made clamps as shown in Figure 13-3. Everything must be covered with wax or plastic to prevent sticking. It is said that a lamination must have at least four layers to be of good quality, but I have made and seen many beams made of three layers of 1 x 4. The deck layers constitute the rest of the lamination. The advantage to triple-laminated beams is that they finish at only $2^{1}/_{4}$ inches high, a particular advantage in gaining headroom in flush-decked vessels.

Only two beams per day can be made on one jig, and these must be planed on both sides to true up the layers to each other and remove excess glue. Use a try square during planing to prevent the beams from getting out of square. After planing, belt-sand the beams smooth with a #80 belt.

CARLINS

Major carlins for trunk cabins, some cockpits and large cargo hatches are similar in size to the major deck beams. When sawn from solid timber, the timber is "visualized" in the plane of the deck at the place where the carlin will be. (See Fig. 13-4.) Curved carlins, cut in that plane, will be parallelogram-shaped in section and will match the curves of the hull sheerline adjacent to them both vertically and horizontally. (In other words, the carlins will be parallel to the sheerlines.) Generally, the sheer curve in the vertical plane is automatically duplicated in the carlin, because as the ends of the carlin curve inboard they also lift slightly due to the pitch of the deck. Lay out the top of the carlin on the appropriate stock (4 x 12 for *Teresa*) by holding the timber next to the hull where the carlin will be, tilting the timber to the plane of the deck, and duplicating the hull sheerline on the timber by making equal measurements along its length from the hull to the timber every foot or so. Spring the batten through these and connect the

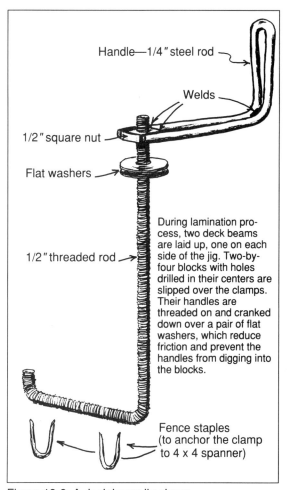

Figure 13-3. A deck beam jig clamp.

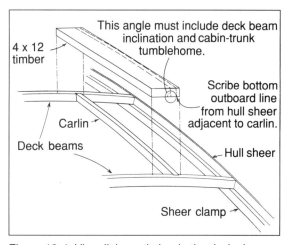

Figure 13-4. Visualizing a timber in the deck plane for carlin layout.

Photo 13-3. Solid carlins are cut from 4 x 12 timbers, notched for side deck beams, routed and sanded before being prefinished.

Photo 13-4. Laminated carlins can use the hull sheer outboard of their intended location as a laminating jig. Here three 1 x 6 laminates are used. The sheer will also be used as a template to scribe and cut the finished lamination to the desired deck curve by holding the lamination outside the hull at the desired trunk cabin tumblehome angle and scribing it.

Photo 13-5. This shows the same thing from a different perspective.

dots. Use a compass set to the desired width of the carlin to reproduce a second curved line parallel to the first. Draw the appropriate carlin section on each end of the timber, and re-create the top curves on the bottom. Set your circular saw to the correct bevel using the end sections, and carefully cut out the carlin from both sides. The cuts are made at a bevel so the sides of the carlin will be either vertical or parallel to the trunk sides (which should have a little tumblehome). For vessels with a relatively flat sheerline, place the timber right on top of the hull sheer and trace the curve onto the bottom of your timber. Then follow the above process working from the bottom instead of the top. Hulls with dramatically curved sheerlines will require starting with a thicker timber. After the carlin sides are laid out and cut, as above, place the carlin alongside the hull and trace the sheer onto it twice (for the bottom and top), and make those cuts. I know this all sounds incredibly complicated, but I believe when you get out there and do it, things will become clear.

Straight carlins can be cut from a slightly warped timber to pick up deck curve, or may be cut from a larger timber and have the curve cut or planed into them. Careful layout of large carlins will pay off later in the harmonious beauty of the lines of deck, sheer and cabin sides. (See Photo 13-3.)

If it is necessary or desirable, large carlins may be laminated. *Sarah*'s were laminated from three 1 x 6 layers by clamping them right to her hull sheer outboard of their intended location. (See Photo 13-4.) The finished laminations were shaped to fit the deck plane by holding them against the hull sheer outside the boat at the angle of trunk cabin tumblehome, scribing them from the sheer, and cutting them out. The saw was set to the angle (bevel) of the athwartships deck inclination where the carlins were to be installed. This created the same parallelogram section we use for sawn carlins. The bevel angle is taken from the longest deck beam the carlin intersects at the point of intersection. Use a protractor and level—the number of degrees of cabin trunk tumblehome is added to the vertical protractor angle. This angle is also scribed onto the beams (or bulkheads) where the carlins terminate, and notches or mortises are made for the carlin ends to fit into.

NOTCHING THE SHEER CLAMP

When the deck beams meet the sheer clamp at such an angle that they rest on its inboard edge, the clamp must be notched so that the beams rest flat. (See Photo 13-6.) If wedges were used, the sheer of the hull would be raised more than the precalculated height of the deck beams. When the deck beams rest only on the outboard edge of the sheer clamp, as in hulls with tumblehome, the bottom of the beam is usually shaved until it lies flat. This lowers the finished hull sheer, which is better than raising it. If this situation is anticipated early, the sheer clamp can be placed higher during lofting or construction to compensate.

PREFITTING, ROUTING AND FINISHING

When prefitting the deck beams, take care to cut their ends to the correct compound bevels (and not too short!). You can cut one end, set the beam in place, and use a level to determine where the cut on the other end starts. (Place the bottom of the level down in the corner between sheer clamp and hull planking.) The beams should fit snugly in place without pushing on the hull. As I mentioned earlier, bulkhead cleat/beams are laid out to stand vertically (they must interface with bulkheads). Their bottom edges must be beveled at the sheer clamps and they must be

Photo 13-6. The carlin is clamped in place temporarily while the sheer clamp notches are laid out and cut to their correct angles and depths.

made from straight stock. Deck beams are set perpendicular to the clamps, and hence cant inward at each end of the vessel as the sheer lifts. This simplifies their installation as well as that of the deck, and is traditional.

Prefit all the beams in the vessel, mark them where they intersect sheer clamps, carlins and bulkheads, and remove them. I rout the beam bottom edges to my pencil marks with a 3/8-inch quarter-round bit, leaving the beams square where they join the sheer clamp, intersect a carlin or interface with a bulkhead. Then I carefully sand them with a belt sander, orbital sander and by hand. Prefinishing follows. I have found that the easiest way to varnish the beams with the desirable six or eight coats is to spray them with clear polyurethane, two coats per day, sanding between every two coats. If the beams are to be painted, the best results may be achieved by spraying a two-part epoxy (such as Tile-Clad II Enamel) with an anti-mildew additive. Thicken the first coat with talc to make sanding primer and apply three coats minimum. The tops of the beams are left unfinished because the deck will be glued to them. Mask the ends and any other gluing surfaces before varnishing or painting.

Main beams and occasionally bulkheads are notched or mortised to receive the carlin

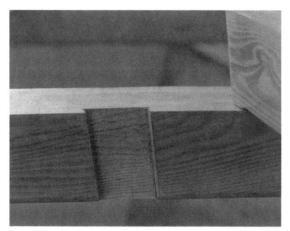

Photo 13-7. Main deck beams are notched to the proper angle for the carlin ends with a backsaw or circular saw using a fine-tooth (plywood) blade.

Photo 13-8. Carlins are notched for side deck beams; bullnose routs end just shy of the sawcuts (the carlin is upside down to show this).

ends and the carlins are notched to receive side deck beams (both carlin and sheer clamp notches are shown in Photo 13-6). The sides of these notches are usually cut at an angle, as the intersections are rarely at 90 degrees. Make the cuts with a backsaw or circular saw with a fine-tooth blade and chisel out the waste between them. Rout bulkhead mortises with a 1/2-inch flute bit; bevel the sides with a chisel, or leave the mortise square and chisel the carlin end to fit.

Carlins are set in place to determine the angles of the ends of the side-deck beams. The layout for side-deck beams along the carlins must correspond to the layout along the sheer clamp. Traditional beam-to-carlin joints (half dovetails) are unnecessary when plywood is used in the deck, as it acts as a huge gusset to relieve tension at the joints. When the carlins and side deck beams are installed (Chapter 16), the joints will be bedded in thickened epoxy and fastened with two 3-inch #14 stainless steel screws, which are countersunk and bunged. When the side-deck beams have been laid out along the carlins and their intersection angles have been determined, write the angles on top of the carlins next to each notch. (These reference

angles will be used later when cutting the ends of the side-deck beams.) Then remove the carlins and cut the notches to the angles with a backsaw or a circular saw with a fine-tooth blade (plywood blades are handy for this). Rout a bullnose on the bottom edges of the carlins, stopping shy of the joints. Photo 13-7 shows a notched main deck beam ready to receive the end of a laminated trunk carlin; Photo 13-8 shows an upside-down carlin notched for a side-deck beam. Note how the routed bullnose terminates at the notch. After the carlins are notched and routed, they are prefinished (varnish or paint) in the same manner as the deck beams.

Photo 13-9. Deck beam ends are epoxy-bedded and lag-bolted to the sheer clamps.

In forepeak lockers, lazarettes, cockpit lockers and cargo holds, it may be more practical to install all deck substructure unfinished and paint the entire compartment before decking—after decking the light will be poor and the paint fumes more concentrated. Always wear a fume-filtering mask when applying epoxy paint.

INSTALLING THE MAIN BEAMS

All deck beams that span the hull are now installed. Their ends are bedded in epoxy (thickened with Cabosil) and lag-bolted to the sheer clamps. In large, heavy vessels through-bolts may be used; small craft use two large stainless-steel screws. The bolts or lags may be hot-dipped galvanized steel or stainless steel. (See Photo 13-9.)

While setting beams in place to be drilled and fastened, a plank strongback should be used to align the beam centers to a fair curve. Examples of these may be seen in Photo 13-10.

Bulkhead cleat/beams are installed the

Photo 13-10. The main deck beams are aligned at the centers before drilling and fastening by means of planks. Crown is checked with the deck beam template (at left). The forward centerboard trunk post has been glued into its mortise-and-tenon joint.

same way, being careful to keep them straight and vertical for the bulkheads. The tops are planed later if necessary to the deck angle; hence they are often made slightly higher than necessary. In some cases this top bevel may be anticipated and made in the initial cut to reduce planing later. However, the whole deck substructure surface will be planed before decking.

CHAPTER 14
THE CENTERBOARD TRUNK

Layout/ Construction/ Removable Top Plugs/
Finishing the Slot

Modern centerboards have come to include many strange and wonderful devices, but the cases or trunks that enclose them still perform the same function. The important factors in their construction are high strength, watertight integrity and troublefree use. This last involves the board as much as the trunk; included are nonbinding operation, without excessive rattling around, and access for maintenance and repair, especially under adverse circumstances.

LAYOUT

Basic dimensions and configuration come from the plans, but final layout must be done in the boat. In general, trunks have posts fore and aft; blocking and plugs along the top; logs (large cleats) joining the sides to the hull, and pivot-pin bearings of some kind, with a way to seal the pin.

Assuming the slot has been cut in the hull in its proper location, post location is just fore and aft of the slot. Post width is equal to slot width. Narrow slots are a curse because a thin

board is fragile, too flexible and inefficient as a hydrofoil. In addition, a narrow trunk is hard to maintain and repair. I find $3^1/_2$ inches to be about the minimum practical size for all but vessels below 25 feet. Posts are usually vertical, but by no means always. I use 4 x 4s or 4 x 6s mortised and tenoned to the hull for most trunk posts. Mortises should be deep (about two-thirds of the hull thickness) and their respective post-end tenons should fit snugly. Cover the inner faces of the posts with epoxy and Xynole-polyester cloth where they will be in contact with water. Bed post mortises in slightly thickened epoxy— the mortise-and-tenon joints will be the sole mechanical fastening for the posts.

To create the trunk sides, lay a plank or plywood template the length of the trunk on edge along the slot, and trace the curve of the hull on its bottom edge using a compass. Cut the template to that curve and lay it back in place. Use tape measures and straightedges to make and record measurements up from the template to the top of the proposed trunk, up the posts, diagonally to all upper corners

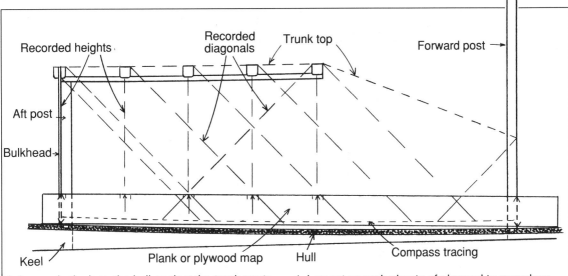

Recorded heights · Recorded diagonals · Trunk top · Forward post →

Aft post

Bulkhead→

Keel · Plank or plywood map · Hull · Compass tracing

1. Lay a plank along the hull against the trunk posts.

2. Trace the hull along the plank using a compass. (Cut this line or leave it and trace a line onto the trunk material using the same compass setting plus 1/8 inch.)

3. Use tape measures and straightedges to map out the trunk perimeters and intersections with deck beams.

4. Lay out enough sheets of plywood to reproduce the trunk map; align the grain vertically.

5. Cut the plywood and dry-fit the sheets in place, making adjustments to the cuts when necessary.

6. Use the cut and fitted sheets as templates for making the remaining laminates for both trunk halves. Offset all seams.

Figure 14-1. Mapping out a centerboard trunk.

and the tops of deck beams—to all structures the trunk will intersect. (See Fig. 14-1.) The resulting map will have all dimensions starting at marked points on the template. The more measurements you make, the more accurate the map will be. The plank is laid out on as many sheets of plywood as necessary to form the trunk (arranging these so their grain is vertical), and all measurements and tracings are carefully transferred. The plywood is cut and set up in the hull to see if everything fits. After any necessary adjustments, the plywood sheets are used as templates for reproducing the remaining trunk laminates; remember to offset (stagger) all seams.

CONSTRUCTION

I usually lay up each trunk side on a perfectly flat surface (this is very important),

epoxying together two or three plywood layers, staggering seams as far apart as possible. I have never felt it was necessary to scarf the plywood butts when three layers are used, but in light vessels using two plywood layers this is a good idea. The inner faces are covered with fabric and epoxy, leaving glue joint surfaces bare for posts, top framing and blocking. (See Photo 14-1.)

Install the top framing, which usually consists of a header plank the same width as the posts notched into undersides of the beam (see Photo 14-2). Fasten the top framing with epoxy and screws. Leave openings for plugs or lifting eyes, unless these will be drilled later. I recommend placing lifting eyes at both ends of the centerboard, and allowing easy access to them in case the board ever has to be removed in the water (which in some cases is the easiest way to remove it). It

Photo 14-2. The header for the centerboard trunk is let into the bottoms of the deck beams for additional strength. After the trunk sides are installed, the gaps above the header are solidly blocked in.

Photo 14-1. Centerboard trunk sides are three-part plywood laminations. Inner faces are covered with fabric and epoxy except where glue joints are located.

is for this reason that I avoid placing pivot pins below the waterline inside the hull. In addition, these are potentially hazardous in a centerboard collision and sometimes leak. Pins can be designed above the waterline or located outside in the keel, although this last option is somewhat inconvenient.

The finished trunk sides are set in place, checked for fit and then epoxied and thoroughly fastened in place. Remember to grind away the epoxy hull coating around the slot both for the trunk sides and logs. Carefully align the trunk bottoms with the slot edges, and remove all excess epoxy while checking that there are no voids along the bottom joint. Many large screws (at least twice as long as the trunk sides are thick) are installed into the posts and top framing in a closely staggered pattern. Vessels over 50 feet with large centerboards should use through-bolts to fasten

the trunk sides to the forward post. A long piece of PVC pipe is used to make fillets from oozing epoxy in the inside corners of the trunk. These cannot be made perfectly, but that is not essential. The goal is to seal the inside corners.

Above the top framing, epoxy the blocking in place and fasten from the trunk sides, thus bringing the trunk up to deck level and providing a gluing and fastening surface for the deck. In V-bottom and wineglass hulls having low centerboard trunks that don't extend to the deck, floor timbers, bulkheads or both will provide lateral strength for the trunk; in some cases the cabin sole is fastened across the top framing.

After the trunk sides are in place, the trunk logs are installed. In all but small vessels, these are stack-laminated in place, using narrower planks higher up. (See Photos 14-3, 14-4.) The trunk logs are fastened both to the hull and the trunk sides. (Grade screw lengths so that their points do not come within 1/4 inch of the outer hull skin or inner trunk skin.) These beveled trunk logs act as huge cleats or fastened fillets, providing incredible strength. The centerboard trunk becomes a massive box beam in the heart of the hull. Moreover, integrating the trunk with the deck spreads compressive loads between keel and deck. I extend the forward trunk post up to the coach roof as a compression post and to add lateral strength. Finally, I incorporate one or more major athwartships bulkheads (preferably watertight) into a structural joint with the trunk, deck and hull. Centerboard hulls built in this manner are the strongest and safest I know of, ranking on par with heavy steel construction.

REMOVABLE TOP PLUGS

I make T-shaped removable top plugs that drop into the opening between the trunk sides. Screws are installed from the trunk sides into the plugs. These are neither countersunk nor bunged, to allow for easy removal. All other screws in the trunk assembly except through-bolts, if used, are now bunged or filled. The whole trunk assembly is sanded, epoxy-coated and varnished or painted. The plugs should fit snugly; foam gaskets along the top trunk edges add extra insurance against leakage in a pounding seaway. On vessels over 35 feet, the lower part of the plug should be a 4 x 4. A 1-inch or $1^1/_2$-inch plank can be the top, or cap, which is glued and fastened to the lower part.

FINISHING THE SLOT

When the keel was covered with fabric, back when the hull was upside down, the slot should have received one layer of cloth and epoxy. During trunk construction, all inside surfaces also received one layer. Now coarsely sand the slot-to-trunk inside joint, and lay up another layer of fabric and epoxy across it. This ensures watertight integrity and also provides abrasion resistance where it is most needed. Working on your back under the keel makes this a nasty job.

Photos 14-3 and 14-4. The centerboard trunk logs are stack-laminated in place; they are fastened both to the hull and the trunk sides with #14 stainless-steel screws graded to come not within 1/4 inch of the inner trunk skin. Each progressive layer is fastened both to the layer below and the trunk.

CHAPTER 15
INTERNAL STRUCTURE

Bulkhead Layout, Cutting and Fitting/
Bulkhead Installation/ Mast Steps/ Floors/ Engine Beds/
The Cabin Sole

BULKHEAD LAYOUT, CUTTING AND FITTING

I use plywood for all bulkheads, even if they will be paneled later. Nothing can match its low cost, strength and utility. Thickness varies from 1/2 inch in small vessels to $1\frac{1}{8}$ inches in large vessels, but most cruising sailboats and medium to large powerboats can use 3/4-inch plywood for structural bulkheads. In most cases, seams can be butted in epoxy, which is troweled smooth. I sometimes cover the seams with a decorative batten, especially when the plywood is finished bright (as with teak veneer or birch plywood). In vessels over 50 feet, two layers of 1/2-inch ACX plywood may be used, C faces in, staggering the seams of each layer. Subfloor plywood is also useful in very large or commercial vessels; it is $1\frac{1}{8}$ inches or thicker, with one paintable face and tongue-and-groove edges. If both sides of a bulkhead will be paneled, the plywood may be thinner but the panel seams should be staggered from the bulkhead seams.

In Chapter 12, we laid out the bulkhead

positions on the sheer clamps. Bulkhead cleat/beams were installed so that their faces were vertical. The bulkhead side of those cleats was left square or unrouted. Now a level or plumbline is used to ascertain where the bulkhead will contact the hull and chine log (or bilge stringer). Mark these points with a felt tip pen. Place a straight plank the same thickness as the bulkhead where the first seam (vertical) will lie (usually 4 feet from the hull). Level the plank both fore and aft and athwartships, and clamp it firmly to the cleat/beam (use a plywood pad to prevent damage). The plank edge adjacent to the hull represents the first plywood seam. Mark where the top of the bulkhead will be on the plank and label it. Clamp stickers (small stiff planks) to the vertical plank with their ends touching key points on the hull, such as under the sheer clamp and above the chine log. (See Fig. 15-1.) Now, carefully unclamp and remove the vertical plank, with stickers attached, and lay it on a sheet of plywood with the plank edge running along what will become the vertical seam. The sticker ends de-

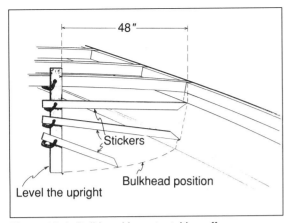

Figure 15-1. Bulkhead layout—taking off.

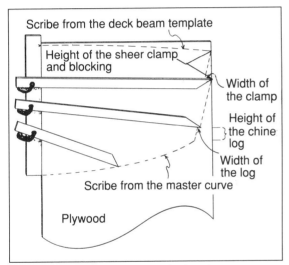

Figure 15-2. Bulkhead layout—laying down.

Photo 15-1. Bulkheads are scribed with the deck beam template and the master curve.

fine the rest of the bulkhead; mark these points and transfer the top and bottom points from the vertical plank, then remove the plank with stickers. Connect the dots with battens, thus defining the bulkhead's perimeters. (See Fig. 15-2.) The deck beam template defines the top, and the master curve defines the bottom. (See Photo 15-1.) If the the topsides are straight (flat), a straightedge connects the dot under the sheer clamp to the dot above the chine log. Since the sheer clamp is square to the topsides, use a rafter square to draw the notch in the bulkhead that receives it. Leave the top of the notch open for the blocking that will later fill in between the beams. This can also be used to draw the notch for the chine log, if it also is parallel to the topsides, as in the example. More complex logs are laid out by using a sliding pin contour gauge in conjunction with a bevel gauge and measurements. A piece of copper or lead wire (solder) can also be bent around the log and traced onto the ply- wood.

The bulkhead is then cut out with a circular saw and hand jigsaw, taking care to get the bevels right if the bulkhead is near the ends of the hull. If it's not a perfect fit the first time, a little trimming with a grinder usually corrects it. Trace the bulkhead onto the hull, then remove it and grind away the epoxy hull sealant out to where the cleats, if used, will lie. In small, light vessels, fillets or fabric tape and epoxy often are used to reinforce the bulkhead-to-hull joint. In larger vessels, wood cleats are epoxied and screwed into the hull and sometimes into the bulkhead (usually this is unnecessary). Often cleats are placed on only one side of bulkheads near the bow and the stern, as the diminishing hull shape will prevent them from kicking toward the ends of the vessel. In any case, the hull must be ground to achieve a good glue joint.

BULKHEAD INSTALLATION

Bulkheads are glued with epoxy thickened with Cabosil, and fastened to cleat/beams with nails, screws or staples. Cleats, taping and filleting should all be done at once to achieve chemical bonding throughout. If cleats are installed, "finger fillets" are created from oozing epoxy against the hull and bulkhead. These will prevent the tiny voids that can turn into problems later. Use two layers of latex gloves or heavy rubber gloves to keep epoxy off your skin. (See Photo 15-2.) Use a short piece of PVC pipe to make larger fillets. Epoxy for filleting may be poured into a Ziploc plastic bag and applied by squeezing it from a cut corner. (See Photos 15-3, 15-4.) Clean away the excess with a putty knife. Consistency of the epoxy used for fillets is discovered largely by trial and error but the mix should be stiff enough that it won't drip off the stir stick or sag once it is in place. Nail or screw holes are puttied over at the same time filleting is done.

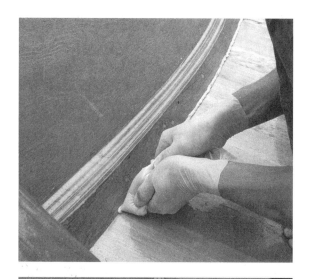

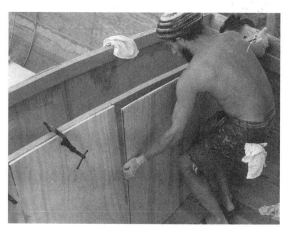

Photo 15-2. Bulkhead sections are butted with epoxy glue; they are likewise glued to the hull and cleat/beams. The bulkhead-to-hull joint is further reinforced with cleats glued and fastened to the hull on one or both sides. Near the ends of the hull large fillets are used on the side closest to the bow or stern. Stainless steel ring-shank nails or hot-dipped galvanized box nails are used to fasten the bulkheads to cleat/beams; staples are used in smaller vessels.

Photos 15-3 and 15-4. Epoxy thickened with Cabosil is applied from a Ziploc bag with one corner cut off to make fillets. Shaping is done with short pieces of PVC pipe, and excess epoxy is cleared away with a putty knife. All joints are filleted to keep moisture, dirt and insects out of any voids, and to add strength.

Photo 15-5. When a major bulkhead intersects the centerboard trunk, mortises are routed for cleat/ beams on both sides. Likewise, cleats are installed on both sides of the bulkhead where it joins the hull and centerboard. Battens reinforce butt joints in the bulkhead on both sides.

Continuing bulkhead sections are laid out, cut and installed in essentially the same way. In vessels where interconnecting bilges are desired (I am against this for safety reasons), the bottom of the center section is left out or cut away in some manner. Fore and aft bulkheads can be laid out similarly to the template/map method used for the centerboard trunk sides in Chapter 14, or, if carlins are in place, using the same plank and sticker method described previously. Bulkheads that butt each other at angles may be attached with cleats or with fasteners through one into the edge of the other. Major bulkheads that intersect centerboard trunks should be cleated to the hull, deck and trunk on both sides in all but small vessels, and the cleat/ beams should be mortised into the centerboard trunk (see Photo 15-5).

MAST STEPS

I usually stack-laminate mast steps, using both solid timber and plywood. I believe in designing and building them strong enough to support the masts without rigging in all sea conditions, regardless of whether the vessel will carry standing rigging.

The first layer is usually solid fir, yellow pine or oak, $2^{1}/_{2}$ inches to $3^{1}/_{2}$ inches thick by at least $11^{1}/_{2}$ inches wide, and as long as practical. If any perimeters can butt against a structural bulkhead, centerboard trunk or other structure, so much the better. I then build up subsequent layers with 3/4-inch plywood, cutting the mast mortise into each layer. There are at least two of these layers. The first component, of solid timber, is epoxy-glued and heavily fastened to the hull, often down into the keel if possible. In V-bottom and wineglass hulls, the mast step is often beveled to fit snug to the garboards. In many cases a limber hole or trough is cut into the bottom of this block to allow water under it (make it big—at least $1^{1}/_{2}$-inch square by the length of the block). This won't weaken the step, but be sure to seal the exposed wood with epoxy and paint. The subsequent plywood layers are heavily screwed and glued to the block, taking care to thoroughly seal all end grain. A trough or weep hole should be cut out of the lowest plywood layer on its low end to drain off any water that may accumulate in the step mortise; remember to seal the exposed end grain. If the solid block has a limber hole (trough), a hole may be drilled and epoxy-sealed to drain water out of the step instead of cutting the plywood layer. The hole should be 3/8 inch in diameter, drilled from the lowest part of the mortise down into the limber trough. In large vessels (over 45 feet), I add one more plywood layer that encloses the whole base of the mast above the mortise. (See Fig. 15-3.)

Bridge steps must be carefully designed, because they transmit part of the mast load to parts of the vessel other than the keel. I usually incorporate a large, heavy, athwartships timber against a structural bulkhead and place solid compression posts under it to the

keel. Another partial structural bulkhead boxes the exposed side of the bridge to the hull
and compression posts, creating a very strong
structure. All components must be heavily
fastened to the hull, bulkheads and each
other. Bridge steps are usually needed only
where a shaft, stuffing box or transmission
interferes with mast placement. The bulkheads have apertures cut in them to allow
placement of the mechanical components.

FLOORS

Floors, or floor timbers, play a different
role in cold-molded construction than in
plank-on-frame construction. The difference
may vary from a matter of degree to their total
absence. Canoe or flat-bottom hulls will only
need floors if they have fin keels, and then
only above the keels. These may be solid
wood, laminated wood or metal, as I said
earlier. For deep, ballasted keels I prefer
welded stainless-steel floors of I-beam section.

V-bottom and wineglass keel hulls of the
construction described in this book will need
very few or no floors for structural reasons. In
a keel hull with outside ballast there should
be several floors above the ballast area. These
should be through- or lag-bolted to the keel
plank, to which the ballast is bolted; deep,
heavy ballast should be bolted from the ballast through the keel and the floors in the traditional manner. These floors should also be
fastened to the hull with large screws installed from the hull. This should, ideally, be
done during planking before the hull is covered with fabric and epoxy to avoid violating
the fabric layer (holes made in any fabric/
epoxy skin cannot be repaired with epoxy
putty; the existing fabric must be feathered
back and a cloth/epoxy patch overlaid). If
weight and space are not restrictions, these
floors should be solid timber. In light, ul-

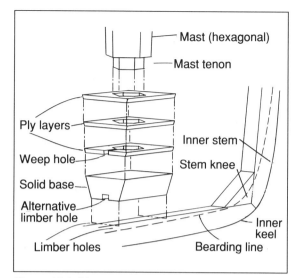

Figure 15-3. Mast step, exploded view.

tralight and shallow-bodied or very open
hulls (as in flat-out racing machines), the
floors should be laminated or fabricated from
metal. Figure 15-4 shows four different hull
sections and their respective floor arrangements.

Deep wineglass hull sections may either
use two floors—one above the keel plank
and one to support the cabin sole—or one
floor at the sole and a heavy plywood gusset
glued and fastened to the side of the floor,
and glued to the hull and keel plank. Epoxy
fillets should be made for hull and keel contact areas; larger vessels might employ glass
or Kevlar tape under the fillets. The plywood
should be fairly thick—twice what the bulkheads are; exposed grain at limber holes and
air vents should be epoxy-sealed and
painted.

V-bottom hulls can employ solid floor timbers, though half (or less) the number used in
conventional plank-on-frame construction
will be required. Floors should be lag- or
through-bolted to the keel-plank and fastened with screws and epoxy to the hull.
Heavy outside ballast should be through-
bolted to floors in the traditional manner.

Engine stringers, particularly for powerboats, may be through-bolted to floors right through the hull.

Deep ballasted fin keels in canoe or flat-bottomed hulls can make use of I-beam section welded stainless-steel or aluminum floors. Heavy wall pipes receive the keel bolts; the cabin sole can be laid above.

Where there is room and the hull shape suits it, floors may be stack-laminated wood. Keel bolts should terminate in a metal block or heavy plate, and a straight floor timber can be fastened alongside to support the cabin sole.

These hull types will also need cabin soles to walk on. In most cases, the floor timbers may also support part or all of the sole. Exceptions are very deep keel hulls, where the sole is well above the floors, and laminated floors which are not flat on top. Extra floors, often just 2 x 4s, can be installed across the hull to support a cabin sole. These should be attached to the hull with epoxy and screws from inside, grading screw sizes so as not to come closer than 1/4 inch from the outer hull surface. Firm attachment to the hull will render these floors very strong and stiff, but if a long span is called for, they may need to be larger or incorporate a compression post or gusset to the keel or lower floor. Cockpit deck floors may be similar to these as are those in pilot house decks and raised cabin soles over engine compartments. In some extreme cases, plywood gussets may be used where floors join the hull. In those installations where engine rooms are beneath a cabin sole, as in many powerboats and motorsailers, the floors may even be made re-

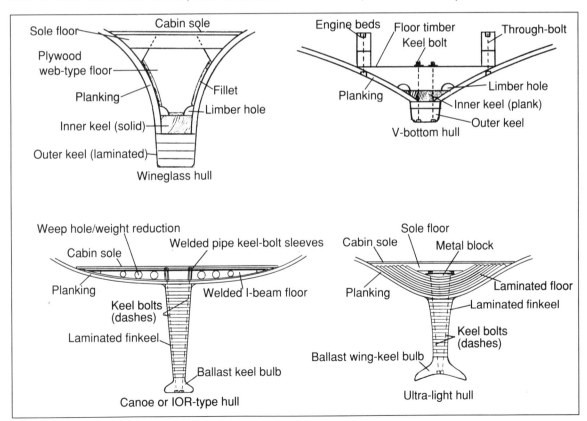

Figure 15-4. Four hull types and their floors.

movable by placing their ends in U-shaped hangers made of 3/4-inch plywood. The hangers are often fastened to large carlins placed inboard of the cabinets and furniture.

ENGINE BEDS

Engine beds may be solid timber or stack-laminated. Their design, construction and shape will depend on the hull, location and type of engine to be used. In general they will be long, tapered, heavy stringers. They must be firmly attached and bedded to the hull, and I prefer to integrate one or more structural bulkhead into their construction. Stack-lamination is best for larger beds, as it is easier to fasten the first layer to the hull skin, and the structures will be more stable than solid timbers, although either should be thoroughly sealed with epoxy and paint. The first layer is beveled and tapered such that subsequent layers are just stock lumber. The first layer is epoxy-glued and screwed with plenty of stainless-steel screws (#12 or #14 wood screws). These should be long enough to come within about 1/2 inch of the outer hull surface when countersunk—be very careful that no screws damage the outer hull skin. Subsequent laminations, often just nominal 2 x 4s, are epoxied and screwed to the layer below, using screws that don't penetrate below the layer they are fastened to, as previously explained. Some engines have one pair of motor mounts on a different level; partial beds for these are simply stacked up higher. The higher stack can be beveled shorter as it goes up; the topmost plank need not extend more than 3 or 4 inches beyond the mount location. The finished lamination should be cleaned up and epoxy-painted. If the beds join a bulkhead at the forward (or low) ends, cut or drill large limber holes through the bottoms of the beds at the junction. The beds should be shaped so as to allow access to the engine as much as possible without weakening them. I prefer flexible rubber motor mounts—to reduce vibration, for ease of adjustment, and because they elevate the motor farther from the beds than possible with most rigid mounting.

Whenever possible, the engine should be in its own isolated compartment, with its own bilge. Usually at least one end of the engine beds can be fastened to a watertight bulkhead. Motor mounts should be fastened with long, large-diameter stainless-steel lag-bolts into the beds; phenolic block or dense hardwood plates under the mounts will reduce vibration wear.

In a hull with floor timbers, the engine beds may simply be solid stringers lag-bolted into the floors or through-bolted through the floors into the hull. Through-bolting applies to powerboats and motorsailers with large, heavy engines; install the bolts up through the hull, leaving the nuts and washers on top where they can be tightened. Recess the bolt heads and washers in the hull planking and fill the hole with epoxy thickened with Cabosil. If the hull fabric is already in place, feather it back and apply a fabric and epoxy patch. Note that the bolt heads and washers aren't gaining structural root in the hull planking, but from the floors and hull, which are both epoxied together.

THE CABIN SOLE

I typically make cabin soles from plywood, even if they are to be overlaid with teak. The exception might be in small sailboats where removable planks will suffice if they are well-sealed so they don't swell or warp—a terrible nuisance. In large vessels the sole will typically be permanently fastened with access doors or removable sections. These may rest in part on floors (cut the edge of the lift-out portion over the center of a floor), have additional supporting cleats, or both. Cabin sole plywood is usually 5/8 inch or 3/4 inch thick, but it may be 1/2 inch thick in small vessels with closely spaced floors or when a teak overlay is planned.

The day of the traditional teak and holly sole is over; holly is no longer commercially available. But teak and holly (I'm not sure it's really holly) veneer plywood is available, though it is very expensive. I personally would rather live with painted plywood than this expensive substitute, but if you opt to use it, be aware that the veneer is paper thin. Seal it with a coat of reduced epoxy, be very careful sanding it, and apply 8 to 12 coats of clear polyurethane over it. Not wearing shoes will help too.

The other alternative is a thin (1/4-inch, typically) hardwood overlay. This too will be expensive, but it will not wear out. I prefer to lay it in epoxy without fasteners, using weights and clamps to position it during curing. Most other methods usually result in delamination, particularly around the edges of the removable sections.

Make the removable panels fit snugly, but loosely enough so that they won't bind and stick when dirt and moisture accumulate around the edges. The support cleats should be both screwed and epoxied to the sole. Plywood cleats are less likely to break than solid ones, which split along the grain. Lift rings tend to collect dirt and break off or stick; I prefer finger holes or lift bolts set in a shallow depression. I often don't let the support cleats touch in the corners so that less dirt and moisture will accumulate. Round corners will last longer than square ones on the lift-out panels.

The sole perimeters should be cut to (or close to) the bevel of the hull, and be both epoxied and fastened with screws or nails. The edge should be filleted and fastener holes filled to keep out dirt and moisture. I use three or four coats of epoxy paint unless an overlay is to be installed. I also epoxy-paint the hull, keel plank, floors and sole underside white below the sole level. This way you can see what's going on; white paint bounces light around and foreign objects stand out. Use a mold/fungus inhibitor in the paint.

Plan your cabin sole carefully so that cabinetry and partial bulkheads get good support; you also want to allow convenient access to all of your bilges.

CHAPTER 16
MORE DECK STRUCTURE

Installing Carlins/ Mast Partners/ Bitt Partners/
Breast Hook/ Side Deck Beams/ Blocking and Finishing
the Sheer Clamp

INSTALLING CARLINS

We have already described carlins for trunk cabins, which are frequently curved and usually are as wide as main deck beams (the common exception being when they are laminated). Trunk carlins support both side-deck beams and cabins and thus must be very strong. Hatch carlins usually only span be-tween two (occasionally three) adjacent beams, which must be terminated at and sup-ported by the carlins. Simple hatch (or sky-light) carlins are typically 1½ inches thick, and the same depth as the adjacent beams. When the carlin must support an intermedi-ate beam, I usually shape the carlin to be deeper at the supported beam by at least 1/2

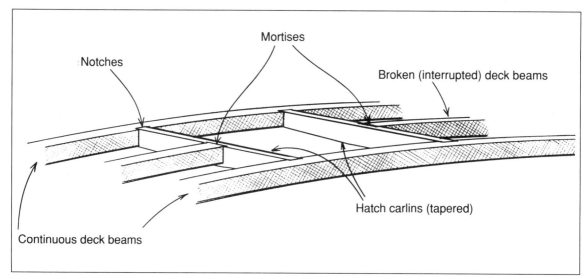

Figure 16-1. Hatch carlins.

inch, and taper it at the ends to the same depth as the beams. I rout a mortise into the carlin for the beam end, and fasten it with epoxy and two screws through the carlin into the beam end grain. An alternative to these truss-type carlins is simply to make the carlins thicker by 1/2 inch and notch the intermediate (broken) beam ends into the sides of the carlins in the same manner as with trunk carlins. I notch the carlin ends into the beams— usually 1/2 inch—and install two large screws through the beams into the carlin ends. If the carlins end at a bulkhead, rout in a 1/2-inch deep mortise and install the screws from the cleat/beam on the other side. All these joints are bedded in thickened epoxy during fastening; finger fillets seal the seams with excess epoxy, again to keep out moisture, mold and insects. Use a rag with denatured alcohol to clean up the joint. The screws are countersunk and bunged. After the bungs are chiseled off, they are carefully sanded (so as not to damage the surrounding prefinished surface), and spot-varnished.

Carlins in cockpit areas may serve merely as cleats to accept fastenings for a longitudinal bulkhead-to-deck joint, in which case 2 x 4 stock works well. If there is no fore and aft bulkhead present, I also use a 2 x 4 carlin notched for side-deck beams to form the outboard support for a cockpit locker seat. Cargo hatch carlins are laid out, made, and installed in the same manner as trunk cabin carlins, except they are straight.

MAST PARTNERS

As with mast steps, I build partners to bear the unstayed mast loading in ultimate heavy weather conditions. I also prefer to use stacklaminated plywood, because the wood end grain supports the compressive loading of the mast athwartships as well as fore and aft, and because the diagonal loading is picked up by the multidirectional tensile strength of sandwiched cross-grain structure.

At this point I should say a little more about plywood. Many wooden boat builders turn up their noses at it. They are often traditionalists who don't wish to take advantage of contemporary technology, or they may be ignorant of the incredible properties of good plywood properly used. Plywood eliminates the need of all knees traditionally used in deck structure, so that mast partners, for example, are just square or rectangular blocks. The interlocking structure of veneers laminated at alternating right angles supplies strength that can be achieved, weight for weight and cost for cost, by no other material or combination of materials known on Earth. And wood can work and flex (watch the trees), as long as it doesn't exceed its natural spring constant (or elastic limit), longer than almost any other known material; in other words, it does not fatigue and weaken. So let's hear it for plywood!

I cut mortises 1/2 inch or more deep into the beams around the partners, usually to more than half the beam depth. The partners for a 45-foot sailboat may be 2 inches thick, using four layers of 1/2-inch plywood (see Photo 16-1). I fasten each layer with epoxy and stainless-steel screws set at an angle into the beam, so that each plywood layer has a mechanical joint (the mortise), a glue joint and a fastened joint. The layers should be installed all at once and clamped until cured. Avoid using fasteners to clamp the plywood layers, because they may be in the way later when the mast hole is cut. In some cases the mast holes may be cut through each plywood layer, using it as a template for the next. This must be very carefully laid out and done, as there is usually pitch to the deck and rake to the mast, and the hole should be tapered for mast wedges, to say nothing of getting the mast alignment right both athwartships and

Photo 16-1. Mast partners are mortised into adjacent deck beams as well as glued and fastened (screws are angled into the beams). The four-layer stack lamination shown here will support a 50-foot freestanding mast with less than 5 feet of bury depth. When the deck is laminated, the entire partner depth will be three inches. This in conjunction with the adjacent bulkhead and centerboard trunk creates an incredibly strong structural unit.

fore and aft. If the mast is to be round where it passes through the deck, the holes may need to be precut because of the mechanical difficulty in cutting a round hole through several inches of plywood after the deck is laid. Hex-

agonal and large octagonal holes can be cut later using a circular saw and large reciprocating saw, but the job is no picnic. Often the mast hole is made by drilling large holes around its perimeter.

I rout bullnoses on the edges of the bottom plywood layer and align the sides of the stack carefully so it will look finished. I often varnish the partners if they intersect varnished beams. When the mast hole is cut, I also rout or ease the bottom edges of the hole so that the mast wedges will be less likely to damage the last couple of plywood veneers while they are being driven.

BITT PARTNERS

During the life of a boat, bitts may be called upon to drag her bodily off a reef or beach, and must be strong enough to do this without ripping out the deck. I prefer traditional bitts: large square or rectangular wood timbers that penetrate the deck aft of a major deckbeam and are stepped on or beside the keel. If they can run down a bulkhead and be

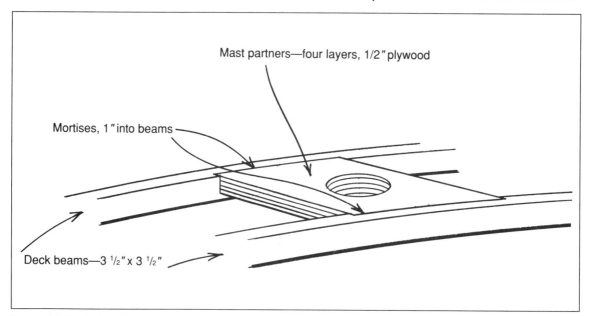

Figure 16-2. Mast partners.

fastened to that also, so much the better. If the vessel has a bowsprit, it should pass between or terminate between the bitts. I prefer two bitts to one mooring post, but both should be very stout. When a single mooring post is used, the bowsprit heel is mortised into it.

Because of this need for strength, the bitt partners should be a plywood stack-lamination similar to and as thick as a mast partner. The bitts may terminate in an actual mortised step, or, if they run down a bulkhead, may be blocked against it; this is discussed in Chapter 20. Remember to provide drainage for any water coming down the bitts. Epoxy-seal the edges of the plywood after the bitt holes have been cut through the partners.

If a bolt-on bollard or a large cleat is to be used, the backing block for this should be made similarly to the partners, and just as thick. Knees from the sides of this block to an adjacent bulkhead will help distribute loading. They should be thick plywood, glued and screwed to the block sides, and attached to the bulkhead by means of through-bolted steel angles. Make it *strong*. A steel plate should be used under the block to through-bolt the bollard or cleat.

BREAST HOOK

Traditionally, the breast hook was a vital structural member; now it serves as a fastening point at the junction of the topsides and deck. It should still be heavy and strong, particularly if a bowsprit is to be attached to it. If so, I use a solid block the same height as the deck beams and two or three times wider. (See Photo 16-2.)

I lag-bolt the breast hook to the sheer clamps, bedding it in thickened epoxy, the same as if it were a deck beam. The timber should be shaped to fit tightly to the stemhead; the remaining gaps on either side

Photo 16-2. Breast hooks are only required by large vessels or those that will be fitted with a bowsprit. The breast hook here is a solid timber lag-bolted to the sheer clamps. The voids on either side of the stemhead are blocked in solid.

of the stem are filled with wood and epoxy.

On smaller vessels without bowsprits, the breast hook may even be eliminated. The blocking above the sheer clamp is extended to the stemhead, and this alone is adequate when incorporated with a plywood deck.

SIDE-DECK BEAMS

Side-deck beams are the same height as major beams but, because of their short span, usually less than half their width. I frequently use 2 x 4s, belt-sanding or band-sawing a slight curve on top to match the deck beam template. For side decks having a span of 18 inches or less, even this is often unnecessary; they may be left flat. An advantage to curved trunk cabin sides, in addition to higher strength and better looks (straight, vertical trunk sides can ruin the appearance of a boat), is that all the side-deck beams will be the same length. Their ends, however, must all be cut to a different bevel in the fore and aft plane, except for a few near the hull's maximum beam. Determine the vertical bevels by laying a straightedge across the carlin to the sheer and, using a bevel square at each end, measuring the angle between straightedge and carlin inboard and straightedge and hull outboard. Frequently these angles will hold good for the whole run of side-deck beams joining that particular carlin. The fore and aft bevels should already be written along the tops of the carlins from the previous operation of notching (Chapter 13). Note that the fore and aft bevel will be the same for both ends of each beam unless the sheer and carlin are not parallel. Side-deck beams intersecting cockpit and hatch carlins are similarly measured and cut.

After all the beams are cut and numbered, fit them in place and mark them for routing. The routing or bullnosing ends just at the carlin joint and at the sheer clamp, so that the joints will be square and clean (see Photo 16-3). Sand and varnish or paint the beams, taking care to leave ends and tops clean for glue joints.

The side-deck beams are installed the same way as the main beams were attached to the sheer clamp: with lag-bolts, through-bolts or screws, depending on size. Two large screws (2$\frac{1}{2}$-inch or 3-inch #14) are set through the carlins into the end grain of each beam, and again a rag and denatured alcohol are used to clean the joint. The holes left from countersinking are bunged, chiseled, sanded and spot-varnished. This often necessitates a light sanding and overall finish coat of varnish to the inner carlin faces to achieve a smooth surface. If the carlins are to be covered by large trim or handrails in the traditional manner, this final varnishing is unnecessary.

BLOCKING AND FINISHING THE SHEER CLAMP

The gaps above the sheer clamps between all the beams are now blocked in solid, using deck beam scrap or 2 x 4 stock if the clamps are 1$\frac{1}{2}$ inches thick. The ends of these blocks

Photo 16-3. The ends of deck beams are left unvarnished where there will be glue joints.

Photo 16-4. The blocking between deck beams above the sheer clamps is dished out slightly with a belt sander to match the curve of the clamps' inner face.

are beveled to fit snugly between the beams. The outer block faces, adjacent to the hull, may be left flat—epoxy will fill the slight gap. The inner faces should be slightly dished out with a belt sander to conform to the sheer clamp curve. (See Photo 16-4.)

The blocks should fit well, their faces exactly aligned to the sheer clamp faces. Joints to the beams should be even and close. The blocks are bedded in thickened epoxy and fastened to the sheer clamps with long nails or screws. In smaller craft (below 50 feet), they may be toenailed to the beam sides with finishing nails. Structural integrity comes from the large gluing surfaces to the hull deck and the sheer clamps; the fasteners function

Photo 16-5. The blocking is epoxied in place and toe-nailed into adjacent beams. After curing, the blocks and clamps are sanded and varnished, taking care not to damage the prefinished deck beams.

Photo 16-6. *Teresa*'s finished deck substructure is ready for plywood planking.

to hold the blocks in place until the epoxy cures. (See Photo 16-5.)

After installation, the blocking and sheer clamps are lightly sanded and varnished or painted. Take care not to damage the prefinished deck beams. The structure is now ready for a final surfacing and decking. (See Photo 16-6.)

CHAPTER 17
THE DECK

Preparing the Surface/ Layout and Prefitting the First Plywood Layer/ Scribing and Painting the Underside/ Laying the First Layer/ The Second Layer/Countersinking, Trimming, Routing, Filling and Fairing/ Fabric and Epoxy/ The Foam-Core Deck/ Teak Overlays

PREPARING THE SURFACE

Examine the deck substructure for fairness using long battens and the eye. True the surface with a power plane and hand plane. Bring down the rough plywood edges of the hull sheer and the sheer clamp blocking to the plane of the deck beams. There should be no hard spots in the deck plane; these will be revealed by the battens. A low beam will necessitate planing the tops of adjacent beams until it fairs in; a high beam is planed down until it fairs in. The sheer must be one long, fair, flowing curve the length of the hull. At this point any flaws should be subtle, of a magnitude of less than 1/8 inch, and easy to correct. During planing take care that the nose of the plane does not damage the sides of structural members at right angles to the one you are planing. Think of the whole surface as one smooth, fair, compound-curved plane. Lay the battens out in all directions and examine the surface. On a large vessel this can entail a full day's work or more for one

person. Good workmanship here will result in clean, fine glue joints between beams and deck underside as well as a fair deck.

LAYOUT AND PREFITTING THE FIRST PLYWOOD LAYER

Plywood decks use the simplest form of "tortured plywood" methodology. The deck has a compound curve, though a very gentle one. This involves two considerations: First the deck substructure must be stiff enough not to deform during fastening (and the plywood must not be so thick or stiff that it cannot conform to the curves); second, the plywood seams will not be straight lines, but must be cut or planed to slight curves or epoxy-filled (you pay in labor or material—your choice).

I usually make a scaled sketch of the whole deck, 1 inch equaling 1 foot, on a piece of scrap plywood, showing all deckbeams. Then I lay out imaginary sheets of plywood, two layers thick, such that I gain the most economical use of material while staggering all seams as far apart as possible. I do not scarf plywood edges; all athwartships seams must fall on main (wide) deck beams or bulkhead/cleat/beams wide enough for fastening two plywood edges. Fore and aft seams have their grain spanning the beams (the plywood is always laid with the grain aligned fore and aft, across the beams) and don't need further support. However, if this troubles you, add internal seam battens later, or even inlay them across your beams. If the deck is only one plywood layer thick, as in the TERRA-PIN schooners, seam battens are essential. Athwartships plywood seams should be two beams apart; fore and aft seams should be a half sheet (2 feet) apart.

After you are satisfied with your layout, place full sheets on the deck for the first layer. To get tight butts, the fore and aft seams (which will be seen from below), are planed through the middle areas of the sheets. Use long battens to determine athwartships cuts for deckbeam butt joints. After the edge of one sheet is cut, the next adjoining sheet is tucked under the cut edge, which is traced onto it and cut. Trace the hull sheer onto the sheets undersides and cut them. Leave a little

excess overhanging the hull sheer; it can be planed off later. Hatch, cockpit and trunk cabin openings are also traced from beneath and cut out. Make slightly oversized cuts for the openings so you won't have a lot of trimming to do—hatch coamings and cabin joints will cover the joints. When all the sheets are cut and in place, position them accurately and nail the corners down temporarily (don't sink the nails) so that from underneath there are no gaps between the deck substructure surface and the plywood. Any flaws in your surface preparation will show and can be corrected. (See Photo 17-1.)

SCRIBING AND PAINTING THE UNDERSIDE

From below the deck, use a sharp pencil to trace all deck structure onto the underside of the plywood. Then remove the plywood, lightly sand and paint it with three coats of epoxy paint having a mildew-retarding additive (this item I keep mentioning is a powder available from most paint suppliers—I get mine from Sherwin-Williams). Try not to overlap your pencil lines with paint more than 1/4 inch, as they represent the glue joints; a little bit won't hurt, and masking the

Photo 17-1. Plywood is laid out and cut so that seams butt on deck beams. The corners are tacked down and the substructure is traced from underneath, then the panels are removed and painted, except where glue joints will be.

Photo 17-2. *Sarah*'s first deck layer is painted and ready to be laid.

whole thing off takes too much time. I use high-quality 3/8-inch nap by 9-inch roller covers (often called "all-paint/phenolic core") and white or off-white paint, and the results are beautiful. Cheap roller covers will leave fuzz all over the place. Good rollers leave a subtle, uniformly textured surface with no brush marks. In tight spots, use a 3-inch roller. (See Photo 17-2.)

LAYING THE FIRST LAYER

The first layer is now epoxy-glued and fastened in place. I use 3-inch rollers to apply slightly thickened epoxy to beam tops (as neatly as possible and not too much) and plywood. Use throw-away brushes to apply epoxy to gluing surfaces narrower than $3^{1}/_{2}$ inches. It is helpful to spread tarps inside the hull to catch the drips, but here it really pays to get the epoxy just the right thickness so it doesn't drip, and to apply just the right amount so a lot of excess doesn't squeeze out. The plywood butt edges must be coated and carefully aligned; a small plywood scrap screwed across a butt halfway between beams with plastic under it will align problem areas, but these are rare.

Use a batten to scribe the locations of beams on top of the plywood to locate fasteners. Remember that bulkhead/cleat/beam tops will have to be scribed as curves near the ends of the vessel, whereas the beams are flat to the deck plane and present straight lines.

Fastening may be done with staples or nails, usually pneumatically driven to save time (it's a big job and you have to finish, and clean up inside, before the epoxy cures). I've nailed off several large decks by hand and it involves several people working at a furious pace, including one or more people inside cleaning up all the time. It is also important to check periodically, or preferably constantly, for fasteners breaking through inside (miss-

ing the substructure), particularly when pneumatics are used. I almost always nail off the deck perimeter by hand with #4 or #6 (big boat) hot-dip galvanized box nails or stainless-steel ring-shank nails about 2 inches on center. (See Photos 17-3, 17-4, 17-5.)

The real challenge here is the cleanup inside. It's a big job and it must be done meticulously, before the epoxy cures. Wear a fume-filtering mask and use denatured alcohol on a clean white rag to wipe the substructure-to-deck joints. When this job is finished prop-

Photo 17-3. The deck is epoxy-glued and stapled using a pneumatic gun. Note the stagger pattern; staples are aligned with the grain to minimize surface damage.

Photo 17-4. The perimeters are nailed off with stainless-steel ring-shank nails or hot-dipped galvanized box nails for extra strength.

Photo 17-5. Oozing epoxy must be wiped up both inside and out before it cures. This is done with white rags and denatured alcohol. When working inside, a fume-filtering mask must be worn.

erly, the results are stunning: The gleaming varnished beams end in a razor-sharp line against the white-painted deck underside. This quality finish work could never be done as well from inside, and attempting it would take forever and give you a permanent stiff neck. The epoxy-paint/polyurethane-varnish surfaces will last nearly a lifetime with no more maintenance than an occasional cleaning. Household window cleaner works well.

THE SECOND LAYER

The second layer is laid out in the same manner as the first except that all the seams are located away from those of the first layer. It is cut and fit, but the fastening planes (substructure surfaces) must be carefully drawn out using battens. Fasteners that miss the substructure will still break through to the inside.

Epoxy is rolled onto both plywood surfaces and the deck is laid the same way as the first layer, including nailing off the perimeter. Take care not to trap air voids between the layers by walking around from one side to the other between the beams. Areas that separate or pull apart for some reason can either be screwed down in the field (removing the screws and repairing the damage later) or be compressed with weights.

Repair any damage to the inside finished surface with epoxy thickened with sawdust for natural or varnished wood and epoxy thickened with titanium dioxide (white pigment) for painted surfaces.

COUNTERSINKING, TRIMMING, ROUTING, FILLING AND FAIRING

All fasteners that are at or above the surface must be countersunk. Trim the plywood edges with a power plane and/or hand plane, using care not to damage the hull skin. Final trimming is usually done with a belt sander or disc grinder. An industrial router with a large cut-off (edging) bit and roller wheel does this job best, but is expensive. When the deck edge is flush to the hull, it is bullnose-routed, even if a bulwark or toerail is to be added later; this is usually inset by the radius of the routed edge. In any case, this edge must at least be eased enough to allow the fabric covering to wrap and cover the plywood end grain.

Now fill all flaws, cracks and countersinking holes with thickened epoxy, including plywood core voids visible at the edges. After curing, the whole deck is sanded and faired smooth with a body grinder and a soft pad with #80 paper. Take particular care along the sheer to create a smooth, fair line.

FABRIC AND EPOXY

Clean and cover the deck surface with Xynole-polyester cloth. Lap the edges down to where they will be covered by the rubrail. If no rubrail is to be used (the height of folly—rubrails are to a boat what bumpers are to a car), or in areas not covered by a rubrail, lap the cloth down to an inch or so below the lower deck edge. Masking tape is applied at this point, and the cloth is lapped over it; this will help create a straight, finished edge later. The hull's epoxy primer is sanded along the sheer to provide a good bond with the deck covering.

The cloth is then saturated with epoxy (usually three coats). After curing, the edge beneath the rubrail location is trimmed and sanded off more or less to a straight line. In other areas feather out and fair the cloth into the hull surface with thickened epoxy (as in the glazing process described in Chapter 10), or the edge above the masking tape may be finished as a paint line. Use silver paper or plastic masking tapes; some of the cheap paper varieties are penetrable by epoxy and stick to the surface beneath. Above plank-overlaid transoms, the cloth should end just below the plywood edge (approximately 1/8 inch) and be carefully finished to reveal a clean seam along the planking. Again, masking tape will simplify this process.

The basics of the decking method de-scribed above were taught to me by West Coast marine architect/shipwright Patrick Cotten. Part of the system's beauty is its simplicity, but high strength and versatility of application are other strong points. The method can be used on any frameless hull, including fiberglass and ferrocement. Appearance from beneath is traditional and very beautiful, but the construction incorporates the strength, stiffness, light weight and watertight integrity of modern cold-molded construction.

However, the system is also rather labor- and materials-intensive, heavy by some modern standards, and has very little insulative value. Insulation can be incorporated either by adding an intermediate hard-foam layer between the plywood layers (this creates many problems, and necessitates two thin plywood layers above for strength), or by adding foam sheets below the finished deck

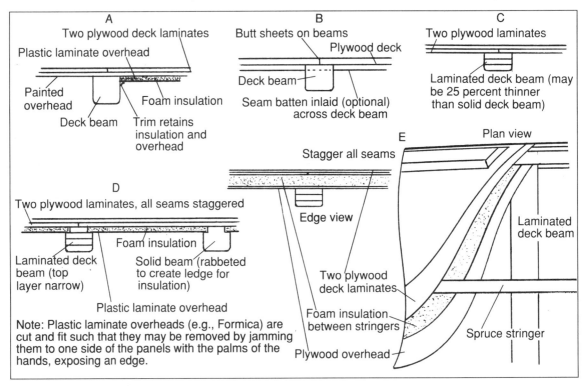

Figure 17-1. Deck sections.

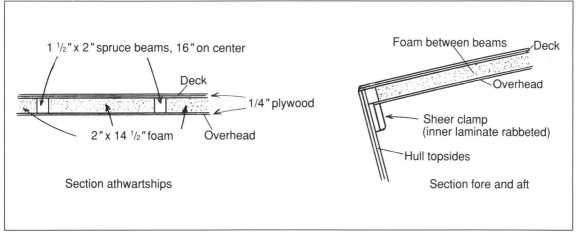

Figure 17-2. Foam-core decks and coach roofs.

between beams. (See Fig. 17-1.) In Figures 17-1A and 17-1D the insulation does not increase overall height; rather it decreases beam exposure. The insulation also provides a convenient hiding place for wiring and deck hardware back-up blocks, including access to them. Plastic-laminate panels (Formica) are carefully cut so that they can be removed by shoving them to one side to expose the opposite edge. The panels are centered when installed; the deck curve keeps them flat between beams. Figure 17-1E shows a composite deck having a foam core installed between fore and aft longitudinals laid above a first plywood layer over beams.

THE FOAM-CORE DECK

Another alternative is the foam-core deck (see Fig. 17-2). The method I will describe here is a plywood/foam sandwich that incorporates 1½-inch square or 1½-inch by 2-inch spruce beams. This deck is very strong, light, thin and stiff, and a little less labor- and materials-intensive than the one just described. Because there are no exposed beams, it is very plain inside. It also provides no internal access and lacks the ultimate strength and flexibility of the other deck systems. I would recommend it for light and ultralight racing vessels and for multihulls.

The sheer clamp is stepped on top by the thickness of the inside plywood layer (1/4 inch in the example) to form a continuous rabbet, either by using a wider plank for the outer lamination during layup, or laying a wood strip 1/4 inch by 3/4 inch along the top of the outer laminate. Spruce deck beams are installed 16 inches apart at the sheer (or the distance of the width of the foam to be used, not to exceed 24 inches). Cleat/beams are placed on both sides of structural bulkheads. These must be beveled to the fore and aft deck pitch for their specific location. Carlins are made and installed; they are just butted, glued and screwed in place—very quick and simple. A plank strongback (two for wide-beamed vessels) is placed over the deck beams and temporarily screwed in place to stiffen the deck.

Precut, prepainted plywood panels are glued and stapled in place from underneath, sliding them into position over the sheer clamp rabbet. Careful measuring and fitting are essential here. Staples are countersunk and puttied with titanium-dioxide–pigmented epoxy; from above the panels are stapled to the sheer clamp rabbet. Prefinished seam battens (varnished wood or just painted plywood) are glued and fastened in place; these are optional on athwartships seams, which may be puttied, but provide tensile strength across the unsupported fore and aft seams. If a seamless overhead is desired, cloth tape (Xynole-polyester or fiberglass) is applied across the seams from above, between beams. In this case all seams are puttied from below with titanium-dioxide–pigmented epoxy. It is also possible to install this plywood layer unfinished and finish it later from below, perhaps with an airless spray system.

Block in the gaps between beams above the sheer clamps and fasten the blocks down into the clamps. Blocks are the same thickness as the sheer clamps and the same height as the beams, and may also be spruce. Backing blocks may be installed now or later wherever deck hardware is to be located (this is described later in this chapter). Mast and bitt partners are stack-laminated in place using plywood, in the manner already described, except that the laminates will start at the plywood bottom sheathing already in place and finish flush to the beam tops. Notching the beams is not necessary; fasteners are placed through beams into the edges of the finished *cured* stack. The laminates are, in this case, each fastened to the layer below, as clamps cannot be used, unless the mast holes are precut (a good idea in this instance).

Glue foam panels in place with epoxy or industrial contact cement (get the low-odor stuff and wear a fume-filtering mask). Due to deck curvature, the edges of the foam panels may have to be shaved near the centerline, as the beams will be closer together (use a Stanley Surform and *wear a particle mask*). Be careful to get a very tight fit. Fill gaps with insulating foam available in spray cans. It is important that there be no large air voids. All foam used should be high-density, closed-cell polyurethane, or its equivalent.

Lay in electrical wires now by cutting troughs in the foam with a razor knife (stay away from beams as much as you can to avoid the possibility later of a deck staple hitting a wire). Drill holes down where fixtures are to be located and leave plenty of wire hanging out; remember, it will be all but impossible to replace these wires, so use good-quality marine cable. When crossing beams, cut the trough and lay a small steel plate over the wire so staples can't penetrate.

All deck hardware will require solid blocking in the deck to provide compressive strength for the through-bolts. After determining hardware location, draw an accurate plan of it. Blocking should butt adjacent deck beams and blocking. It may be solid wood or stack-laminated plywood, and is installed either before foam-paneling or after cutting out the foam with a razor knife and epoxying it in place.

When all deck framing is complete, check the surface for fairness and smoothness. The sheer is faired with a power plane and hand plane as in the other method. Trim the foam with a Stanley Surform.

Lay out and install two plywood layers as in the first decking method, staggering all seams and fastening to beams. In the illustrated example, the layers are 1/4 inch thick. Finishing and covering with fabric and epoxy are the same as in the other method.

The deck described here would be adequate for vessels between 35 feet and 50 feet, using 2-inch-thick foam, 1/4-inch plywood and 1$\frac{1}{2}$-inch by 2-inch spruce beams 16 inches apart. Vessels between 20 feet and 35 feet might use 1$\frac{1}{2}$-inch foam, 3/16-inch plywood, and 1$\frac{1}{2}$-inch square beams 12 inches apart. Ultralight multihulls might use 3/4-inch or 1-inch foam, 3-millimeter plywood and 3/4-inch square or 3/4-inch by 1-inch plywood beams 12 inches apart, using only one layer of plywood on each side of the beams and scarfing the joints. (One would have to walk gently on such a deck.) Vessels over 50 feet might use 3/8-inch plywood, and thicker foam as size increases, or use the decking method described in Figure 17-1E.

TEAK OVERLAYS

Teak decks are expensive, require high maintenance and are hot in the tropics both to the feet and inside the hull. But people love their beauty and want them. Their single crucial problem comes from using fasteners to hold them down. This practice will, in every case, eventually destroy the deck and deck beams and cause interior damage. It cannot help but fail. Solid wood expands and contracts. Seams open up and bungs get loose, particularly as the deck wears thin with age. Water will always find its way in. It will run right down the fasteners and will travel between the teak layer and plywood subdeck until it soaks into the plywood where all those convenient fastener holes are. Then the subdeck will rot—every time. Shortly after that, as water continues along the fasteners down into the beams, carlins and other substructures, they too will rot. This is how many shipwrights are kept in work.

If you must have teak decks, use heavy enough material so that it will have some stability, and don't fasten it down. You can use thinner plywood in the deck, but it is still best to use two layers. Cover the deck with epoxy-saturated Xynole-polyester cloth. Scratch it up after curing, and lay the teak in slightly thickened epoxy or a synthetic rubber compound such as 3M 5200, Sikaflex or polysulfide (Thiokol). Wash the teak gluing surface with acetone to dissolve some of the natural teak wax that makes the stuff resist gluing. Use many weights to hold the teak planks down; bar or pipe clamps from the sheer can be used to spring the planks to a curve if that is the planking style you choose. Avoid air voids. It is best, of course, to wet out the cloth as you lay the deck, thereby achieving a chemical bond from plywood to teak through the fabric, but this requires careful prefitting and a larger work crew. Caulk the planks with a high-quality compound such as two-part polysulfide (Thiokol). Use a good grade of teak oil and maintain the wood instead of letting it go gray. Teak does rot when all the natural wax is cooked and washed out of it. It also warps, shrinks, cracks and breaks.

The final threat to decks involves their hardware, and teak-overlaid decks are especially vulnerable. Because of the tremendous loads imposed on deck hardware, their through-bolts and bedding often allow water to penetrate the deck. My solution is to drill oversize holes and install PVC pipe bushings in them, thoroughly set in epoxy, so that all wood end grain is epoxy-sealed. The hardware then is bedded in Thiokol rubber, 3M 5200, Sikaflex or another rubber bedding compound. The fasteners also are coated.

If you follow these instructions, your teak deck should last a very long time, perhaps 100 years or more. There is so much information on decking in books and articles in *WoodenBoat* magazine that I won't go into detail on specific planking styles.

CHAPTER 18
INTERIOR

Cabinet and Furniture Layout/ Tank Layout/ Integral Tank Construction/ Metal or Plastic Tank Installation/ Cabinet Faces/ Doors and Drawers/ Horizontal Surfaces/ Trim, Paint and Varnish/ Companionway Ladders

If at all possible, the interior should be at least roughed in before trunk cabins are built. To do otherwise is like building a ship in a bottle.

Basic interior layout comes from the design, but often details and the exact placement of furniture are unclear or omitted altogether. Also, during construction, the vessel's future inhabitants may have revelations concerning living arrangements. It then becomes the builder's responsibility to lay out the interior in place. This process will determine the livability of the vessel, and should be thoughtfully undertaken.

CABINET AND FURNITURE LAYOUT

In general, counters should rarely exceed 36 inches in height; berths narrower than 24 inches and shorter than 6 feet 3 inches are uncomfortable; and headroom while seated on finished upholstery should be at least 35 inches. There are many books on both yacht interiors and joinery; several are listed in the back of the book. There are myriad considerations in interior layout, and careful planning is essential. You can use mockups to test the height and extension of galley counters, navigation desks, heads and showers, engine area access, berth sizes, etc. Just clamping 2 x 4s and scrap plywood in place will help you visualize furniture location. Account for hull curvature and intersection angles of cabinet faces and bulkheads when locating drawers, stoves and other appliances. Sinks should drain on both tacks and, if possible, be incapable of flooding the cabin during a knockdown. In general, sinks located within 15 percent of the hull's maximum beam from the fore and aft centerline will fulfill these criteria. Stoves should be in a stable part of the hull (preferably aft) and have good ventilation. Hulls roll about an axis fore and aft through their centerline at the waterline, and tend to pitch about an athwartships axis, also at the waterline, usually about a third of the way forward from the stern. The most stable part of the vessel in a seaway will be at the intersection of these axes, and the closer the stove can be to that point, the calmer will be the pots and pans used on it. In vessels that are intended to make regular sea passages, a gimbaled stove with fiddle rails is very useful; at times it will represent the only surface on which anything may be placed without needing to be secured. Vessels that will rarely make sea passages, as is the case of most American coastal cruisers and island-hoppers, can get by with an ungimbaled stove placed athwartships beside the companionway, which I feel is an ideal location. Heads likewise need ventilation; sleeping areas need fresh air but not rain or spray; navigation areas should be accessible to the cockpit, and so on.

If you have a knack for visualizing through drawings, trace your hull onto several sheets of paper (don't draw on your blueprints) and try sketching different interior plans. Remember that very few items in a hull can touch the perimeter or sheer outline. Refer to the body plan to see how close furniture will be to the perimeter at the level of its location (settees and bunks are a good example of this—often their outboard edges are several feet inboard from the hull's sheer perimeter).

To lay out cabinet faces, countertops, berths, etc. in the hull use a felt tip pen (or pencil on unpainted surfaces). Use a level to establish vertical and horizontal planes, and indicate thicknesses of surfaces to establish cleat locations. Calculate and record drawer and door sizes. Make sure everything will fit where you want it, and that cabinet stiles and rails will be uniform and harmonious. Locate partial bulkheads, shelves, storage areas and the access to them. Make sure doors will be able to open without hitting anything. Keep in mind the location of plumbing, electrical conduits and fixtures, and machinery and tanks with fills and vents.

TANK LAYOUT

Integral tanks can often be built into settees and berths or other furniture. They must be built very strongly and include baffles and access panels. Cleats with rounded (bull-nosed) inner edges must be laid out for all sides, baffles and tops. During layout, consider fill, drain, vent and access panel location. Obviously the drain or pickup will need to be in the deepest part of the tank. Fuel tanks are best built of stainless steel or aluminum and should be removable without destroying any part of the boat. All tankage should be in the lowest and most central part of the hull possible. Avoid placing tanks above the waterline, far outboard (unless balanced port and starboard), and in the ends of the hull. This can be a real challenge, and often compromises must be made. Consider the location and function of your tanks under dynamic conditions—at various angles of heel, pitching and rolling.

INTEGRAL TANK CONSTRUCTION

Cleats are glued and fastened with stainless-steel screws to the hull and bulkheads, and tank walls are glued and screwed to the cleats. More cleats are installed around the interior of the tank perimeter for attaching the lid. Baffles are fastened and glued to cleats; cut out all four corners of all baffles to allow fluid and air to transfer. Add cleats to baffle tops for lid attachment. Make finger fillets along all edges. Cover the tank interior with Xynole-polyester cloth saturated with epoxy, paying attention to corners so as not to trap air voids or leave holes or gaps. Cut and fit the lid, allowing a large enough access panel so that all corners of the tank can be reached through it. The lid underside is also coated with fabric and epoxy, including the cleats to which the access panel will be fastened. Holes are cut or drilled in the lid for plumbing fittings (often plastic through-hull fittings are used), and the holes are epoxy-sealed. The plumbing fittings may be installed now or later, but now is better. Seal them with rubber gaskets (inside) or with nonpoisonous caulking compounds. The tank and lid underside are now coated with epoxy potable-water tankcoating (available from International Paint Co.; *wear a fume-filtering mask*), taking care not to paint the gluing surfaces for the lid perimeter and baffle tops. After two coats have cured thoroughly (allow several days), wash the surfaces with hot water, gentle detergent and baking soda.

Glue and fasten the lid in place, making sure to fasten the baffle tops, too. Large fillets are made along the lid-to-cleat seams by reaching through the access panel, and before they cure, they are painted with tank coating. Large tanks (over 50 gallons or so) will need epoxy and cloth tape reinforcement around the inside of the lid perimeter. The areas where the tape will be applied must be masked off during tank coating to provide adhesion, and painted later. Remember that epoxy surfaces must be coarsely sanded and cleaned with reducer before further lamination or painting. In tanks with baffles, the access panel will have to span them so that all corners of the tank can be reached. In some large tanks there may have to be more than one access panel.

The access panel, which is covered with fabric and epoxy and painted with tankcoating, may be fastened with a gasket or glued and screwed in place. The latter is undesirable because it eliminates further access; a gasket must be carefully made or the panel may leak. The tanks shown in Photo 18-1 were assembled without access panels. Don't do it that way! It was a bad experiment. The Delrin through-hull fittings are in place for fill, vent and pick-up. The tanks are separated by the aft end of the centerboard trunk.

METAL OR PLASTIC TANK INSTALLATION

I prefer to make water tanks integral and fuel tanks separately of metal; in the event of integral tank failure, a fuel leak into the hull material is very harmful. Well-made plastic tanks for water are fine, if you have room for them; I usually avoid plastic fuel tanks unless they are of heavy industrial quality.

Custom-made stainless-steel tanks are the best, but I have also had good success with heavy-walled aluminum (3/16-inch minimum), using plastic tank fittings. Tanks must be very well supported on dogs or cleats. Blocking must be installed on all sides of the tanks so they cannot shift; imagine the vessel violently turned upside down with full tanks and install them so they won't move. Thoroughly epoxy-paint all areas around tanks to protect them from condensation and fuel leakage. Plastic tanks are not as strong as metal ones and will need more careful blocking. Enough blocking should be removable so that the tank can be removed, but make it strong. Leave a space between tanks and the hull for air circulation, and allow for plumbing access.

CABINET FACES

Cabinet faces are typically made from solid lumber 3/4 inch or 13/16 inch thick. The faces contain doors and drawers or bins, and should be carefully laid out so that all components fit well, function easily and provide good access to their interiors. Cabinet construction is described in detail in many books, and I just want to briefly discuss the joints between stiles and the rails. Traditionally, these joints were doweled together. This method is time-consuming and usually involves the purchase of a doweling jig. Other methods include mortise-and-tenon joints (even more time-consuming), half-lapping or just butting with glue with or without fasteners. As versatile as epoxy is, neither it nor any other glue can be expected to bond end grain to side grain; such a joint will fail eventually. Adding a plywood butt block across the inside of the joint, glued and stapled (or nailed or screwed) in place, improves this joint somewhat. In Photo 18-1, the drawer-stack cabinet face shown on the left is made with this method. The narrow slot at the top is for a slide-out chopping block—a handy addition to any galley.

I often add two long screws through the sides of the stiles into the end grain of the rails. This involves laying up cabinet faces with stiles (which are usually $1^1/_2$ inches or 2 inches wide) of full cabinet height, and setting the rails (anywhere from 2 inches to 6 inches wide) between them. The screws are 3 inches by #10 and are spaced far enough apart to make a very strong joint. I typically lay out the cabinet face on a flat plywood table covered with plastic, glue and clamp the stiles and rails together, and install the

screws after curing. Installing them before curing may misalign the joints and force out the glue (remember that epoxy needs a larger glue gap than other glues to develop strength).

Often cabinet faces, such as berth faces, may be made from plywood, especially if they also act as a partial bulkhead (see Photo 18-2.) An inexpensive alternative to drawers is stuff holes (see Photo 18-3), or bins.

Photo 18-2. It is much easier to build the interior before the trunk cabins are built. The plywood partial bulkheads forming the Vee berth are cut out for drawers; the tall partial bulkheads will form large hanging lockers.

Photo 18-3. Stuff holes, or bins, are a cheap alternative to drawers. The area below the cabinet has been covered with fabric and epoxy to be the shower pan.

Photo 18-1. Settees can double as integral tanks. The bulkhead plywood seen here is parana from Brazil. The dark trim is from Paraguay, and the cabinet faces are rock maple. Access panels were cut into the tank tops after they were installed. This was a mistake—it's much easier to do it ahead of time. In the foreground is a compression post located near the center of the cabin, where it is very handy as a handhold.

DOORS AND DRAWERS

I prefer to half-lap my door joints: I have never seen one fail, and the process is easier than making mortises and tenons or using dowels. I plan the door so that the stiles will overlap the rails on the side exposed; I don't mind that the rails overlap the stiles on the backside. The lap joints can be made on a radial arm saw or a table saw using the sliding crosscut guide that comes with most table saws. Make a series of cuts and chisel out between them. The roughness of the cuts will provide excellent tooth for the glue joint. Photo 18-4 shows *Teresa*'s drawers, sanded between varnish coats, the dish cabinet face with dividers (foreground), the backside of a door before caning and the centerboard trunk plug (at right). Photo 18-5 shows the finished drawers, a companion ladder, desk top, battery compartment door and caned doors with half-lapped joints varnished and ready for installation.

I will leave door types to the reader to research, whether they are flush mount or rabbeted surface mount, the type of paneling, etc. However, provide as much ventilation as possible, by incorporating scalloped cutouts in the top and bottom rails, caning or metal screens, louvers or decorative cutouts in the panels. (See Photo 18-6.)

Use good-quality hinges made of brass or stainless steel, with screws of the same material. They are well worth the extra money. Even wood, leather or heavy rubber hinges are better than plated steel ones.

Drawers are a mark of craftsmanship. They should be well-made. It's not that hard to do. Whatever style you choose, faces should be solid wood. The sides and back may be solid wood or high-quality plywood, usually 3/4 inch thick. Bottoms should be 3/16-inch or 1/4-inch plywood. Faces should be rabbeted for the sides; the sides should be rabbeted for the backs; and all should be grooved (two

Photos 18-4 and 18-5. Various cabinet parts (described in the text) for *Teresa*.

Photo 18-6. Varnished hardwood makes a beautiful contrast to painted plywood as seen in this photo of *Lucayan*'s foreward cabin. The treads of the companionway ladder have been varnished with fine silica sand in masked-off patterns for non-skid. Note the louvered doors.

passes through the table saw) for the bottoms. Leave about 3/8 inch of wood below the bottom so it won't break out when heavy loads are placed in the drawer. (See Fig. 18-1.) The traditional way of keeping drawers from sliding out when the vessel is heeled is to cut notches in the sides behind the faces, which hold onto the rail below. (See Photo 18-4.) I know of no better way.

There are many ways to support drawers. If there are bulkheads on each side, cleats are used as tracks. If not, a bottom support and two side supports will work fine. Avoid store-bought tracks altogether—they will rust, break, take up valuable space, and won't stay shut. Install your tracks true and make them

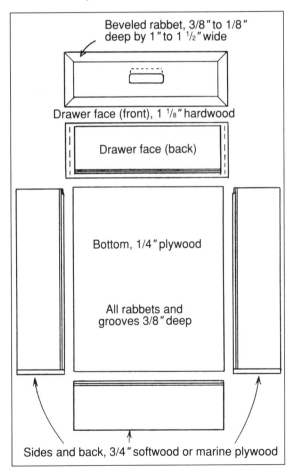

Beveled rabbet, 3/8" to 1/8" deep by 1" to 1 1/2" wide

Drawer face (front), 1 1/8" hardwood

Drawer face (back)

Bottom, 1/4" plywood

All rabbets and grooves 3/8" deep

Sides and back, 3/4" softwood or marine plywood

Figure 18-1. Drawer construction.

strong. Drawers that are too loose or too tight are a nuisance. Hardwood tracks won't need paint but should be sealed. Use two or three coats of epoxy paint on softwood tracks. Do not use beeswax on drawer tracks because it makes them stick. Use paraffin.

HORIZONTAL SURFACES

Countertops and berth tops are usually made of plywood and supported on cleats fastened to the hull, bulkheads and on cabinet faces or partial bulkheads. These latter should be backed up by cleats behind their perimeters so they can't kick in under impact. Large surfaces will need field support, like floors under a cabin sole. These can be 1 x 2s, 1 x 4s, 2 x 2s, or 2 x 4s, depending on application, span and load. Access panels are usually supported by 1 x 2 cleats glued and screwed to the plywood underside. Horizontal surfaces should be glued and screwed in place; they lend great structural support and stiffening to the hull, becoming large horizontal bulkheads. Their thickness is usually from 1/2 inch to 3/4 inch

Photo 18-7 shows ballast boxes lined with fabric and epoxy (alongside the centerboard trunk), berth framing on the left (three center sections will lift out for access), an integral water tank ready for its lid (top right), a shower pan (with rag), and partial bulkheads and support cleats for the lavatory countertop (right). The 4 x 4 post in the foreground is mortised into the hull, joins the centerboard trunk sides, and will continue as a compression post and handhold to the coach roof. The top of the centerboard trunk will use the plug shown in Photo 18-4. Photo 18-3 shows this area after installation of the cabinet face and countertop.

Plastic laminates such as Formica make excellent counter surfaces. Tile is too heavy for most boats, paint eventually wears out,

Photo 18-7. All cabinet interiors are prepainted. Ballast boxes on each side of the centerboard trunk are also covered with fabric and epoxy prior to loading lead pigs and fastening gasketed plywood lids over them.

Photo 18-8. An old cabinet door with holes drilled in it makes a great router table. The finger guide holds trim against the fence and router bit and prevents kickbacks.

and solid wood may warp, crack and leak as well as trap food particles and bacteria.

TRIM, PAINT AND VARNISH

Trim varies tremendously. Styles are personal and I won't go into them much. Fiddle rails should be rabbeted both for strength (they double as handrails) and to cover the edge of the countertop or shelf. Install them with epoxy glue and screws, taking care that the joint is tight to keep out dirt and moisture. Leave gaps or cleanouts in the fiddle rails, usually in the corners.

As mentioned earlier, I often use batten trim to cover and reinforce bulkhead seams. These are glued and finish-nailed in place. Colored wax (available at the lumberyard or hardware store) may be used to fill the nail holes, before or after varnishing.

Trim can create a beautiful contrast to either varnished or painted wood, and will cover rough corners and joints as well as protect these areas from wear. I prefer dark hardwoods finished bright with varnish, clear polyurethane or hand-rubbed oil. Good trim can make an otherwise plain interior come alive (as, for example, satin-varnished cherry trim over plywood painted off-white).

Photo 18-9. All the trim is made and installed before the trunk cabins go on.

A router with a 3/8-inch quarter-round roller-wheel bit can be used to make all your trim. More bits create more possibilities. After basic shapes for corners, fiddle rails, panel trim, window trim and hatch and skylight trim are cut out and surfaced, they may be run through a router table quickly and easily. (See Photo 18-8.) Use a finger guide to hold wood to the fence and prevent kickbacks. Always make extra. Shaping may also be done with only a block plane and sandpaper. Photo 18-9 shows *Teresa*'s trim ready to be installed. Cut corners and butts carefully; by them your craftsmanship will be judged. Use a backsaw, with or without a miter box, and true the cuts with a sharp block plane.

Finishing nails used in trim should be either brass or hot-dipped galvanized steel. Predrill in hardwood to avoid splitting. Cover the heads with colored wax as mentioned earlier.

I use epoxy paint for all interior surfaces, particularly in storage compartments and bilges, which I always paint white for visibility. (See Photo 18-10.) I also use porch and floor enamel and industrial enamels; these are high-quality oil-based coatings, but they take longer to dry. You can pigment your own paint colors with universal tints and dyes (available from any paint supplier), but they must be thoroughly mixed, especially in epoxy. Measure and record your tints so you can match them later. Totally avoid latex paints and other cheap house paints—they won't hold up.

As mentioned, I use polyurethane for varnishing interiors because it lasts almost indefinitely and resists wear and abrasion. Oil-based varnishes and some oils are slow to dry inside; drying can be accelerated by the addition of very small quantities of Japan drier or other additive driers. Using too much will cause the finish to dry flat; this phenomenon

Photo 18-10. The ice box in the corner dog-legs behind the bulkhead to an ice hold loaded through the flush hatch at the top of the photo. The heavily insulated compartment can hold 200 pounds of ice and stay cold for as long as three weeks. Most of the ice remains aft of the compartment seen here, so that it can hold more food. After the ice is loaded from outside, a case of beer goes on top, accessible from the cockpit.

can be used to develop a hand-rubbed effect (satin finish) or to reduce gloss.

Hand-rubbed oil finishes have been all but forgotten today. They are perhaps the most beautiful and natural of all; they are also the most work, and the most vulnerable. But they are the easiest to repair. I use WATCO oil with wet/dry #320 paper and 4/0 bronze wool to apply and rub the oil. The wood must be previously sanded to #280 or finer, and have no scratches. After six or more coats of oil, use several coats of satin wax to seal and protect the surface. Counters, tables and shelves finished this way will take water stains, like any fine furniture. Oil finishes of lesser quality can be used also; often just an oil-saturated surface that has only been planed and/or scraped (no sanding) can be very natural and beautiful. I have seen incredible results in Third-World countries where a craftsman scraped the wood with fragments of broken glass and oiled the wood with lard (rendered animal fat), coconut oil, nose grease or even kerosene. Log oil, boiled or raw linseed oil, and tung oil also work. Oil finishes soak into the wood and densify it, as opposed to coating it, which all other finishes do. Because of this, the wood surface should be finished, whether planed, sanded or scraped, to a much higher degree.

COMPANIONWAY LADDERS

Strong simple companionway ladders can be made from plank sides with mortised-in steps. When using softwood, 1¹/₂-inch stock is required; when using hardwood, 7/8-inch stock is adequate unless the treads are longer than 15 inches, in which case use 1-inch or thicker stock.

I prefer at least 5 inches of "reveal" for the treads. "Reveal" is the amount of the tread that is openly exposed beneath the step above. Five inches allows people to safely

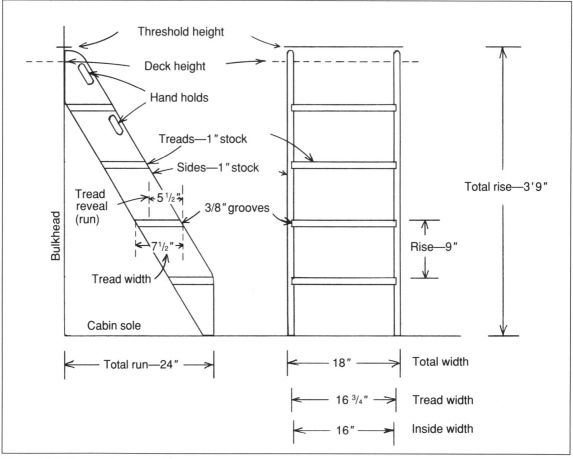

Figure 18-2. Companionway ladders.

walk down the companionway ladder without having to turn around and back down it. The maximum rise, or height of each step, should not exceed 1 foot or be less than 8 inches. To find rise, compute how many steps will divide into the total height that must be climbed and yield an amount between 8 inches and 12 inches. When possible, make all companionway ladders throughout the vessel equal in tread rise and reveal for safety and convenience.

Make the treads and risers (sides) from the same size stock. Five-and-one-half-inch is the minimum comfortable width for treads—I prefer $7\frac{1}{2}$ inches or $9\frac{1}{2}$ inches for large vessels. If you wish to be meticulous about

matching tread and riser width, rip the necessary amount off the risers to match the diagonal distance that the treads will form when installed. (Because of the ladder angle, the treads will not reach across the risers.)

I like to curve my risers at their tops, to prevent possible injury, and I cut away the fronts of the risers below the bottom step vertically to keep from tripping over them. (See Fig. 18-2.) Cut hand-holds into the risers between the top two treads and above the top tread.

Mortise the treads into the risers one-third the thickness of the latter. I like to bevel the very ends of the tread edges to blend into the risers. Bullnose all edges with a router and a quarter-round bit. Use epoxy glue and screws to fasten the treads in place, and bung the holes.

Be sure to fasten the ladders firmly in place at both top and bottom. This will vary between vessels—I often use small pieces of stainless-steel angle screwed to the adjacent bulkhead and cabin sole, and bolted to the ladder risers. Wing nuts are handy here to allow easy removal of the ladders. Avoid any protrusions, such as bolt ends, that could cause injury.

CHAPTER 19
TRUNK CABINS

Trunk Sides/ Coach Roof Structure/ Hatch Openings/
Coach Roof Decking/ Finishing, Fabric and Epoxy

TRUNK SIDES

Trunk cabin size and shape must be transferred from the plans. Most trunk sides are
curved, have some tumblehome, and therefore won't literally conform to the flat plane
drawings; they will be slightly larger and
contoured.

The three general modes of construction
are: solid planks (high trunks often consist of
two planks edge-glued); stack-lamination
using from 1½-inch to 3½-inch high planks
(also edge-glued); and plywood, using either
one or several laminated layers. I have come
to prefer the last because it is lightest, strongest and most economical.

Trunk thickness will come from the design. In general, trunk sides are at least as
thick as the deck, and usually thicker. Solid-
plank trunks and stack-laminated trunks
rarely use material thinner than 1¼ inches,
except in small vessels (under 30 feet). A
trunk side laminated of three layers of 1/4-
inch marine (5-ply) plywood would be about
as strong as a solid trunk of 1½-inch lumber.

In working with solid-plank construction,
the general dimensions are transferred from
the plans to the plank (allowing for curve and
tumblehome), and the plank is sprung into
place, usually after rabbeted corner posts are
at least temporarily installed. The deck at the
carlin where the plank will be installed is
traced with a compass to the plank, the bevel
is measured (it may vary along the length),
and the plank is cut or planed. It is put in
place again, and the ends are traced from the
corner posts, cut, and then the top edge is
laid out. Use a batten to determine the curve
of the top. Determine the bevel for the coach
roof angle by laying a coach roof beam or the
beam template in place (the angle may again
vary, particularly toward the ends of the
house). When dealing with rolling (varying)
bevels, either slowly change the bevel angle
on your circular saw during the cut (this takes
practice), or make the cut to the largest bevel
angle and plane in the decreasing bevel by
hand. The way I usually lay out rolling bevels
is to write the angle of the bevel on the material every 2 or 3 feet—or for every 2½ degrees
of change (my circular saw gauge is marked

in five-degree increments). I start the cut with the saw locked to the first bevel, and as soon as the saw blade is enclosed in the cut, I unlock the bevel gauge and slowly roll the saw toward the next bevel mark as I cut. Rolling the saw while it is running but still stationary is very dangerous, as this binds the blade and can cause the saw to jump backward out of the cut. Never try this procedure with any other than commercial right-angle (gear-driven) saws such as a Skilsaw model #577 or #367 (my own preference). Do-it-yourselfer saws, with the motor and handle offset from the blade, are dangerous and limited.

When two planks are needed to achieve cabin height, they may be edge-glued first or laid up in place and glued during installation (it will be harder to align the edges if the trunk is very curved).

Plywood trunk sides are laid out similarly, especially if made from one thickness. When laminated from two or three layers, they may be laminated in place during installation or on a jig first. Determine jig curvature by laying a plank flat along the carlin/deck edge and tracing it from below onto the plank. Cut the jig from two 2 x 8s or wider planks to the carlin curve, adding 1/2 inch additional curve to allow for springback. The laminates may be screwed to the jig, clamped or both. When laminating in place, use upright 2 x 2s to clamp the plywood layers, in pairs (one on each side), about one foot apart. If you make the trunk sides on a jig, make them a little oversize and trim them to fit.

Stack-laminations are laid out in place during construction. The first layer is beveled along the bottom for the trunk-side tumble-home and subsequent layers are stacked from square-edge stock. Ends may be cut to fit corner posts during lamination or later, in which case upright guides are securely clamped in place. In curved trunks, one or more of these may be required along the length of the trunk to prevent the lamination from trying to flatten out in the middle. If the plank ends overlap alternately in the corners to form finger joints, plywood templates (essentially big bevel guides) may be used to keep the lamination true, or temporary corner guides may be securely clamped in place. When finger-jointed corners are made, the trunk-side laminates will have to be milled to a parallelogram shape in order to integrate with the trunk end laminates.

In trunk cabins laminated with wide stock (2 x 4s), the planks won't be able to conform to the deck crown or curve fore and aft. Hence, cut the first layer to fit by laying it in place and tracing the deck curve onto it with a compass. Measure the bevels and cut the first layer to fit the deck. Subsequent layers are square stock, and corner posts are used.

Windows, deadlights and portlights or other apertures must be laid out prior to fastening or laminating cabin trunks so that fasteners can be located out of the way of the cuts that will have to be made for them. The cutting is often done in place after trunk installation to avoid deformation, particularly in stack-laminated trunks. Apertures in solid trunk sides of flat or gentle curve may be cut before installation, as may jig-laminated sides, but both should be laid out, cut and fitted first so the holes end up in the right place.

Plank sides are traditionally fastened with solid rods threaded at each end for nuts and washers. Take care while drilling to keep the hole in the center of the material. Figure 19-1 shows a simple jig for this. Avoid making these rods out of stainless steel, because it is difficult to cut threads onto them. Use bronze, or buy stainless threaded rod (all-thread). Also avoid electroplated steel unless you have no choice, in which case use it but bed the rod in rubber and countersink and seal both ends in rubber. Normally the bottom is left recessed but exposed under the carlins so

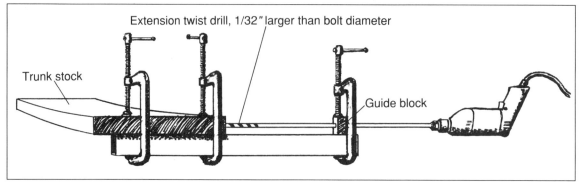

Extension twist drill, 1/32″ larger than bolt diameter

Trunk stock

Guide block

Figure 19-1. Trunk-side drilling jig.

that the nut may be periodically tightened. In traditional craft, water eventually finds its way between deck and trunk and causes corrosion and rot, hence the preferred use of bronze rod.

Stack-laminated sides are fastened each plank to the next, but often extra-long screws are used in the second layer to penetrate down into the carlin. Subsequent laminations should avoid long screws; they will penetrate into the second strip below the one you are fastening into, pushing it away slightly, thus creating a gap and ruining the lamination. For example, when stacking 1½-inch square stock, use 2½-inch by #12 or #14 flat-head wood screws countersunk 1/8 inch to 1/4 inch; when using 3½-inch stock (lumberyard 2 x 4s) use 5-inch by #14 or #16 screws countersunk 1/4 inch to 1/2 inch. Fill the screwheads with epoxy during lamination. Hot-dipped galvanized nails may be used in place of screws; drill first, about 1/32 inch smaller than the nail diameter. Countersink the nails with a punch and use bar or pipe clamps if necessary to achieve tight (but not too tight) joints. Remember that epoxy needs a thicker glue joint to achieve strength than other glues.

Plywood trunks are usually fastened to the inner face of the carlin or into a rabbet in the carlin. (See Figures 19-2B and 19-2C.) This joint must be carefully glued, leaving no voids and using plenty of fasteners (screws or large ring-shank nails) in double rows. In stack-lamination, all the layers are epoxied as well as screwed or nailed together. In all lamination above the deck, the fabric and epoxy deck covering is scuff-sanded for tooth, but left in place to protect the deck in the event of leaking. Solid plank trunks must be bedded in something flexible, as they will have the greatest expansion and contraction—do not use epoxy. Polysulfide rubber, 3M #5200, Sikaflex or the like may be used as bedding/adhesive, or bedding compounds such as Dolfinite may be used. The same is true for corner post joints: Solid planks should be bedded, but stack-laminations and plywood sides are epoxied and fastened.

Corner posts are traditionally rabbeted for the sides and ends; this is still the best and easiest way (see Figure 19-3), as exposed end grain always leads to trouble. Even mitered corners will end up with exposed end grain when they are rounded, and they lack the strength necessary for trunk corners. The exception is finger-jointed corners, which need no corner posts and are extremely strong (see Photo 19-1). However, the exposed end grain will have to be covered with fabric and epoxy. We tried finishing *Teresa*'s trunks bright, and no matter what we did, the joints eventually leaked from expansion and contraction, which broke the cross-grain cor-

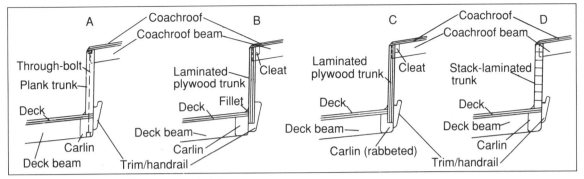

Figure 19-2. Trunk cabin to deck/carlin joints.

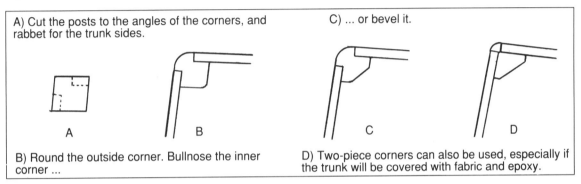

A) Cut the posts to the angles of the corners, and rabbet for the trunk sides.

C) ... or bevel it.

A   B

C   D

B) Round the outside corner. Bullnose the inner corner ...

D) Two-piece corners can also be used, especially if the trunk will be covered with fabric and epoxy.

Figure 19-3. Trunk cabin corner posts.

Photo 19-1. Stack-laminated trunk cabins can employ finger-jointed corners, but after trying it I have concluded that traditional corner posts are much better.

ner lamination. We even tried 4-ounce glass cloth, epoxy and clear polyurethane—within months the glass cracked and failed. The final solution was Xynole-polyester cloth and epoxy, finished with epoxy primers and industrial enamel. I have concluded that finger joints aren't worth the trouble.

Trunk ends are made and installed in pretty much the same manner as the sides. When the trunks are fastened either on the inner face of the carlins and beams or in rabbets in the same, the corner posts must be installed after the ends and sides are in place by sliding them down from the top. The exception might be the aft ends, which include companionway openings; these can be made in halves and slid into the corner rabbets. Note that corner posts should extend to the bottom edge of the carlin/beam (or carlin/bulkhead) joint, or very nearly so, if possible, to provide extra strength and to provide corners for the trim or handrails that will cover the inside trunk/deck/carlin joint.

Many modern yachts have very raked, curvaceous forward cabin ends. These are either laminated in place or on a jig, and may involve joinerwork too specific to each case to go into here.

Plywood sides and ends are so much lighter and stronger than either stack-laminated or plank sides that the only reason for using the latter two is if a bright finish is desired both inside and outside. This can, however, be achieved by laminating thin planks over the plywood using the transom overlay technique described in Chapter 9. Or veneers may be laminated over either side, but I don't recommend their use for the outside unless you cover them with 4-ounce glass cloth and epoxy. Thin veneers don't last long exposed to sun and salt water. A final alternative is to use teak or mahogany veneer plywood for either (or both) the inner and outer trunk plywood layers, but the outer layer will still require a glass and epoxy skin. Remember that epoxy deteriorates in sunlight, and use many (8 to 12) coats of high-quality polyurethane varnish with ultraviolet filter additives to protect such finishes.

With all but solid-plank trunk sides, use large epoxy fillets at the deck-to-trunk exterior joint to prevent damage from moisture or dirt. Make a finger fillet during lamination. The final fillet is made after covering the trunk with fabric and epoxy. The fabric covering should lap out onto the deck at least 1/2 inch. Low-stick masking tape makes this easy: The tape is placed 1/2 inch to 1 inch away from the trunk sides; the cloth laps and ends on the tape, and, after curing, a body grinder with a softpad cuts away the excess cloth to the tape without scarring the deck. Then the tape is removed. As previously mentioned, the silver-colored paper tape or plastic tapes are best for this; some of the cheap paper tapes will soak through with epoxy. Shape large fillets of Cabosil-thickened epoxy with a short piece of $1^1/_2$-inch or 2-inch PVC pipe.

Traditionally the trunk sides were set in bedding compound. If you use solid trunk sides, I suggest you bed them in Dolphinite or a synthetic rubber compound, with no fillet or trim on the outside to trap moisture.

Apertures are cut before or after fabric covering, depending on the trim style. If portlight rings and window trim are to be surface-mounted, the cloth may be applied before or after cutting. If rings and trim are to be flush-mounted or recessed into rabbets, these should be cut oversize first, and the cloth should lap into the rabbets. The point is that the cloth should end beneath the rings or trim if they are to be recessed to keep moisture away from the wood. The same is true for large windows, which are rabbeted in from outside (never rabbet them from inside)—the cloth should lap behind the windows to protect the wood and add strength. Large windows, especially plastics (Lexan [polycarbonate sheet] is best), will expand and contract at different rates and amounts than wood, eventually breaking the seal between them. The right bedding to use is 3M #5200, polysulfides, Sikaflex or an equivalent. The best installation uses many small stainless-steel through-bolts. These can be covered both inside and out with trim. If the trunks are to be finished bright with no fabric covering, recessing or rabbeting rings and trim will invite moisture and water into the cracks that will eventually form due to differing rates of expansion and contraction.

When designing large windows for trunk cabins, keep in mind what a rogue wave might do to them when breaking against the vessel from abeam. Never make a window that relies on fasteners alone; always install windows from outside so that they will have the trunk cabin behind them forming a rim or lip. Make this lip as large as possible (3/4 inch minimum in most cases), and don't rabbet deeper than half the trunk thickness. While it is true that portlights are installed from inside, they are made of metal and are also through-bolted to an exterior metal ring. All I will say about plastic portlights is that your life depends on them. Chapter 22 covers portlights in more detail.

COACH ROOF STRUCTURE

Skylight and hatch placement determine beam placement; hence they must be laid out first. Normally placement comes from the design, but skylights in particular vary greatly in size. I recommend using the largest skylights and hatches possible, especially if you intend to sail in the tropics, or anywhere else in the summer.

If you use manufactured skylights, it is good practice to have them on hand to accurately measure their coach roof apertures. Figure out how you are going to trim out the aperture, because this will affect its dimensions.

Do your layout along the top edge of the trunks in the same manner as laying out for the trunk cabins and deck hatches in Chapter 12. Beams will be placed at hatch and skylight ends, allowing for trim thickness. Then the other beams are determined and laid out, as close as possible to the coach roof beam schedule specified in the design. Hatches and skylights that span more than two adjacent beams will require larger carlins to support the broken beam. Carlin location is laid out on the trunk ends.

A beam template is made of plywood to the design-specified crown in a manner similar to the deck beam template discussed in Chapter 13. Beams are cut from solid stock or laminated. Coach roofs should be as light and thin as possible, both to reduce weight and windage aloft as well as to increase headroom. Hence they especially benefit from the foam-core construction methods described in Chapter 17.

The primary difference between coach roof and deck construction, other than scale, is in the beam attachment to the trunk sides. There is frequently no sheer clamp or beam shelf except in very large vessels; the beam ends are often simply mortised, or routed, approximately one-third of the way into the trunk sides. Beam ends should fit tightly and cleanly into the mortises. In this case, I usually edge-rout my beams using a quarter-round bit right to their ends and rout the mortises with a flute bit the same radius as the quarter-round bit. The joints are epoxied and fastened with two screws from outside into the beam ends. Finger fillets seal the joints. It doesn't matter if the trunk sides have already been covered with fabric and epoxy, because the coach roof covering will lap down far enough to cover the holes made by these fasteners.

Compression posts that miss coach roof beams should end at a stout block that is mortised into each adjacent beam and fastened with epoxy and screws. An example of this may be seen in Photo 19-2.

I notch beams and carlins where they join, end my routs just before the joints and prefinish all woodwork in the same manner as with deck construction. All joints are fastened with screws and epoxied in a similar manner. Because the coach roof framing is so highly visible, the joinerwork and finishing should be meticulous. Photo 19-2 shows *Teresa*'s aft coach roof in frame before surfacing for plywood. Masking paper inside keeps epoxy off interior joinerwork; this may be seen in Photo 19-3.

Examples of coach roof design and construction may be seen in the designs in the Appendix. The TERRAPIN 45 shows a foam-core coach roof design.

HATCH OPENINGS

There are as many ways of building companionway hatches as anything else, and I

Photo 19-2. Coach roof beams don't require a sheer clamp except in very large vessels; beam ends are mortised into the trunk sides.

Photo 19-3. Sliding hatch carlins become knees mortised into the cabin trunk. Handles are cut into them where you most need them going up the companionway. Beam ends are mortised into the carlin sides; carlin ends are mortised into a beam. The pipe sticking up at the left is a tank vent which will terminate in two elbows and be clamped to the trunk. The masking paper will help keep epoxy off the interior while laying the coachroof.

will just describe the way that has evolved for me. Even though I don't assemble hatch components until after the coach roof is on, the parts are integrated and the carlins have to come first.

Because companionway openings break the structural continuity of both the coach roof and the trunk, they must be carefully designed and strongly built. I shape my carlins to act as knees between coach roof and trunk (see Photo 19-3). The outboard sides of the carlins are mortised to contain the ends of the coach roof beam broken by the hatch opening. The aft ends of the carlins are mortised into the trunk aft end on either side of the companionway, and the forward ends of the carlins are set in notches in the continuous coach roof beam at the forward end of the hatch opening. Further structural reinforcement is provided later by the hatch track supports, which will be the same width as the carlin and fastened both to it and the coach roof farther forward. I cut handles into these carlin/knees; they are exactly where you want to grab something when ascending a companionway, particularly in rough weather, and they don't appreciably weaken the knees. I install these carlin/knees flush to the trunk companionway edges. These details are apparent in both Photos 19-2 and 19-3.

Next make a threshold. I like this to be high enough that a modest amount of sea water or wash-down water sliding across the deck won't come down the companionway. This doesn't have to be very high—3 inches to 6 inches is enough (consider that your drop boards or doors should be in place if a lot of water is anticipated on deck). The exceptions are companionways that open into cockpit wells. These should be quite high, perhaps a foot above the well deck, to minimize the amount of water that could enter the cabin during pooping by a breaking following sea. When practical, I design bridge decks between cockpit and trunk cabin for safety, strength, storage and seating out of the helmsman's way. Bridge decks also provide an excellent location for an inboard diesel engine.

In most cases I build up the trunk end a few inches high under the threshold, and groove, or slot, the threshold to fit down over this built-up lip. I notch the ends of the threshold to extend beyond both ends of the companionway opening to slightly beyond where the jambs will lie. When building the trunk ends with plank or stack-laminated wood, a lip is left at the bottom for the threshold (in stack-laminating, this lip is formed by the first one or two laminates). When plywood trunk ends are used, a filler piece is added to form the lip, being careful to make a tight, well-glued joint, and covering it with fabric and epoxy; you don't want a leak or a weak spot here. The notched and slotted threshold ties the whole thing together. I usually make it from oak, bed it in epoxy or rubber compound and screw it down. The top of the threshold is beveled and stepped (rabbeted). (See Fig. 19-4.) The step is placed so that the outside surfaces of the doors or drop boards, when in place, will line up with, or be in the same plane as, the outside surfaces of the trunk, as shown in the drawing. The inside surfaces of the doors or drop boards will contact the step when closed, and their bottom edges are cut to the same bevel as the rabbet of the threshold.

The jambs are likewise grooved to fit snugly over the edges of the trunk ends. The jamb bottoms are cut to fit tightly to the threshold, and the tops extend flush to where the tops of the hatch track supports will lie. Inside the cabin, the top outboard jamb edges are cut away to fit snug to the carlin knees, and outside the cabin, the top outboard edges are cut away to fit against the hatch track supports, which will extend beyond the coach roof and end flush with the jamb outer faces. The depth of these cuts is the same as the depth of the groove: They all end in the same plane. The jamb inboard edges are grooved if drop boards are used, or rabbeted if doors are to be hung. I know this sounds a like Japanese jigsaw puzzle, but as you start to build it, things will become clear. Figure 19-4 will help, too. The key to the whole thing is making the jambs longer than you need, grooving them, and holding them against the threshold. Trace the threshold to the jamb and cut it out. The groove or rabbet for the doors has to line up to the step in the threshold; mark it and cut that. Then the grooved outboard edge has to fit over the trunk edge; it does at the bottom, but the carlin/knee is stopping it from fitting at the top. Trace the bottom of the knee onto the jamb and cut it away so it fits. When you make the tapered hatch track supports later, they will interface with the jamb ends sticking up. The jamb is traced and cut away above the coach roof to allow the hatch track support to overlap it, as shown in the drawing. The jambs are screwed in place, using epoxy or synthetic rubber compound for glue. Take care to align the jambs properly, both parallel to each other athwartships and parallel to each other fore and aft if doors are to be hung. If tapering drop boards are to be used, the jambs are set closer together at the bottom, and all your angles and cuts become compound. I prefer vertical jambs even with drop boards, as I usually make them into one or two louvered panels, described in Chapter 22.

These companionway components aren't necessarily made or installed at this point, but an understanding of them is helpful in planning and cutting the companionway rough opening, as well as fitting the carlin/knees.

COACH ROOF DECKING

If plywood trunk sides and ends are used, cleats are installed between the beams (and carlins on the ends) to reinforce the trunk-to-coach-roof joint and increase the gluing surfaces between them. These can be 3/4 inch by $1^{1}/_{2}$ inches for a vessel between 30 feet and 50 feet. They are glued and screwed to the trunks, often from trunk to cleat (outside in) to avoid having to bung screw holes inside. All the screw holes we have made around the upper perimeter of the trunk cabin are

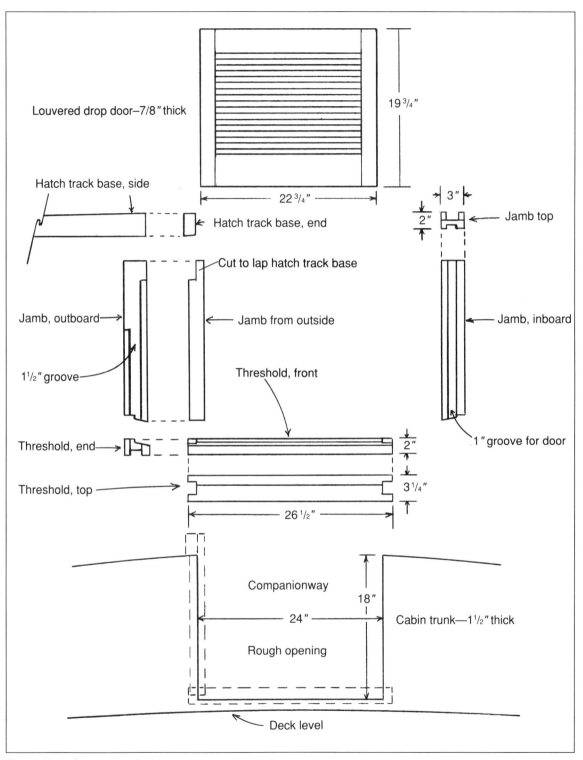

Louvered drop door–7/8″ thick

19 3/4″

22 3/4″

3″

Hatch track base, side

Hatch track base, end

Jamb top

2″

Cut to lap hatch track base

Jamb, outboard

Jamb from outside

Jamb, inboard

1 1/2″ groove

Threshold, front

1″ groove for door

Threshold, end

2″

Threshold, top

3 1/4″

26 1/2″

Companionway

18″

24″

Cabin trunk—1 1/2″ thick

Rough opening

Deck level

Figure 19-4. Companionway components.

epoxy-puttied; they will be covered by the fabric used to cover the coach roof.

An alternative for the trunk ends, particularly if they are plywood, is to make cleat/beams (coach roof beams of half-thickness) similar to those used for bulkhead-to-deck joints. The result is stronger and better looking than continuing the cleats along the end joints.

The top of the coach roof substructure is surfaced fair and smooth just as the deck was. Plywood is cut to fit, then laid out and tacked in place, traced from beneath, removed and painted between the lines as was done for the deck, then glued and fastened down. Take care inside to keep epoxy off your finished interior and to clean the seams with denatured alcohol as before. Lay out the second layer with staggered seams and cut, glue and fasten it. Trim and rout the edges or round them by hand if a large-radius bullnose is desired. In cases where a very large (more than a radius equal to the trunk thickness) bullnose is desired, it is necessary to increase the size of those interior cleats, as you may actually cut into them.

Dimensions of the components in a coach roof are substantially smaller than those of a deck for the same vessel. *Teresa*'s coach roof beams are 2$\frac{1}{2}$ inches square and placed on approximately 16-inch centers, and her coach roof decking is 1/4-inch plywood over 3/8-inch plywood. Two layers of 1/4 inch would have been better, to save weight. Likewise, her cabin trunks could have been three layers of 5/16-inch plywood to save weight, instead of 1$\frac{1}{2}$-inch stack-laminated fir. To maximize headroom without increasing cabin height, laminated beams, though expensive, are useful. So are foam-core coach roofs, which can often be made half the thickness of conventional framed roofs. Increased coach roof crown also allows slightly smaller scantlings, though at the expense of dimin-ished headroom outboard from the cabin centerline.

FINISHING, FABRIC AND EPOXY

After bullnosing the edges of the coach roof, the whole surface is inspected, fasteners are countersunk, and all defects are filled with thickened epoxy, including the fastener holes in the cabin sides. Sand and fair the surface and cover with epoxy-saturated Xynole-polyester fabric. The cloth laps the trunk sides and ends to just below the screw holes. Use masking tape to create a clean line to sand to with the body grinder, as with the trunk-to-deck cloth. This joint is usually covered with wood eyebrow trim. If you elect not to use this, fair in the lap or deliberately finish it proud to create a paint line or just a visual line. I usually apply only two coats of resin to the coach roof, deliberately leaving a fabric-texture finish. This is scratch-sanded before painting. The result is a natural appearance very much like traditional canvas coverings, with nonskid properties. The coarse finish will also be easier on the eyes than a highly finished glossy surface, not to mention saving the cost and weight of the extra epoxy used in supersaturating and fairing, and the extra labor of applying it. Then there is the cost of nonskid work areas on the finished roof. On working vessels and cruising boats built on a budget, this technique of "nonfinishing" may be used on the decks also, though I recommend use of nonskid particles, too.

The most durable, low-maintenance finish I know of is epoxy-saturated Xynole-polyester cloth painted with a two-part polyurethane. This will require less maintenance than a polyester gel coat, which needs to be waxed. Using different colors for the deck, trunks and coach roofs will avoid the institutional fiberglass-boat look.

CHAPTER 20
ABOVE THE DECK

Scupper Layout and Laminating Bulwarks/ Rubrails/ Bowsprits/ Bitts/ Bulwark Caps/ Taffrails/ Fife Rails/ Cockpit Coamings and Caps

SCUPPER LAYOUT AND LAMINATING BULWARKS

Scupper and freeing port layout generally come from the plans. Confirm the location of the lowest scupper on the deck of the constructed vessel, as it may differ. Set a marble or large ball bearing loose near the lowest point on deck and note where it rolls off the side; do this several times. Make that point the forward end of the middle or lowest scupper (most boats will sit either level or slightly bow-high). From that point the scuppers may be laid out and deck puddles will be least likely to form.

Many yachts have closed toerails and drain-type scuppers in the deck. These cause many problems: They clog, the hoses or fittings eventually fail and leak inside the hull, puddles form if the hull isn't perfectly trimmed (and often if it is), and they take a long time to drain the deck. Their intended use is to avoid stains on the topsides from dirty deck water running through scuppers on vessels without rubrails. I strongly believe that omitting rubrails on any vessel is absurd,

for the obvious reasons. Properly made rubrails have a drip-lip (just a saw cut) so that the water doesn't get to the topsides. (See Fig. 20-1.)

There are many ways of building bulwarks. Traditionally, either the frame heads came above deck and plank bulwarks were affixed to these, or wood stanchions (bulwark pins) were placed alongside or between frames to which plank bulwarks were affixed. Bulwark pins are like small frames or ribs that penetrate about as far below deck as above deck and look like frame heads. These eventually leak and cause rot. In the old days, deckhands sloshed salt water all over the decks several times a day every day, and leaks were kept caulked up, so there was little problem. Today we don't want any more holes in the deck than absolutely necessary, and only very large vessels have high bulwarks, anyway. Most contemporary yachts have small toerails or very low bulwarks. Too often this is because these vessels already have a ridiculously high freeboard to try to contain a condominium inside and so cannot

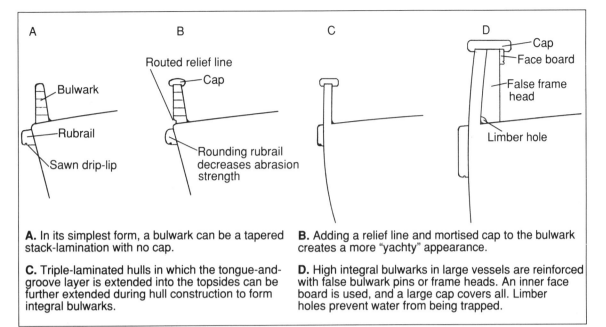

A | B | C | D | Cap
Face board

Routed relief line
— Cap

Bulwark

False frame head

Rubrail

Limber hole

Sawn drip-lip

Rounding rubrail decreases abrasion strength

A. In its simplest form, a bulwark can be a tapered stack-lamination with no cap.

B. Adding a relief line and mortised cap to the bulwark creates a more "yachty" appearance.

C. Triple-laminated hulls in which the tongue-and-groove layer is extended into the topsides can be further extended during hull construction to form integral bulwarks.

D. High integral bulwarks in large vessels are reinforced with false bulwark pins or frame heads. An inner face board is used, and a large cap covers all. Limber holes prevent water from being trapped.

Figure 20-1. Bulwarks, caps and rubrails.

afford the additional windage and weight of anything as practical and safe as real bulwarks. These same vessels always seem to lack rubrails, too!

The two types of bulwark I will describe are a continuation of the triple-laminate hull topsides (when plywood topsides are not used), and stack-laminated bulwarks, which have become the norm today.

Stack-laminated bulwarks are usually made from $1\frac{1}{2}$-inch Douglas fir or southern yellow pine, though they can be teak or mahogany if you can afford it. If they will be fabric-covered and painted (for low maintenance), they may be made of spruce or hem-fir to save money.

The first layer is broken at the scuppers. Segments between scuppers and in the ends of vessels with "curvy ends" (on the flat) will need to be cut out of wide plank-stock to match the deck curve. The bulwarks should be tapered from a wide base; this is determined by the finished height. (See Fig. 20-1.) *Teresa's* $7\frac{1}{2}$-inch-high bulwarks are $2\frac{1}{2}$

inches wide at the base; *Sarah's* 9-inch high bulwarks are 3 inches wide at the base. Both are $1\frac{1}{2}$ inches wide at the top. (See Photos 20-1, 20-2.) The bottom of the first layer is cut to a bevel that will determine the angle of the outer face of the bulwark. In the bow area, this bevel usually diminishes or even reverses as the deck flattens out and the bulwarks flare out. On vessels with very flaring bow topsides, this bevel may become so pronounced that a continuous wedge must be added under the first layer (an extreme bevel might cut away too much of the finished bulwark height in the bow). This will again be a rolling bevel, and is usually cut with a power plane, checking the bevel angle every 2 feet or so. You can take the bevel angle from the plans if they are very accurate, but it is best to take angles off the deck edge every few feet and lay them out along the first layer. This is a little tricky and must be done carefully; your eye is your best tool. The first layer is epoxied and screwed to the deck. Set it in from the sheer about 1/2 inch. The screws should be large (3 inches by #14 or #16) and staggered on close centers (6 inches maximum). The outer edge gets a finger fillet, and the inner edge gets a large fillet made with 1½-inch PVC pipe.

In starting to stack-laminate the gradually narrower planks, often the second layer cannot make the bow curves. Cut it 1/8 inch wider than the top of the first layer and try to spring it into place with clamps. If it won't go, rip it in half and lay it up in two pieces side by side (see Photo 20-1). If it does go, cut off the 1/8 inch and install it. This will rarely be necessary in subsequent layers (as they become progressively narrower). The exceptions are canoe and round sterns, all of whose layers either will have to be cut out of wide stock or steam-bent. Steam-bent laminates will have to be made on a jig and allowed to dry before lamination. Of course the layers may also be ripped into narrower strips and laminated side by side as the second layer in our example was.

As mentioned previously, don't use screws that penetrate below the layer you are fastening into except during lamination of the second layer. In this one instance, it is desirable to fasten all the way down into the sheer clamp blocking, if possible. During subsequent lamination, screws that are too long will push the next layer down away as they break through, ruining the lamination. Use 2½-inch by #14 screws countersunk 1/8 inch to 1/4 inch. Epoxy-fill the screwheads as you laminate. The top-layer screws should be countersunk 3/8 inch and bunged (always align the grain).

Scarfs in the layers can be glued before or during stack-lamination. They should be at least 6 inches long, and I usually make them in the vertical plane so that diagonal lines don't show in the bulwarks. In curvy bows, (like *Teresa's*), the scarfs may need to be made before lamination to avoid hard spots,

Photo 20-1. The second lamination in these bulwarks had to be made in two halves to make the curve near the bow. Subsequent laminations were narrower due to bulwark taper higher up and made the curve in one piece.

Photo 20-2. Here the bulwark stack-lamination is finished and ready for sanding.

or long planks will be needed to avoid scarfs in the first third of the bulwarks altogether. Scarfs should be staggered at least 4 feet apart between adjacent laminations.

Neatness counts in this laminating process, as it will save work in finishing the bulwarks, which is awkward, particularly on the inboard side. This must be done with the softpad, *keeping it moving*. Final sanding is done with an orbital sander and by hand, with the grain, first with #80 grit paper then with #120.

The finished bulwarks may be capped or just bullnosed. You can cover them with cloth and epoxy and linear polyurethane, paint them (oil-base enamel is best over bare wood), varnish them or oil them, which is my preference (I use many coats of Flood's Deks Olje #1 and #2).

On large, traditional vessels, particularly those with raised quarter decks, bulwarks often included a relief line or "waist," in which the highest planks were thinner than the lower ones. This can be visually duplicated in cold-molded construction by terminating the outermost diagonal planking layer at the desired waistline, and planking above it with thinner material, either plywood or fore and aft planking if a bright finish is desired. If planking is used, install it as described in Chapter 9 during the teak transom overlay.

RUBRAILS

Rubrails should be hardwood (although yellow pine will work). I prefer white oak or ironbark (New Zealand red eucalyptus). They should be prominent from as close to the bow as convenient, right back to near the transom, which so often gets clipped clearing docks and pilings. By "prominent" I mean that if something vertical hits the hull, it should contact the rubrail and nothing else.

The surface of the rubrail should be vertical or nearly so, even if it is curved. Half-rounds will be damaged easily because they present less surface area. Tops should pitch down to shed water, but be flat enough to get a foothold on, though this is impractical on smaller vessels.

Rubrail segments should be long-scarfed (5 to 1) before installation. A drip-lip is cut about 1/2 inch in from the bottom outer face, 1/8 inch wide by 1/8 inch deep or a little larger; this keeps deck run-off water from staining the topsides. A good practice is to

seal the back of the rubrails with epoxy, old varnish or clear preservative before installation. Fasten the rubrails with large screws (3-inch by #14 for 35-foot to 50-foot hulls) staggered on close centers (around 6 inches). Bed them in rubber compound (such as 3M 5200, etc.) or bedding compound. Don't use epoxy—rubrails, being made from solid stock which is alternately dunked in salt water and exposed to sunlight, expand and contract too much for a glue joint to survive. They are also susceptible to damage and during the life of a vessel are bound to be replaced. During installation and bedding, be very careful not to form air pockets in which water can get trapped. I use oil mixed with pine tar to finish rubrails because they take abuse, and that kind of finish doesn't show it so readily. *Teresa*'s rubrails are about $2^3/_4$ inches high at the base, $1^1/_2$ inches thick on top, and present a flat abrasion surface of about 2 inches.

BOWSPRITS

Like so many other things, bowsprits have either disappeared or changed so much as to be unrecognizable, or worse, laughable. Several other books cover the many new types, and most plans are pretty specific, so I will describe only the heavy plank type, which I feel is best. I prefer deck-mounted heavy plank bowsprits because of their ability to support large, strongly constructed anchor rollers, and because they are easy and safe to walk on, compared to round ones. In profile they look traditional, having about the same thickness and taper of a round or square-to-round sprit, and ending in round section.

For vessels 25 feet to 35 feet the sprit might be made from a nominal 4 x 10 or 4 x 12 timber. It would taper from $3^1/_2$ inches at the stem head to around 3 inches at the collar (end). On the flat, it might taper from $9^1/_2$ inches (or $11^1/_2$ inches) at the stem head to the same 3 inches at the collar, and taper aft to around 6 inches or 8 inches For vessels from 35 feet to 50 feet the sprit could be made from a 6 x 12. It would taper to $3^1/_2$ inches or 4 inches round at the collar, and to 8 inches or 9 inches aft.

Solid timber is better than a lamination for two reasons: first, expense, both in labor and materials; second, a large laminated structure exposed to the weather would probably not hold up well unless painted or covered with fabric and epoxy.

As mentioned in Chapter 16, I prefer to step the bowsprit between the mooring bitts; they complement each other structurally. I cut away or taper the sprit underside so it conforms to the deck (if it is to be deck-mounted) at such an angle that the line of the sprit continues the sheer; this just happens to please my eye.

The edges of the sprit are rounded or bullnosed as desired, and, going forward, this bullnose increases until the end of the sprit is perfectly round. At that point, a shoulder is cut for the collar. The sprit end is often determined by the sizes of pipe available from which to make the collar, but they will be close to those sizes given earlier. The sprit, if deck-mounted, is through-bolted into the breast hook, deck beams and mooring bitt partners. It should extend back on deck at least a third of the amount that reaches off the bow. There are usually three or four places to bolt it down. Use pairs of large bolts, 1/2 inch or larger. Seal the underside of the sprit (I use several coats of clear Cuprinol or other preservative followed by oil or varnish—epoxy is too brittle for this), and bed it heavily in Dolfinite or an equivalent. It's plain that a good fit will save money on bedding compound. Bedding compound is used instead of synthetic rubber because the bowsprit may

have to be replaced during the life of the boat. Countersink and bung the bolt heads. The bungs will be large (washers are needed under the boltheads), deep (minimum 3/4 inch), and carefully epoxied in place. Large bungs can be cut out with a coping saw or made with a hole saw in a drill press by removing the center-guide twist drill.

The bowsprit will move around some; it is a large timber that will expand and contract, and it may at times be under thousands of pounds of compression from the rigging. For these reasons it must be made from a good-quality timber and carefully installed. I always step it against the mooring bitts so that the compressive loads are picked up by something more than just the bolts. If bowsprit anchor rollers are used, they should include a solid shaft through the sprit. Both the sprit and the roller assembly will need to be strong enough to absorb the deflective, torquing surge loads placed on them when anchored in large seas. I have personally seen my own 6 x 12 Douglas fir bowsprit on *Fishers Hornpipe* twist and deflect a full inch at the rollers while anchored in short steep seas during a Caribbean squall.

In many large traditional craft, you will see bowsprits that are not deck-mounted. If you are building such a vessel, the sprit will have to be very securely stepped against large, heavy bitts or a mooring post. Such sprits are usually square and/or hexagonal on deck, and taper and round out toward the collar end. They are supported where they leave the deck between knight heads—heavy, long, vertical timbers that pierce the deck on either side of the stem and also contain the hawse pipes. Also incorporated in their support are a large stem head, gammon iron and, frequently, clipper head gear.

I prefer oil finishes on bowsprits, often incorporating pine tar; these finishes are not slippery. If you varnish or paint the bowsprit, use fine-graded (#1) silica sand for a non-skid surface. This will finish out clear used with varnish; it is what I use on companionway ladders. When masked into patterns it is handsome and you can see the wood grain through it, as with textured satin finish.

BITTS

I have already said a lot about bitts. The remaining considerations are how they are stepped and how to seal the deck where they pass through. One good stepping procedure is to lag-bolt 4 x 6 timbers both in front of and behind the bitts where they meet the lower stem or keel. Another wood block is lagged between the bitts. If their outer edges lay up against the hull, it is a good idea to place a fairly large piece of 3/4-inch plywood there to distribute the load. Otherwise, sculpted wood blocks are fastened outboard of the bitts against the hull. All these timbers are epoxied together and capped by a layer of 3/4-inch plywood epoxied and screwed to all. Allow for water drainage through and under the step. Use epoxy paint to seal and protect it. The bitts may be painted, varnished or oiled. If oiled, soak them with several coats of clear wood preservative first, allowing several days for it to dry. The bitts are not fastened to the step, but may be bedded if desired. If the bitts come down a bulkhead, they may be fastened to it, but position the fasteners where you can remove them and don't use adhesives, as the bitts may need to be replaced some day.

The bitt partners, already described in Chapter 16, should be thoroughly sealed with epoxy and paint. When the prefinished bitts are set in place, they should have about 1/8 inch or more of play on all sides. The bitts are centered, and masking tape is used to seal the gaps between them and their partners from below. Fill the gaps with a liquid rubber compound (like two-part Thiokol, 3M #5200 or Sikaflex). The old way was to caulk them, driving in first oakum, then cotton, then pouring hot pitch over the top. The only drawback to using poured rubber compound is that it might be very difficult to replace the bitts, but this disadvantage is offset by the fact that they probably won't ever leak, as long as no air voids are trapped in the rubber compound. An alternative might be to drive caulking in the traditional manner and use two-part Thiokol rubber in place of the hot pitch. In the event that damaged bitts need to be replaced, cut them off above and below the deck, and drill them out.

Above decks the bitts are hollowed out slightly around the top third, to keep hitches in place. The tops are usually covered with lead or copper sheet or heavily painted; this is still essential to protect the exposed end grain. Use tar or raw linseed oil under the lead or copper. Painting the top 3 inches white helps you locate the bitts in a squall at night when you need to pay out scope!

BULWARK CAPS

Bulwark caps vary according to taste and vessel size. Their proportions are sensitive in terms of achieving a balanced look. If you aren't satisfied with the information presented by your design (or if you are adapting a design), the best source of information is traditional craft. Refer to books (such as those of Howard I. Chapelle) or vessels that look right to your eye.

The first step in making the caps is laying out planks to locate the scarfs. Make sure the planks are long and wide enough by looking underneath to see if there is enough overhang when laying them out in place. Avoid placing the scarfs too close together, and make them symmetrical port and starboard. The scarfs should have cut ends as opposed to a straight diagonal line; this is called a common scarf (see Fig. 20-2). I make the scarfs first, before cutting the caps to shape. A scarf is centered in what will be the finished cap width, cut, and the adjoining plank end is traced from the scarf and cut, and so on. When all the planks are scarfed together and laid out around the bulwarks, weigh them down so they touch and lie flat. Plan to leave extra length at the ends because when the caps are mortised to fit down over the bulwarks, they will be further out on the arc of the circle determined by the hull sheer, and hence will need to be longer.

Use a compass to trace the inner and outer edges of the cap, usually 1/2 inch to 1 inch beyond the bulwark faces. If a wider cap is desired, extend it inboard where it won't be as vulnerable. Also trace the bulwark faces under the caps, so there will be four lines on the underside of each plank. Cut the inner

lines first, to the depth of the mortise. If the material is to be chiseled out (as opposed to routed with a flute bit), make several parallel cuts 3/8 inch to 1/2 inch apart between these first cuts. Before chiseling or routing make the edge cuts; these must be fair and true. Any obvious defects in the bulwarks that trace onto the caps should be faired out with a batten. After cleaning out the mortises, lay the caps back in place and check that the scarfs fit tightly. Then cut the fore and aft ends. At this time the transom cap and quarter knees are laid out and made, if your bulwarks and caps continue around the transom. (See Fig. 20-2.)

Lay out the fastener holes and drill them, countersinking at least 1/4 inch for bungs. If the bulwarks are wide enough, the hole pattern should be staggered; fasteners can be 6 inches or 8 inches on center. Both the tops of the bulwarks and the insides of the cap mor-

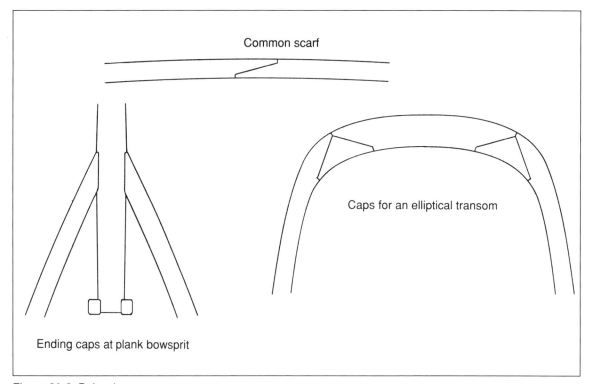

Common scarf

Caps for an elliptical transom

Ending caps at plank bowsprit

Figure 20-2. Bulwark caps.

tises should be coated with clear wood preservative and oil or varnish. If they are to be painted, seal them with oil-base paint. Bedding should be Dolfinite or its equivalent, both for mortises and scarfs. The tapered scarf ends are fastened horizontally into the adjoining cap. Caps are periodically replaced during the life of a vessel and must be easy to remove. Bungs are epoxied in, taking care to match color and align grain.

A modified spade bit is a handy tool for removing epoxied bungs. Take a spade bit the same size as the bungs and grind down its starting point until it is just barely longer than the cutting faces. Use this to drill out the bungs. The starting point will usually go into the center of the screw slot, causing no damage to the fastener.

After the caps are fastened and bunged, fair them along the edges (they should be very close already) using a batten, plane, belt sander and sanding board. (A compass plane is the ideal tool for planing curved surfaces. A sanding board can be made from a 2-foot long 3-inch by 3/8-inch plank by gluing and screwing a handle on each end and contact-cementing #50 closed coat sandpaper (the kind used for floor sanding) onto the bottom. The sanding board is used in fairing. It will leave prominent scratches on high places, will conform to concave and convex curves and will finish fair curves with minor flaws. Be very careful using a belt sander for this kind of work, because it can do a lot of damage quickly. The only place you should need it is to fair up the scarfs. Keep a try square handy to check that the sides are staying square to the top. Sand the tops smooth and fair. The edges may be bullnosed with a router, or sometimes the whole top of the cap is clamshelled and the edges rounded with a power plane, hand plane or both, and sanders. Use a plywood template to maintain consistent shape. It may not be possible to use a router on the lower edges of caps that are only a little wider than the bulwarks, because there won't be room for the guide wheel. These edges are either shaped by hand using a block plane and sandpaper, or are routed before the caps are fastened and trued up after they are in place.

Caps, after a final sanding, may be oiled, varnished or painted. Areas of high traffic and abrasion will benefit from chafe strips.

TAFFRAILS

I usually lay out my taffrail stock on top of the bulwark caps and trace it from them. The taffrail is the same size or larger than the cap, so I use a compass and trace it larger to the inboard edge. Taffrails are cut, scarfed, shaped and finished similarly to the caps, except they are not mortised for a bulwark, and the scarfs (if any) are epoxy-glued and screwed to each other.

Turnposts are made to support the rail; I usually mortise these into the underside of the rail but not into the cap, where the mortise could trap moisture and cause rot. I then drill from the rail down through cap, bulwark, deck, blocking and sheer clamp. Install long, threaded rods or bronze rods that are threaded at each end and recess nuts and washers on both top and bottom. Leave the holes in the sheer clamps to tighten the nuts and allow moisture or water to get out; carefully bung the holes on top of the taffrails using epoxy glue. Bedding compound or a liquid rubber compound is used between all components, including around the fasteners.

An alternative to turnposts is to use brass pipes with brass plates brazed to each end. The top plates are screwed into the rail bottoms; the bottom plates are screwed or bolted into the caps or set just inside the bulwarks and bolted to both deck and bulwarks.

FIFE RAILS

Fife rails are placed around masts and contain belaying pins for mast halyards, topping lifts, etc. They often have three rails, the fourth side being the forward edge of a house aft of the mast. The two forward corners, or all four corners if there is no house, are supported on turnposts (see Photo 20-3). A third alternative, typical of American fishing schooners, employed bitts at the forward corners of the fife rails into which the rail ends were notched and mortised. Beams mortised between the bitts supported a boom crutch in slots, and held the fore sheet cleat. Large thumb cleats on the bitts took the tension of tops'l halyards, which led to the fife rail belaying pins. (See *The American Fishing Schooners*, by H.I. Chapelle.) Threaded rods are used to through-bolt from the rails to backup blocks or a deck beam below the deck, or even through the mast partner if it extends far enough. Fife rails should be at least 16 inches or 18 inches high to facilitate looping the halyards under belaying pins and hanging the coiled lines. The rail corners should be half-lapped and epoxied. Eye nuts are often used over large washers for the tops of the threaded rods. The turnposts are mortised into the caps, but not into the deck. They are bedded in a rubber compound or Dolfinite. In very large vessels, the halyard tension may be too much for the fife rail; in this case deck irons (large hooks) are through-bolted to the deck beneath the fife rail. Halyards are looped under the deck irons and then made off to the fife rail pins.

COCKPIT COAMINGS AND CAPS

A strong and simple way to make cockpit coamings is to laminate them from four layers of 1/4-inch plywood on a jig of two 2 x 6s cut to the desired curve of the coamings. The cured laminations are held on edge where

Photo 20-3. The aft ends of this fife rail are mortised well into the trunk cabin. The corners are half-lapped, and 1/2-inch threaded rods are through-bolted up from the mast partners, ending in eye nuts. The turnposts are oak, as are the belaying pins. At the right is a tank vent.

Photo 20-4. Cockpit coamings are made on a simple jig (the two curved planks on the left) from four layers of 1/4-inch plywood. Both sides are covered with fabric and epoxy, and the coamings are fastened to the deck from inside the cockpit seat lockers. The tops are epoxy-sealed and capped with teak.

they are to be positioned on deck, traced from the deck and the cabin trunk with a compass, and cut to fit. The tops are drawn as desired using a batten, and cut. The coaming faces are then covered with fabric and epoxy, and glued and screwed to the deck. Fasteners come up through the deck into the coamings (trace the coaming, remove it, and drill down first to locate the holes; replace the coaming and drill up into it from beneath). The coamings are fastened to the trunk cabin by drilling and screwing from inside the cabin into the coamings. Make large fillets from epoxy thickened with Cabosil on both sides of the coamings at the deck. Photo 20-4 shows a laminated coaming in the rough; the jig is seen at the left. Caps may simply be made from flat stock and offset outboard (so you don't lean on a protruding cap edge in the cockpit). They are often a little narrower and thinner than bulwark caps. The coaming tops are epoxy-sealed, and the caps are bedded and fastened down, bunging the holes. Finish is the same as for other caps and rails.

CHAPTER 21
THE COCKPIT

Layout/ Footwell/ Seats and Lockers/ Outboard Wells, Aperture Doors and Engine Covers/ Finishing (Fabric and Epoxy)/ Grates

LAYOUT

The basic cockpit was laid out during the initial interior layout, at least insofar as the footwell location, deck beams, bulkheads and carlins are concerned. To backtrack, some considerations during that process are helm type and location, footwell shape and location, and seat and locker size and shape.

If the vessel is to have wheel steering, the size and location of the wheel must be considered. A large wheel will need either a wide cockpit or a T-shaped well. If a pedestal is employed, it will need to be located such that the steering machinery can be installed and maintained by someone other than a midget contortionist. The cockpit sole or deck will need stout athwartships floors and a backup block under the pedestal; it is absurd to have a helm that wriggles around while steering (I mention this because I have seen it). There should be enough space around the wheel so that hands and legs can't be pinched or injured; crew movement around the cockpit must be considered.

Tiller steering requires that the cockpit be designed around the tiller. The helmsman will need clear sitting space on both sides of the tiller end and footwell room to change sides without interfering with other crew members.

Sheets should be easily accessible to the helmsman, but their location should also allow a crew member to work them without getting in the helmsman's way.

Footwell depth should be comfortable both for sitting (12 inches to 18 inches from grate to cushion top) and standing, and high enough above the waterline to ensure self-bailing. It is ideal to have large scuppers in all four corners of the well, with separate drains and through hulls. This is both expensive and complex, plus it increases hull vulnerability by increasing the number of through-hull fittings. Tying scuppers into common drains and through hulls decreases the drainage rate and increases the chance of clogging at the junctions. When using outboard wells, the cockpit deck pitches down aft and drains through the outboard transoms into the wells. Most other cockpit decks pitch down forward and have forward scuppers only. This arrangement is potentially vulnerable during "pooping," when a cockpit full of water holds the stern down and the drains are at the wrong end. A stronger pitch will somewhat alleviate this. Cockpit deck pitch angle does not affect standing position; the grate is set to the desired height and angle (I usually set it horizontal or parallel to the seats). The well should only be as large as necessary, and scuppers should be as large and simple as possible; they should drain just above or just below the waterline if possible. Provide seacocks to close them in event of a ruptured hose (the old-style scuppers often drained straight out with no seacocks—a dangerous arrangement). What I usually opt for is a cockpit deck sloped down aft at least two degrees, incorporating large (at least $1\frac{1}{2}$-inch) scuppers in the aft corners. The one circumstance in which it might be acceptable to eliminate seacocks would be if the scuppers were plumbed in the cockpit lockers, where the throughhull fittings are visible, and a leak or broken pipe would be limited to flooding only the seat locker. In this case a wooden plug should be tied with a lanyard to the through-hull, and the plumbing should be located where it is unlikely to be damaged by gear stowed in the locker. An advantage of placing the scuppers so far aft is that they can empty just above the waterline without requiring much pipe or hose. However, the well may partially fill with seawater when the vessel heels.

Open access under cockpit seats through their well faces is undesirable on any but daysailers intended for protected water (or in center cockpits in large vessels), as the total volume of water that can be shipped becomes dangerously large. Well width should consider the length of human legs, particularly on tender vessels. When sitting on one seat, crew will need to brace their feet on something across the well. Wide cockpits (over 2 feet 6 inches) are uncomfortable and potentially dangerous; the farther you can be thrown, the worse you can be hurt.

Cockpit seats can be a nuisance if they are poorly designed and built. In cold-molded construction, the use of plywood bulkheads joined to a smooth inner hull surface makes it easy to create large, dry lockers. Leaking seats will make their contents vulnerable and necessitate either drains or pumps (I prefer the latter; a long-bodied portable hand pump kept in the cockpit can be used in seat lockers and lazarettes). I like the seats to be the lids of the lockers (rather than accessing them through doors in their faces—for the same reason of vulnerability), and I make the openings as large as possible for convenience.

Outboard well layout is complex and should be undertaken very carefully. The motors will determine a lot; shaft length will have to be long, but not extremely so (20 inches is best). The propellers will need to be set at the proper depth and located so as not to hit the rudder when hard over. The motors will determine inner transom height and possibly angle; they should, ideally, be on the site when the cockpit is being laid out. The hull apertures are typically located as close as possible to the centerline (whether one or two engines are used), and located such that the forward end is about at the waterline. I prefer teardrop-shaped apertures that allow the motors to be tilted up, thus the after ends of the apertures must allow the propellers to clear. A box or opening will have to be designed under the aft deck, usually incorporated into the lazarettes, to allow the motor lower units to clear the hull far enough that doors or hull plugs can be put in place. Several of the designs in Appendix A show outboard well arrangements.

In hulls with inboard engines mounted

under a bridge deck forward of the cockpit, the well might shift farther aft, and the aft end will simply be a bulkhead extending from hull to deck, behind which will be a large lazarette.

FOOTWELL

Typically the athwartships bulkheads at each end of the well are installed first. Then fore and aft bulkheads are installed at each side of the well. Vertical cleats for these are located outboard on the athwartships bulkheads. Well deck cleats are installed on these fore and aft bulkheads at the desired height

and angle to drain the well. Athwartships support cleats are mounted on the athwartships bulkheads; if outboards are used, the aft cleat is installed on the outboard well transom (this will be described shortly). Before the well deck is installed, the void beneath must be sealed, filleted and epoxy-painted. If a pedestal is to be installed, floors and blocking are now installed, and access channels cut. The well deck is epoxied and screwed down, all exterior bulkheads and the deck are covered with fabric and epoxy, and corners are filleted. An access door, such as a round screw-plate type, may be cut in and installed, making sure to maintain watertight

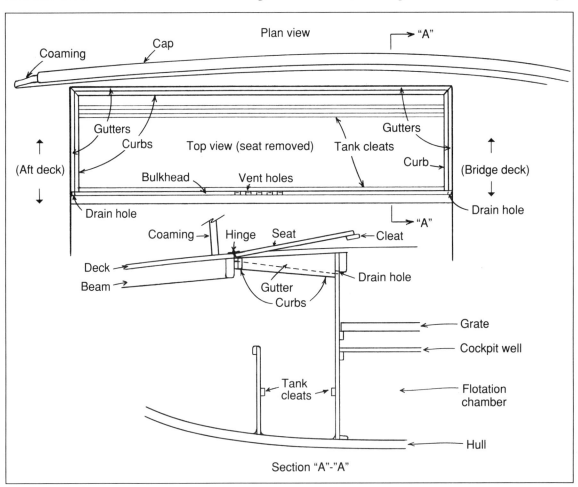

Figure 21-1. Cockpit seat lockers.

integrity. This void, if not violated by machinery, plumbing or wiring, is an airtight and watertight box and may be used as a flotation chamber or storage compartment for things rarely needed (because of its difficult access beneath the grate). It may also be used as an integral water tank in large vessels, though the location of that much weight must be carefully considered.

SEATS AND LOCKERS

The areas outboard of the well become seat lockers. The seats are best built like box-top lids. Large double lips line three sides of the opening—outboard, fore and aft. (See Fig. 21-1.) The outer lips act as gutters and the inner lips act as curbs. The inboard seat/lid edge has a cleat underneath to keep water out from that side. I like to extend this cleat beyond the seat so that a filler platform can be dropped in place to cover part or all of the cockpit well: This can cover outboard motors for additional seating and noise insulation, and can convert the cockpit into a double bed or yoga/exercise platform. Lips fastened to the underside of the rest of the seat/lid are optional; if the lid fits tightly they aren't really necessary except possibly on the aft, or high end.

Vents for these compartments are cut into the fore and aft bulkheads as high as possible. If the fore and aft top stiffener or cleat for these bulkheads is a 2 x 4 fastened inboard (as in the Fig. 21-1), vents may simply be 1-inch holes drilled under these 2 x 4s; water will rarely get in. If outboard fuel tanks are incorporated (the tank cleats shown in Figure 21-1 support three such tanks), fuel hoses and wires to motors may lead through these holes. Photo 21-1 shows *Teresa*'s cockpit under construction. Seat/lid hinges, if used, must take into consideration the fore and aft curve of the deck, if any. A full-length piano

Photo 21-1. Here *Teresa*'s cockpit is under construction. The flush hatches in the foreground are for the ice hold and a scuppered propane locker that vents into the cockpit well. The hatch openings aft open into the lazarette. Between are the cockpit seat lockers, which will contain six outboard fuel tanks, fenders, line, diving gear and much else.

hinge usually won't work. If wires from the batteries pass through these lockers, they should incorporate terminals with studs to pass through bulkheads (outboard starter/ charging wires will need to be easily removable—use wing nuts), so as not to violate watertight integrity or allow fuel fumes to pass into another compartment. If any other wires pass through a hole, they should be rubber-sealed. Any holes in plywood bulkheads should be epoxy-sealed first to prevent rot.

OUTBOARD WELLS, APERTURE DOORS AND ENGINE COVERS

The outboard transom is located at the aft end of the cockpit well deck. It must be heavily constructed (several plywood laminations to a finished thickness of at least $2^{1}/_{4}$ inches), and solidly cleated on both sides to the fore and aft bulkheads. Cleats are placed on the hull forward of the transom, a large fillet is made aft of it during installation, and a cleat on the forward side supports the aft end of the well deck. Scuppers are drilled through the transom to drain the cockpit well (these

Photo 21-2. The outboard transom is roughed in and the well apertures have been cut out. The bulkhead at the top of the photo encloses the lazarette, which has a bridge box above the wells to allow the motors to be tilted up. Doors made from the aperture cut-outs are used to plug the well when sailing, creating a totally smooth hull surface with nothing dragging in the water. It is partly because of this that *Teresa* is capable of speeds over 10 knots under sail.

Photo 21-3. Here the aperture edge is being covered with epoxy-saturated Xynole-polyester fabric—note the darts. The cloth will be sanded to a feather edge and faired in with thickened epoxy. Inside you can see the finished transom; the round holes are cockpit well scuppers and the elongated holes are for the outboard brackets.

should be at least $1^1/_2$ inches); the holes are epoxy-sealed and painted. The transom, which receives much abuse, is covered with two layers of epoxy-saturated Xynole-polyester cloth. The apertures are cut with a circular saw and saber saw. Photo 21-2 shows the well apertures cut and the transom being installed. Photo 21-3 shows the fabric and epoxy covering the exposed aperture grain; note the darts cut in the cloth. Photo 21-4 shows the proper motor depth for cavitation plates and finished apertures.

The aperture doors are made from the cutout plugs by fastening 1/2-inch plywood lips to the top surfaces. All edges and tops are then covered with fabric and epoxy, taking care that the doors will fit in their holes afterward (there should be a full 1/8-inch or more gap around the edges prior to any covering). Handles are attached at the forward ends of the doors, and a method for holding them down must be devised; a wood yoke slid under a large thumb cleat fastened to the horn timber works fine. (See Fig. 21-2.) The

Photo 21-4. Cavitation plates are located two inches below the waterline. Shown are twin Yamaha four-cycle motors with 3-to-1 gear reduction and 11-inch propellers, which push *Teresa* at $7^1/_2$ knots.

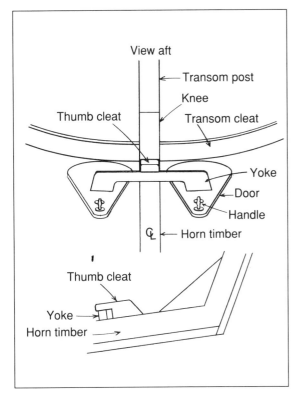

Figure 21-2. Outboard well door yoke.

Photo 21-5. Motor controls are the stock handles removed and mounted on an aluminum bracket fastened to the transom. The cleats on the undersides of the cockpit seats support a platform that is used as a seat and engine cover. It also converts the cockpit into a double bed.

door handles should have lanyards attached so they can't be lost overboard.

Even the new four-stroke outboard motors are noisy enough to be a discomfort, if not a hazard to communication. The cockpit seat cleat, which extends inboard (refer again to Fig. 21-1), can be used to support an engine cover (which doubles as the seat/bed/platform described above). Foil-backed engine room insulation glued to the underside of a plywood panel will help, and a front cover may also be made. Keep in mind easy access to the motors as well as their air requirements. Airtight compartments (or nearly so) will need vents for exhaust, water and intake air. Many engine manufacturers supply spec sheets for such installations. Often the outboard motor control handles are inconvenient and separate controls are installed. (See Photo 21-5.)

If a diesel engine is installed under the bridge deck at the forward end of the cockpit, large portions of the athwartships bulkheads and deck must be removable for engine access; this will be discussed in Chapter 25.

FINISHING (FABRIC AND EPOXY)

All surfaces exposed to sunlight, water and chafe should be covered with fabric and epoxy and painted, except for trim. The edges of the seat lids should be rounded slightly to facilitate covering, and particular care must be taken on corners. Cut darts with sharp shears (these must be kept clean—wipe them with solvent after working around wet epoxy), to allow corner wrapping. One edge should slightly overlap the other to ensure a seal. Carefully sand out the bump later, taking care not to break through the fabric. Masking tape may be used to hold the corners down (underneath) during epoxying. Seat undersides may be just painted. Vents and drain holes may be cut before or after the fabric and epoxy covering, but the exposed endgrain, again, must be epoxy-sealed and painted to prevent rot and delamination. If cut before, lay the fabric/epoxy right across the holes and cut them out again with a razor knife when the epoxy is almost cured.

Use epoxy primers and polyurethanes for finishing. Inside surfaces will only need epoxy paint.

GRATES

Much has been written about grate construction elsewhere, and all I want to say is that the larger members should span the short distance (almost always athwartships). These may be notched for the smaller, longer members to lie across them by taping them all together and running them collectively across the table-saw blade with the crosscut sliding guide. The blade is set to the depth of the smaller members, and the whole raft of support members is slid over 1/8 inch at a time (blade width) to cut the grooves (which will be the notches when the pieces are separated). Before assembly, wash all glue joints with acetone (assuming that the grate is teak) to dissolve the natural wax from the wood pores to allow the epoxy glue to bond. Support the grate on cleats fastened to the well bulkheads. If outboards are used, it may be necessary to make the grate in two pieces to facilitate removal.

CHAPTER 22
COMPARTMENTS, HATCHES AND WINDOWS

Hatches and Coamings/ Sliding Hatches/ Doors and Drop-Boards/ Skylights/ Propane Lockers/ Ice Holds and Boxes/ Lazarette and Forepeak/ Cargo Hold and Hatches/ Engine Room/ Portlights, Deadlights, Windows, Prisms and Ventilators

HATCHES AND COAMINGS

As with everything else, there are numerous ways to build hatches and skylights, and every book on boatbuilding shows several. I will show you the way that has become easiest for me, and that best applies to the construction methods we have used so far.

After decking, hatch openings are a rough hole. Plywood deck end grain lies above the inner faces of deck beams and carlins, or, in some cases, bulkheads. I rabbet my hatch coamings so they cover this vulnerable joint and are thereby "self-trimming." The coamings bear half on the deck and lap down several inches over the beam, carlin or bulkhead. (See Fig. 22-1.) For most vessels, the coamings are made from 2 x 4s or 2 x 6s. The rabbet is usually half the coaming thickness, which for most hatches is $1^1/_2$ inches, making the rabbet 3/4 inch. I miter the corners and

fasten them to each other. The part of the coaming that overlaps the beam, carlin or bulkhead is fastened to it. The coamings

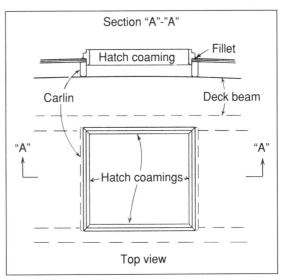

Figure 22-1. Hatch coamings.

should be carefully fitted, both to square up the hatch opening and to ensure that the opposite coamings are parallel to each other in both planes. The lower inner edges of the coamings are bullnosed or beaded; the coamings thus trim the hatch opening.

The upper edges of the coamings are also rabbeted half their thickness by an equal height (for a 1½-inch coaming, the rabbet would be 3/4 inch by 3/4 inch). The face cut is beveled down so that it will shed water. I also usually bevel the top edge of the coaming to the same angle.

Carefully drill and install the corner screws so as not to pull the corners out of alignment. Tighten the screws gently, leaving plenty of epoxy in the joint. A rough but true saw cut will provide better tooth for the joint than a smooth one. The inner face fasteners (into beams, carlins or bulkheads) should not be overtightened, because this will pull the corners apart. Use plenty of epoxy, take care to leave no voids and fillet the joints. A finger fillet will suffice at the bottom and inside corners. The outside fillet should be larger and

formed using a short piece of PVC pipe of about 3/4 inch inside diameter, which will create a fillet having about a 1/2-inch radius. Screw countersink holes are epoxy-puttied or bunged. (Photo 22-1 shows a hatch coaming being filleted.)

Hatch frames are made of stock of the same thickness. They are rabbeted to fit over the coamings snugly, but with enough play that subsequent painting won't cause binding. Corners may be simply mitered and fas-

Photo 22-1. Hatch coaming fillets are made with 3/4-inch PVC pipe.

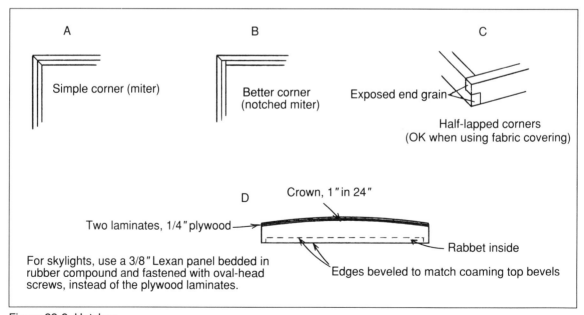

Figure 22-2. Hatches.

A — Simple corner (miter)

B — Better corner (notched miter)

C — Exposed end grain
Half-lapped corners (OK when using fabric covering)

D
Crown, 1" in 24"
Two laminates, 1/4" plywood
Rabbet inside
Edges beveled to match coaming top bevels
For skylights, use a 3/8" Lexan panel bedded in rubber compound and fastened with oval-head screws, instead of the plywood laminates.

tened, but a notched corner (see Fig. 22-2B) will be much stronger. Many carpenters half-lap hatch corners; the reason I don't is to avoid exposing end grain. However, if the hatches are to be fabric-covered, half-lapped corners are excellent. The total finished height of these hatches and coamings is usually around 3 inches to 4 inches. The edge of the outer rabbet in the coamings might be 1 inch above the deck, and the covered hatch frame might be $2^1/_2$ inches high. I cut a slight crown into the athwartships hatch frames of about 1 inch per 24 inches. This looks better than a flat top and adds much strength. The hatch tops are 3/8-inch plywood, preferably marine grade, or (better) two laminates of 1/4-inch ACX plywood with interfaced C faces. The tops are epoxy-glued and fastened (staples or nails) with the hatch frames in place on their respective coamings to ensure alignment. The edges and corners are bull-nosed (usually 1/2 inch), and the hatch is sanded and covered with fabric and epoxy. Take care with the corners.

If the hatch is to be used as a skylight, the top may be plastic. Lexan, or polycarbonate sheet, is much better than acrylic (Plexiglas), which so often cracks at the fastener holes. In any case, drill the holes oversize and countersink them so the screw heads will be flush to the surface or slightly above it. (I prefer oval-head screws in this application.) The plastic should be no thinner than 1/4 inch and no thicker than 1/2 inch. Cut the same crown as before into the athwartships frame ends. Very large hatches and skylights (36 inches long or more) will need an intermediate support in the middle cut to the same crown as the ends and mortised into the sides. The plastic cover should finish flush to the hatch frame perimeter just like the plywood cover. Use a rubber compound to bed the plastic, and also coat the screws with it. Don't overtighten the screws, and use plenty of rubber, taking care

not to create air voids. (I prefer 3M #5200 here because it can be cleaned up with mineral spirits or paint thinner.) A belt sander may be used to bring the top perfectly flush to the frame sides and to round the corners. A sharp block plane is best for easing the top edges (take care not to scratch the plastic), but a router will also work (leave the protective paper on the plastic while routing to prevent scratches—but don't expose the paper to sunlight). Be aware that some solvents will attack the plastic and make it cloudy. Mineral spirits are safe.

The hatch frames and coamings may be painted or finished bright (especially skylights). If the coamings are to be bright, they are masked off at the top of the outside fillet, and the fillet is painted with the deck (or coach roof); the coamings are then sealed and finished bright above the fillet. Hatch covers are painted as they are covered with fabric and epoxy , but the coamings may still be finished bright, if so desired, creating a decorative strip of natural wood between the painted surfaces. Remember that brightwork requires a lot of maintenance.

SLIDING HATCHES

I usually frame sliding hatches from $1^1/_2$-inch stock, making the frame 5/8 inch narrower than the distance across the outside edges of the tracks on which it will ride. I cut a crown into the hatch frame ends (also 1 inch in 24 inches), and then rabbet them for the covering planks or plywood. The hatch side frames are covered by the hatch top, and the ends are higher by the thickness of the top because it is rabbeted into them. The frame ends also drop down between the hatch tracks to finish flush with the tops of the hatch track supports (which will also be flush with the top of the drop door). By now you're scratching your head, and it might help to look at Figure 22-3. The frame ends are notched on the bottom corners to fit over the hatch tracks. I usually make the hatch tracks 1/2 inch thick by 2 inches wide. I also rabbet, or notch, the ends for the side frames, and glue and screw the frame together on a perfectly flat surface, taking care to keep the corners square. The frame sides are beveled for the top, and end flush with the rabbet in the frame ends. Long hatches (over 30 inches) may require an immediate support, or beam, between the frame sides to reinforce the hatch top. This beam must be flat on the bottom, crowned on top and thin enough to clear the curb at the hatch opening. Mortise the ends into the frame sides. Then cut, glue and fasten the hatch top to overlap the hatch frame sides and fit into the rabbets in the frame ends. I usually use tongue-and-groove planking 7/8 inch to 1½ inches thick with

caulking grooves on top that are 5/16 inch to 1/2 inch deep and 1/4 inch wide. These may be rabbeted on the tongue sides of the plank edges prior to planking or routed in place later, but they should not destroy the tongue-and-groove joints. Epoxy the tongue-and-groove joints together during planking. The hatch top may also be laminated from two layers of 5/16-inch or 1/4-inch plywood.

After curing, the side edges are planed flush to the frame sides, and side planks are made with longitudinal grooves 1/16 inch wider than the track thickness (usually 1/2 inch) and about 3/8 inch deep. This amounts to 1/16 inch of play both in height and width between the finished hatch sides and their tracks to allow for expansion and contraction. Very large hatches may need a little more. These side planks should be at least 3/4 inch thick, and are glued and screwed to

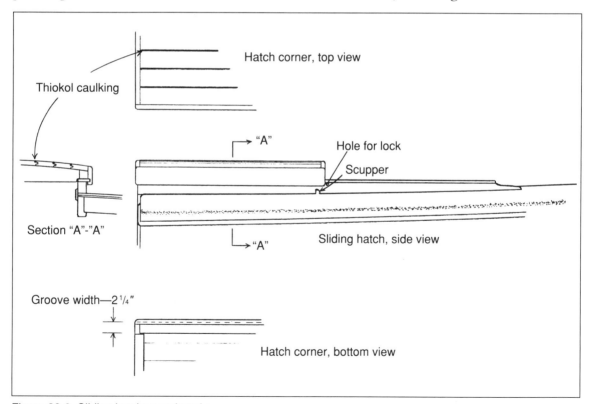

Figure 22-3. Sliding hatches and tracks.

the hatch frame sides and ends such that the upper edges of the grooves are flush to the frame side lower edges and the notches in the frame ends. (See Fig. 22-3.) The tops of the hatch tracks interface with this flush surface, and the slots in the hatch sides fit over the sides of the tracks so that water can't get in and the hatches can't come off.

Bung all fastener holes. Caulking grooves are not necessary between the top planks and the sides, because there is such a large gluing surface involving side grain to side grain. At the corners, however, where the sides lap the ends, the joint becomes side grain to end grain, and eventually stress lines or hairline cracks may form in the glue joint. This is particularly a problem in the tropics, where a canvas cover placed on a varnished hatch is advisable.

The hatch is then belt-sanded, and all edges and corners are bullnose-routed. The grooves are caulked with two-part polysulfide rubber or black Sikaflex, taking care not to trap air voids. (See Photo 22-2.) The hatches are again belt-sanded so the hatch top is a fair arc (use a batten to verify). The hatch is finished bright (or covered with fabric and epoxy and painted if the top is plywood).

Hatch track bases are made from $1^1/_2$-inch stock, and usually taper from 2 inches or 3 inches at the opening (high) end to about $1^1/_2$ inches at the far (low) end. Where a high hatch may create a visibility problem, the trackbases may be decreased in height until the hatch sides just clear the deck (as little as 1 inch high). I usually let the far ends extend several inches beyond the tracks and cut them into a decorative S-curve. The bottoms of the track bases are scribed and cut to fit the coach roof (or deck); bevel the bottoms to make both track bases parallel vertically (consequently making the tops parallel horizontally). Offset hatches may simply be paral-

Photo 22-2. Two-part polysulfide rubber (Thiokol) is troweled into the hatch seams.

lel to the coach roof (really tangential) or horizontal athwartships. In the latter case, the outboard base must be higher. The track base tops must be perfectly parallel or the hatch will jam. If the tracks run uphill, as is often the case on forward houses, scuppers must be cut to allow water out just beyond where the curb or stop will be located.

Fasten the bases above the hatch carlins aligning their inner faces. They are glued and screwed in place, and small fillets are made along the coach roof joints. The door jambs, which were previously notched to allow the track bases to overlap them outside, are now trimmed off to just below the track base top surfaces, and the jambs are fastened to the bases.

The hatch tracks are typically 1/2-inch by 2-inch oak. These are fastened and bedded (use Dolfinite or an equivalent non-adhesive) on top of the bases so that the inner edges are flush and the outer edges overhang 1/2 inch. Take care when installing the tracks that no fasteners will be trapped under that portion of the hatch adjacent to the curb, because these will always be inaccessible. Fastener holes are bunged. The tracks are coated with clear wood preservative or penetrating oil, but don't use anything that can gum up or stick (I use Deks Olje #1). An alternative to oak is aluminum, which I have used with success. The tracks may be covered with plastic laminate, Teflon or metal. I prefer natural wood because the tracks have just the right amount of friction; the hatch stays where you park it. Too much or too little friction is a nuisance (there's nothing like having hatches sliding open and closed while pitching in a seaway).

After carefully sliding the hatch onto the tracks from the opening end, install a curb at the end of the hatch opening above the deck beam aligning the inner faces. Fasten the curb from the sides by installing screws through the track bases into the end grain of the curb. Bed the curb in 3M #5200 or Sikaflex (both ends and the bottom). Take care to eliminate air voids; a leak here can be frustrating. I usually place thin foam strips on both sides of this curb to cushion the hatch as it opens and closes. Once this curb is in place the hatch cannot be removed, so make sure it slides freely all through its travel without binding, leaving room for expansion and contraction. If and when it is necessary to remove the hatch, drill out the track bungs, remove their fasteners and lift the hatch and tracks off their bases.

The inner faces of the hatch opening are now covered with flat trim to cover the exposed plywood deck or coach roof end grain. The finished construction, including door jambs and threshold, is usually finished bright, but may also be painted.

DOORS AND DROP-BOARDS

Companionway doors are almost always made in pairs, and hung on open hinges so they can be lifted off and stowed away. In some cases they can be folded back against the cabin trunk and latched in place. Door construction is covered in so many books that I will not go into it, except to say that you

should build strong doors. The jambs must be parallel to each other in both planes, and are usually vertical (plumb), at least during construction. The after ends of cabin trunks are usually vertical (whereas the forward ends usually rake back—often parallel to the mast). Both the jambs and the threshold are rabbeted for the doors as explained previously. I often build the doors from solid $1\frac{1}{2}$-inch plank stock (or 7/8-inch to 1-inch hardwood) with rails inset top and bottom having mitered corners (see Fig. 22-4) so that no end grain is exposed. The meeting edges are rabbeted, male and female, to fit together when closed. The rails are glued and screwed (or nailed) to the doors. Leave room for expansion, and keep the doors well sealed, whether painted or finished bright.

Drop-boards are so common that the conventional types are well known. I prefer one or two drop-in sliding louvered panels. The jambs are made the same way except that they have grooves instead of rabbets. The threshold is the same as before, to shed water.

I make the drop panel frames with half-

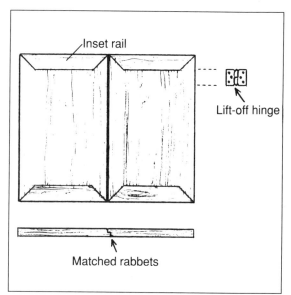

Figure 22-4. Plank companionway doors.

lapped corners. The bottom rail is wider than the top rail, and the latter is the same or wider than the stiles, as in typical door construction. I cut diagonal slots in the inner edges of the stiles to the thickness of the louvers, which are cut out to be parallelograms in section so that their edges will be flush to the door faces (see Fig. 22-5). The bottom louver should slightly overlap the bottom rail, the edge of which is planed to the same diagonal angle.

Assemble the panels carefully; the louvers must be exactly the right length and care must be taken to align everything and square it up. Epoxy is used and no fasteners are required. When using teak, wash the gluing surfaces with acetone or toluol.

After curing, the doors are sanded flush and finished bright or painted. When a single drop door is impractically high (say it hits the fore boom before it comes out of the jamb slots), two doors are made with adjacent rails that are thinner than usual. These rails are rabbeted to interlock (and shed water) and the two panels are hinged together on their faces so that as the top panel is pulled clear of the slots it may be folded forward to clear the boom, and the bottom panel lifted free. The folded panels are easier to stow than one large one and the hinges make the panels slide in and out more easily (they don't jam) than two individual panels.

Three rabbeted cleats are fastened to the panel backs, leaving the top open. A Lexan or acrylic (or even plywood) panel is slid in behind the louvers during cold or violent weather. Weep holes are drilled at an angle down from the rabbet of the bottom cleat through the rail to drain water out; these should be 1/4 inch. Hinged drop-doors use a split cleat at the break so that only one weather panel is needed.

One simple locking system uses a hole drilled through the track base just behind the sliding hatch (in the closed position) through

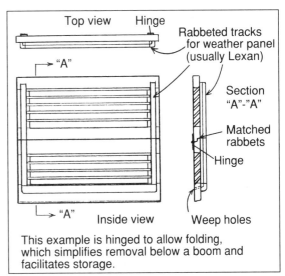

Figure 22-5. Louvered companionway drop-boards.

which a long-shackle lock is inserted. Another system uses a sliding-bolt type lock with a round lock face that emerges through a hole drilled in the drop-board (or active door). The lock body is screwed or bolted to the back of the door and the sliding bolt drives up behind the face of the closed hatch (or into it). The more conventional hasp is easily broken into.

SKYLIGHTS

Simple skylights may be made like hatches, as already described. The old-style hinged-side skylights are notorious leakers. Every boatbuilder tries to make one that won't leak, but few succeed. One secret to all skylight construction is to let the glass or plastic panels (called lights) overlap their frames at the bottoms instead of inlaying them in the traditional manner. Because all materials have different rates of expansion and contraction, sooner or later the seal between the light and frame is broken and leaks start. Allowing the light lower edges to overlap the lower members of the frames solves this problem, as water is less likely to come in along the tops or sides. Slotting the inner edges of the frame tops and sides to receive the lights, which are then slid into place (in rubber bedding) from the bottom, looks good (as the lights are recessed) and is even less likely to leak. It also eliminates the need for fasteners, except for several in the bottom frame members where the lights overlap them. The remaining construction is traditional; make the waterways and interlocking lips large enough so dirt won't inhibit water flow.

By taking advantage of lamination, epoxy and the flexibility and bulletproof strength of Lexan, innovative shapes and styles may now be incorporated into skylight construction. An example is *White Hawk*'s hexagonal skylight. I like round ones, too.

Then there are the manufactured skylights. These are very expensive, and many are poorly designed and poorly made, particularly involving gasketing and light thickness. I personally have had to repair or replace gaskets on new skylights right out of the box. However, installation is often simple, especially if the skylight has the same crown as your deck (some are made that way). Sometimes a low wood base can be built up to adapt deck crown to a flat skylight base. Often skylights can be installed by cutting out a deck opening without disturbing deckbeams or installing carlins by spanning a beam instead of cutting it. The stiffness of the metal skylight frame is often sufficiently strong that no carlins are needed (as long as no beams are cut); trim is made for the exposed plywood deck edge. Of course, if a beam is broken, carlins will be needed. I usually bed these skylights in 3M #5200 or an equivalent compound, and fasten them with large oval-head screws (rubber-coated before insertion) or oval-head through-bolts (likewise coated). The biggest advantage to manufactured skylights is their low profile.

PROPANE LOCKERS

Propane is heavier than air and extremely explosive! I know you know, but it bears repeating. Storage lockers must be vented and scuppered in such a way that the gas cannot accumulate inside the boat. This means that lockers must not be located in living spaces or where a gas leak can get into living spaces, bilges or places where any flame or electrical spark can occur. I often build a separate locker on deck for the bottles and regulators, providing at least two large scuppers (1 square inch or larger). On some vessels I build propane lockers into the bridge deck and scupper them into the cockpit well; this involves pitching the locker floor so that the scupper is at the lowest point. In this arrangement, the scupper is usually a $1^1/_2$-inch hole drilled in the lowest corner of the aft locker bulkhead. It enters the cockpit below the grate but at least an inch or two above the well deck. For this arrangement to work, the cockpit well deck must be designed to be several inches lower than the propane locker bottom. Ventilation also must be provided near the locker top by drilling several holes near the deck in the same bulkhead. In the event of a propane leak, the gas will exit the locker into the cockpit well, where it will dissipate or run out the cockpit scuppers (another reason to place the scupper through-hull fittings above the waterline).

I prefer to minimize all gas plumbing on the grounds that fewer fittings mean fewer sources of trouble. I disagree with the use of extra valves, fittings, gauges, crossovers and solenoid cutoffs. I use one regulator with one fitting and one hose that leads directly to the stove. Gas is turned on and off at the tank. When a tank runs out, you change the regulator to the next tank (there should be two tanks on any but very small yachts). I use heavy-duty rubber gas hose and the best quality brass fittings available. I carefully seal the hole where the hose passes out of the locker with a rubber or silicone compound; the locker should be airtight except for its intended scuppers, vents and hatch. Anything sharing the locker should be nonflammable and nonelectrical. The only additional fitting in the system might be a high-quality manual shutoff valve with a long stem so that the valve handle can be located inside the cabin (not directly over the stove), and the valve body located either in the propane locker or somewhere outside where a potential gas leak would be harmless. I am absolutely opposed to the location of shutoff valves inside the cabin. There are those who disagree with me, of course, and you must make your own judgment.

I recommend buying conventional 30-pound or 5-gallon gas bottles with conventional U.L. listed valves, reliefs and 5 percent bleeders. These bottles are inexpensive and are available in hardware stores, lumberyards and from gas companies. They can be filled anywhere in the U.S., Canada, the Caribbean and Central America. If you travel beyond, you may need adapters. Because the bottles come with inferior paint finishes, I recommend the following treatment: Sand them thoroughly with #120 grit paper, and treat any rust spots with Ospho (rust remover), taking special care around welds at the base, handle and valve fitting. Spray-paint the tanks with two coats of epoxy primer and two or three coats of linear polyurethane (all white). Then glue a piece of garden hose to the base, sliced open with a razor knife so it slips onto the steel ring. Tanks treated this way will last many years; make sure you specify that you want your empty tanks refilled, not swapped for full tanks. Scratches and dings should be sanded, Ospho-treated and touched up with epoxy paint.

Propane refrigerators and hot-water heat-ers should be, in my opinion, treated like propane bottles. They should not be installed in living areas, but rather in their own lockers with proper vents and scuppers. Propane refrigerators are wonderful, but need to be plumb, as they work by convecting gases instead of using a compressor. This is only likely to present a problem on long tacks, such as during ocean crossings. The ultimate solution is to gimbal the whole refrigerator. Wherever appliances of this kind are located, keep in mind that they are cheaply made of sheet steel, which rapidly deteriorates in a marine environment.

ICE HOLDS AND BOXES

On most of the world's waterfronts, ice is still cheap and easily obtained, especially in the Third World, where electric refrigeration is rare and there is a local fishing fleet. Block ice lasts longer than "soft frozen" and "compressed chips," but chip ice used by commercial fishermen makes efficient use of space. *Teresa*'s ice hold can take about 40 gallons of chip ice, which lasts three weeks in tropical heat.

There are three tricks to good ice refrigeration: good insulation (ideally 6 inches minimum on all sides, top and bottom), top-loading access and good gaskets on doors and hatches.

Most yachts have lousy ice boxes. Electric refrigeration using 12 volts has improved over the years, but uses a shocking amount of electricity and requires excellent insulation. Mechanical refrigeration is an expensive nightmare; it is by far the biggest cause of breakdowns, fuel consumption, noise, stinking diesel fumes and heat. And those little ice boxes that come as standard equipment on Tupperware yachts can't hold enough ice, or keep it cold long enough, to be worthwhile.

Hence all my designs have ice holds.

Holds and boxes both have an outer and inner shell. The outer shell should be finger-filleted along the seams and epoxy-painted to seal and protect the wood. The inner shell is formed in place, usually held there by its hatch or throat; that should be the only bridge between the shells (wood conducts heat). If possible, the outer surface of the inner shell should be epoxy-painted. Two-part closed-cell polyurethane foam is then mixed thoroughly and rapidly (a drill motor with a paint mixer is almost essential), and dumped into the compartment between the shells. Repeat this process until the void is almost filled, at which point the counter or deck is glued and fastened in place after dumping in the last carefully estimated batch of foam. (Sometimes I just set the final covering in place and stand on it, using plastic to keep the foam from bonding.) Be sure to leave one or more overflow holes to allow foam to escape. Brace the inner shell with blocking or it may burst inward under the pressure; the inner shell is frequently just 1/4-inch plywood.

The inner shell is coated with fabric and epoxy, filleted and epoxy-painted. Drains or scuppers can be installed ahead of time with PVC pipe, or drilled and installed later, which is more difficult. They should be small

Photo 22-3. Two-part polyurethane foam is poured in place to insulate ice holds and boxes. The ice-hold hatch will be the opening to the left; the hold dog-legs inside the cabin under the galley countertop.

enough to minimize cold loss but large enough not to clog easily. I usually use 1/2-inch CPVC pipe plumbed directly to a small plastic diaphragm pump, as the compartment bottom is usually below the vessel waterline. Photo 22-3 shows *Teresa's* ice hold being foamed. The loading hatch will be to the left; the hold dog-legs and runs inside the cabin where there is a countertop access lid. The ice is loaded from outside through the hatch, and beer is loaded on top. Food is stored inside in plastic trays accessed through the countertop lid. At the time of the photo, the hold is about to receive its last foam batches and be decked over. The drain pump is in the adjacent propane locker (see the plans in the Appendix). Photo 18-10 in Chapter 18 shows the interior dog-legged portion of the ice hold after foaming and ready for the countertop. Overflow foam is shaved off with a Stanley Surform. Plug overflow holes with wood plugs epoxied in place.

LAZARETTE AND FOREPEAK

If at all possible, the lazerette and forepeak should both be isolated from the rest of the hull by watertight bulkheads. In the event of a collision, explosion, fire or other catastrophe, these may save your boat and even your life. The two together could float most boats even if the whole vessel in between were flooded. Hatches of the design I have described (having sides flush with their coamings) can be sealed with duct tape in an emergency or prior to anticipated rough passages. I prefer to invest my money, energy and knowledge in possibly saving my vessel and her contents rather than to rely on a life raft or rescue in the event of an extreme emergency.

Centerline or near centerline hatches are safest in a capsize, broaching or swamping, although they don't provide adequate access into lazarettes in beamy sterns. My solution to

overlapped, half-lapped or mitered. Second, timbers of the same thickness are made to be installed inside the first ones; these will extend nearly to the bottom edges of the carlins and beams, and up at least $1\frac{1}{2}$ inches higher than outer timbers. The corners may be made any way. I prefer to miter them. If the outer coamings are made from 2 x 4s, the inner coamings can be made from 2 x 8s.

The top edges of the outer and inner coamings are beveled to shed water. The top and bottom edges of the inner coamings are bullnosed. The outer coamings are epoxyglued and fastened with large (#14 or #16) screws through the deck into the beams and carlins. The inner coamings are glued and fastened both into the outer coamings and the beams and carlins. All seams are filleted, and the whole coaming may be covered with fabric and epoxy if it is to receive regular abuse from cargo transfer. Galvanized common nails can be used in place of screws in this kind of construction—but they should be drilled for, countersunk and their holes bunged.

Cargo hatches are framed similarly of two laminates having beveled bottom edges to match the coamings. If the hatch is not too large, two or three layers of plywood are laminated to a crown (usually the same as the deck's) cut onto the tops of the frame ends. Large hatches made this way will be pretty heavy; one or more intermediate beams can be notched into the inner frame sides to reduce the number of or thickness of the plywood layers. Or a foam-core hatch may be made, both for its light weight and insulative value. The inner frame members can be made thin (as little as 1 inch) and 3/16-inch or 1/4-inch plywood laid over them as an inner skin (it is glued and fastened in place). Spruce or hem-fir beams are laid up over this skin, cut to the deck crown and depth of the foam sheets to be used (usually $1\frac{1}{2}$ inch). They are

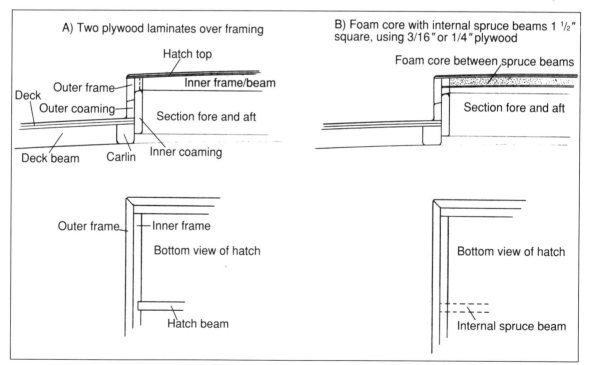

Figure 22-6. Cargo hatches and coamings.

epoxied in place, screwed to the frame and stapled or nailed up through the bottom skin. Blocking is installed around the perimeter to bring the inner frame height up flush to the beams (beams are installed at the ends). Foam sheets, typically 24 inches wide, are contact-cemented (or epoxied) between the beams and perimeters, and two layers of 1/4-inch or 3/16-inch plywood are laminated over the whole, using epoxy and staples or nails. (See Fig. 22-6.) Edges and corners are trimmed and bullnose-routed; the hatch is sanded and covered with fabric and epoxy, then primed with epoxy and painted with polyurethane. The foam-core hatches are light, stiff and easy to handle. I attach a pair of handles at each end as far apart as a person can comfortably reach, so that two people can handle the hatch easily. Eyebolts can be installed beneath the handles for lashing down the hatch cover, and the flush joint between hatch and coaming can be duct-taped. For insulated holds, $1\frac{1}{2}$-inch-wide foam strips can be installed on the tops of both inner and outer coamings (or to the undersides of the hatch frame).

ENGINE ROOM

Diesel fumes, heat, noise and engine-room bilge water are repulsive things to live with. The dangers of fire and poisonous gases that can emanate from batteries and other sources provide all the reason I need to isolate the engine, generator, batteries and heat-generating equipment away from living spaces in the hull.

This is easy to do in cold-molded construction. Watertight bulkheads easily isolate engine bilges from the rest of the hull; a separate bilge pump is installed at the low end of the compartment. The advantage of this isolation is the elimination of oily, stinking bilge muck from all but one sump and bilge. In

many vessels, I locate the engine under a bridge deck between the cockpit and cabin trunk. Because this location is usually too far aft to permit conventional straight-line shafting, a V-drive is used. In smaller vessels in particular, an angled watertight bulkhead flush to the back of the companion ladder allows the engine installation to be shifted as far forward as possible, providing better shaft angle. (See Fig. 22-7.) This bulkhead joins triangular fore and aft bulkheads, which join the major athwartships bulkhead at the aft end of the cabin forming a watertight engine compartment. The bilge sump is immediately aft of the companion ladder, which must be easily removable. Built into the bulkhead is a removable door or panel to provide access to the transmission and stuffing box located beneath it (as well as the sump). This door should be well sealed and insulated, and should start at least 12 inches above the bilge. It will rarely be removed, perhaps as infrequently as a few times a year.

Primary engine access is provided by a large hatch in the bridge deck and another in the aft bridge deck athwartships bulkhead. These two may even be joined together or hinged, and removed as one unit, especially on smaller vessels: The cleat/beam that would normally span the aft end of the bridge deck is removed with the hatch, which sits on channeled cleats fastened to the adjacent fore and aft bulkheads. These bulkheads are usually extensions of the cockpit-well sides. The cleats are made similarly to the ones that support the cockpit seats, to shed water. With this large L-shaped hatch removed, the whole engine is exposed and easy to work on. The mechanic can sit comfortably on the cockpit grate with one foot on either side of the engine, and tools laid out conveniently on the cockpit seat/lids. The only concern is that the bottom of the bulkhead hatch should end on a rabbeted curb high enough so that, in the

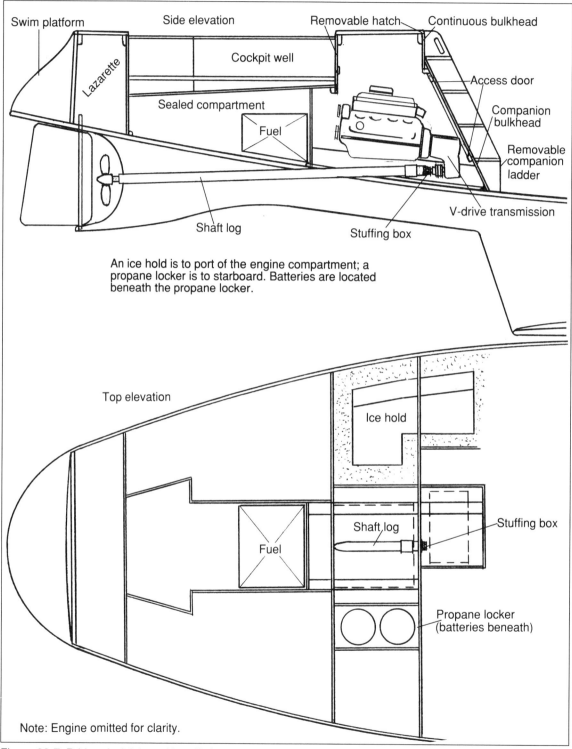

Swim platform   Side elevation   Removable hatch   Continuous bulkhead

Lazarette

Cockpit well

Sealed compartment

Access door

Fuel

Companion bulkhead

Removable companion ladder

V-drive transmission

Shaft log   Stuffing box

An ice hold is to port of the engine compartment; a propane locker is to starboard. Batteries are located beneath the propane locker.

Top elevation

Ice hold

Fuel

Shaft log

Stuffing box

Propane locker (batteries beneath)

Note: Engine omitted for clarity.

Figure 22-7. Bridge deck inboard installation.

event of the cockpit being flooded as when pooped by a following sea, little or no water would be likely to leak into the engine compartment. One foot above the well deck should be enough.

A bulkhead defining the aft end of this engine compartment may be placed as far under the cockpit well deck as desired. The rest of that space may be a fuel tank, flotation void (as previously mentioned) or storage bin. Access would be provided by a reasonably watertight hatch under an easily removable split grate.

Another alternative engine installation involves the use of hydraulic pumps and motors; this allows the engine to be located anywhere. Hydraulic hoses lead from the diesel to the hydraulic motor/transmission, which is installed in its own isolated compartment with propeller shaft end and stuffing box. This arrangement is more expensive than a Vee-drive transmission, and results in a power loss of approximately 10 percent. But with it, the engine may be located in the cargo hold or other isolated compartment.

Engine compartments should be as well insulated as you can afford, to create barriers against heat, noise, fumes and fire. The common material used today is a composite foam/plastic/foil engine-room insulation. It is very expensive and very good. Closed-cell rigid polyurethane sheets $1^1/_2$ inches thick or thicker are excellent, but they emit a toxic gas when ignited, and must be covered with a fire retardant. I use cork, which is U.S. Coast Guard approved, and available in rolls of varying width and thickness (usually around 1/4 inch). In an engine compartment, two layers are desirable (stagger all seams). The cork can then be painted with a white fire-retardant paint, such as Arabol latex rubber lagging compound, the same material used for wrapping exhaust pipes.

All hatches and doors should be well sealed. (Ideally they should be airtight.) This can be done with 1/4-inch-thick foam strips that come in rolls with adhesive on one side. When applied to clean, freshly painted surfaces, this material lasts for years. I prefer the dense black kind that resembles wet-suit material.

Generous ventilation provided to engine compartments will promote air circulation and the dissipation of heat build up. Ventilation requirements will vary for each engine, and the system should be carefully designed. Large cowl vents with or without Dorade boxes are common, but these should be located near the deck centerline. In bridge deck installations, the compartment can be vented into the cockpit by drilling holes through the bulkhead hatch near the top and using clamtype covers.

I paint everything in bilges and engine compartments white or very light gray. These colors reflect light all around so there are virtually no dark corners. Small nuts or parts may be easily found, and it will be obvious when it's time to clean the bilges. Try to use emulsifying detergents that are biodegradable, and remove oil first.

A note here about our environment: Oil, fuel and other mechanical wastes do not belong in our oceans! It is our individual responsibility to keep them out. Maintaining our machinery to a high degree of excellence (no leaks) and cleanliness is the beginning. A good, clean system for changing oil is essential, such as a small piston pump permanently connected to the oil drain plug with a shut-off cock, high-quality fittings and rubber hose. The pump body may be bracket-mounted to a bulkhead, and oil should be discharged into containers that are taken ashore to a proper disposal facility. In remote areas and many Third World countries, you will have to dispose of drain oil yourself or take the oil to a dump or incinerator where it will be burned at high temperatures. Recycling is best, but doesn't much exist outside of North America and Europe. If your cruise is for a year or less, you can store drain oil into plastic jugs (even used milk bottles) and dispose of it properly when you return.

PORTLIGHTS, DEADLIGHTS, WINDOWS, PRISMS AND VENTILATORS

There is a plethora of portlights on the market these days, but the best ones are bronze. Many companies now import good-quality (as well as some less than good quality) bronze hardware from the Far East, made to American patterns. These are reasonably priced, and I have had good luck with those from A & B Industries in Costa Mesa, California and from Doc Freeman's in Seattle, Washington. Examine hinges, dogs and gasket quality, as well as casting and finishing flaws. I recently installed some very expensive, French-made cast-aluminum portlights at the insistence of a client. These had plastic hinge pins and snap-up plastic dogs which were starting to fail before the yacht was completed. What else can I say?

Traditional sliding windows are cheap and easy to build, but are not seaworthy. Neither are the old-type windows that lean in against dogs and are wedged closed with wood. Both are adequate on vessels used only on protected waters but require an emergency back-up system consisting of precut plywood panels with small nails predriven in place. A full knockdown in a squall could easily submerge portlights for several minutes: Once large quantities of water flood the cabins, the hull is sluggish to come up, the vessel is in serious trouble and lives are endangered. Good portlights are worth the expense. I capsized *Teresa* during a violent squall (60 knots) in the middle of the 1985 Mayor's Cup Schoo-

ner Race in New York Harbor. She was brand new, under-ballasted and we had only sailed her for a few days. Her ABI cast-bronze portlights were submerged for about 20 minutes and didn't leak a drop!

Deadlights may be bought or made. If they are made, always inset and trim them from the outside. I use either thick tempered glass, safety glass or Lexan. Bed the light in rubber, and fasten a trim or retaining ring from outside with screws if the cabin trunk (or hull) is thick enough (use bolts if it is thin.) A trim ring may also be made for the inside. I have come to prefer Lexan because it is virtually indestructible, even though it scratches easily and must be carefully maintained.

Underwater viewing ports are a wonderful application for Lexan deadlights in cold-molded hulls. The joy of seeing ocean life through the bottom of your boat, particularly the Cetacea, is in itself reason to go sailing. The lights are strongest when made round or elliptical, and should have a large lip or mounting surface (1$\frac{1}{2}$ inches or 2 inches for a 9-inch to 12-inch deadlight). The Lexan should be 1/2 inch thick. The hole is cut, the lip is routed to the thickness of the Lexan, and the rim is covered with fabric and epoxy. The light is bedded in rubber and fastened with 1/4-inch stainless-steel flat-head machine screws coated in rubber. (Flat-head machine screws are often incorrectly called flat-head bolts.) The outside surface is totally flush. If this makes you nervous, a well may be built around the viewing port to a height above the waterline, or just high enough to ring it with a flange to which a watertight lid may be secured by bolts. Properly installed, this kind of underwater viewing port does not at all compromise the integrity of the hull, although it should be located alongside the keel where it will be less likely to directly contact rock or coral. The primary problem is the different rates of expansion and contraction of the different materials—a thick, carefully made rubber seal is the secret to long-lasting success. During initial installation, take great care not to trap air bubbles, and don't overtighten the bolts, which would squeeze out rubber and deform the plastic. After curing, the bolts may be tightened a little more. Use large washers inside the hull. As always, the bolt holes should be epoxy-sealed first. By *rubber*, I mean one of the usual three compounds: 3M #5200, Sikaflex or two-part Thiokol; once again, I prefer 3M #5200 because it can be cleaned up with mineral spirits, which doesn't attack the Lexan.

The integration of Lexan with plywood and cold-molding allows big windows that just a few years ago were totally imprudent. The biggest factor limiting size is the flexibility of the plastic and the type and size of the connecting joint between the window and the trunk side. The ultimate danger is of a large sea breaking against a window during broaching. The window can flex so much that it can burst completely inside the cabin, possibly breaking the wood/epoxy/fabric lip to which it is secured and tearing the fasteners right through the lip with it. The Lexan itself will not break; the lip will. This is why the lip absolutely must be made as strong as possible, and the larger the window the thicker it should be (I use 1/4-inch to 3/8-inch Lexan for cabin windows and skylights). The fabric covering over the cabin trunk should extend under the window perimeter lip as previously stated. Through-bolts are best, unless the cabin sides are quite thick; the windows are always installed from outside and bedded in synthetic rubber (I use 3M #5200). Trim installed outside covers the joint up to the edge of the interior lip. If the windows are inset deeply into the trunks such that the trim is flush to the outer surface, bed the trim carefully in rubber. It may be necessary to drill several small weep holes at the bottom to drain any water that gets behind the trim due, again, to differing rates of expansion and contraction. The rules regarding using plenty of rubber and not overtightening the fasteners hold true here too.

Deck prisms are used in areas of the boat that don't receive enough light. They come in two general shapes: triangular and acorn (rectangular and round from on deck). They usually have a bronze fitting and trim ring, are bedded in rubber and screwed down from on deck. They are rare today, because other technologies have provided better lighting, but are still useful and attractive. Don't install them where you can bump your head on them. If you have a creative bent, you can buy acrylic blocks and 1/8-inch bronze sheet (or brass or aluminum) and make your own.

Good ventilation can make the difference between comfort and misery in a boat, particularly where you sleep. For the most part, those little 12-volt fans are noisy, use a lot of electricity, get in the way, and do not move much air. Large cowl vents mounted on Dorade boxes are good. I have already described louvered drop-doors. Skylights, even small ones, over bunks are best, set to open forward into the most likely wind direction. Wind scoops are nearly essential on cruising boats; you can buy them or make your own. I won't describe Dorade box or wind scoop construction, as they are described so often in other books and magazine articles.

Keep in mind that air passing over a hollow body creates higher pressure at the back; hence, the natural direction for air flow, and the most efficient, is from aft forward. Skylights aft should open forward and skylights forward should open aft. The only problem with this arrangement is that people tend to sleep forward (as in a V-berth), and need direct outside air blowing on them on hot, sultry nights. Ventilators, however, can take advantage of natural air flow direction. The more open a hull is, the more comfortable it will be. Hence, light curtains have an advantage over doors, which, even when open often block some air flow.

Large PVC pipe can be used to make ventilators by cutting away one-third of the side of a cap and cutting a gap in the top of the pipe to correspond. Putting the cap on backwards will close it. Slip connectors cut into rings are used above and below the deck, roof or Dorade box top to hold the pipe in place; the whole is bedded in synthetic rubber. Epoxy-seal any plywood end grain exposed by cutting holes first.

CHAPTER 23
CENTERBOARDS
AND RUDDERS

*Centerboard Core/ Lead Ballast, Lifting Eyes and
Plywood Skins/ Shaping and Covering, Pin Bushings
and Skid Plates/ Rudderstocks, Cores, Plywood Skins,
Shaping and Covering/ Gudgeons, Pintles, Alignment,
Shaft-Pipes and Supports, Bearings and Stuffing Boxes*

CENTERBOARD CORE

Centerboards need to be very strong and stiff, as do their trunks. I prefer to cold-mold them using a solid core of 2 x 6 Douglas fir, yellow pine or hem-fir, with one or two plywood layers laid at right angles to the core on each side. I align the core lumber fore and aft and stack-laminate the planks edge-to-edge with epoxy (no fasteners) on a perfectly flat surface. The core is made to the approximate shape of the board, and after curing, the actual shape is carefully lofted onto the core from the plans. Double-check all angles and dimensions by measuring them directly from the actual centerboard trunk; don't forget the diagonals. There should be about 1 inch of clearance on both ends and along the top when the board is full-up. Side clearance should be about 1/4 inch maximum on each side, so you can see how critical it is that both

board and trunk be made perfectly flat and true (no twist!).

Centerboard shape is cut onto the core with a power plane. The shape should taper more aft than forward. Consider that a foil

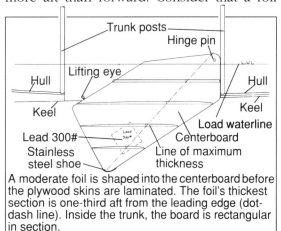

A moderate foil is shaped into the centerboard before the plywood skins are laminated. The foil's thickest section is one-third aft from the leading edge (dot-dash line). Inside the trunk, the board is rectangular in section.

Figure 23-1. Centerboard shape and ballast location (TERRAPIN 45).

shape would be diagonally imposed on the board, in line with water flow across it when down. (See Fig. 23-1.) In most applications, it is not practical or effective to treat centerboards as highly developed airfoils; they aren't thick enough and their positions vary. In general, however, the leading edge is somewhat blunt, the section is thickest one-third of the way aft, and the trailing edge is fine, coming from a long, fairly flat taper. Avoid knife edges. They are fragile, too flexible and actually cause turbulence at sailing speeds rather than alleviate it. A narrow, squared trailing edge is the best shape. (See Photo 23-1.)

Because the plywood layers will thicken the board section and are difficult to taper (they will be full of fasteners), virtually all shape comes from the core-planing. This means that the leading edge may be about 1/2 inch thick and the trailing edge 1/4 inch or thinner. One or more plywood templates may be made to help achieve consistency of shape, especially side to side. The central part of the board maintains its full thickness right to the lowest point. This thickness is important for maintaining strength and stiffness and because, near the bottom, board shape more closely resembles an airfoil. (It is the highest aspect location.) Also, the bottom is the most likely point of impact, and needs to be broad enough to accept an abrasion plate.

Photo 23-1. Centerboard shape is power-planed onto the core prior to skinning with plywood.

It can be argued that putting any shape into the board at all is a waste of time; that the speed and windward efficiency gained are infinitesimal. I personally believe the gains are subtle but worthwhile, especially in vessels that really perform. In slow, heavy cruisers or working craft, shaping is less important. If nothing else, a shaped board will weigh less; it will have less flotation and need less lead ballast.

A note here about ballasted boards: They should be weighted only enough to amply compensate their flotation, so that they go down all the way. Trying to contribute to a vessel's righting moment by use of a heavily ballasted board is generally a bad practice, except in very small vessels. The reasons for this are: the board will be difficult to raise, imposing tremendous strains on pivot-pin, hardware and tackle (a large winch and wire rope may be required); the board, when fully down, will impose tremendous loads on the keel, centerboard trunk sides and on itself; when raised, the center of ballast will be higher than it should be (heavy boards, even thick ones, distribute their weight over a very large plane—a solid steel board illustrates this dramatically). Finally, the board will be difficult to build, install and, especially, to maintain and repair. Solid metal boards corrode where they cannot be easily scraped and painted, are too heavy and cumbersome to remove for maintenance, and can bend (this happens surprisingly often), preventing their being raised or jamming them in the trunk. For these reasons, many designers of steel and aluminum vessels (such as Tom Colvin) specify wood boards.

Properly ballasted laminated wood boards have nearly neutral buoyancy when the entire board is submerged. In most installations, part of the board is always above the waterline even when fully down. Hence I design my pivot pins to be located either above the waterline or outside in the keel, and locate lifting eyes at both ends of the board, so that it can be removed easily when the vessel is afloat. In actual practice, a thorough application of several coats of bottom paint inside the trunk and on the parts of the board that are always up inside can last for many years. There is little erosion of the paint, and the constant slight motion and raising and lowering seem to effectively discourage marine growth inside the trunk; there is also no sunlight. A vessel that gets regular use, such as a working or cruising boat, might go many years without any maintenance inside at all. In this case, all that is necessary is to paint the accessible parts of the board during haulouts and repair abrasion damage to the lower leading edge (common). But it is nice to know that the board can be removed if need be, and that in the unlikely event of damage to the pin, it won't leak inside the boat.

LEAD BALLAST, LIFTING EYES AND PLYWOOD SKINS

The total flotation value of the board is computed to determine ballast. This is usually done by the designer, but if you are adapting a design, you may need to figure it yourself. Consider the board to be uniformly as thick as at its thickest point, and consider that all of it will be submerged. After computing this volume, the board's density is found (the type of wood used) and multiplied by the volume to find total weight. The difference between this figure and the weight of an equal volume of water will equal the amount of ballast necessary to eliminate the board's buoyancy. Because we didn't subtract for the tapered sections of the board, it will actually be heavier than water, and hence, it will sink. I usually add another 50 pounds (for large boards) to make sure; a board that won't go all the way down is a bummer. I use lead for

Photo 23-2. After shaping, the ballast hole is cut, one side of the board gets its first plywood skin, the board is turned over and the lead is installed. Epoxy is poured into the ballast to eliminate air voids and seal the wood.

ballast because it is compact (dense), stable and easy to work with. Ballast location is in the thickest part of the board and low without being closer than about 9 inches from the perimeter. (See Photo 23-2.)

Most of my centerboard trunks are $3^1/_2$ inches wide inside, and the centerboards are about 3 inches or $3^1/_8$ inches thick at the center. A $1^1/_2$-inch core would be skinned with 3/8-inch plywood, one layer per side, then 5/16-inch plywood, one layer per side. Keep in mind that plywood is rarely the thickness it's supposed to be; measure your sheets in several places. Epoxy glue joints, fabric/epoxy skins and several coats of bottom paint can add up to 1/4 inch to finished thickness. *Teresa*'s board has 3/16-inch clearance on each side and moves absolutely freely with virtually no friction when the boat is trimmed and not moving. A really loose board will rattle around in its trunk, especially when you are running off the wind in full-up position, or trying to sleep in a 'roly' anchorage, or, and I swear this is true, when some poor crew members (or charter guests) are trying to make love with rhythmic gusto and don't want to be heard.

After the volume of required lead is figured and translated into the size and shape hole ($1^1/_2$ inches thick) necessary to contain it, this hole is cut into the board. Then one side of

Photo 23-3. Each side of the centerboard receives two plywood layers; large scraps can be used as long as they span the board. Grain direction opposes the core grain, and all seams are staggered.

the board is plywood-skinned (one layer), being careful not to put twist in the board (keep it flat). The skin is epoxy-glued and stapled or nailed; I prefer to nail the perimeter. (See Photo 23-3.) It may be necessary to clamp the leading edge curve in place, as shown.

Turn the board over and install the lead, being careful to support the plywood skin thoroughly from underneath to prevent bulging or even breaking through. *Teresa's* ballast weighed 350 pounds and consisted of six "pigs" weighing 55 pounds each plus some small scraps. After installation, epoxy or polyester resin is poured on the lead, bringing the surface flush to the top of the wood. Lifting

eyes are installed at this time also. I make stainless-steel plates $1^1/_2$ inches by 3 inches to 6 inches and at least 1/4 inch thick. The eyes are large shoulder eye bolts, hot-dip galvanized steel, 1/2-inch or larger diameter. The stainless-steel plate is mortised into the core on edge at least 3 inches down from the top of the board with a 9/16-inch or other appropriate size hole drilled in its center. (See Fig. 23-2.) A hole for the eye bolt is drilled down from the top of the board through the plate hole, and a space is mortised beneath the plate for a nut. All holes and mortises are epoxy-sealed; the plate, bolt and nut are installed, and epoxy resin is poured in to fill any gaps and the space around the nut. Many years later it may well be possible to unscrew the worn eyebolt and screw in a new one.

Then the other plywood skins are laid on. Remember to stagger the seams. The finished board for *Teresa* weighs 750 pounds. You can see why an even heavier board would be hard to build—it could break under its own weight while being turned over the first time, assuming you could turn it over.

SHAPING, COVERING, PIN BUSHING AND SKID PLATE

After skinning, final shaping and fairing are done; I make the board entry round in section, and rout a 1/2-inch bullnose on the trailing and top edges. Any flaws, countersink holes and plywood voids are now filled as usual, and the board is covered with epoxy and fabric. I build up three or four layers on the lowest edges, which usually round into each other. This juncture then receives a stainless-steel skid plate bedded in rubber compound and screwed in place.

The last step is to carefully locate and drill the hole for the pivot bearing. For this I use heavy wall pipe (usually schedule 40, series 304 stainless steel, bought surplus or scrap).

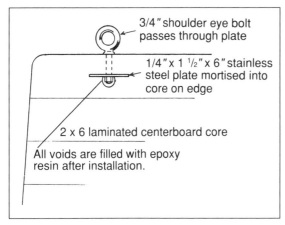

3/4" shoulder eye bolt passes through plate

1/4" x 1 1/2" x 6" stainless steel plate mortised into core on edge

2 x 6 laminated centerboard core

All voids are filled with epoxy resin after installation.

Figure 23-2. Centerboard lifting eye.

A typical size for most yachts is $1^1/_2$ inches inside diameter, which will perfectly fit a pivot pin of $1^1/_2$-inch stainless-steel shaft stock; both are readily available sizes. The rough hole should be a little oversize. It is epoxy-sealed, and the pipe is inserted. The pipe should be 1/8 inch shorter than the trunk width, and similarly about 1/8 inch longer than the board width. It is essential that the hole, and bearing installation, be exactly perpendicular to the board and trunk surfaces. After the pipe bearing is centered (protruding equal amounts from each side), masking tape seals the lower side, and epoxy resin is poured around the pipe to glue it in place. In the unlikely event that the outside of the pipe is polished, scratch it up so the epoxy glue will have some tooth to hold it in place. The finished board is now painted with high-build epoxy primer.

RUDDERSTOCKS, CORES, PLYWOOD SKINS, SHAPING AND COVERING

I will describe two types of rudder construction: Transom-hung, using a wood stock; and keel-hung, using a stainless-steel stock covered with wood. The latter type is mounted in a lower gudgeon and pierces the hull through a stainless-steel pipe or extended bronze stuffing box. I will not deal with spade-type rudders specifically, though they are built in the same manner as keel-hung rudders, by simply using much larger shafts and hardware. Every vessel I have ever owned or traveled in has bounced its rudder on a hard bottom many times, and I personally would never use a spade-type rudder on any but professional racing machines.

Rudderstocks of wood must be strong and well seasoned. They should be of fairly large section, as wide as possible without creating excessive drag; typically they are equal in thickness to the aft end of the keel on which

they are hung. When driving hard to weather under too much sail, as in clawing off a lee shore or during a race, tremendous torque loads are placed on a rudder that is fighting strong weather helm. An inferior or under-sized rudderstock can twist itself to splinters at the worst possible time.

I prefer Douglas fir for rudderstocks, but yellow pine and oak are excellent also. Red oak has very long cell structure and transmits water along the grain even after curing, hence it is much more rot-prone than white oak. In rudderstocks this shouldn't present a problem as long as care is taken to seal the wood thoroughly at the top and at fittings. Douglas fir and oak are flexible, which I consider to be a good quality (to a limited degree) in a rudderstock, for shock absorption.

The rudder in the example (*Teresa*'s) starts out as a 4 x 6. The post is slotted to receive the fore and aft core planks (see Photo 23-4). These planks are 2 x 6's, as were the centerboard core planks. They may be fir, yellow pine or hem-fir. The planks are stack-laminated in place with epoxy and epoxied into the slot in the rudderstock. Screws in pairs are also installed from both sides, as shown in the

Photo 23-4. Two-by-six planks form the rudder core. In the case of transom-hung rudders, the core is mortised into the rudderstock, and is glued and screwed in place. Rudder shape is power-planed into the core. The tiller is mortised into the rudderstock, and plywood cheeks are laminated to each side of the rudder head and heavily fastened.

photo. A common problem with transom hung/tiller-steered rudders is that they float up to the side when the vessel is not moving, depending on the degree of rake to the stern-post. For this reason, heavier wood is an advantage, or even a little lead ballast installed in the core as in the centerboard. I install tiller combs on vessels with tiller steering (see Fig. 23-3), which solves the problem because the tiller is always immobilized when not being held. (A tiller comb is a slotted bar beneath the tiller. A metal cleat is fastened to the underside of the tiller so that it drops into the slots of the tiller comb.)

The rudder core is shaped with a power plane and grinder with softpad to a taper aft, in this case nearly to a point, as it is desirable for the rudder trailing edge to be smaller than that of the centerboard. A single layer of plywood is glued and stapled or nailed to each side (1/2 inch in the example). The edges are trimmed, shaped (1/2-inch routed bullnose),

filled, sanded and covered with epoxy and fabric, again building up two or three layers on the rudder bottom edge. The rudder trailing edge tapers to a finished thickness of 1 inch, which is totally rounded by routing.

The edges of the rudderstock may be left square, rounded or beveled (see Photo 23-5). A fairing block may be added to the trailing edge of the stock to create a curve, and tiller cheek blocks are added at the head to reinforce the tiller socket or mortise (see Photo 23-6). On large vessels, these should be through-bolted above and below the socket. I prefer the mortise to be tapered on very small vessels; the tiller is held in with a Bungee cord. On larger vessels, the mortise is square and larger than the tiller end, which is through-bolted in place using large, thick flat washers, or stainless-steel plates covering the cheek blocks on very large vessels. The tiller can then pivot up and down, a great convenience to different helmsmen, as well as allow-

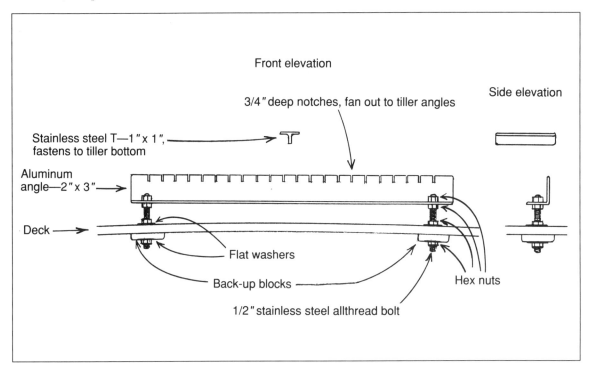

Figure 23-3. Tiller comb.

Photo 23-5. The plywood skins build up the rudder blade, and the stock is shaped as desired.

Photo 23-6. Shown is *Teresa*'s finished rudder, including hardware.

ing use of a tiller comb. The fit at the socket should be tight, to limit side-to-side play.

The rudderstock may be finished bright or painted; the rudder is painted with two coats of high-build epoxy primer prior to bottom paint.

Rudders incorporating metal shafts can be built with an internal plate(s) or external straps. I no longer use the latter method, which involved fitting the shaft to a rounded slot in the leading edge of the rudder and welding two heavy straps to the front and sides of the shaft. These lay along each side of the rudder for perhaps one-third its length, either on the surface or let in flush, and are through-bolted. One through-bolt on each

strap is left long for the attachment of zincs, the others are trimmed to the nuts. The cold-molded rudder blade is covered with fabric and epoxy, including under the straps, even if they are let in. All drilled holes are epoxy-sealed, and the shaft and straps are bedded in rubber compound.

The method I now prefer is to encapsulate the rudder shaft with the blade. This method is cleaner and smoother, and lends itself well to counterbalanced rudders, which I use extensively. A stainless-steel plate, usually of 1/4-inch stock, is edge-welded to the aft side of the rudderstock, extending at least two-thirds of the blade height and at least 6 inches wide. If the rudder is counterbalanced, a similar plate (perhaps narrower) is welded to the forward edge of the shaft (see Fig. 23-4). Welds should be deep, continuous, ground and over-welded. If the plates sheer off, you have no steering. The heat generated by welding will likely deform the shaft, which may have to be trued before laying up the rudder; this is an important step to remember.

The rudder blade is stack-laminated of 2 x 6 stock as before. The planks are slotted to fit over the steel plates and beveled or hollowed to fit against the shaft; the plank stock is typically equal to the shaft diameter ($1\frac{1}{2}$ inches) so planks and shaft finish flush on both sides. These proportions will work for vessels from 25 feet up to 50 feet. Above that, add 1/2 inch for both shaft size and blade core stock. Vessels between 25 and 30 feet use $1\frac{1}{4}$-inch shaft and stock; smaller vessels use 1 inch. The planks are fastened to the plates either by machine screws tapped into them or by through-bolts and epoxy-glue. Of course, the rudderstock and plates may also be bronze-brazed together, but I prefer stainless steel because it is much stronger and more durable, as well as being less expensive. Bolt-heads or nuts and washers are countersunk and epoxy-puttied.

The rudder core is now planed and sanded to shape as before; a proper airfoil may be incorporated if desired. The core is then planked with one or two plywood layers (two would be used only on large rudders of difficult shape), glued and stapled or nailed in place. These layers span the shaft and cover it; the grain should be oriented fore and aft. Any voids along the shaft should be filled with thickened epoxy. The edges are trimmed and shaped (mostly routed; the leading edge may require some grinding if an airfoil if incorporated). The whole is filled, sanded and covered with fabric and epoxy and painted, taking care to get a close seal around the protruding shaft ends.

GUDGEONS, PINTLES, ALIGNMENT, SHAFT-PIPES AND SUPPORTS, BEARINGS AND STUFFING BOXES

I choose to make gudgeons and pintles entirely from fairly heavy stainless-steel plate (1/4 inch minimum) $1\frac{1}{2}$ inches wide or wider. For transom-hung rudders, three of these fittings are mounted on the rudder, two on the transom and one near the bottom of the keel. Instead of traditional pintles, I prefer to weld one flat plate to each rudder fitting and two to each hull fitting. These are drilled for bolts (1/2 inch minimum). The plates act as thrust bearings and eliminate all vertical forces on the bolts. (See Fig. 23-4 and Photo 23-7.) The fittings are through-bolted both to rudder and hull and to each other; the pintle bolts should receive lock nuts also. The holes through all fittings should line up; attach the rudder fittings first, sighting through all the holes. Obviously, if the rudderstock is not straight, there will be a problem: Leave the bottom hole undrilled and sight it by eye through the other two, mark and drill it. Epoxy-seal all holes through the wood, and bed the fittings in rudder compound, coating the bolts also. Position the rudder against the hull and block and suspend it in place, then locate the hull fittings and mark and drill their holes. Sometimes a shim may be needed under one of the transom fittings, as shown in Photo 23-7. Epoxy-seal these holes and bed everything in rubber.

For vessels 25 feet or less, the plate stock can be 1/4 inch by $1\frac{1}{2}$ inches, the pintle bolts 3/8 inch, and through-bolts 1/4 inch. For vessels 25 to 40 feet, the plate stock could be 1/4 inch by 2 inches, the pintle bolts 1/2 inch, and through-bolts 5/16 inch. For vessels 40 to 50 feet, the plate stock could be 3/8 inch by 2 inch, pintle bolts 5/8 inch or 3/4 inch and through-bolts 3/8 inch or 7/16 inch. For vessels 50 to 60 feet, the plate stock can be 1/2 inch by $2\frac{1}{2}$ inch, the pintle bolts 1 inch, and

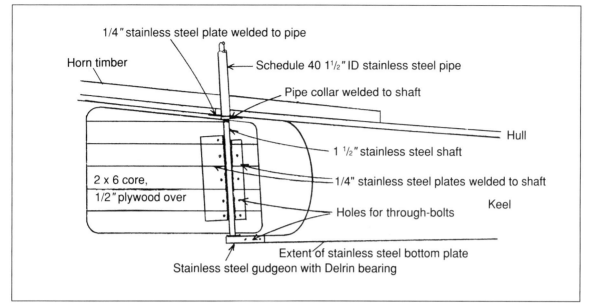

1/4" stainless steel plate welded to pipe

Horn timber

Schedule 40 1½" ID stainless steel pipe

Pipe collar welded to shaft

Hull

1 ½" stainless steel shaft

2 x 6 core,
1/2" plywood over

1/4" stainless steel plates welded to shaft

Keel

Holes for through-bolts

Extent of stainless steel bottom plate

Stainless steel gudgeon with Delrin bearing

Figure 23-4. Shaft-hung rudder.

through-bolts 1/2 inch. Vessels larger than this are unlikely to have transom-hung rudders with wooden stocks, although years ago they did; the fittings should increase in number and be carefully designed and made. All stainless-steel fittings should be ground very smooth and polished; if facilities are available, they should also be chemically passivated. Care must be taken that all metals used, including the welding rod, be of the same series. Any pinholes or crevices in stainless welds will corrode.

Shaft-hung rudders ride in a large, heavily built gudgeon bolted to the lower aft extremity of the keel. Plate sizes for this fitting are similar to those listed above for similar sized vessels. The fitting consists of a U-shaped strap, which extends at least 12 inches forward along the bottom of the keel end, its sides being let in so as to finish flush (see Fig. 23-6). A bottom plate is welded on inside the strap and likewise let into the keel bottom to finish flush. A short piece of stainless pipe is welded inside the aft end of the strap, such that the top finishes flush. The pipe may fit

Photo 23-7. Stainless-steel rudder hardware is heavily welded and polished to prevent crevice corrosion. A teak shim was used to align the three fittings properly. Bedding compound is 3M #5200.

tight to the rudder shaft, or a larger pipe may be used and fitted with a Delrin bearing; this is especially desirable on larger vessels. A 1/4-inch hole is drilled in the bottom of the fitting centered in the shaft pipe. The fitting must be designed and made to compensate for any difference in angle between keel bottom and rudder shaft by angling the pipe appropriately. This involves cutting the bottom of the pipe to a bevel. The 1/4-inch hole is drilled at this angle also. The gudgeon is through-bolted into the keel, and on large vessels screws or bolts may also be installed up from the bottom. One lateral bolt is left long for the attachment of a sacrificial zinc anode. On very large vessels (over 50 feet), it is desirable for any or all of the plates to extend as far forward as reasonable. The bottom plate could extend 3 feet or more and double as a protective skid plate for the keel bottom. All holes should be epoxy-sealed, the let-in wood surfaces covered with fabric

Keel fitting   Rudder fitting

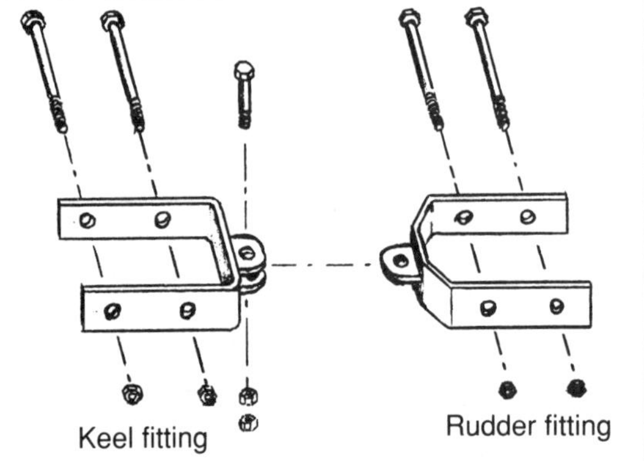

Transom fittings have a flat strap instead of the U-shaped strap shown. For the fittings below the water, one bolt is left long to affix a sacrificial zinc anode.

Figure 23-5. Transom-hung rudder hardware.

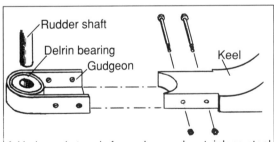

Rudder shaft
Delrin bearing
Gudgeon
Keel

A U-shaped strap is formed around a stainless steel pipe section fitted with a Delrin bearing for the rudder shaft, and a plate is welded to the bottom. One bolt is left long so that it can take a zinc anode. The bottom plate may be extended further forward.

Figure 23-6. Shaft-hung rudder gudgeon.

and epoxy, and the fitting and bolts bedded in rubber compound.

The hull usually has a metal pipe installed to hold the upper portion of the shaft. The bottom of this pipe should have a flange plate welded to it to fit against the hull. This plate is fit to the shape and angle of the hull and is either through-bolted or screwed and bedded in rubber compound (as usual, all holes are epoxy-sealed). If the vessel is tiller-steered, the pipe extends through the hull interior and above the deck about 1/4 inch. Another plate is made to fit around it as a collar, but it is not welded, only screwed and rubber-bedded to the deck and pipe. There should be a 3/4-inch plywood back-up block epoxied and screwed underneath the deck through which the top of the pipe passes. The rudder shaft extends the desired distance above deck, and is either machined and drilled for the tiller end fitting, or a keyway is cut for a bolt-on tiller fitting.

If the vessel is to be wheel-steered, the pipe usually ends above either the horn timber or a special floor timber or fairing block, and the top is fitted with a rubber hose and conventional stuffing box. In this instance, the flange plate may be located inside the hull if desired (it is still welded to the pipe), providing there is room to install the pipe from inside.

Another alternative is a stuffing box with its own integral pipe. This may either be purchased or made by brazing a piece of bronze pipe to a conventional flange-type bronze stuffing box. If brazed, the job must be very thorough (strength and alignment are critical) and have no pinhole leaks. A fairing block is epoxied and fastened to the top of the horn timber for the flange.

All these components are aligned by installing the gudgeon temporarily and drilling a pilot hole up through the hull with a long 1/4-inch bit *through the 1/4-inch hole in the gudgeon*, taking care not to flex the bit while drilling. This bit is easily made by brazing or welding a section of 1/4-inch rod to a 1/4-inch twist drill. An oversize hole is drilled for the pipe, using the 1/4-inch hole as a pilot. If the pipe extends through the deck, it is pushed up through the lower hole, and sighted through the gudgeon hole; when true, the deck hole is scribed and cut. Don't forget the backup block.

The pipe or stuffing box is bedded in rubber, and the flange is screwed, lagged or through-bolted in place, after epoxy-sealing all holes. The top of the rudder shaft is cut, squared and fitted with a tiller arm or quadrant (in some cases, the shaft head is cut for a keyway; this is not as reliable, particularly in large vessels). When the pipe extends through the deck, the top trim plate is installed after rubber is poured around the pipe hole (mask the bottom off).

A final consideration is to prevent the rudder shaft from riding up in its pipe. This could obviously be very dangerous, particularly if the shaft can jump free of the gudgeon. Because the rudder could be pushed up during grounding, some positive device is needed to prevent this. One solution is to weld a collar onto the rudder shaft outside the hull that will ride just below the pipe end; another (when the pipe ends inside the hull) is to install a dodge bearing or pillar block fixed in place somewhere above the stuffing box, having set screws set into shallow holes in the shaft (use anti-seize compound). This last arrangement is particularly useful in large vessels, where friction is reduced by using the bearing to center the shaft and absorb tiller arm or quadrant loads that would otherwise be borne by the pipe and stuffing box. Salt water must not be allowed near these bearings, and they must be kept greased.

CHAPTER 24
FINISHING

*Epoxy Primers/ Polyurethane Topsides and Bootstripe/
Deck Patterning, Masking, Non-Skid/ Polyurethane
Finishes for Decks, Trunks and Coach Roofs/
Bottom Paint/ Annual Maintenance*

Much of the information in this chapter has been covered elsewhere as the need to paint has arisen. Like so many people who must work with limited financial resources, I have been frustrated by the cost and and price markup (as much as 500 percent) of so-called marine products, and have looked for alternatives. I have also been angered by the plethora of products whose sole purpose is to separate consumers from their money.

Long ago I came to the conclusion that modern marine paints don't really work well on wooden boats. They tend to be hard and brittle, and the constant flexion, expansion and contraction of wood cause them to chip, peel, blister and delaminate. When it comes time to refinish, they don't sand out to a nice feather edge; as they thin down, they flake off, so that the whole paint surface needs to be removed. These paints do, however, work well on fiberglass, steel, aluminum and ferro-cement, and also on cold-molded boats that are skinned with fabric and epoxy. The basic

rule that an old-time professional painter taught me is: Use a hard paint on a hard surface, and use a soft paint on a soft surface. So I began using good-quality oil-based enamels on wood, usually porch and floor enamel or exterior window and sash enamel. I mostly bought these in white and used universal paint colorant to create my own traditional colors—pale creams, pale blues, grays, greens and off-whites. (I still do this, as these colorants work well with the paint products I am about to describe.) Light colors reflect light and hence keep the surface cool. Dark colors absorb light and heat up, both dessicating and shrinking the material over which they are applied and radiating heat to adjacent areas. In your boat, this results in an uncomfortable interior and creates a benign environment for rot, mold and fungus. In the tropics, dark colors should be totally avoided; in the extreme north and south, they are beneficial.

Cold-molded wood covered with epoxy and a flexible fabric such as Xynole-polyester becomes a different material from the separate components. There is a great deal more flexibility of choice in colors and paint types, especially for hull topsides. If there is insulation present, there is even more flexibility—hull topsides may really be painted any color. Decks and coach roofs should still be very light colors; no insulation stops heat transfer well enough to ignore the heat-gathering and radiating qualities of horizontal surfaces exposed to intense sunlight. I have painfully burned my feet walking on tan-colored decks in the tropics. But pure white decks are so blinding as to be equally uncomfortable to the eyes. Pale cream works well.

So now we are confronted primarily by economic factors—how to save money and beat the marine mark-up. My personal solution has been the Sherwin-Williams Paint Company. Their commercial catalog of products is so extensive that I still haven't figured out most of them. Many years ago someone turned me on to their epoxy enamel, Tile-Clad II. This two-part epoxy coating is remarkably tough, durable and flexible. It is also very economical. Tile-Clad II has less odor than any other epoxy paint I have ever used; and the only disadvantage I know of is that it chalks when exposed to sunlight. This doesn't seem to compromise its durability, but the finish gradually changes from semi-gloss (which I like very much on decks, coach roofs and interiors) to a satin approaching flat, and of course it rubs off on things, especially human bodies, which come in contact with it most frequently. Periodic washing greatly diminishes this problem, as does the application of wax. The advantage of paint that chalks is that it is easy to sand off the oxidized layer periodically (once every 5 years seems right for Tile-Clad II) and repaint. Because Tile-Clad II is somewhat soft, it flexes well and sands to a feather edge without losing its adhesion; in short, it acts like an oil-based enamel but has the durability, adhesion and abrasion resistance of epoxy. When not exposed to sunlight, it does not chalk and seems to last indefinitely. For these reasons, I use it exclusively for all interior paint work, including bilges, engine rooms, cabinet interiors, hull interiors in living areas and deck and coach roof undersides. In these applications, it retains its semi-gloss finish and covers in two heavy coats. Three coats may be considered a life-time coating; it just doesn't deteriorate appreciably.

EPOXY PRIMERS

Tile-Clad II comes in a white enamel and a high-build red primer (Tile-Clad II Hi-Bild Primer); both are of excellent quality. The "enamel" finish coating is heavy-bodied and sands well, hence I often use it as a primer for polyurethane finish coats, and as an intermediate protective coating for surfaces (such as hull topsides) that may need to sit in the primer stage for as long as several years. I often create my own sanding primers by the addition of dry talc powder to white Tile-Clad II; this must be very thoroughly mixed with the paint. It is not wise to leave conventional sanding primers exposed to sun and weather for more than a month or two because they deteriorate rapidly and can lose their adhe-

Photo 24-1. Spraying epoxy primer. Wear protective clothing, including a fume-filtering mask.

sion. Tile-Clad Hi-Bild Primer is excellent for priming metal surfaces and for use below the waterline and on rudders, keels and centerboards. It also holds up well when left uncoated for long periods of time, and holds bottom paint well after a rough (80- or 100-grit paper) sanding and washing with the specified reducer for the bottom paint to be used.

Sherwin-Williams also makes an excellent sanding primer for their polyurethane paints: Polane Sanding Primer, also a polyurethane.

I should state here that the other epoxy and polyurethane paint products on the marine market are mostly of excellent quality; indeed I know of nothing quite as good as Awlgrip, but these products are extremely expensive, often costing twice what the Sherwin-Williams industrial products cost.

POLYURETHANE TOPSIDES AND BOOTSTRIPE

I don't paint hull topsides until a vessel is near completion and nearly ready for launching because the hull gets dirty, scratched and smeared with various chemicals during construction, to say nothing of the graffiti that seems to end up all over the hulls I build—everything from construction notes to poetic polemics reflecting on the quality of the management. (We also sign our mistakes.)

I use Sherwin-Williams Polane H.S. polyurethane industrial coating for all exterior painted surfaces from the masts, steel davits and aluminum day tanks to decks, coach roofs, cockpits, cabin trunks and topsides: literally everything. When ordering these products, it is important to specify that they are for exterior use and require nonphotochemically reactive catalysts and reducers. Failure to do this may result in slight eventual chalking. Sherwin-Williams has industrial or commer-

cial outlets in large American cities, and the staff of these warehouses will know what you want and be more likely to stock it than the untrained personnel in the neighborhood stores, who will stare at you blankly until you prompt them to get out their catalogs.

Either Tile-Clad II or Polane Sanding Primer (better) may be used as primers prior to applying Polane H.S. to the hull topsides. Typically, the hull has been left for months with two coats of Tile-Clad to protect the epoxy/fabric covering and fairing compound (which, remember, deteriorates rapidly when exposed to sunlight). At this point, the Tile-Clad is thoroughly sanded with #120 paper using orbital sanders (the pneumatic jitterbug is dramatically faster than electric models). Any nicks and scratches are filled with a glazing putty, such as Z-Spar #2 Glazing Compound. Two coats of Polane Sanding Primer are applied, sanding after the first coat with #180 paper, and with #220 paper after the second coat. The surface is cleaned with compressed air and wiped with reducer using clean white rags between coats, then two coats of Polane H.S. are applied. The first coat is sprayed lightly, as a tack coat; the second coat follows immediately (working around the hull) and is sprayed more heavily.

The bootstripe is typically painted first, to avoid the possibility of getting overspray on the topsides (getting a little on the primer won't hurt), and because the bootstripe is easier to mask off. Buy several rolls of masking paper, with or without a self-adhesive strip, and use low-tack masking tape—the silver stuff is the best.

Spray painting requires a fair amount of expensive equipment, skill and experience, but is well within the reach of most people who work at learning it. A good spray job greatly increases the quality, beauty and resale value of a boat, but many cruisers feel it isn't worth the trouble. One alternative for these people is to use brushable Awlgrip, which, when properly applied, can look very handsome. I think there is nearly as much skill involved in good brushwork as in spraying, but certainly the equipment is less expensive. A decent spraygun (I use siphon-feed external-mix) costs at least $100. You also need a compressor (which you might have if you followed my advice about staple guns and pneumatic tools), hoses, a water filter (I use in-line disposable types), goggles and a fume mask (which you should aready have for working with epoxy paints inside the hull). By the time you spray all the primers and urethane varnishes during the whole project, you will probably be ready for spraying Polane, which is pretty user-friendly.

Another alternative is to apply high-quality marine or industrial enamels with a roller, followed immediately (within 10 seconds) with a wide bristle or sponge brush. This technique produces results close in quality to a spray job, but it must be done by two people working as a team on a cool, windless, overcast day.

DECK PATTERNING, MASKING AND NONSKID

Earlier I mentioned that Xynole-polyester for decks and coach roofs can either be super-saturated (three resin coats) or left with a coarse texture by applying only two coats of resin. "Professional yacht-quality decks" are super-saturated and sanded fair, usually without requiring glazing. After sanding, the perimeters surrounding nonskid areas are coated with epoxy primer. Then, non-skid patterns are accurately laid out, often using pencil and batten and compass or template for corners. These are masked off carefully, the hardest part being tight outside curves. Inside curves are more common and easy to do, randomly bunching the tape on its unimportant side; the outside curves require careful, uniform folds or laps in the tape. The more neatly the layout and masking are done, the better the finished job will look; but keep in mind that very few people are likely to look at your corners from closer than 5 feet or 6 feet away.

A thick coat of epoxy paint is laid down, followed immediately by nonskid sprinkled on with a big saltshaker (either one of those huge old plastic ones with extra holes drilled in it or a commercial one from a restaurant kitchen). I use graded #1 kiln-dried silica sand for nonskid, available from any lumberyard for several dollars a sack; you will need only a pailful or so. Check that the holes in your shaker pass the sand neither too quickly nor too slowly; practice on something to perfect your wrist motion and to determine how thick you want it (more will make a coarser nonskid; a light dusting will be less coarse). It is important to apply the epoxy evenly with a roller; a heavy buildup will create a different texture. The same sprinkling pattern must be used for the whole deck to create a uniform texture. After the paint cures, the deck is swept off and vacuumed or air-blown clean. Another coat of epoxy paint is rolled on. When this cures, the masking tape is removed, the perimeters lightly sanded, and three coats of polyurethane are sprayed over the whole deck. If you want to go all out, you can first paint all your perimeters one color, then mask them off and paint the non-skid areas another color. In either case, the results are very professional and durable. With three paint coatings over the sand it is not too abrasive. Over years the sand will just barely start to show through, but it will usually do so uniformly and not hurt the appearance of the deck, especially if the color is a pale cream. It will not wear out like many of the other nonskid products available, and will cost a fraction of the price.

This same technique may be used for companionway ladders or even cabin soles (I don't find the latter necessary), even if they are finished bright (clear), by using clear silica sand (usually available in little bags at the hardware store) with polyurethane varnish. The results are a textured transparent to translucent finish through which the wood grain may be plainly seen. By masking off adjacent clear areas, some very beautiful effects can be created.

As mentioned in Chapter 19, coach roofs may be finished with nonskid like the decks, or left textured, lightly sanded and painted with primer and polyurethane. I greatly prefer the latter, which looks very much like a traditional canvas covering.

POLYURETHANE FINISHES FOR DECKS, TRUNKS AND COACH ROOFS

The only additional things to be said about this are that the techniques involving priming, sanding, masking and application are similar to those described for painting the topsides earlier in this chapter, with the exception of the non-skid deck areas, which cannot be sanded between coats. Because of this, it is important to follow coat on coat with as little delay as possible, not allowing dirt, chemicals, moisture or total curing to affect the previous paint layers.

Both the nonskid and textured coach roof effects greatly diminish the glare of high-gloss polyurethane coatings, and the contrast to perimeters and trunk cabins finished glossy is handsome. I usually finish my coach roofs a shade lighter than the decks, and I often paint the cabin trunks a different color altogether, or a considerably darker shade of the same. To mix different shades of the same color, use the same pigments in the same relative proportions, varying instead the total quantities. All my on-deck colors are essentially different shades of the same color and therefore harmonious to the eye. Keep an accurate record of the mixes you make so you can match them later.

I usually make my color or shade breaks at the bottom or top of the fillet at the base of the cabin trunk and at the eyebrow trim around the top of the trunk. If there is only a fabric overlap line, the paint break is there. In any case, this line is usually 1 inch to 3 inches below the edge of the coach roof, and the fillet line is about 1/2 inch out on the deck, or the same amount above the deck.

BOTTOM PAINT

Bottom antifouling paint should not be applied until the vessel is nearly ready for the water. Today there is growing controversy surrounding the ecological damage being caused by these paints, and the marine industry may soon seek alternatives; already the use of tributyl tin products is being limited. *All bottom paints are deadly poisons and should be treated as such.*

The self-destructive fool sanding bottom paint and applying fresh coats with absolutely no protective clothing, gloves, eye protection or respirator is a tragic and stupid scene. And yet I see this every time I go to a boatyard. Please don't do this to yourself, your employees or your crew. If a professional yard sends out bottom painters with no protective clothing, complain to the management; we are all responsible.

My preference for years has been the high-copper, vinyl-type bottom paints that gradually slough off. I believe it is good practice to haul out once a year when practical, and high-copper vinyl paints are usually in good condition after this time period. Maintenance during haulouts consists of washing the bottom paint (pressure washers are best), perhaps scuff-sanding (wear protective clothing and a fume-filtering mask) the band at the waterline just below the bootstripe (mask off the bootstripe so as not to scratch it) with #80-grit paper. Any loose or flaking paint will also need to be scraped off and sanded; this is rare. The bottom should be recoated before the paint is exposed to air for more than a few days, as most bottom paints deteriorate rapidly out of the water. I typically add two coats, the first being reduced between 10 and 15 percent, and the second being nearly full strength—reduced no more than 5 percent.

Bottom paint should be very thoroughly mixed, as the heavy copper compounds accumulate on the bottom and rapidly settle out after mixing. I usually stir the paint with a paint stick, scraping the copper loose from the bottom (it is often helpful to pour a little out to prevent it from slopping over the sides). I then stir it thoroughly with a drill motor and metal stirring rod at slow speeds so as not to splatter; this takes a surprisingly long time (about 10 minutes). The paint is then stirred each and every time it is poured into painting buckets or trays. I paint from heavy-duty plastic trays using heavy-duty 9-inch roller frames with sturdy wood extension handles about 5 feet long. These keep you as far from the fumes and splatter as possible and allow you to paint the keel and hull underbody without actually crawling under the boat. I use 3/8-inch nap, 9-inch good quality roller covers (such as Corona Glass-Koters); the cheap ones come apart and leave fuzzies. The two coats are painted the same day, one after the other.

When a new hull is being painted for the first time, the epoxy primer should be thoroughly sanded with 80-grit paper to provide tooth for the bottom paint. The hull surface is then thoroughly dusted off (compressed air used simultaneously with a stiff whiskbroom works best—wear a mask) and then wiped down with the same solvent used to thin the bottom paint (usually xylene). It is vital that the surface be clean, dry, uniformly scratched up and absolutely dustless, and that it contain no chemical residue. Washing the hull with solvent without first dusting it off results in spreading a dust paste into the sanding scratches and defeats the purpose. Three coats of bottom paint are applied the first time. The first is reduced about 15 percent, the second 10 percent, and the third 5 percent or less.

ANNUAL MAINTENANCE

If these above processes are followed, barring accidents, yearly maintenance consists of washing the bottom (usually done by the yard with a pressure washer) and recoating it as described. Haulouts should not take more than three or four days. The less time the paint, fresh or old, is exposed to air, the better. If a boat has to be drydocked for a long time, one alternative is to apply the first coat of bottom paint within a few days, and apply the second coat prior to launch. Always, however, read the directions that come with your paint and follow them.

The higher the copper content, the more effective and longer lasting the paint will be. The advantage to sloughing-type paints is that they are self-cleaning. As marine organisms try to attach themselves, the paint surface slowly erodes away, taking them with it. Because the paint gradually erodes off, three coats are applied the first time and two more each yearly haulout. Sailing is good for the bottom, and washing it while in the water is easy and fast, though a nasty job. The best way to scrub the bottom is to anchor in a good current (one or two knots), and start scrubbing from aft forward, keeping upstream from your work to minimize exposure to the paint. Wearing a wet suit as protective clothing helps too. Plastic handles with rubber suction cups are the greatest thing going for holding on, as are one or more lines over the side.

As previously mentioned, the centerboard and trunk should be very carefully painted when new, just prior to installing the board. Four coats are ideal. Each year, often when the boat is in slings so that the board can be lowered all the way, as much of the board and trunk as you can get at are recoated. The rest will fend for itself, often for 10 years or longer at a time. Many yards will let you hang in the slings overnight and launch you first thing in the morning. Also, try to position blocking, cribbing or jackstands in a different place each year so that these oft-neglected areas get treated. Often they receive only a quick slather of paint just before launch. Again, hanging in the slings overnight is helpful to give them more attention.

CHAPTER 25
INBOARD DIESELS

Beds, Mounts, Shaft Log, Shaft, Stuffing Boxes, Couplings and Props/ V-Drives/ Fuel Tanks and Systems/ Cooling Systems/ Exhaust Systems/ Machinery and Systems/ Insulation/ Fire Prevention

BEDS, MOUNTS, SHAFT LOG, SHAFT, STUFFING BOXES, COUPLINGS AND PROPS

Engine beds depend largely on the engine used, and it is best not to make the beds until you have studied the engine specs from the manufacturer containing engine dimensions, or, better still, until you have the engine itself available. The beds should allow access under the motor, particularly to the oil pan and drains. As mentioned, an oil drain pump permanently installed is ideal for oil changes. I have even seen professional installations where fresh oil and drain oil tanks are installed with transfer pumps, electric or manual, to drain and refill the crankcase. Refer to Chapter 15 for a complete description of engine bed layout and construction.

As stated previously, I prefer rubber-based motor mounts because they are flexible and absorb vibration. They usually have a slot in one of the base holes for athwartships alignment, and have fine-thread nuts on upright bolts for height adjustment. Fore and aft location is carefully chosen, and after the mounts are installed, there is no way to adjust the location; position them right the first time. The mounts are lag-bolted into the beds. Use fairly long lags (3 inches minimum) of the largest diameter that will fit through the mount holes. Drill two holes: one for the shank and one for the threaded portion. If this second hole is too large the lag may strip; if too small, the bolt could break, split the bed or just be very difficult to install. Lags can be hot-dipped galvanized or stainless steel. I use 1/2-inch- or 3/4-inch-thick phenolic plates under the mount bases to reduce vibration wear to the wood beds, and to increase clearance between the engine and the beds.

I strongly recommend rubber shaft couplings because they isolate the engine, batteries and the electrical system from the water, as well as absorb vibration. The advantages to this are many: Zincs deteriorate more slowly, electrolysis is all but impossible and batteries cannot discharge into the water. With conventional steel couplings, the dissimilar metals in engine, shaft, propeller and batteries are all grounded into the natural electrolyte of salt water, and then charged with 12 volts of negative electricity, creating numerous possibilities for electrolysis and corrosion. Consequently all other dissimilar metals underwater are involved in an accelerated corrosive process, and all fittings must be protected with larger zincs, which deteriorate at a greater rate. The practice of bonding all these fittings together further closes the circuit between them in the natural electrolyte of salt water, creating an even more efficient galvanic corrosion cell. This increased vulnerability is eliminated by the inclusion of one or more sacrificial zinc anodes in the circuit, whose job is to protect all the fittings. This protection is conditional on correct zinc size, location, electrical connections and conscientious maintenance. However, a break in the bonding system, which is very common, may isolate interconnected fittings from their zincs, accelerating corrosion or electrolysis even further. In my extensive restoration experiences, I have seen the damage done so many times that I am totally against this way of doing things. Alternatives will be discussed further in Chapter 28.

Shaft log holes may be drilled or cut in during keel stack-lamination as described in Chapter 7. Trying to drill through an existing stack-laminated keel may be one hell of a trial, especially if stainless-steel fasteners are encountered. If drilling is intended, great care should be taken during keel lay up to keep fasteners off to the sides of the log hole. The shaft log I prefer is the hand-laid-up fiberglass type (see, fiberglass is good for something!). The log inside diameter should be 3/4 inch or 1 inch larger than the shaft diameter to allow for the Cutless bearing used at the prop end of the shaft. The outside diameter of the log usually matches that of the standard bronze stuffing boxes available for the matching shaft. The stuffing box is attached to the log by means of a heavy-duty marine rubber hose and large, heavy-duty clamps (the kind cast in steel or bronze and tightened by a through-bolt—don't ever use cheap hose clamps). There are other types of stuffing boxes on the market now, and other ways of attaching them, but I still believe this way is best. The rubber hose completely seals the shaft and log, yet allows for vibration and flexion in the shaft. Stuffing boxes rigidly mounted often wear faster and are more likely to score the shaft because they cannot flex. The tallow-soaked hemp packing traditionally used is great, but now there are Teflon packings that may be better. I think traditional packing glands are superior to the new shaft seals because you can repack them anywhere in the world, anytime, with no materials or tools. You can make the packing yourself from old hemp rope and rendered animal fat if necessary.

The shaft log is carefully positioned and aligned in the hole, the lower end is masked off, and epoxy or polyester resin is poured into the surrounding void from above until filled. The log must protrude from the deadwood or sternpost enough (usually 1 inch) to drill and tap holes in it (one from each side) to hold the Cutless bearing shell in place. The latter should fit snugly but easily in the log end and, when in place, be centerpunched for the locating screws. The bearing is removed and very shallow holes (1/8 inch deep) are drilled with a drill point. It is then reinstalled (use an anti-seize compound), and set screws are installed in the tapped holes in the log and into the locating holes in the bearing shell. I use 1/4-inch SAE stainless-steel bolts for set screws, and I grind their points to match the drill-point holes in the bearing shell. After they are gently tightened (don't strip out the fiberglass threads), they are cut off 1/8 inch from the log, vertical slots are cut in the ends with a hacksaw, and a Monel wire is seized around them and the log end so they can neither unscrew nor come out. There are other ways to do this; this happens to be the method I have found best and easiest.

The propeller shaft is installed and carefully lined up for the propeller location, with the Cutless bearing and the stuffing box in place. If the shaft weight seems to depress the stuffing box, block up the shaft to its proper location. Next install the shaft flange, put the coupling in place and sling the engine by chain hoist, crane or tackle in place over the logs. Set the motor mounts in place, and maneuver the engine until the transmission flange meets the coupling. The engine is approximately aligned until the coupling flanges are true to each other. The motor mounts are traced onto the beds, the engine is lifted clear, the beds are drilled and the mounts installed, and the engine is replaced. Alignment is performed by using a feeler gauge around the perimeter of the coupling, with bolts lined up and in place. Tolerances should be within 0.002 inch. Do not use the rubber coupling to compensate for poor alignment: The alignment must be perfect. After tightening the motor mounts, recheck the coupling before tightening the coupling bolts. After the vessel is launched and run in, check the alignment again.

I use stainless-steel alloy shafts, bronze or phenolic shell Cutless bearings and bronze self-feathering Max-Props (Swedish made) for fast sailboats. Two-blade props have considerably more vibration than three blades, but less drag. Proper diameter and pitch are vital for all propellers, and are best computed by a highly experienced professional who is familiar with your engine and hull type.

V-DRIVES

The use of a V-drive allows the engine to be mounted aft of the propeller shaft inner end. The great advantage of this is removing the engine from the cabin and isolating it from the living space, the merits of which have been described earlier. There are many V-drive transmissions on the market today; most engines list them as an option. There are also V-drives that are mounted independently and must couple to the transmission and to the shaft prop.

When ordering an engine, make sure that the V-drive angle and dimensions will fit in your boat. When laying out engine space and shaft log location, be sure to provide access to the stuffing box (underneath transmission or bell housing in most installations).

FUEL TANKS AND SYSTEMS

Fuel tanks are best made of stainless steel or aluminum. Mild steel tanks are sometimes made, sandblasted, Ospho-treated and epoxy-painted outside, but they eventually rust out from the inside due to condensation. Tanks should fit snugly in place, and be blocked so that they cannot move in any direction, including up. I prefer them located between structural bulkheads, with several wood skids beneath so they don't contact the hull, and held in place by wood cleats screwed to the hull and structural bulkheads. I often incorporate a shelf above and cabinet face or cover in front. Fuel tanks should be removable, and an access or cleanout port is desirable, though not essential. All plumbing should enter through the top or near it so that hose or fitting failure cannot drain the tank into the bilge. Tank plumbing and fuel systems will be described in Chapter 27. The areas into which tanks are installed should be thoroughly painted with epoxy, including all cleats and skids, and room should be left behind and under the tanks for air circulation and for water and condensation to escape.

Almost all diesel failures involve the fuel system, specifically the filters. Diesels must have either two filters (one of which is a water separator), or a two-stage filter. Diesel fuel is often dirty, especially when purchased from questionable sources—a problem in Third World countries in particular—and it often contains water and microorganisms. Filters should be large, a separate water separator is best, and both must be serviced frequently. Water condenses faster in a partially empty tank, hence diesel tanks should be kept as full as possible. Dual systems, with switching valves such as described for water-strainer systems, are the ultimate. Vessel stores should include a good stock of filter elements, and containers will be needed for storage of dirty fuel and contaminated water. Do not dump fuel overboard—it is illegal and immoral. All fittings, pipes, hoses, filters and valves should be of high quality and designed for their purpose. Hose and pipe runs should be as short and simple as possible, and sharp turns and high loops should be avoided. Tank fittings will be discussed in Chapter 27.

COOLING SYSTEMS

Virtually all modern marine engines used in yachts are freshwater (or coolant) cooled. The cooling water is in turn cooled by salt water in copper heat exchangers. Hydraulic transmission fluid is typically cooled in the same manner. Direct saltwater cooling is seldom used, though I have restored some old saltwater-cooled gasoline engines that are still in service after a life of 30 or 40 years. Another alternative is the keel cooler, which usually makes use of a pipe loop outside the hull. This method creates some drag and is vulnerable to damage; as a result it is rarely used in yachts today.

In designing a conventional cooling system, use large through-hulls and seacocks, and large-diameter hose with the shortest possible runs and gentlest possible curves. Avoid using more elbows than absolutely necessary. Use the largest and best water strainer you can afford, particularly if you plan to travel waterways and rivers, and mount it where you can easily service it. I often use the modern plastic ones, though the old bronze and glass ones are excellent; they are just too expensive now. An ideal system would use two water strainers installed "in parallel" with shut-off or Y-valves for both sides. When one is switched off for cleaning, the parallel strainer is ready to go. The raw-water intake should have a grill over it, if possible.

EXHAUST SYSTEMS

Today the vast majority of yachts use "wet" exhaust systems, employing water-lift-type mufflers. Raw (salt) water is introduced into the engine exhaust system just after the exhaust manifold via a mixing elbow. These elbows can be purchased or made by welding a pipe that fits the raw-water hose exiting the heat exchanger at approximately a 45-degree angle into a pipe that threads into the exhaust manifold. The mixed water and exhaust gases are then introduced into a small tank via a pipe the same size as the exhaust pipe; these are connected by a heavy-duty rubber exhaust hose. Another pipe exits the top of the tank and loops high under the deck before dumping the water outside, usually through or near the transom. (See Fig. 25-1.) The exit pipe ends about 1 inch or $1\frac{1}{2}$ inches above the bottom of the tank; exiting exhaust gases lift the water at the pipe mouth and carry it out. The water cools the pipes and

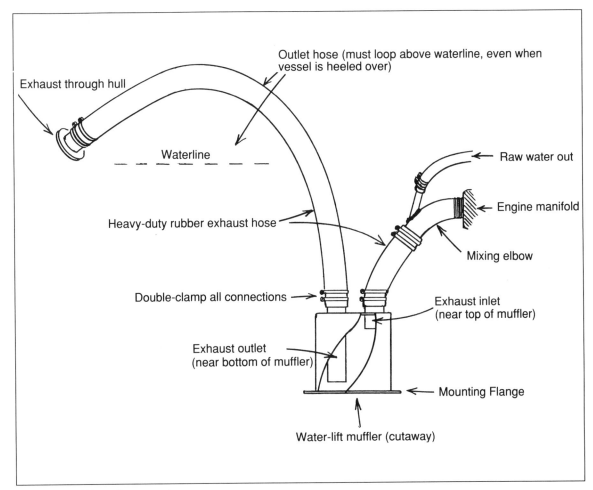

Figure 25-1. Wet exhaust system.

muffles engine noise. The mufflers, commonly called Aqualifts, can be bought or made. I have seen several laid up by hand of fiberglass using cans and pipe and even cardboard for molds, and I have made several from PVC pipe and sheet. Ten-inch or 12-inch heavy-wall (schedule 40) pipe is cut into a 12-inch length; this pipe can most easily be found where municipal waterlines or sewers are being installed by trading a six-pack of beer for a piece of scrap. Sheet PVC is bought (3/8 inch thick) from a plastics supplier. A PVC slip connector the size of the inlet/outlet pipe is cut into 1/2-inch rings, and two tight holes the size of the pipe used are cut into

what will be the top of the muffler. One pipe is installed such that the pipe ends 1 inch inside the muffler; the other pipe extends $10^{1}/_{2}$ inches inside. Both stick up about 6 inches above the top. Rings are cemented on the inlet/outlet pipes on both sides of the top plate for each pipe: Use PVC cleaner first and use heavy-duty PVC cement liberally, wiping away the excess with a clean rag. The top and bottom plates are cemented on the top and bottom of the large pipe (all cuts must be very accurate as PVC cement is not gap-filling). Then holes for small, flat-head stainless-steel machine screws (3/4-inch #12) are drilled, tapped and the screws installed around the perimeter of both top and bottom plates, about 1 inch on center. The bottom plate may be left square to facilitate mounting, and the top plate is usually cut round to a diameter slightly larger than the pipe.

There should be no elbows in the exhaust system after the mixing elbow unless absolutely unavoidable. Large-radius sweeps in galvanized pipe may be purchased from plumbing or electrical warehouses. Heavy-duty rubber exhaust hose connects all components in the exhaust system. The exhaust through-hull is normally a purchased item, and is often the only one in the boat with no seacock. For this reason, and to avoid back pressure, it should be located above the waterline in such a place that it would very rarely be immersed in seawater.

In engines installed low in a vessel, it is very important that there be a high loop in the raw-water output between the final heat exchanger and the mixing elbow. Obviously the raw-water intake must always be immersed, and the whole cooling system is frequently below the vessel waterline. Without the loop, water can seep past the raw-water pump and circulate through the whole system (hoses and heat exchangers) until it dumps into the mixing elbow. It then fills the exhaust system until it overflows into the exhaust manifold and enters whichever pistons have open exhaust valves, seeping past the piston rings and into the crankcase. When the engine is turned over, the pistons are compressed against water, often resulting in bent connecting rods. In vessels where the engine is mostly above the waterline and located on the vessel's centerline, such as some of those under a bridge deck using a V-drive, this is not a concern.

The other type of exhaust system, commonly used in commercial vessels, is the "dry stack." This involves running a steel exhaust pipe through a heat-insulating deck fitting straight up into the air. A freestanding muffler is typically installed above deck. The pipe is often supported somewhere near the top, or in several places, if the run is long. Sometimes the system is encapsulated by an enclosure, sometimes it is lagged with asbestos or fiberglass cloth and Arabol (latex rubber lagging compound); more often it is left exposed with a cage or steel shroud around it to prevent injury to the crew. Raw cooling water is simply dumped through a through-hull. Occasionally, sailboats with metal masts will use an exhaust pipe inside an aft mast passing right through the mast-head truck and exiting well aloft; I installed such a system in the sailing commercial fishing boat *Prelude*, using a stainless-steel exhaust pipe inside a steel mizzenmast made from a light pole. Often a dry stack will angle aft at its end to keep rainwater out. The principal advantage to the dry stack is getting the exhaust gases away from the crew on a vessel where the engine is frequently used; conversely, the disadvantage of the wet exhaust is that there will always be times when the crew will have to breath noxious diesel exhaust fumes.

MACHINERY AND SYSTEMS

Hydraulic systems have great utility on very large yachts and commercial vessels. Their pumps should be securely mounted and driven by two or more belts. Pulley ratios need to be engineered to provide the number of pump r.p.m.s specified by the manufacturer. Excessively long belts tend to slap and wear. Hydraulic lines and fittings should be of high quality and carefully installed. Give some thought to where the fluid will end up in event of a leak or rupture; I once had an accident that ruined a young woman's clothing and she never forgave me. Where lines pass through living quarters, I prefer to run them through large-diameter PVC pipe, sealing the pipes where they pass through bulkheads to maintain watertight integrity. Hydraulics can be used to drive bow thrusters, windlasses, winches and net- or trap-hauling power blocks. Some commercial vessels employ jack-shafts—belt-driven auxiliary power shafts mounted alongside the engine in pillar blocks or Dodge bearings and driven by three or four belts by the engine. Jack-shafts are used where there are too many auxiliary devices to be mounted and driven by the crankshaft pulley, such as alternators, generators, refrigeration pumps, air-conditioning compressors, air compressors and hydraulic pumps. The advantage is that the front of the engine is unencumbered and exposed, and all the auxiliary machinery is isolated and neatly laid out where it can easily be inspected and serviced. Large, sophisticated yachts can also benefit from jack-shafts.

FIRE PREVENTION

The Halon systems now available are considered to be the best fire extinguishers, but the gases they release must be isolated from people, as inhalation can be fatal. Conventional fire extinguishers should be of high quality and rated for all types of fires. They must be replaced or recharged when their gauges indicate low pressure. U.S. Coast Guard regulations govern the number and type of fire extinguishers to be carried on all vessels; failure to conform to these results in a citation or even termination of a voyage.

Real fire prevention consists of careful layout of all components that present a fire hazard. Proper installation procedures, good maintenance and a high state of awareness and conscientious behavior of everyone on board are keys to success. Often simple rules involving fuel handling, stove use, lamps and smoking, as well as shutting down propane and some electrical systems when not in use, are helpful. Certain materials, including PVC, give off highly toxic fumes when ignited; these should be thoughtfully used and installed, anticipating worst case scenarios. I keep an army-surplus gas mask in a scuttle box where I can quickly don it if I have to go below deck to fight a fire, and I can locate all my fire extinguishers in the dark. It is good practice to teach this to every crew member when they first come on board, as well as the location of life preservers, rafts, medical supplies, and other safety equipment.

CHAPTER 26
BALLAST

Kinds/ Inside Ballast/ Outside Ballast/
Casting Lead/ Trim Ballast

KINDS

Today yacht ballast is almost always lead or iron; other heavy items placed low in a hull, such as the engine, machinery, tankage, stores and cargo, may function as ballast. True cargo vessels typically have no ballast, which would diminish cargo capacity, and hence are loaded with anything available to make passages when not carrying cargo. Many vessels carried stone as ballast, which could be discarded and replaced with cargo. Yachts have often carried concrete as ballast, and even today it is not uncommon to use concrete to fill the gaps between iron, steel or lead ballast.

External ballast is most desirable because it provides the lowest center of ballast, and hence lowers the vessel's overall center of gravity and gives her a stronger righting moment. This translates into greater stiffness and reduces the possibility and severity of a knockdown. Extreme shoal-bodied hulls frequently are not self-righting without external lead ballast, usually in the form of a shoe several inches thick and quite long—in some cases the length of the keel. A good example of this is the *Meadow Lark* by L. Francis Herreshoff, a short-gaff ketch with nearly equal-height masts 33 feet long with a draft of 15 inches. *Meadow Lark* was fitted with a 2,500-pound lead shoe, which was integrated into her keel, and also carried 1,000 pounds of internal ballast. I believe that a combination of inside and outside ballast is the most versatile. The vessels of Commodore Ralph Munroe, often called Presto boats after his first model of that type, had all internal ballast. These hulls were shoal-bodied but were deep enough for the necessary ballast to make many of them self-righting. Many of their hulls had very flaring topsides and a deep, hard turn of the bilge. Their bottoms were narrow and almost flat; they are vaguely reminiscent of a rounded dory hull, one of the most seaworthy of all small craft. The commodore's hulls were lightly built, carried light spars, and as a result had a high ballast ratio. His reasoning for all inside ballast was low cost, simplicity and the ability to remove the ballast. If caught in a really severe storm at this is to place two lazarette hatches just inside (above) the vessel's capsize waterline. Because beamy sterns have excellent flotation, this allows the hatches to be placed far enough apart to allow total access to lazarette space.

In frameless cold-molded construction, lazarette and forepeak compartments are large and open. To take advantage of this, the hatches should be large enough to climb in and out of and allow you to pull through your largest sail bag. Steps made of wood blocks epoxied and fastened to the forward bulkhead are simple and convenient in the forepeak. Chain lockers can be installed with drop-boards between cleats or using plywood partial bulkheads. A pump will be useful in the forepeak to remove water coming in with the anchor rodes. Pegs or hooks set in the sheer clamp are great for hanging spare lines. All seams should receive fillets and the lockers should be epoxy-painted. Lazarettes can be pumped (usually only after cleaning) with a long-bodied piston pump. As mentioned earlier, I use the contemporary plastic version to pump both lazarette and cockpit seat/lockers.

Chain and ground tackle should be stored as low as possible in the forepeak; avoid stowing heavy gear in the lazarette. I usually use the latter for life jackets, fenders, line, fishing tackle and perhaps some snorkling gear.

These compartments can be vented by partially opening their hatches in harbor. If not hinged, there should be secure tie-downs. Permanent venting, other than near-centerline Dorade boxes, is not worth the compromise to the flotation value of the compartments. The forepeak may be vented through deck pipes, which could be plugged with rags in the worst possible kinds of emergencies. Many mechanical windlasses have built-in chain/deck pipe collars to feed chain

below as it comes over the gypsy. Some of these have lids, but they don't seal unless you remove the chain and turn the lid. I often use PVC pipe for deck pipes and chain fairleads to bins below. PVC "slip" connectors can be cut into rings, and the rings can be glued one above and one below the deck, the whole unit being bedded in rubber compound. This will be further described in Chapter 31. A PVC end cap can be modified as a lid.

CARGO HOLD AND HATCHES

Cargo holds in these vessels make excellent use of space, as there are no obstructions of any kind and no bilge water to damage cargo. In many cases there are no floors, cabin sole or ceilings and cargo is loaded right to the hull. Tie-downs are made by installing eyebolts through bulkheads and/or by bolting wood cleats (2 x 4s or larger) to bulkheads, hull and centerboard with holes drilled in them for lashings. Skids, pallets and blocking may be used. The hold and deck may be insulated with spray foam over epoxy paint, or foam sheets may be contact-cemented directly to the painted hull and under-deck surfaces. The foam may be covered with plywood, fabric and epoxy or may even be fiberglassed with glass cloth and polyester resin. If uninsulated, the cargo hold should be covered with fabric and epoxy for abrasion resistance. Plumbing and wiring passing through hold bulkheads should be high out of harm's way, and the holes should be rubber-sealed. Wiring should be protected in PVC raceways.

Hatch coamings are typically large in section, and I prefer to make them in two laminates. First, 2 x 4s or 2 x 6s are scribed to the deck curve above the hatch carlins and deck beams, cut and fit into place so that their inner faces align with the inner faces of the beams and carlins below. The corners may be sea, his boats could literally be driven ashore up a beach, with centerboard full-up. After the blow, ballast was removed, the vessel inspected and floated, and ballast again loaded. This was, of course, a worst case scenario; but he was serious. The commodore's boats have greatly influenced my own designs of shoal-draft vessels, which I believe are more suited to cruising than deep-draft vessels. (It depends, finally, where you want to cruise.)

Ballast should be concentrated as close to the center, both fore and aft and athwartships, as possible. Large concentrations of ballast in the ends of a vessel will contribute to pitching, as the ballast will promote a pendulum effect, and to sluggish turning.

Iron was the poor man's choice for ballast throughout most of this century, but because it is difficult for the amateur to cast, it is more rarely used now for outside ballast. Lead can be cast easily by melting it in old cast-iron bathtubs and pouring it into wood or earth molds.

INSIDE BALLAST

In keel vessels, lead or iron is purchased in any form available that will fit down into the keel. Cold-molded construction allows internal ballast to be loaded deeper and much more efficiently than ever before possible in a wooden vessel, to an extent that it is often more practical than and nearly as effective as outside ballast.

The areas where ballast is to be placed should be covered with fabric and epoxy and epoxy-painted to protect the wood from abrasion and moisture absorption. Ballast may be lead, iron, steel, concrete or combinations thereof. If pigs are stacked in the bilge, fit them tightly and compactly between floors so that they cannot shift. Firmly secure dogs, floors or plywood panels over them so that in the unlikely event of the vessel being turned

completely upside-down, the ballast will remain in place.

If ballast removal is unimportant, any form of metal scrap may be used, such as boiler punchings, window sash weights (now becoming too valuable), battery lead, ingots, rebar cut-offs and used bullets or lead shot. A common procedure to ensure that the ballast cannot get out is to drill two or more holes through the floor timbers and install pieces of rebar through them fore and aft. Seal the holes with epoxy before installing the rebar. Next, apply a skim coat of Portland cement over the fabric-epoxy–covered bilges, about 1/8 inch to 1/4 inch thick. Before it sets up, the ballast (usually small pieces) is loaded with batches of concrete having small aggregate (no stones). Tamp the mixture with a 2 x 4, driving out air bubbles and forcing the metal down low. The top is finished with a concrete layer roughly 1/2 inch thick, contoured concave and sloping down to the sump or bilge pickup area. This surface is finished smooth with a sponge (texture will be needed to provide tooth for paint). Take care that water coming down the hull cannot be trapped, particularly between ballast and bilge, but will be channeled to the sump instead. Burlap or canvas is laid over the finished surface and kept moist for as long as is convenient, up to 30 days (the ideal curing time for concrete). The cured concrete is then allowed to dry thoroughly; fans will aid in this. After drying, vacuum the surface, clean and paint it with three coats of white or light gray epoxy paint. Another option is to cover the concrete with fabric and epoxy firmly bonded to the hull.

In flat-floored vessels with no bilge or hollow keel, such as *Sarah* and *Teresa*, shallow boxes are built along the sides of the centerboard trunk, using the stack-laminated trunk logs for their inboard sides. Ends often employ at least one bulkhead; the outboard side

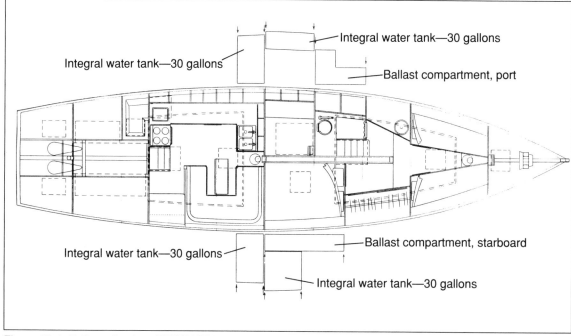

Figure 26-1. Ballast plan for a TERRAPIN 45.

and other end are often 2 x 4s glued and heavily screwed into the hull bottom (don't let the screw ends get closer than 1/4 inch to the outer hull skin). The insides of the boxes are covered with fabric and epoxy, and epoxy-painted. Ballast, typically lead pigs, is stacked in as densely as possible, and 3/4-inch plywood lids are screwed down over a thin sponge-rubber gasket. Both sides of the lid are epoxy-painted. (See Fig. 26-1.)

OUTSIDE BALLAST

Very large ballast keels are best left to professionals; the temperatures, times, hazards and forces involved in casting are dramatic. Since lead poured in stages doesn't bond to itself well, castings should be made in one pour. There are very real dangers involved: Trapped moisture in either the lead or the mold can cause a violent explosion of molten lead, molds can break, pipes and valves can fail, and the fumes are toxic.

Small keels and shoes, however, can be poured by the amateur. Molds are made of dry wood, securely nailed together and gusseted from outside and bridged across the top. Bolt holes and countersinking holes can be ceramic or wood dowels. An old cast-iron bathtub is blocked up (use steel) high enough so a large, roaring fire can be built under it. Don't block with concrete blocks—they can explode. An elbow, pipe and large gate valve lead from the tub drain to the center of the mold. A large, hot charcoal fire must be built under the pipe and valve or the lead will congeal as soon as it starts down the drain. All of the lead is loaded into the tub gently (tossing pigs will crack the tub). The fire is built—a large amount of wood, preferably hard and dry, will be needed. It may take as many as four to six hours to melt one or two tons of lead. Full protective clothing, respirators and eye protection should be worn, and workers should stay upwind at all times. The tub enamel will crack and blow off; it and other impurities will rise to the surface of the molten lead and can be skimmed off. It is important to wait for the lead to be completely molten and very hot before attempting the pour. It is also advisable to talk to other people who have poured lead to familiarize yourself with the potential problems. Where the pipe enters the mold, station a worker with a wood baffle to keep molten lead from overshooting the mold, and to help distribute it to the ends.

Keel shoes may be poured in sections, either butted together or having simple lapped scarfs. If a fin keel must be poured in stages, rebar can be planted in the first pour to hold the layers together, but the rebar should not be allowed to contact saltwater—a difficult thing to ensure. Holes can easily be drilled in lead, and it can be cut and chiseled if need be. When grinding it, keep its toxicity in mind, and wear protective clothing.

OTHER BALLAST

Frequently trim ballast must be used, either to bring one end of the vessel down or one side down. This ballast is usually lead, and it should be firmly secured. Water ballast is occasionally used in some vessels, although it has limited effect because of the rather neutral weight of water (it amounts to partially swamping the vessel in controlled areas). One advantage is that water, and fuel for that matter, can be transferred to different locations by means of pumps between tanks. This has obvious advantages for long-distance ocean racers, commercial fishing vessels and cargo carriers.

CHAPTER 27
PLUMBING

Through-Hull Fittings and Seacocks/ Tank Fittings, Fills, Vents and Pickups/ Pumps, Manifolds, Accumulators, Fixtures and Sumps/ Heads and Holding Tanks/ Water Filters/ Pipefitting/ Water Heaters/ Showers and Tubs

THROUGH-HULL FITTINGS AND SEACOCKS

Bronze has long been considered the only proper material for through-hull fittings, to the degree that most insurance companies won't insure vessels without them. In cold-molded construction, I find bronze to be the wrong material: It has very different rates of expansion and contraction from wood, fabric and epoxy; it conducts heat and cold into the hull, causing condensation; and it places metal in the water unnecessarily, creating one more element to deal with in the galvanic cell.

I find high-quality Delrin through-hull fittings to be ideally suited for modern construction of most kinds, including steel, aluminum and ferrocement, as well as cold-molded wood. These fittings are extremely strong, flexible, abrasion-resistant, don't transmit heat and cold rapidly, expand and contract more in harmony with the hull (or at least are soft enough that it doesn't matter), and are galvanically neutral.

The traditional backup block is also unnecessary when Delrin fittings are used in the cold-molded construction described in this book. The hull skin is so thick and strong that reinforcement around through-hulls is redundant. The only possible exception to this might be when a through-hull passes through a laminated plywood topside below the waterline. In this one instance, a 1/2-inch or 3/4-inch plywood backup block could be considered an option, particularly if the fitting is in an engine compartment.

Considerable thought must be given to the layout of through hulls. They should be close to the devices they serve, suitably located in relation to the waterline and they should be isolated in certain instances (galley saltwater intakes should be lower and as far as possible from head discharges). Inside the vessel, they should be located where they can be quickly and easily reached, and their numbers should be minimized. On rare occasion this last can involve multiple uses of fittings, such as combining sink and shower discharges, and engine and refrigeration raw-water intakes.

Installation involves drilling an oversize hole with a hole saw, epoxy-sealing the hole, and bedding the fitting thoroughly in rubber compound. Do not overtighten the fitting, but do take care to eliminate air voids. Apply rubber to both the hole and the fitting. Inside the hull, there should be a seacock, unless the fitting is a discharge or engine exhaust mounted well above the waterline.

I strongly recommend the new, all-plastic PVC seacocks, which have Teflon or Delrin ball valves and no metal parts. Never use gate valves or globe valves for seacocks—these are totally unsuitable and compromise the safety of the vessel. The plastic valves exist in harmony with the Delrin through-hulls, never corrode or jam, are very economical, easy to operate and have no galvanic properties. One caution: They shouldn't be stressed or overtightened during installation; use Teflon tape to seal the threads, one layer thick only and provide deep thread penetration without bottoming out the fitting (see Fig. 27-1). In many cases, particularly where fittings are located in the thick hull bottom, the flange nut is not used, and the seacock is tightened directly against the hull. This increases the strength and integrity of the installation by eliminating a component and shortening the leverage arm that can be placed on the sea-cock.

Plumbing to the seacock may be PVC schedule 40 pipe, or threaded hose barb to rubber or plastic hose. Fittings below the waterline should receive two all-stainless hose clamps at each hose termination. Avoid metal pipe and fittings until in close proximity to the engine or machinery; then bronze should be used.

In engine room installations, through-hulls and seacocks should be located in protected areas where exposure to heavy shifting objects, extreme temperatures and fire is as lim-ited as possible. In some cases, it may be worthwhile to create safety barriers around the fittings.

When insuring a vessel, copy the relevant parts of this chapter, including Figure 27-1, and present them to your insurance company; I have in several cases demonstrated to underwriters the superior value of these installation techniques and materials over the previously accepted ones.

TANK FITTINGS, FILLS, VENTS AND PICKUPS

As previously mentioned, tank fittings, particularly in fuel tanks, should be located on or near the top, to prevent draining into the hull in the event of a failure. Instead of sight tubes for fuel tanks, I keep log entries of when tanks are filled, how much, what tank is being used and engine hours to monitor fuel use. I prefer to use oversize threaded flanges welded to the tank top, but in thick-walled aluminum tanks (1/4 inch or more), holes can simply be drilled and tapped. I use PVC threaded fittings in the flanges or holes of aluminum tanks. In the case of integral water tanks, I typically use $1\frac{1}{2}$-inch or 2-inch fills, and 1/2-inch or 3/4-inch vents and drains. The fittings are usually PVC male-thread-to-slip. Vents and drains are typically all PVC schedule 40 pipe; fills are PVC schedule 40 pipe up to the deck fitting, where I often use a short piece of plastic or rubber hose to compensate for expansion and contraction, and to facilitate installation and removal of the deck fitting and its alignment to both deck and pipe. In the past, I have terminated the fill pipe top at another PVC male-thread-to-slip fitting screwed directly to the deck fill and later found leaks through the deck due to misalignment or expansion. PVC pipe may be easily bent into gentle shapes by heating it carefully over a stove burner. Constantly ro-

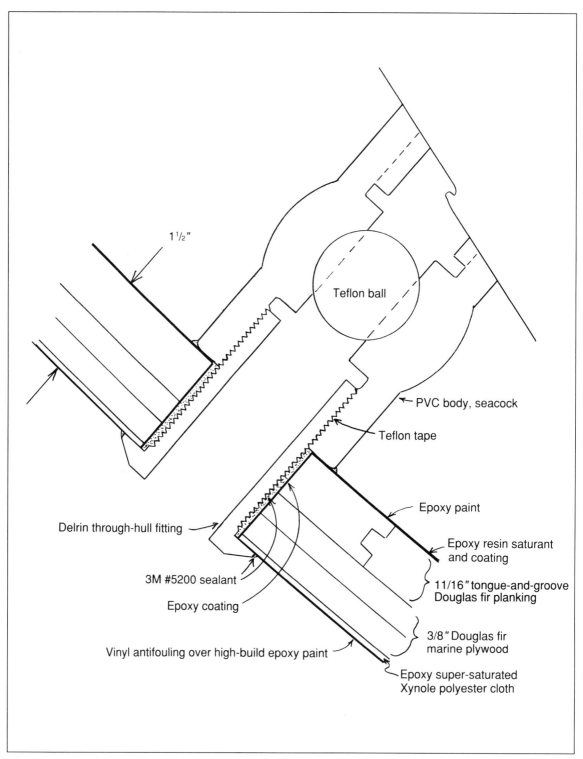

1½"

Teflon ball

PVC body, seacock

Teflon tape

Epoxy paint

Epoxy resin saturant and coating

Delrin through-hull fitting

11/16" tongue-and-groove Douglas fir planking

3M #5200 sealant

Epoxy coating

3/8" Douglas fir marine plywood

Vinyl antifouling over high-build epoxy paint

Epoxy super-saturated Xynole polyester cloth

Figure 27-1. Delrin through-hull installation (EXUMA Series) using a PVC seacock.

tate the section where the bend is desired, several inches from the flame. Do not scorch the pipe; the fumes are poisonous. When the pipe becomes soft and rubbery, bend it to the desired shape without collapsing it, and wipe it with a wet cloth to fix the shape.

Deck fills can be bronze, stainless steel, aluminum or plastic. The hole should be drilled oversize, epoxy-sealed and the fitting bedded in rubber compound, coating the screws, fitting and hole, and taking care to eliminate air voids. Give some thought to deck fill location, both above and below deck. Water fills placed outboard are convenient for rainwater collection; after the decks are rinsed, towels or anything are used to block the scuppers and the fills are opened. In some cases, trim is installed around coach roofs, which are easier to keep clean, and permanent pipe nipples installed in their low corners are connected to hoses, which lead to the fills.

Fuel-tank fittings may be plastic or bronze, though bronze must not come in contact with aluminum, or severe corrosion will occur. I generally use hose barb fittings with rubber fuel hose, clamped with all-stainless hose clamps. For fuel lines, it is important that air not be allowed into the system, or it may stall the engine and necessitate bleeding the fuel system. I typically make fills and vents with PVC pipe in the same manner as for water tanks, except that I use a short section of rubber hose near the tank fittings to facilitate removal. Often hose can be purchased in sizes that fit over PVC pipe, simplifying the system by eliminating slip-to-thread adapters and hose barbs. Valves used in fuel systems should be designed and made for that purpose—usually the bronze conic type.

Vents should end higher than the fill whenever possible. They should turn and open down so that dirt and water cannot enter. Coarse bronze wool loosely tucked into the opening will keep insects out. I usually make vents entirely of PVC or CPVC pipe and brace them to something on deck (a cabin trunk) out of harm's way, but where they are audible and visible to the fill location. Tanks should be very carefully topped up, both to avoid possible damage to the tank due to head pressure, and to avoid forcing liquid up the vent and onto the deck; it is best that no liquid sit in the fill pipe after topping up. Vents should be near the vessel's centerline and at least 6 inches above deck so that when decks are awash or in a knock-down, salt water cannot enter.

Tank pickups should enter from the top, to avoid the tank draining its contents in the event of a plumbing failure. The pickup pipe should end about 1 inch above the lowest point in the tank bottom. Use PVC or CPVC pipe and slip-connectors cut into rings to fix the pipe in position in integral tanks. For metal tanks, I modify slip-to-male-thread PVC fittings by drilling through them and cementing the PVC pickup pipe through the fitting. Or I simply weld a metal pickup pipe in place in the tank top from both sides before welding the top in place.

PUMPS, MANIFOLDS, ACCUMULATORS, FIXTURES AND SUMPS

Choose the size of electric pumps according to plumbing distance and number of turns (the longer and more, the bigger the pump required), height of lift and number of fixtures supplied. The belt driven Par-Jabsco pumps with 3/4-inch fittings have become the standard of the industry, and can supply more than 10 years of troublefree service if not abused. Stock rebuilding kits and spare motors for long voyages.

Complex vessels with several tanks may require a manifold to facilitate switching from different sources (tanks and watermakers) to pumps. The manifold is a gang of incoming and outgoing valves interconnected in a line or loop. I make these with PVC elbows, tees and pipe, using PVC valves (the same as seacocks). These valves come with either slip-to-slip bodies or threaded bodies; the only problem with the former is that in the unlikely event of failure, they would have to be cut out of the system. (See Photo 27-1.)

An accumulator, or water-ballast tank, should always be installed on the pressure side of each pump. This tank is entered and exited from the bottom, and is mostly filled with trapped air compressed by the pump; this prevents the pump from rapidly starting and stopping during low-flow usage, thereby greatly prolonging motor and pressure switch life. The air is eventually dissolved into the water, and the tanks must be drained periodically. Tanks can be made of PVC pipe or purchased.

It is a good practice to install a PVC valve in the supply line just before each filter or fixture, to facilitate repair or changing elements without shutting down the system.

Quality and type of fixtures vary in the extreme; you should buy the best you can find or afford. I often use single-faucet "bar" spigots (available from plumbing suppliers) in the galley and lavatory; the high spigots are convenient for filling containers. I use plastic showerheads, often drilling out the feeder hole inside the swivel body, which is usually too restrictive for low-pressure water systems. Metal showerheads corrode and clog.

Smaller vessels with tanks fairly close to fixtures can use manual hand or foot pumps, of which I prefer the latter. Fixtures then become simply spigots, of which I prefer the high, swivel type.

Sinks for marine use are compact, often lack fixture-mounting holes and are deeper of body than household sinks, hence they are

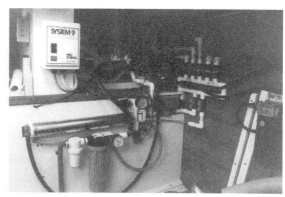

Photo 27-1. *Lucayan*'s water manifold is near the right side of this photo. The water-maker at the left converts salt water to fresh water.

very expensive. They are often made of a higher grade of stainless steel and have heavier construction. Bar sinks are one alternative; check your local plumbing supplier for alternatives to marine suppliers. The more fittings and fixtures you purchase through him, the more money you will save. I prefer to mount sinks under countertops if possible, so that water doesn't stand outside around the rim, always needing to be sponged up. This involves finishing the plywood counter edge with plastic laminate (heat it to go around tight corners), epoxy resin, or by making metal or sculpted wood countertops that drain into the sinks (the latter is my preference). Small round sinks, which are readily available from plumbing suppliers, are commonly used in lavatories.

Many yachts use sumps for waste water, accumulating quantities of water before either discharging it overboard or into holding tanks. Sumps are often small plastic tanks, often open on top, with a float switch and electric sump pump nearby. These are common for showers because the pan is below the waterline. I prefer to make a fairly large shower pan with a teak grate over it. When 3 gallons or so accumulate in the pan, your feet start to get wet, telling you that you are using too much water. The water is pumped out with a manual or electric pump, either switched manually or with a float switch. There is a description of integral sumps at the end of this chapter.

Electric bilge pumps are commonly of the Par-Jabsco type mentioned, but often of the next model below, having 1/2-inch fittings and no belt drive. These are mounted anywhere convenient, and are activated by a float switch with a manual override. They are fed by strum boxes in the lowest bilge area. Simple strum boxes are made from large PVC tees and caps and pipe: The tee is $1^1/_2$ inches by 1/2 inch or 3/4 inch reduced with a 1/2-inch bushing; short pipe nipples (6 inches) are added with caps at the ends, and numerous 3/16-inch holes are drilled in the bottom of the assembled unit. One-half-inch PVC pipe leads to the pump and is connected by rubber or plastic hose.

HEADS AND HOLDING TANKS

The marine toilet is undoubtedly the most repulsive and problematic device on any boat. My personal conviction is that human toilet functions should not be performed inside the living space of a boat, and certainly the discharges should not be stored there. I subscribe to the bucket-and-chuck-it method, or straight-over-the-side procedures; unfortunately, these are both at times impractical, illegal or antisocial. Ideally, an isolated small compartment with a comfortable wooden seat and a plastic bucket can be incorporated in a yacht; the bucket is partially filled with seawater, slid under the seat, used, removed, tossed, rinsed and put back under the seat.

Typically (for people who cannot cope with these procedures), a marine toilet is installed. Plumbing should be as simple and direct as possible, and a loop on the discharge side that will stay above the water on any angle of heel (being close to the centerline helps) should be installed, usually with a siphon break (a small rubber valve on top of the loop to let in air). I avoid heads with electric pumps and macerators; they require more maintenance and energy.

The discharge through-hull is ideally located just below the waterline; a common problem is for toilet paper to clog at or near the opening, so quick access to clearing it is necessary. Locating the discharge slightly above the waterline is, again, antisocial. The intake through-hull should be well below the waterline on any normal angle of heel.

In the U.S. today, U.S.C.G. regulations and laws require the use of sewage-holding tanks on all vessels within defined areas, particularly enclosed and partially enclosed bodies of water, where pollution has become a problem. The tanks may be discharged at sea or pumped out by land-based facilities in marinas. Marine toilets often employ a Y-valve so that the head may be discharged overboard at sea or into the holding tank. To discharge at sea, the tank must either be located above the waterline and fitted with a drain and through-hull, or have a pump system, both of which are undesirable.

There is no easy solution to the holding tank dilemma. Pump-out stations are often hard to find or nonexistent in many places. I suspect some pump-out stations just straight-pipe the waste back into the harbor—after charging the boatowner a suitable transfer fee. Some vessels have heads that chemically treat sewage and discharge it overboard. Many vessels have holding tank systems installed but never use them. Others use portable toilets and empty them ashore. I'm happy with the bucket!

WATER FILTERS

Water tanks tend to accumulate particles,

minerals, bacteria and possibly other growth. Water quality varies extremely, particularly among arid islands and Third World countries. A good practice is to add one-half capful of pure chlorine bleach (such as Clorox) per 50 gallons of water to kill potentially harmful bacteria. After this treatment, drinking water may be decanted into open-mouth jars and allowed to sit for an hour or so, during which time the chlorine will evaporate. I do this even if I employ filters, because bacteria may pass through them.

In the galley, I install charcoal filters. These are the plastic-bodied, removable-cartridge type, which come in two sizes, and are available from local plumbing-supply houses. They are installed after the pump, just before the fixture. The large size is best, as it offers less resistance to the pump and doesn't need to be serviced as often. The charcoal removes virtually all flavor from the water, including the chlorine taste, and removes all particles; it does not, however, remove bacteria. Be sure to carry several filter cartridges on voyages; dirty water causes them to plug up rapidly, creating pump back pressure.

PIPEFITTING

PVC pipe ends should be cut square, the burrs filed or sanded off, cleaned with PVC cleaner, and both pipe and fitting coated with PVC cement. The pipe is immediately inserted with a 90-degree rotation and held in place for 10 seconds; excess cement is wiped away with a clean rag. Threaded PVC pipe should receive one layer of Teflon tape, and the fittings should not be overtightened.

Bronze fittings are assembled either with Teflon tape or plumber's pipe dope and made very tight, taking care not to damage the soft pipe.

Galvanized steel pipe and fittings are normally used only in exhaust systems. They should be assembled very tightly using an anti-seize compound. The pipes are frequently lagged with either asbestos or fiberglass tape with either pipe cement or Arabol (latex rubber lagging compound), particularly when not water-cooled.

Elbows should be minimized; 45-degree turns are better than 90-degree turns, and sweeps are better than elbows. PVC pipe can be bent by careful heating as described earlier. Bronze and steel are bent with a jig or hickey; but large steel pipe must be bent in a hydraulic jig or purchased in sweeps (commonly used in the electrical industry and suitable for exhaust systems).

WATER HEATERS

The solar water heater can simply be a day tank, painted a dark color, with a large flat surface exposed to the sun. It is usually mounted on a coach roof, and gravity-feeds a shower, lavatory or galley sink. The tank is completely filled each morning, so that water contacts the heated surface. A fill is installed on top through which you may add kettle-heated water for showers in the event of no sun; otherwise, the tank is usually filled by hand or electric pump from a bilge tank. Tanks may be metal or PVC, but aluminum painted flat black works best. Usually no mixing with cold water is necessary; in the unlikely event that the water may become too hot, a wet white towel is placed over the tank to prevent overheating.

Electric hot-water heaters made for the marine industry are usually of slightly higher quality than for land homes, but they still rust out after several years and are poorly insulated with fiberglass. They are usually 120 volts or 220 volts, and must be used with a generator. Care must be taken that the tanks are kept full, or the elements may burn out, steam might be generated or even an explosion can occur. These tanks are usually supplied with a heat exchanger that circulates hot water from the diesel engine; these normally work so well that the electric element becomes a backup system. Plumbing distances for the heat exchanger should be minimal and use as few elbows as possible to minimize back pressure on the diesel water pump.

Propane water heaters are dangerous and should be located where gases can be scuppered overboard in case the flame goes out. They are often cheaply made and should be isolated from water and salt spray. All fuel-burning devices deplete oxygen from the air and therefore constitute a health hazard in enclosed living areas.

Manifold heaters often consist of copper coils tightly wrapped around the engine exhaust manifold. Water may be used on demand, providing inconsistent temperature (affected by usage rate), or stored in an insulated tank by filling it very slowly while the engine is being run.

SHOWERS AND TUBS

Showers are often incorporated into head areas on small yachts. The truth that people don't realize until they become involved with the cruising lifestyle is that these showers are so awkward to use that they rarely if ever are. Most cruising people, at least in warm weather, use solar showers on deck, consisting of black plastic bags hung in the rigging. Serious washing is often done in the sea, and the solar shower is used for a fresh water rinse. Real land-type showers are entirely too extravagant for the small yacht. They use copious amounts of water, electricity (pumping), energy (to heat water) and space. Hence I think either really practical showers should be built (especially if the vessel is to be lived aboard in cold climates), or there should be

virtually no shower at all. As I mentioned earlier, conventional showerheads may need to be drilled out to provide reasonable water flow. Hand-held units have become popular, also—some types include an overhead fitting to which they may be affixed. I have already described the shower pan that acts as a sump and uses a teak grating. Showers need to be in the part of the yacht with the most headroom if a tall person is to wash his or her hair while standing on a grate under a showerhead; in a keel hull this is no problem, but in a flat-floored vessel, such as *Teresa*, it involves being close to the centerline amidships. The alternative, and a very good one, is to have a bench in the shower, and use a hand-held showerhead while sitting.

Bathtubs are normally reserved for very large yachts, but they can be eminently practical on smaller vessels, if made small, by just adding a very high curb to a large shower pan. Their primary use is for bathing small children and for washing clothes, though both these functions are better performed in a plastic tub on deck in favorable weather. All shower pans and tubs should incorporate bulkheads and strong curbs (or partial bulkheads). If a drain fitting is to be used, as in keel yachts where there is a bilge and possibly a sump under the pan, the hole is drilled and recessed so that the drain flange will be lower than the pan bottom. Fabric and epoxy are laid up in the pan and drain depression; the hole is epoxy-coated. Corners are filleted, and the pan is epoxy-painted. If the pan will have no grate, or if it will double as a tub, a non-skid area is masked off and made in the same manner as the deck non-skid areas described in Chapter 24. The drain is installed with rubber compound or plumber's putty; I prefer to use fittings with a stainless-steel or brass screen—the kind made from domed plate stock with holes drilled in it. This keeps debris out of the sump and pump. Pans that are formed right on the hull are drained by a curved PVC pipe laid into the lowest edge of the pan with several holes drilled along its bottom edge. The end is plugged.

A sump box may be made integral to the hull in keel vessels by covering with fabric and epoxy the space between two floor timbers. A float switch and strum box are installed, leading to a pump. A partial top on the sump, open in the middle to allow cleaning, will stop water from slopping over the sides in rough weather. Limber holes between the floors are fitted with PVC pipes to transfer bilge water under the sump; the fabric and epoxy covering goes over them after they are filleted to hull and keel. The strum box may be of the PVC type described earlier in this chapter.

CHAPTER 28
ELECTRICITY

Raceways/ Electrical Fixtures/ Wiring and Junctions/
Distribution Panels/ Generation Systems/ Grounds,
Bonding and Zinc Anodes

Ideally, all electricity in a boat should be free-floating, or isolated from the hull, salt water, machinery, metal fittings, bilge water and other electricity. (Twelve-volt systems, 110/220-volt systems, lightning grounds and bonding systems should all be isolated, with no grounds commonly shared.)

There is much disagreement today about the efficacy of bonding systems. My own experiences have placed me in the "opposed" camp. I strongly believe that there is no longer any reason to place large numbers of metal objects in the water, due largely to the invention of Delrin through-hull fittings, all-plastic seacocks, rubber couplings and radios that no longer need large ground plates.

Metals are rated in a "Galvanic Series," which range from "most noble," or protected metals, to "least noble," or corrodable metals. In an electrolyte, the metals ionize as electricity flows between them, destroying the less noble of the metals involved. Where common marine metals are involved, their relationship is as follows:

Most Noble
Monel
Stainless steel (passivated)
Silicon bronze
Copper (and bottom paint with copper oxides)
Lead
Stainless steel (active or common)
Cast iron
Mild steel
Aluminum
Zinc
Least Noble

There is obviously a dramatic difference between passivated and active stainless steel. Passivation is an electrochemical process. If you live near an industrial area, it may be possible to take your stainless-steel hardware and fittings and have them passivated and polished; this will greatly increase their life-span, particularly for fittings that will be installed underwater.

There are two basic processes that cause underwater deterioration of metal fittings: galvanic and electrolytic corrosion. Galvanic corrosion occurs when two or more dissimilar metals are placed in an *electrolyte* (battery acid is an electrolyte). Because seawater is a natural electrolyte, immersion of dissimilar metals causes very slow molecular transfer between them, at greater expense to the less noble metals. At this level there is a very poor electrical connection between the metals; the circuit is incomplete and hence molecular exchange is slow. Joining the immersed metals with an electrical wire creates a circuit between the metals on one side and through the salt water electrolyte on the other. Now there exists a "galvanic corrosion cell," or simple battery, basically short-circuited by the wire. Molecular exchange is now accelerated. By installing a sacrificial zinc anode (a least noble metal) on the less noble of the metals, the very ignoble zinc will deteriorate instead of the slightly more noble metal to which it is attached.

Electrolysis (electrolytic corrosion) occurs when an electrical current is introduced into the system. Electricity greatly increases electron flow, accelerating the molecular exchange between the dissimilar metals. The most dramatic example of this occurs when a boat with a water-grounded electrical system lies in a body of salt water that is electrically "hot," such as when a 110-volt extension cord is immersed in water nearby. Let's speculate that your boat is correctly grounded, such that its 110-volt system is oriented the same as land-based electrical grounds, and that the boat is properly plugged into the marina electrical system. Then let's speculate that the immersed wire has a deep nick, cut or weather crack in its insulation, such that the hot, or ungrounded, wire is exposed to salt water. There is now a 110-volt electroplating tank established between your vessel's underwater metal fittings and the local power plant. All underwater metals can, in this instance, literally turn into porous, sponge-like remnants of their former dense constitutions, frequently resulting in the sinking of your boat. This has been known to happen in as little as 48 hours. If the wires involved happen to be 220-volt, the process is even more dramatic.

Bonding consists of interconnecting all metal fittings on a vessel (except, perhaps, for those on deck), with copper wire, and placing sacrificial zinc anodes in the system. As long as all connections are good (low voltages need excellent connections), no breaks in the wires occur, and zincs are properly installed and maintained, the system protects all metals involved. In reality, the bare copper wires and the metals to which they are connected corrode in the salt water and air of the bilges, resulting in broken wires and poor connections. This often leads to various dissimilar metals being interconnected, frequently without the benefit of zincs, causing accelerated galvanic corrosion of the components involved. Traditional wood and metal boats are further damaged by this current flow: Wood soaked in salt water is structurally damaged, appearing rotten, punky and discolored; metal is electrolytically corroded, often becoming so thin or porous that no structural integrity remains. The evidence continues to mount against bonding. The choice is yours.

ELECTRICITY RACEWAYS

When practical, raceways are ideal for carrying wires to different parts of the boat. I use PVC schedule 40 pipe, placed behind ceilings or cabinetry, or placed high under the cabin sole when necessary. Pipe diameter should be as large as possible so extra wires can be installed at a later time. Where the pipe passes through structural and/or watertight bulkheads, it should be thoroughly rubber sealed. Access is gained by installing tees in the pipe, or by leaving the ends open.

Small, open yachts with very simple electrical systems (lamps, radios and navigation lights), often don't need raceways; the few wires involved may be run under the sheer clamps or under the deck and coachroofs through holes drilled at the tops of the beams. In some cases slots are cut in the beam tops and epoxy-sealed before laying the deck, taking care to keep fasteners out of them. Exposed wiring of this kind should be kept away from bilges and exterior metal fittings, and should be of good quality. The type commonly used today is insulated stranded copper grouped in twos or threes in a plastic jacket.

ELECTRICAL FIXTURES

Electrical fixtures on boats should be of better quality than their household cousins. Twelve-volt electricity operates at a higher current than 110 volts, and therefore requires larger wire and better connections. Metals used in fixture housings should be brass, bronze, copper or stainless steel; often connection terminals are tin or lead/tin coated to ensure good conduct and limited corrosion. Fixtures should be located where they will be protected from salt spray, if possible, and where they won't endanger crew members' heads. The common flat, round overhead lights that used to be distributed by Perko are made in the Far East, and some are of very good quality; the same is true of reading lights and fluorescent strip lights.

Radios and navigation equipment are highly specialized and require close scrutiny and personal choices. Their location is determined by their function and convenience, but they should be protected from salt spray and excessive moisture unless they are designed to be located outside.

I have found 12-volt electric fans to be disappointing: Most of them don't move enough

air to be worthwhile, are noisy and consume too much electricity. Properly located skylights with wind scoops work much better.

Sophisticated vessels with AC electrical systems often have many of the appliances of a land-based household. All I want to say about them is that electricity is much more critical and dangerous in boats than on land, and these items should be of high quality, internally grounded or double-grounded, and wired very carefully, particularly as to grounding. They should also be isolated from metal fittings, plumbing (use PVC for appliances that use water), bilges and other electrical devices.

WIRING AND JUNCTIONS

Wire connections to terminal fittings are ideally soldered. Today this is rarely done except for large heavy-current carriers such as battery cables and feeds to large motors in winches, windlasses, starter motors, bow thrusters and so on. A good solder joint requires clean wire and fittings. Both items to be joined are tinned: heated until solder easily flows around them; then joined together, more solder added and the joint held motionless until cool. The fitting is then sealed with electrical tape or heat-shrink tubing, a plastic that contracts when heated.

Today most marine terminals are of the automotive type—tin-coated copper covered with plastic sleeves. These are placed over the stripped wire ends and crimped in place with a special tool. They tend to loosen and corrode, but are highly accepted nonetheless. I have found that their life span and reliability can improve by coating them thoroughly with rubber sealants made for the purpose, such as Scotch-Kote.

As stated above, 12-volt wire carries higher current loads than higher voltage wiring for the same amount of power or energy consumed (P=IE, or power in watts = current in amps times voltage). Wire sizes therefore should be larger, as higher current at a fixed resistance requires greater voltage, and since voltage is fixed, resistance must be decreased by using larger wire (R=E/I, or resistance in ohms = voltage divided by current in amps). In general, #12 stranded copper wire is used for circuits containing several lights or radios. Motors and some navigational equipment (such as radar) may require larger wire. The longer the distance the electricity must travel, the larger the wire must be, as the cumulative resistance causes a voltage drop (or must be overcome by an increase in current, which consumes more power). Besides depleting batteries more rapidly, voltage drop can damage electric motors.

Wire runs should be as direct and short as possible, but ample amounts of wire should be left at the ends to allow connections to be made comfortably. In 12-volt DC, black is ground and white is hot. In 110-volt AC, green is ground, white is neutral, and black is hot. In 220-volt AC, green is ground, and black and white (or red) are both hot (each is 110-volts 180 degrees out of phase, so they push and pull each other).

Terminal blocks are used for junctions where wires supply fixtures or devices, where circuits branch out or where it is convenient to terminate a wire and start another (for example, where masthead running light wires are interconnected near the base of the mast). These are usually hard black plastic (such as Bakelite) with banks of tin-coated copper strips, each containing two screws, with raised ridges between the strips. The terminal blocks should be located away from water, spray and moving objects that might damage or short-circuit them. After junctions are made, the screws and connectors are best coated with a liquid rubber such as Scotch-Kote.

DISTRIBUTION PANELS

Twelve-volt panels frequently consist of a stiff, nonmetallic sheet in which circuit breakers and/or switches are installed. Fuses and fuse blocks have become less popular except when used in-line as backups or to protect specific devices, such as radios.

Typically, the panel is installed in a hinged frame to provide access to the wiring behind. Circuit breakers and switches are carefully laid out, including spares for future needs. Labeling is often done by sending the drilled panel to an engraver, having custom-engraved panels added to the face of the electric panel alongside the breakers and switches, or using stock labels. Custom and stock panels are listed in most comprehensive marine catalogs. Wiring should be very neatly laid out and bundled to the hinged side of the panel-back to facilitate its opening. I coat all connections with Scotch-Kote or an equivalent. Panels should be installed away from spray and high moisture areas; where this is unavoidable, such as in cockpits or other exterior switch panel locations, cover the switch panel with a clear plastic lens. These are often hinged or set to slide in teak tracks. Twelve-volt panels are set in cabinet faces or boxes; it is essential that nothing be able to interfere with the exposed wiring and devices behind the panel. Frequently one or more voltmeters are installed to monitor battery levels.

One-hundred-and-ten-volt panels may be conventional steel or plastic electrical boxes or custom made similarly to 12-volt panels. The greater danger of the higher voltage in terms of shock, fire and electrolysis must be considered. Most 110-volt wiring should start and terminate in enclosed containers well away from water and metal structures, plumbing and uninvolved machinery. Plastic boxes, commonly used today by residential electricians, adapt well to boats. Grounds must be carefully installed and isolated. Shore-power fittings should be designed and made for that purpose, even though they are very expensive. Three-wire, twist-lock extension-cord terminals and pigtails rated for the proper amperage of the systems involved should be used. Interior wiring should be stranded copper marine wiring, no lighter than #14, and that should be limited to lights only. Install wiring in PVC conduit and raceways; never run it exposed in bilges or other high-moisture areas. Panels also need to be carefully located away from moisture and protected from damage by stored objects or machinery.

All panels should be accessible during emergencies, and placed away from stoves, appliances or machinery that constitutes a potential fire hazard.

GENERATION SYSTEMS

Twelve-volt generators are now virtually obsolete, having been replaced by alternators, which are more efficient, particularly at low r.p.m.s. I prefer alternators with internal regulation systems and an output of at least 55 amps. There are many kinds and sizes now available, most automotive and some made specifically for marine application. They are typically activated after the diesel engine is running, often by a wire from an oil pressure switch. Alternators should be very firmly mounted, and have the correct size pulleys and belts. Carry replacement belts in a spares kit. Isolation devices ensure that electricity can't transfer from batteries back to alternators when they are not running. Often, on large and complex vessels, two alternators are installed to charge separate battery banks; occasionally the engine-starting batteries and alternator are isolated from the ship's electricity. Switches, used in the event that something fails, allow either system to back up the other. Banks or even individual batteries generally are wired to heavy-duty battery switches.

Large and/or sophisticated vessels often have diesel power plants for generating 110/220-volt AC. These are treated much like the main engine in that they must be mounted on beds and have fuel systems, saltwater cooling systems, exhaust systems and ventilation. An alternative is to employ a belt-driven AC generator beside the main diesel, but both voltage and frequency (alternating current in the U.S. is 60 cycles per second) will depend on engine r.p.m.s. An optimum speed will have to be chosen at which the diesel will be run when generating, and appropriate pulleys will have to be used to provide the desired generator speed.

Solar panels are popular on small yachts with modest electrical use. They require as much direct sunlight as possible, and put out very small amounts of charging current unless there are large numbers of them, but they are a good way to help maintain batteries in areas and times of good sunlight.

Solar-cell technology becomes more sophisticated and efficient each year, and the newest marine-use cells are made into flexible panels, often with grommets in their corners. These can be moved for optimum sunlight exposure, can conform to the curves of decks and coach roofs, and may even be incorporated into bimini tops and awnings. A panel of this type measuring 2 feet by 4 feet puts out an average of 2.15 amps at 14 volts or 33 watts (peak power) at 12 volts, and retails for about $480 (1989). Regulators required with the panel retail for about $110. Wind generators are also popular on yachts today, and produce more generating current than solar panels on small yachts. They can, however, be awkward, noisy and even dangerous, and require daily attention. There are many kinds on the market, and considerable research is justified before choosing one.

Towed generating systems are rare, but at least one wind generator has an adaption system, and there is at least one other being marketed. These systems consist of a propeller and shaft towed behind a moving sailboat in similar manner to a taff-log spinner, spinning a small alternator on board. I have seen one homemade system consisting of an outboard motor prop on a stainless-steel shaft connected by stiff braided line to an alternator in a plywood box.

Shaft-driven systems are similar to towing systems, but use the vessel's free-wheeling propeller and shaft to drive an alternator via belt drive between the two.

High-quality watertight connectors should be used for generator systems and devices used on deck or for devices that must be frequently disconnected. Wiring passing through the deck should be carefully sealed with a rubber compound, after epoxy-coating the drilled hole. Location should be as protected from harm as possible.

Inverters have become very efficient for converting 12-volt DC to 110-volt AC, as compared to the old, inefficient motor generator converters. They are solid state with transformers. But there is still some power loss in conversion, and it should be remembered that many household-type appliances and devices use more electricity than may be prudent for a vessel's batteries. Most inverters also have a relatively low ability to supply current; for example, a right-angle-drive circular saw cannot be used with most inverters. They should be installed where their heat can be dissipated, out of areas subject to salt spray and high moisture.

GROUNDS, BONDING AND
ZINC ANODES

Terminal blocks for ground wires, usually solid copper with screws mounted on a plastic or phenolic block, are mounted in electric panel cabinets or boxes, both for 12-volt and 110-volt systems. Scotch-Kote applied over the terminal and connections will retard corrosion.

Some navigational equipment needs to be grounded to a metal plate in direct contact with seawater, but these grounds don't necessarily include the ship's electrical system. If they do, check to see if the on/off switch for the device disconnects the ground, and if it does not, I strongly suggest that a ground-disconnect switch be placed between that device and the electrical panel to prevent stray-current leakage to ground. Another application for ground-disconnects is for windlasses with grounded casings that can connect your battery's ground to the sea via your anchor chain.

Lightning protection systems are essential, even for all-wood vessels. Lightning will strike mastheads and travel down wiring of any kind, destroying everything it encounters on its way to the sea, including radios, batteries and the hull beneath. I have personally experienced this, and the results are awesome, expensive and sometimes fatal. A lightning rod should be installed for each mast, preferably higher than any other metal; it can be simply a stiff, large-gauge copper wire. It should make the straightest possible path to the bottom of the boat, where it is connected to a lightning ground plate via a bronze bolt through the hull. The hole should be epoxy-sealed and the bolt bedded in a liquid rubber compound such as 3M #5200. The ground plate may be about 1 square foot of sheet copper (see Photo 28-1) glued or nailed to the hull with bronze ring-shank nails. If nails are used, they should be bedded in liquid rubber to prevent water violating the hull skin along the nail holes. The whole may be covered with bottom paint. Inside the hull, an eye connector should be soldered to the end of the wire (the wire should ideally be unbroken right to the mast head with no junctions) and sandwiched tightly between two nuts on the bolt through the hull, then coated with Scotch-Kote or an equivalent. There are also porous bronze grounding blocks on the market that are suitable for this purpose; I don't use them because they are very expensive and stand proud of the hull. I also suspect that, at the high voltages of lightning, the larger "apparent" surface area of a copper plate will be more effective than the larger "actual" water contact surface area of the porous block grounds. Number 6 bare or insulated solid copper ground wire is suitable for the lightning ground system. It is my firm belief that standing rigging should not be employed in any way in lightning ground systems.

If a bonding system is to be employed, the wire should be #6 or heavier solid copper, eye fittings should be soldered, bolted and coated at every junction, the wire should be insulated or at least isolated as much as possible from the hull skin and stored objects, and more than one zinc anode should be included in the system. Zincs should be located away from each other, usually one near each end of the vessel and/or one on each side. Holes for bolts through the hull to zincs should be epoxy-sealed and the bolts bedded in rubber compound. Stainless steel is a poor conductor of electricity, hence bronze should

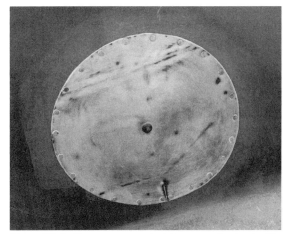

Photo 28-1. Copper ground plates are attached with 3M #5200 and bronze ring-shank nails. The bronze carriage bolt at the center connects a lightning ground.

be used; typically, threaded rod is employed so that nuts and washers can be placed snugly against the hull, and another set of nuts and washers used both to attach the bonding wire inside the hull and the zinc anode outside. Zincs must be inspected and replaced as necessary, and the entire bonding system should be inspected regularly.

As previously stated, I am against bonding systems, and prefer to isolate and individually protect underwater metals. Zinc anodes used to protect isolated fittings outside the hull, such as prop shafts, rudder gudgeons and bobstay chainplates, should be firmly bolted in place and must not be painted. They should be inspected and tightened regularly.

CHAPTER 29
HEAT AND REFRIGERATION

Stoves and Fuel/ Refrigeration Systems

STOVES AND FUEL

Stoves used strictly for heat in boats have traditionally burned wood, coal or charcoal. These work as well today as ever and are still in common use. Cast iron is a better stove material than steel, which burns out rapidly in a marine environment. The burning of driftwood should be minimized because the salt and heat together cause accelerated corrosion of the stove interior and chimney system.

Single-wall steel chimneys radiate much more heat than double-wall chimneys, which is an advantage considering the short run of boat chimneys and the fact that most of the heat generated is lost to the atmosphere. This can be improved by angling the chimney, running a nearly horizontal pipe for several feet and adding corrugated pipe radiators or other devices designed to extract heat from the pipe. The disadvantages of single-wall chimneys are the danger of burns to crew members and heat damage to items in close proximity. Any flammable objects will need to be shielded with tile, sheet metal, asbestos or some other insulative/reflective material. Two types of deck irons still commonly in use are the cone type and dish type, which holds water to cool the iron. Both are generally cast iron and are through-bolted to the deck. The hole cut for the iron is much larger than the pipe, which fits inside the iron. The exterior pipe fits down over the iron and is held in place by two or three sheet-metal screws (self-tapping panhead) in holes in the iron. Often the above-deck pipe section is removed during warm weather and a canvas cover placed on the deck iron. The hole cut through the deck should be sealed with epoxy paint and fitted with an insulative ring, usually copper or aluminum folded over asbestos paper and nailed in place in the hole. Asbestos paper may be placed between the deck iron and the deck; no bedding will then be needed. If the iron is bedded, a heat-resistant compound such as silicone should be used.

The areas around the stove also must be protected from heat damage. In vessels where weight is not a consideration, tile is the most attractive material, though copper sheet (often over asbestos paper) can also be very attractive. I don't know of an alternative to asbestos paper, which is a known carcinogen. When I use it, I wear a respirator and totally seal the material by folding sheet-metal covering over its edges and nailing these to the bulkhead, sole or overhead it is protecting. Silicone used along the perimeters before nailing should completely eliminate any health hazard, but a less hazardous alternative would be welcome. Asbestos can be bought in thick paper rolls, in cloth (perhaps the most hazardous) and in pressed rigid sheets. Today it may be difficult for nonprofessionals to purchase.

Photo 29-1 shows the Sears Roebuck solid-fuel stove in the aft cabin of *Fishers Hornpipe*. The firebox on the left holds coal, charcoal or wood. The stove pipe makes a 4-foot horizontal run under the deck before exiting through a deck iron. The drying rack on the right is excellent for drying and warming gloves and socks for the deck watch; the photo was taken during a fall passage from New England to the Caribbean. Beneath and behind the stove is copper sheet over asbestos paper.

The spontaneous-combustion hazard of large quantities of stored coal or charcoal allowed to become wet or moist is well known. This rarely poses a problem on yachts, but it cannot be ignored. Combustible materials should be stored in dry, ventilated compartments. Coal is a dirty fuel, and it will blacken decks and sails. Stovepipes should be carefully located and sails kept covered when not being used.

Diesel stoves are in wide use in northern climes both for heat and cooking, as are multifuel stoves, which in many ways are ideal for large or commercial vessels used in cold weather. My favorite is the kind with a propane range, oven and broiler on one side and a coal/wood firebox on the other. These stoves are heavily constructed of cast-iron tops and thick sheet-metal sides. Others of this type burn diesel fuel and are generally kept burning for long times. Diesel stinks up the galley and cabin, but is economical and effective.

Other liquid fuels include alcohol and kerosene. I personally find these stoves obnoxious to live with and agree with Donald Street, who once said he would rather risk a quick death with propane than a slow living death with any other fuel, or words to that effect.

Compressed natural gas (CNG) has become a recent alternative to propane. The principal advantage to this fuel is that it is lighter than air and hence is less likely to accumulate and explode. Different jets are required in these stoves, and different bottle fittings are used. Outside of the U.S., CNG may be hard or impossible to find, and I would suggest that vessels cruising out of the U.S. carry propane gas jets, bottles and fittings (the jets are easy to change).

Again, all fuels consume oxygen during combustion, and ventilation must be provided both for the stove and the people. Seri-

Photo 29-1. *Fishers Hornpipe*'s Sears Roebuck solid-fuel stove does double duty drying shoes, socks and gloves for the crew during a fall passage from New England to the Caribbean, while keeping the coffee hot. Note homemade fiddle rails.

ous injury or death may result from oxygen deprivation or carbon-monoxide poisoning. Poorly designed or installed stoves may also pose health hazards if smoke or noxious gases are allowed to leak into occupied cabins.

REFRIGERATION SYSTEMS

Ice has already been discussed elsewhere in this work and is my obvious preference. The alternatives are electric (12-volt and 110-volt), mechanical and propane systems.

I have found 12-volt systems to be unsatisfactory; they consume very large amounts of electricity, must run nearly constantly and rarely make ice. I doubt solar cells or small wind generators can keep up with any but very small ones, hence the diesel or a generator must be run on a daily or near daily basis to maintain refrigeration. One-hundred-and-ten-volt systems include household refrigerators and mini-refrigerators; they run off either inverters or diesel generators, which run constantly or twice a day for long periods. When run off inverters, the batteries must typically be charged by the diesel once a day.

The most common refrigeration now is mechanical, consisting of an automotive-type compressor belt-driven off the diesel. Through a plethora of plumbing and equipment, cold plates in refigeration and freezer compartments are charged by Freon expanding from liquid to gas. The systems are expensive and complex, often including 110-volt backup compressors to handle the frequent problems of the mechanical system. I may have been wrong earlier when I called the marine toilet the most repulsive and problematic device on the boat. Mechanical refrigeration systems are by far the biggest cause of canceled and disrupted cruises and repair expenses. No matter how careful and thorough the installation, no matter how expensive the components, the damn things break down frequently. They also require running the diesel several hours twice a day. As I mentioned earlier, anchoring in an idyllic location next to some cruiser pumping diesel fumes and noise in your face while you are trying to share a bottle of good, cheap French wine and an exquisite tropical sunset with your love is much worse than dealing with the ubiquitous Mexican disco on the beach at 2 a.m.

In the event that you go with this system anyway, which most people do, make the boxes in the same manner as the compartments described in Chapter 22. There are various do-it-yourself books available and component suppliers, but I suggest you have the installation done by an experienced, reputable local professional who will swear on his mother's grave to fly immediately into whatever godforsaken corner of the planet you happen to be in when your refrigeration breaks down—which will probably be no further than the first available port. In any case, you can always rip out the massive, bulky cold plates and get some ice.

Propane refrigerators work by convection instead of compression, and tend to be efficient. They are, unfortunately, household appliances cheaply made of sheet metal and poorly insulated. They also need to be upright, at least most of the time, for convection to work. This might require gimbaling, but is only likely to present a problem on long passages on one tack. There is also the danger of having on board a device that is constantly burning propane. As mentioned earlier, the refrigerator should be mounted in a vented, scuppered compartment, preferably somewhat isolated from living spaces, yet away from high moisture and salt spray. Because of these problems, propane refrigeration is rarely seen on boats, even though it might, in many ways, be the answer everyone is seeking. I think vessels with pilot houses might benefit from the installation of a modest propane refrigerator, carefully vented and scuppered onto the deck or into the cockpit in such a way that salt water would be unlikely to enter the compartment. Gimbaling is probably unnecessary as most vessels don't roll and pitch through the vertical plane enough to disrupt convection.

CHAPTER 30
MASTS AND BOOMS

Selecting Lumber/ Layout and Cutting/ Scarfs/ Layup Jigs/ Cores/ Internal Wiring/ Radar-Reflecting Foil/ Layup/ Mast Shaping, Fairing, Sanding, Sealing and Finishing/ Mast Collars/ Booms and Jaws

Virtually all masts and booms today are aluminum, which does not excite me. Aluminum is inflexible, corrodes rapidly and severely in the proximity of bronze and stainless steel (which is always present), is very expensive and makes a horrible racket when halyards slap against it. Aluminum masts that are made strong and durable enough to be worthwhile on a long-distance cruising or working vessel are no longer particularly lightweight and are expensive.

Wood masts also have deserved a lot of their bad press, in that the box-section spruce masts so popular in the first half of this century weren't very good. On the other hand, well-made laminated Douglas fir masts seem to last indefinitely. I recently sailed on the Alden schooner *When And If*, and her original 1934 laminated Douglas fir masts were perfect. The hollow-laminated Douglas fir mast for the 1929 Alden sloop *Imagine*, which I restored in the early 1980s, was also in nearly perfect condition even after years of

neglect. Solid wood masts of spruce or Douglas fir are excellent, but have become virtually obsolete because of unavailability, weight and curing time necessary for a high-quality spar (one year per inch of diameter for the tree with bark intact). Slender masts common to the modern marconi rig tend to be too flexible when made solid, and larger-diameter, stiffer spars are too heavy except for the gaff rig, which is approaching extinction in new construction. Rot is also a hazard at fittings, partners and step, though this is strictly a design/construction/maintenance problem, and generally involves spruce more than fir.

Multihull designer/builder Chris White made hollow-laminated hexagonal Douglas fir masts for his cruising trimaran *Juniper* some years ago, and I have found this to be an excellent concept for mast construction in cruising and working sailboats. Hence the construction techniques I am going to describe will be for hollow hexagonal Douglas fir and epoxy masts. They are excellent for both freestanding and stayed rigs, are strong, stiff and durable, and can be made reasonably light. Hexagonal construction also provides the easiest layout and construction. (See Fig. 30-1.)

SELECTING LUMBER

Douglas fir mast lumber should be clear heartwood having vertical or diagonal grain (quartersawn), and should be air-dried if possible. For vessels with masts over 9 inches in diameter and 40 feet in height, the stock should be 2 inches or more thick in the rough, and should finish out to about $1^7/8$ inches or more. The grain should be long, straight and even; pitch should not be flowing, and the planks should be straight, without twist or warp. Density should be medium, and grain size should not be overly large, as in some of the reforested, "forced" trees.

This will be the most exotic wood in the boat, and consequently the most expensive. The lumber for *Sarah*'s masts, purchased

Photo 30-1. Mast lumber for *Sarah* is clear, air-dried Douglas fir heartwood with vertical grain, the best on Planet Earth!

from McEwan Lumber in Delray Beach and Miami, cost $2,500 in 1984 (See Photo 30-1). It made two 11-inch–diameter (at the partners), 50-foot freestanding masts of ultimate quality and durability. With maintenance (paint), they can be expected to last several lifetimes.

Kiln-dried wood may have to be used; the longer it has been stored the better, because it will slowly reabsorb moisture. The finished mast will be epoxy-sealed both inside and out, so the threat that rot normally poses to kiln-dried wood is greatly reduced.

For smaller spars, conventional $1^1/2$-inch lumberyard stock may be used, still in clear heartwood, quartersawn. Mast-quality spruce may also be used—I prefer fir for its grain-crushing resistance, flexibility, rot resistance and high strength. I have seen so many soft, punky, rotten spruce masts that I don't use it; I find fir to be much more durable. It also holds fasteners, fittings and rigging hardware better than spruce, and has much better chafe and wear resistance. I find that these qualities more than compensate for the increase in weight, which may be partially compensated for by decreasing the wall section. This is made possible by fir's higher strength. However, the use of epoxy coatings with spruce may greatly improve its performance in certain applications (such as for high-aspect

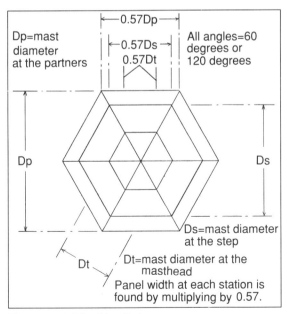

Dp=mast diameter at the partners

0.57Dp
0.57Ds
0.57Dt

All angles=60 degrees or 120 degrees

Dp

Ds

Ds=mast diameter at the step

Dt

Dt=mast diameter at the masthead
Panel width at each station is found by multiplying by 0.57.

Figure 30-1. The friendly hexagon.

multipaneled marconi rigs); I have yet to try it.

Mast lumber should be purchased in the longest lengths possible, usually 20 footers. Careful thought should be given to how the panel segments will be laid out on the stock, and where the scarfs will lie (keep in mind the extra length the scarfs will use). Typically, two panel segments can come from one 12-inch plank by cutting one from one side and one from the other, taking advantage of the 60-degree side bevels of the mast panels to gain additional face widths on opposite sides of the plank.

LAYOUT AND CUTTING

A 50-foot mast is laid out in six panels, each running the full height of the mast and constructed of three segments scarfed together. A taper schedule is laid out on plywood or paper; this is a lofting, and comes from the plans (see Fig. 30-2). Some architects include mast size information; if your plans do not (often sailplans have very inaccurately drawn masts), you will have to figure it out or get help. Skene's *Elements of Yacht Design* has some useful information on mast diameter and taper, as does Chapelle's *Yacht*

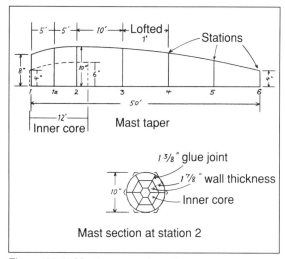

Figure 30-2. Mast taper and section.

Designing and Planning. The only problem is that both works are pre-epoxy, don't deal at all with truly contemporary mast types (such as wing masts) and don't specifically discuss hexagonal-section masts rounded on the outside. Mast taper is a function of mast type, height, rig, number and layout of stays, shrouds, spreaders and so on.

I loft masts into stations every 10 feet, but the lofting is contracted 10 to 1, or laid out with each 10-foot length drawn as 1 foot. Thus a 50-foot mast, having six stations, will be lofted in 5 feet. Station height equals mast diameter at that station. I usually add an extra station at the mast partners, as that will normally be the location of maximum mast diameter, even though the mast may be cylindrical or untapered for the distance between it and the next station aloft. Figure 30-2 shows a 10-inch–diameter freestanding mast 50 feet tall with an extra station (labeled 1a) at 5 feet from the step. This station is lofted 6 inches from the first station, and represents the partners, below which the mast tapers to an 8-inch diameter at the step. The mast above Station 2 tapers to 4 inches at the head. Note that mast diameter is calculated to the flat portions, or centers of each panel of the hexagon, as the finished mast will be rounded to this dimension.

Masts with oval or elliptical sections are laid up with proportionately wider side sections. (See Fig. 30-3.) Some mast design sections may need slight modification (or thicker planks) to provide adequate glue joint dimensions.

Because the masts are rounded after layup, wall or plank thickness determines glue joint size in conjunction with mast diameter. The planks used for a mast of 12-inch diameter must be at least 2 inches thick dressed; for an 11-inch mast, $1^7/_8$ inches; for a 10-inch mast, $1^3/_4$ inches; for a 9-inch mast, $1^5/_8$ inches; for an 8-inch mast, $1^1/_2$ inches, etc. For lofty marconi rigs requiring lightweight spars, the above dimensions may be reduced by 1/8 inch and the insides of the finished panels may be backed out, or cut hollow (concave). The mechanics of this will be difficult. Without a special tool (such as a round-blade power plane), I would make a series of sawcuts varying in depth from shallow near the panel inside edges to deep at the center. The material between the cuts would have to be broken out and the surface chiseled smooth with a large gouge or body grinder. Care must be taken not to diminish the glue joint surfaces. You can see that this process greatly increases the labor cost of the mast. The weight savings might be around 10 percent to 15 percent, and stiffness and strength would decrease only very slightly.

As mast taper changes, the panel width changes proportionately. Panel width may be figured as 0.57 times the finished mast diameter. Hence panel width at each lofting station is 0.57 of the diameter at that station (or: station height). In our example, this would yield a panel width of 5.7 inches at the partners, which I would cut as $5^3/_4$ inches; 4.56 inches at the step, which I would cut as $4^9/_{16}$ inches and 2.28 inches at the truck (masthead), which I would cut as $2^5/_{16}$ inches. These represent panel widths for stations 1, 1a and 6. Panel widths for stations 2 through 5 are computed the same way, by multiplying each station height by 0.57.

The panel segments (six for the example— there will be two differently laid out panels consisting of three segments each) are laid out on the surfaced planks. In this case, each panel will consist of two 20-foot segments and one 14-foot segment. Two of the segments will lose 12 inches to the 24-inch scarfs, and one segment (the one in the middle) will lose 24 inches to scarfs, or 12 inches at each end. Hence the lineal footage of lumber for each finished panel adds up to 54 feet;

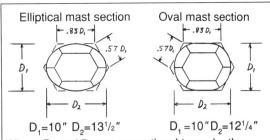

Elliptical mast section   Oval mast section

$D_1 = 10''$ $D_2 = 13^1/_2''$ $D_1 = 10''$ $D_2 = 12^1/_4''$

Where D_1 and D_2 are proportional to each other, only D_1 is lofted for taper. Panel width will still be $0.57 \times D_1$ at each station for the paired panels at the front and back of the mast, but panel width for the sides will use a different multiplier—0.83 in the illustration. To find this multiplier, loft the largest section of the mast (usually at the partners), and divide the measured side panel width by D_1. Use this constant to determine side panel widths for the remaining mast sections by multiplying by D_1 at each respective station.

Figure 30-3. Elliptical and oval mast sections.

a total of 4 feet being lost to scarfs. During layout, stations are laid out to full scale (10 feet apart), keeping in mind that the scarfs overlap and must be added to each panel segment. A centerline is struck with a chalkline, laying out the panel as close as possible to the edge of the plank; the centerline need not be exactly parallel to the wood grain. Panel widths are laid out at each station, and long stiff battens are used to draw the sides. A circular saw with carbide rip blade is set to a 60-degree bevel (this will be read on the saw as 30 degrees), and the panel segment is carefully and accurately cut out. The remaining scrap is turned over, and the largest possible panel is laid out and cut from it.

Obviously, it would be unwise to locate all scarfs in the same places, so I lay out two panel types; one with the short plank at the bottom of the mast, and one with it at the top. During mast assembly, the panels will be alternated to stagger each adjacent scarf. I believe this to be totally adequate, as a 24-inch– long, epoxy-bonded scarf should be equal in strength to a continuous plank, if not stronger.

Photos 30-2 and 30-3. Scarfing jigs make 24-inch scarfs for mast panels. Where the planks are too wide for the circular saw, the cuts are finished with a hand ripsaw.

Photo 30-4. The scarfs are hand-planed true; plywood under the end prevents bending or breaking the feather edge.

Oval or elliptical masts should have a different scarfing pattern, so that the opposite sides are identical. This can be done, for example, by using the short plank in the middle of the side panels, ending up with three different panel layouts.

Before ordering the materials, give thought to exactly what lumber will most economically supply the mast panels. This process may be aided by sketching the sequence described above on paper ahead of time.

SCARFS

After all the panels are cut out, the scarfs are made. I use simple custom-made jigs (see Photos 30-2, 30-3). The jigs are nailed to the end of the plank (one at a time), and a sawcut is made from each side. Wide panels will need to have a final cut made with a hand rip saw, as the circular saw may not cut deep enough. The scarfs are then hand-planed true (see Photo 30-4). The aluminum level behind the worker's left leg in the photo was used to check the flatness of the scarf. The plywood under the panel supports the very tapered scarf end, which otherwise might break or bend away from the plane.

The scarfed segments are then laid up to form the six panels, carefully aligned (the chalklines must form one 50-foot–long straight line), and epoxy-glued. It is essential not to thicken the epoxy too much, as it will lose both tensile strength and penetrability. The scarfs are held in place by screws and clamps; without the screws, the inclined plane effect of the scarfs would slide the segments apart. The screws are removed after curing. Three-quarter-inch plywood panels may be clamped on each side of the scarf, using Visqueen plastic to prevent adhesion during curing. Do not overtighten the clamps and screws; epoxy joints should not be paper thin, and take care not to trap air bubbles. We

Photo 30-5. Scarfs are epoxied and held in place with screws, which are removed after curing.

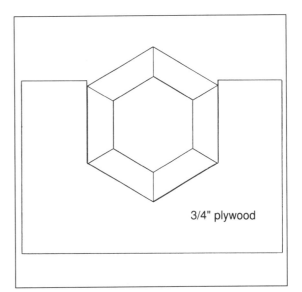

3/4" plywood

Figure 30-4. Mast jig.

Photo 30-6. Mast panels are laid up in open-top jigs, which are clamped to sawhorses anchored to the earth or the floor, and aligned by centerlines visible on the jigs.

scarfed *Teresa*'s panels with screws only, using four pairs (two pairs on each side). We positioned the first pair about 2 inches from the scarf end and the second pair 8 inches from the scarf end. Both scarfs in each panel were laid up together, the panel carefully turned over, and the remaining pairs of screws installed from the other side. In doing it this way, care must be taken to not over-tighten the screws, which would deform the scarf and force out too much epoxy. With this method we were able to scarf all the panels at once (see Photo 30-5). The screws were removed after curing.

After all the scarfs are made, the panel edges are hand-planed to smooth out any sawcut inconsistencies and to fair in the scarfed portions. All curves in the sides must be very gentle, uniform and identical for all panels. A common problem area is at station 1a for vessels with shallow depth of hold: Sometimes the side curve must be faired in a little higher to achieve a gentle shape, making mast diameter slightly undersize at station 1a.

LAYUP JIGS

Masts of this type are so stiff that a conventional spar bench is totally unnecessary. Instead, the mast is laid up in a series of open-topped jigs, one for each lofting station (ex-cluding station 1a). (See Fig. 30-4.) Jigs are not made exactly for Stations 1 and 6, as they would be awkward at the very ends of the mast; rather, the end jigs are made to be placed about 1 foot in from each end. The jigs are designed to fit the spar a little loosely, with perhaps 1/8 inch of play. Photo 30-6 shows the jigs for *Sarah*'s masts. We later eliminated the little tabs at the jig tops, because they got in the way. The jigs form four sides of the hexagonal section at each station,

Photo 30-7. A mast core, at left, will extend below the mast, forming the step tenon. This may be seen protruding from the finished mast at the right which is still in the jigs.

Photo 30-8. A double core for a large freestanding mast is being planed to fit inside the mast, in the jigs at the left.

Photo 30-9. Here the core is being checked for fit during a dry run.

and the sides stick up enough to aid in positioning the last two panels, which are laid up simultaneously. Pencil lines at the centers of each panel laid out on each side of each jig are used to align the jigs; this is done by eye (the pencil lines may be seen in Photo 30-6). Masts that require one side to be totally straight (such as certain marconi rigs requiring a straight mast track) may of course be laid up with the bottoms of all jigs forming a flat, straight line; these masts usually have no taper below decks and are stayed. The flat side should be labeled during all stages of mast shaping and hardware installation. I don't believe this extra trouble is often necessary because an evenly tapered mast can be tuned with rigging to straighten the back side. I mention it because some masts with wide sides may have to be laid out and scarfed with one edge straight, and laid up with the back straight. Sawhorses are set up for each station and staked firmly to the ground (or nailed to the shop floor). Jigs are clamped or stage-nailed to one end of each horse, leaving room beside them for the mast panels.

CORES

An inner core is made to reinforce the first 10 or 12 feet of the mast and to form the tenon for the mast step. This is essentially a mast within the mast, and is laid up of the same quality wood, though vertical grain is not so important. Its dimensions are a little less than those of the inner faces of the mast panels at the same respective lofting stations, and it is made $2^{1}/_{4}$ inches or 3 inches longer to protrude from the bottom, hence forming the tenon (these dimensions correspond to the number of 3/4-inch plywood layers in the mast step). In Photo 30-7, *Teresa*'s second mast core is at the left, and a finished mast with protruding core forming the tenon is in the layup jig on the right. This inner core is epoxied together and clamped with polypropylene rope strops (Spanish windlasses). It is left hexagonal, and must fit comfortably inside the mast (without forcing the mast glue joints open). Cores for very large, freestanding masts may be double-walled to be solid at the step tenon (see Photos 30-8, 30-9). Photo 30-9 shows *Sarah*'s mast being laid up in a dry run to test fits and joints.

INTERNAL WIRING

I typically lay up all wiring on the inside center of one mast panel, stapling the wires in place about every 2 feet. It can never hurt to run too many wires; carefully plan what each mast will need, then allow for future contingencies if possible. Different masts require different lights, and some new masthead navigation light systems use reversed polarity to activate different lights with fewer wires. Antenna wires should be the right size and of high quality, as well as being properly shielded. As stated before, lightning grounds should be #6 solid copper and may be uninsulated.

Where wires exit the mast above decks, the holes should exit down so that water can't enter easily, and they should be epoxy-sealed. After the wires are in place, the hole should be plugged with liquid rubber compound. Below decks, the wires should enter the mast near the deck level if possible, except for the lightning ground, which should enter near the step.

During mast layup, the wired panel is positioned in the bottom of the jigs. A groove or slot is cut in the core so that it will fit over the wiring.

Photo 30-10 shows one of *Teresa*'s panels being wired on layup day. A slow-curing epoxy sealant has been applied under the wires, taking care to keep it off the glue joints. The sealant may also be applied after wiring,

Photo 30-10. On lay-up day, the insides of the panels are epoxy-sealed prior to installing electric wiring, which is stapled in place.

but because it is important to get it under the wires, leaving no dry spots where rot might eventually start, I prefer the former method.

RADAR-REFLECTING FOIL

During mast layup, a roll of aluminum foil may be loosely crumpled inside the top portion of the mast to reflect radar. The wet epoxy sealant will keep it from falling down the mast. Take care that none of the foil is trapped inside the glue joints.

LAYUP

A slightly thinned epoxy sealant is applied to the inner faces of each mast panel immediately prior to final layup. I use a 3-inch roller for this. Avoid getting epoxy on the glue-joint faces (some will be unavoidable—but it must not cure before layup).

The epoxy for layup is slightly thickened with Cabosil, and is mixed in medium-size batches as the work progresses to avoid heat generation and short pot life. Prepare polypropylene rope strops (about one per foot of mast, with some extras) beforehand, and procure as many helpers as can be coerced to show up. Lure these innocent victims to the site by any means available, including large quantities of liquid refreshment (such as cold beer). Provide lots of latex gloves. The thickened epoxy is applied with 3-inch rollers; this must be done very rapidly as the entire mast must be assembled and clamped before the epoxy starts to cure. As usual, all gluing surfaces must be coated.

Lay in the bottom panels first, then each side, then set the core in place (using lots of epoxy, thickened more than for the panel glue joints). Finally, lay in the two top panels simultaneously. Scatter the rope strops along the length of the mast, and tie them in place all along the mast randomly; do not deliberately concentrate on any one area. Place sticks through the strop ends and tightly wind them until the mast panel faces slide into alignment (sometimes a wood mallet will help—one worker should be appointed to this task) and the joints close, oozing epoxy. Add additional strops between the first ones, concentrating on areas where the glue joints seem larger. The area needing the most atten-

Photos 30-11, 12, and 13. Polypropylene rope strops are used as Spanish windlasses to clamp mast panels together. This worker's hands are coated with petroleum jelly to protect them from epoxy, a poor alternative to gloves. The strops are tightened very tightly—damage to corners is cut away during rounding.

Photo 30-14. The initial strops are placed far apart to align the mast panels. A wooden mallet is used where necessary.

Photo 30-15. The whole gang, lured by rumors of copious amounts of liquid refreshment (cold beer) and bikini-clad assistants (who didn't show), crank away with strops. Sticks are tied in place with nylon twine.

tion is typically just below the partners (between station 1 and station 1a). Photos 30-11, 30-12, 30-13 show a strop being tightened. Photo 30-14 shows the first strops going on, and 30-15 shows the whole gang going at it. The strop sticks may be held in place by any method that works—here we used nylon twine. Since then we have come to prefer nailing the stick ends to the mast near the glue joints where the wood will be cut away during rounding later. Photo 30-17 shows *Sarah's* twin 50-foot masts ready to be cleaned up and shaped. Construction time for both spars was less than a week, involving one person for most of the work, with help moving materials and much help during layup.

MAST SHAPING, FAIRING, SANDING, SEALING AND FINISHING

After curing, the strops are removed and the masts are cleaned up and shaped. This is done initially with a power plane, working off all the corners gradually and taking great care not to cut too deeply or to take off material from the flat centers of the panels beyond perhaps one shallow pass to remove epoxy waste. This process is normally done entirely by eye, but templates for the mast loft stations may be made by drawing and cutting half circles on thin plywood. These will at least ensure that the mast is uniformly round at each station; the areas between will still have to be shaped by judgment of the eye.

After power-planing, a long-bed hand plane is used to fair the mast and further refine roundness (see Photo 30-18). I leave the mast hexagonal from the collar (or gooseneck) down. This simplifies cutting and wedging at the partners, mounting hardware and making and installing the boot, and it simply looks good.

The planed mast is sanded first with a #80

Photo 30-16. The clamped mast is allowed to cure overnight in the jigs.

Photo 30-17. It was, of course, more difficult to bribe the same crew back to lay up the second mast; several pizzas were required to do the trick. The bases of these masts were later cut to form a large mast step tenon. The small protrusion seen here was used as a handle for the core during lay up.

Photo 30-18. The masts are rounded initially with a power plane, then faired with the long-bed plane shown here. Final shaping is done with a softpad and pneumatic orbital sander.

soft pad; an orbital sander (I use a pneumatic jitterbug) with #80 paper finishes it. The mast is cleaned with compressed air and epoxy-coated, thinning coats 10 percent to 15 percent with reducer and applying to rejection, but avoiding a surface buildup of more than one coat. The epoxy is then lightly sanded with #120 paper (I often do this by hand to avoid breaking through the surface), carefully cleaned and wiped with solvent, primed with epoxy or polyurethane primer (two coats), and finished with polyurethane (two coats). If so desired, the mast may be varnished with clear polyurethane; this will hold up better than oil-based varnish. Keep in mind that epoxy deteriorates in sunlight, and use products with high ultraviolet-light filters. When finishing bright, a minimum of six or eight coats should be used. Pigmented polyurethane will greatly outlast any clear finish, but nothing looks like varnished wood, and Douglas fir is, to me, especially beautiful. I prefer to apply all of these finishes by spray gun, except for the first resin coats, which are applied by roller. I always paint the top (5 feet or 6 feet) of masts white, so I can see them in the dark.

MAST COLLARS

Many traditional masts use a collar or half collar to support the boom jaws or clapper (the pivoting block between boom jaws that rides the mast) when the sail is being lowered and furled. This is just a large, thick wood ring built around the mast. It may be set perpendicular to the mast or raked to the boom (preferable on very raked masts). It is fastened with epoxy and numerous large screws or lag-bolts. On large vessels, small knees are often used to support the collar. All fastener holes are bunged. A copper or stainless-steel chafe ring is sometimes placed on top of the collar to protect the wood, and sometimes

Photo 30-19. *Teresa*'s freestanding masts are 10 inches in diameter at the partners by 50 feet tall. Collars are epoxied and screwed to the masts, which are painted with epoxy primer and polyurethane. The mainmast is finished bright below decks, as it will be in the aft cabin.

the front center of the ring has a dish cut for the end of whatever boom is forward of that mast. This acts as a crutch or gallows for that boom, particularly during heavy weather when the sail is being lowered and furled, and in 'roly' anchorages. Photo 30-19 shows *Teresa*'s finished masts.

BOOMS

For very large vessels, booms may be made similarly to masts. But in most cases, they can be made from solid lumber, usually Douglas fir. I simply find no advantage to hollow booms on vessels under 65 feet or so. If anything, a little weight is desirable to flatten the sails, and prevent the booms from jumping around when luffing in a strong breeze. I believe that an aluminum boom is probably a bigger health hazard than a wood one, both to gear and human crew. The argument about a lighter boom hurting you less is questionable; they both have the power and speed of the wind in the sail behind them, and the difference in weight is often not much when comparing aluminum to a well-formed double-tapered fir boom.

Booms for vessels up to 60 feet can generally be gotten from lumberyard stock 6 x 6 Douglas fir. Vessels below 35 feet can generally use 4 x 4 stock. Many yards stock Douglas fir timber in up to 30-foot lengths, or can order it. You may have to look around, but you will find it. In some cases, spruce can also be used (if the trees grow near your house and some small ones need to be thinned, for example). Wrecking companies that salvage large timbers from defunct factories, railroad trestles, etc., are an excellent source for spar material. Plugging a few bolt holes is no problem in exchange for the quality in a timber that has cured for many years.

To lay out a boom, strike a centerline with a chalk box on two opposite sides of the surfaced and cut-to-length timber. The maximum diameter in the middle, and the end diameters (usually the same) are laid out. Spring a stiff batten the length of the spar through the three points. One-half of the way in from each end the batten is pulled out a little to make the ends a bit fuller than if the batten merely described the arc of a circle. Make these new points identical. The same shape is re-created and traced for the other edge, and the timber is turned over and the other side traced identically.

The lines are cut from both sides with a circular saw using a carbide-tipped rip blade. The same curves are then laid out on the newly cut faces after striking new centerlines, and these lines are cut. Now shape the square

tapered boom into a round one. Usually the first step is to cut the corners off with the circular saw set to a 45-degree bevel, creating a tapered octagon. The width of each octagonal face will be equal to approximately five-twelfths of the square face, or the octagonal face width is found by multiplying the square face width by 0.417. Lay off half that amount on each side of the chalk centerline on opposite sides of the boom at the middle and at the ends, spring the batten through these points and trace along it. Cut these lines to the 45-degree bevel. Final shaping is done with a power plane, hand plane and sanders. Gaffs are made the same way. The process also applies to solid masts of all sizes.

The booms may be painted, oiled or varnished, but because they are solid timbers, I don't use epoxies or polyurethane finishes on them. My own preference is the two-part oil system Deks Olje, soaking in Deks Olje #1 until it is rejected by laying on six or eight coats, wet on wet, one or two days in a row, and letting the surface dry for a few days. Then I apply six or eight coats of Deks Olje #2, one or two coats per day, weather permitting. If varnish is used, it should be a good-quality oil-based spar varnish, and not a hard plastic. Likewise, if paint is used (I always

Photo 30-20. The boom ends are flattened out with a small adze for the jaws.

paint boom and gaff ends white so I can see them in the dark), it should be either an oil-based enamel, like a porch and floor enamel (not a marine enamel), or a soft epoxy like Sherwin-Williams Tile-Clad II Enamel.

JAWS

If booms and/or gaffs are to be fitted with jaws, the sides of the forward ends of these spars are usually finished flat where the jaws will be fastened. (See Photo 30-20.) I prefer to make jaws of oak, and cut boom jaws flat, rounding the bottom forward ends up slightly and sometimes tapering the bottoms aft slightly after the basic shapes are cut out. Remember to leave room for leather covering when laying out and cutting. I make gaff jaws from thin (1/8 inch or so) laminates, gluing them up with epoxy on a simple jig to form the desired curve. Gaffs with low peaks (less curved) can be made from thicker laminates. When laying out jaws, run the grain diago-

nally for continuity and strength. Alternate the grains slightly when laminating jaws. Photo 30-21 shows correct grain orientation. I attach jaws with stainless-steel threaded rod in holes drilled completely through the jaws and boom end, about 9 inches apart. Nuts and washers are countersunk, but I don't bung the holes, so that the nuts may be tightened and broken jaws easily replaced. I usually bed the jaws to booms with Dolfinite, but I have found that epoxy also works well—except that damaged gaff jaws must be cut off. Another hole and rod are placed through the clapper, if used, which is also leathered. I oil-saturate the boom and jaws before leathering to preserve the wood, and nail on the leather with bronze ring-shank nails (they must be drilled for), avoiding placing nails in chafe areas. After leathering, the booms receive their second oil treatment. Photo 30-22 shows *Teresa's* booms ready for oil and leather.

Photo 30-22. Booms are solid Douglas fir, double-tapered and fitted with oak jaws. The ends are painted white for visibility at night, and the rest finished with the two-part Deks Olje system. The jaws and clappers will be leathered.

Photo 30-21. Boom and gaff jaws for a TERRAPIN 34 (*Tomfoolery*). Note diagonal grain.

CHAPTER 31
HARDWARE AND FITTINGS

Windlasses/ Ground Tackle/ Mastheads/ Mast Hardware/ Boom Fittings/ Boom Gallows and Crutches/ Davits/ Cleats and Chocks/ Winches/ Handrails and Handles/ Steering Systems/ Cabinet Hardware

WINDLASSES

For vessels 45 feet and under, A & B Industries in Costa Mesa, Calif., makes a good bronze and stainless-steel windlass that is compact, well built and extremely durable, for a very reasonable price. (See Photo 31-1.) This windlass comes with a chain gypsy for any size and type chain up to 1/2 inch on the starboard side and a rope head on the port side. Other configurations are available on a custom-order basis. I avoid aluminum fittings or hardware on deck because they corrode rapidly, even when painted. ABI also makes a number of other windlasses, including some fairly large electric models.

Traditional windlasses are still available from Lunenburg Foundry and Engineering in Nova Scotia in hot-dip galvanized cast iron. Some models are bolted to the back sides of the bitts, others are deck-mounted.

West Coast fishing vessels often use large drum winches for windlasses, occasionally employing wire rope anchor rodes. I used

such a windlass for several years and enjoyed the convenience of winding the rode onto a drum and not having to wash it and stow it below decks; however, there is no provision for a second or third rode, and the whole system places a lot of weight on the highest part of the deck.

Windlass placement should be carefully

Photo 31-1. This bronze and stainless-steel windlass is made by A & B Industries (ABI) of Costa Mesa, California. This is an excellent example of high-quality hardware made in the Orient to American patterns.

considered. The rodes should lead properly to gypsies and drums, and there should be enough room both to operate the windlass and maneuver around it while it is being operated. If the distance to hawseholes or bow rollers is far, chafe gear, usually consisting of hardwood troughs, should be provided to protect the deck.

GROUND TACKLE

Modern American yachts almost universally have inadequate ground tackle; evidence of this is experienced in virtually any American or Caribbean harbor during a blow, whether or not it is expected. The best description of ground tackle proportions and anchoring techniques I have found is in the book *Oceanography and Seamanship* by William Van Dorn.

In general, a cruising yacht should have at least three anchors. Rodes should consist of all chain for at least one, and should combine chain and nylon rope for the others. My own preference is for at least two 100-foot chain rodes, with at least 300 feet of nylon available for either or both rodes; often I connect each end of the 300-foot rode to each chain rode. This provides up to 400 feet for one anchor, or 250 feet for two anchors. A lunch hook may use all nylon or nylon with a short length of chain, when anchoring in a sand or mud bottom where nothing on the bottom can chafe through the rode.

For vessels likely to anchor in deep water, much more rode length should be provided. The above configuration is intended for yachts of modest size and draft, anchoring in American and Caribbean harbors.

The rule of thumb for five-to-one rode-to-depth ratio indicates good conditions. Riding out a blow in a deep roadstead may require much more scope, particularly if holding conditions are poor.

I favor the CQR plow as the best all-around anchor, but I have found that it is less effective in smaller sizes, and some of the imitations should be avoided. I have had good luck with ABI anchors of both the plow and Danforth types. Plows seem to be most effective in sizes 45 pounds and above. My second anchor is always a large Danforth type, either high-tensile or heavy-bodied cast steel. These have the highest holding power per weight of any anchor I know, and make the best lunch hook, as they can be proportionately lighter. I often use an all-nylon rode with a good sized Danforth, when there is no danger of chafe and when pull will be from one direction only. A change in tidal current or wind can often trip a Danforth, which frequently then fouls and drags across the bottom. A large plow will almost never do this; I have anchored my large cutter, *Fishers Hornpipe*, in a four-knot tidal estuary for weeks at a time on a single 75-pound CQR plow, and she never once dragged anchor. I have also watched her reverse her position 180 degrees in squalls and during storms without ever tripping that plow—literally several hundred times.

My third anchor is always a large fisherman. Nothing can compare for anchoring in rock or coral, and these anchors very rarely drag once well set. A fisherman should, however, be heavy enough and have large enough flukes to be effective.

A fourth anchor would be a smaller Danforth type, possibly kept aft and used as a kedge and/or lunch hook. The high-tensile type is best for this, as it provides great fluke area for weight. Such an anchor is perfect for rowing or walking out to help free a grounded vessel, usually using an all-nylon rode.

Ground tackle proportions should be based more on vessel weight and windage than on length. Table 31-A gives approximate

Table 31-A. Approximate Anchor and Rode Sizes for Yachts of Light to Moderate Displacement and Windage.				
	Vessel Size (L.O.D., in feet)			
	25–35	36–45	46–52	53–60
Anchor 1 (CQR Plow)	35#	45#	60#	75#
Anchor 2 (Danforth)	25#	35#	45#	50#
Anchor 3 (Fisherman)	50#	65#	85#	100#
Anchor 4 (Danforth)	20#	25#	35#	45#
Chain Rode Size (BBB or proof coil)	5/16"	3/8"	7/16"	1/2"
Nylon Rode Size (3-strand or braid)	1/2"	5/8"	3/4"	7/8"-1"

Note: Nylon rode sizes will typically be one size smaller for Anchor 4 (high-tensile).

anchor and rode sizes for yachts of light to moderate displacement and windage.

Vessels of more displacement and windage (very tall marconi rigs, full working schooner rigs and pilothouse or high-freeboard vessels) should have larger ground tackle.

The chain referred to is BBB or proof coil; I avoid high-test because it is high in carbon and deteriorates faster, often without obvious evidence. Many yachtsmen use high-test chain one size lighter than they should to save weight; I believe this is a bad practice.

The nylon rode is either three-strand or braid. Nylon makes a better rode than Dacron simply because it stretches more, providing shock and load absorbing properties.

Hawse pipes are usually cast bronze, made in two halves and through-bolted through the bulwarks, or bulwarks and knightheads. Hawse pipes passing through the deck and hull generally must be custom made using bronze or stainless-steel pipe. ABI makes cast-bronze bulwark hawse pipes suitable for vessels up to around 50 feet.

Many windlasses have a built-in deck pipe collar on the chain gypsy side. Cast-bronze deck pipe flanges can be purchased from numerous suppliers; both these types have covers. I have often made deck pipes from schedule 40 or 80 PVC pipe, using caps for covers (this requires sanding down the pipe end so the cap can be easily removed). I cut a slot into both pipe end and cap so that the rode can be left in place while covering the pipe. An eyebolt installed in the cap with a hook allows the rode end to be hung just inside the pipe; rotating the cap so the slots don't line up seals the pipe.

PVC pipe is excellent for fair-leading chain to chain bins in the forepeak locker; but the end of the pipe must be at least 12 inches above the chain pile in the bin or a jam-up can result. Keep in mind that the chain can sometimes form a surprisingly high pile if not flaked into the bin. Use schedule 80 if possible—the PVC eventually wears thin and must be replaced.

Bow rollers are almost universal today, but many of them are flimsy, poorly designed and badly installed. I make mine of welded stainless-steel frames and cast-bronze rollers (deep enough so the chain won't jump out), and mount the rollers on a heavy stainless-steel shaft that passes through the bowsprit. (See Fig. 31-1.) The shaft should be at least twice the chain size (for example: a 3/4-inch shaft for 3/8-inch chain). The frames should be through-bolted using 1/4-inch or larger threaded rod. Frame stock for the example would be 3/8 inch by 2 inches, and the threaded rods would be 3/8 inch. Bow rollers

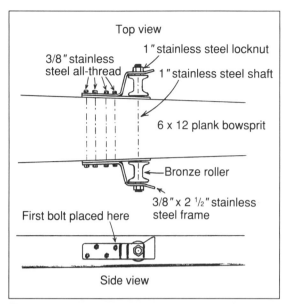

Figure 31-1. Anchor rollers for plank bowsprits.

Photo 31-2. The 6 x 12 Douglas fir bowsprit seen here is fitted with heavy-duty stainless-steel roller frames with cast-bronze rollers. A solid 7/8-inch shaft goes through the bowsprit to support the rollers. A two-laminate inner forestay stainless-steel chainplate passes through the bowsprit. Behind the bits is a drum-type windlass with a ratcheting cast-aluminum alloy handle.

of this type are unlikely to fail under any conditions. (See Photo 31-2.)

Catheads are virtually obsolete except on large schooners and working craft. They are used to lift the crown of large anchors up to bulwark level, where they are lashed in place. On large yachts today, a small but heavily made pipe davit can be used for this purpose to great advantage. I still make wood catheads from laminated stock, setting two Delrin sheaves into the ends to make up the upper tackle. The catheads are useful in handling large Danforth and fisherman anchors that don't work well with rollers. More will be said about cathead tackle and use in Chapter 32.

MASTHEADS

A disadvantage of stainless-steel hardware is unreliability of the welds. Any hairline cracks encourage crevice corrosion that can result in unexpected and catastrophic failure. This is particularly dangerous in rigging components, hence a rule of thumb is to avoid allowing any component of the standing rig in particular to rely solely on a stainless weld.

Masthead fittings are frequently nothing more than a section of pipe with tangs vertically welded to it. If such fittings are used, the welds should be ground and over-welded, then ground very smooth, and the fitting should be electrochemically passivated and polished. Care must be taken that all materials (including welding rod) are of the same series (usually #304). The fitting should be heavily made and the welds should be as long as possible. Photo 31-3 shows *Teresa*'s foremast head, which is of this type, but supports no standing rigging.

An alternative is to form the tangs from straps passed completely over the masthead, welded to a pipe or screwed to a wooden fan-shaped masthead. (See Fig. 31-2.) Stainless-

Photo 31-3. *Teresa*'s stainless-steel mastheads have tangs welded to a capped pipe.

steel eyes can be plug-welded for halyard blocks, or tangs can be welded between pipe and strap. Shroud and stay loads pass completely over the mast head and place virtually no load on the welds. In the event of a shroud or stay breaking, this type of fitting would still be more reliable than one relying solely on welds.

I purchase my stainless steel almost solely from surplus and scrap yards. Because it is so hard to cut, I try to find stock of useful size. I cut it with a Carborundum metal cut-off wheel in either a circular saw or table saw,

wearing protective clothing and eye and ear protection. If extensive cutting needs to be done, it may pay to find an industrial sheer press that can handle stainless steel. Small stock can be cut with specialized hacksaw blades, either mechanically or by hand.

Bending may be done cold unless the angles are extreme or hard, in which case the bend location is heated with an oxyacetylene torch. A large vise may be used for small stock; large stock will require a press made from a hydraulic jack and welded steel I-beam frame. The one-time builder should probably find a reliable local steel fabricator and farm out his custom hardware.

Mastheads also can be made of mild steel and hot-dip galvanized after welding; however, hot-dip facilities are becoming increasingly rare due to pollution problems.

MAST HARDWARE

Lower shrouds, inner forestays and halyards are often attached to masts by stainless-steel or bronze fittings of the type seen in L. Francis Herreshoff's *Sensible Cruising Designs*. These typically have at least one bolt or threaded pipe passing through the mast.

I prefer to attach halyard blocks to large

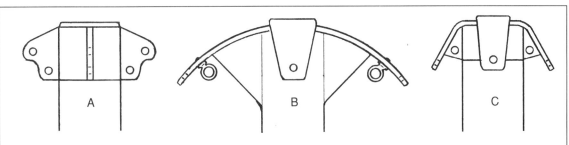

A. Tangs are welded to a pipe section and a cap is welded on top, unless the mast continues above. When fabricated from stainless steel, this type is not ideal for standing rigging since stays and shrouds rely solely on welds.

B. Shown is a fan-type truck using stainless steel straps welded together, so that stay and shroud

C. Straps are used here too, but they are welded to a pipe section. Tangs are welded between straps and pipe for halyards.

Figure 31-2. Mastheads.

shoulder eyebolts either lagged or through-bolted into the mast. I find the traditional spliced loop placed around the mast over an inlaid hardwood thumb cleat to be perfectly adequate; if anything, the old way is superior in the sense of weighing less, having no additional components to fail and costing much less. Lower shrouds in pairs can be passed around the mast and heavily seized together (figure-eight seizings are less likely to slide). An example of this may be seen in Figure 31-3. Shrouds or stays that must be removable or can't be passed over the masthead can be shackled to a wire rope strop with spliced eyes in each end passed around the mast over a thumb cleat. The strop can be of smaller diameter than the stay because it is doubled,

but strop wire working load should be well over half that of the stay.

One big reason for changing from these old methods was the adoption of 1 x 19 wire rope, which cannot be spliced. It can, however, make use of the strops just described, as an alternative to bolted-on tangs.

If mast track is used, it should be of the male type, in which the cars ride on the outer edges. This is less likely to jam in the event that track screws become loose (which is possible during a blow, making it difficult or impossible to get the sail down). The track should be set away from the mast on a hardwood bed, and fasteners should be large and long enough to make failure unlikely.

Goosenecks and tracks should be firmly

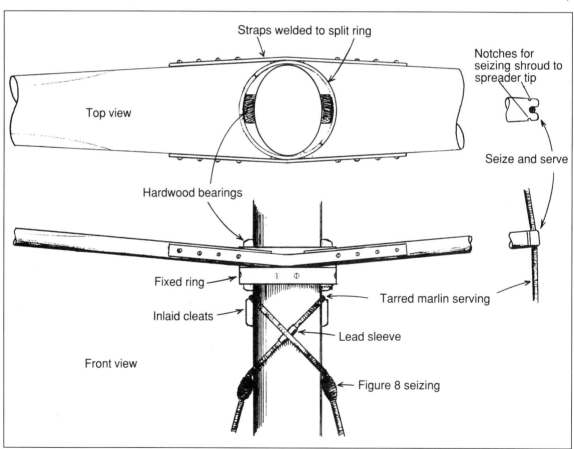

Figure 31-3. Pivoting spreader fittings.

fastened to the mast, either with long, heavy screws or mast bands and bolts. Many of the modern stock fittings available leave me cold, therefore I either look for old cast-bronze and stainless-steel fittings of the type made by Merriman during the first half of this century, or make my own.

Many of my designs use boom jaws and laced-on sails, avoiding much cost in materials and labor. Laced-on sails can be reefed or dropped on any point of sail, a distinct advantage for the short-handed cruiser. They also allow the sail luff to track around to the vacuum or lift side of the mast, sometimes providing a more efficient airfoil than possible with mast track on nonrotating masts, and, finally, there is much less sail chafe. The limitation is that laced-on sails cannot go beyond spreaders, and are limited to freestanding masts, gaff rigs and stayed masts without spreaders.

Spreaders should be strongly made. I like to laminate two layers of Douglas fir together, with their grain running at slight diagonals to each other. Mast fittings for spreaders should allow the spreaders to rotate if possible. My own preference is to mount the spreaders on a split-ring strongly made from stainless-steel pipe. Stainless straps are edge-bent to the spreader angle and welded to each side of the split ring. (See Fig. 31-3.) A second ring is screwed to the mast for the spreader ring to ride on. Compressive loads imposed on the spreaders from the upper shrouds are balanced because the spreaders rotate together. The reason for free-moving or rotating spreaders is flexibility: In a collision of any kind involving shrouds or spreaders, the rig can absorb shock and shift momentarily. Rigid spreaders are likely to break, which in turn can bring down the mast. Worst case scenarios include collisions at sea, particularly glancing blows by ships, collisions with high quays, sea walls, cargo booms and

bridges, and knock-downs and pitch-poling at sea during heavy weather. The spreader arrangement shown in Fig. 31-3 is that used on *Fishers Hornpipe*. A round mast would not require the bearings shown.

Upper shrouds should be heavily seized to spreader tips in such a manner that they cannot shift up or down. It is also important that the spreader angle bisect the upper shroud angle. I usually seize the junction first with stranded seizing wire, then with tarred marlin, to prevent chafe to sails and running rigging. The seizing should be tight and strong enough that two large men standing at the end of the spreader cannot make it slip. We used to have spreader parties on *Fishers Hornpipe*'s large flat spreaders, where six people would go aloft and sit on the spreaders with a bottle of rum to toast the sunset!

BOOM FITTINGS

For clew outhauls, I use a shoulder eye lag bolt on one side of the boom and a cheek block on the opposite side. The outhaul is not spliced to the eyebolt so that it can be end-for-ended as chafing requires. Use a stopper knot (figure-eight knot) at the eyebolt and pass through the clew back to the cheek block. Lead the outhaul forward to a cleat on the side of the boom where it will be accessible at all times. I use a similar arrangement for reefing tackle, which I usually leave rove in position permanently, as I am used to taking reefs in and out quite a lot.

I often use rope strops to attach sheet blocks instead of boom bails, in the old manner: They cost practically nothing, never fail (I have seen two bails break at sea in strong winds, and one did not involve a jibe), and distribute sheet loading to two places instead of one, which is easier on the boom. Inlaid thumb cleats or bronze eye straps are used to prevent the spliced strop ends from sliding

Photo 31-4. This cast-bronze truck was modified for a boom fitting by cutting off the lower tang, and making a stainless-steel bail with threads and nuts at each end. The lace rail replaces a boom track. The construction of this laminated Douglas fir boom is evident at the end.

on the boom. Cast-bronze fittings (see Photo 31-4) can still be purchased, often as masthead trucks for small vessels, and modified by cutting off one tang and installing a stainless-steel bail made from round stock threaded at each end (as seen in the photo). Conventional bails welded to stainless plates still can be purchased from marine suppliers; these should employ at least one through bolt.

Lacing rails (Photo 31-4) are a great alternative to boom track, which I find to be a terrible nuisance, as it interferes with gaskets, reef nettles and straps for vangs and preventers. As of late I have come to prefer loose-footed sails, which I think have slightly better shape; but the tacks and clews must be more heavily reinforced, and fittings should be a little heavier.

Small winches for reef tackle can be mounted on one or both sides of the boom, though they are really unnecessary for any but very large sails (over 450 square feet). Often a block and tackle set up under the boom is used for reefing, but in some cases

the two-part reef outhaul will be too long and the tackle will go two-blocks before the reef is in. The tackle hook must then be reset through a loop in the outhaul, creating a hassle and taking too much time. It is always best to reef on time, when the sail is still easy to manage. During racing, extra crew are usually available for grunt work, and reefing is done at the last moment.

The best use for keeping a block and tackle under the boom is to use it as a preventer and vang; a hook is used at the forward end of the tackle, which is set to cleats, eyes or strops when using the tackle to pull down or forward on the boom. The block at the other end is shackled to a strop, bail or eyebolt (this last being vulnerable to pulling out unless through-bolted).

An eye, eyenut or ring under the gooseneck or between the jaws is used to attach the tackle hook when not in use and also may be shackled to a downhaul tackle for increasing luff tension after the halyard has been set up. It is generally not a good practice to shackle either sail tack or downhaul tackle to the clapper between boom jaws. Instead, a shoulder eyebolt is placed at the front of the boom, having an eyenut at the bottom (from downhaul and boom tackle), so that all tension passes from sail luff to downhaul through the boom end. Sometimes a metal strap is installed first, passing around the boom end between the jaws and being nailed or screwed over and under the boom end. This prevents the eyebolt from splitting out of the boom (it must be installed very close to the end). The other way to attach the tack is with a large ring passed through two eyebolts installed through the jaws on either side of the boom end. Examples of traditional fittings may be studied in *The American Fishing Schooners 1825–1935*, by Howard I. Chapelle. The second half of the book is a "Notebook on Details of Gloucester Fishing

Photo 31-5. A small pedestal supports a gooseneck for a stays'l boom. Stainless-steel straps are inlaid into the boom end.

Schooners," and is a vast compendium of knowledge.

Staysail booms and jib clubs can be attached to a pedestal, sliding truck or stays'l stay turnbuckle via a gooseneck. (See Photo 31-5.) The boom fitting usually consists of a U-shaped strap screwed to each side of the boom, preferably inlaid flush to the surface. An eye welded to the strap fits into a toggle, which forms a gooseneck. The pedestal is placed about one-eighth of the way aft of the stay to the sail clew. This causes the sail to flatten when sheeted in going to weather and to balloon when sheeted out reaching and running. Sliding trunks were used on American fishing schooners, and allowed adjustment of sail shape. They consisted of two parallel rods attached to the bowsprit on which rode a truck supporting the gooseneck. Attaching the gooseneck to the turnbuckle allows for no adjustment of sail shape other than the boom clew outhaul.

BOOM GALLOWS AND CRUTCHES

The utility of a boom gallows is nearly essential to a serious cruising boat. The gallows is the best way to secure a thrashing boom at sea in foul weather, either to reef or furl the sail, and in a 'roly' anchorage. It also provides a real measure of security when working on the stern of many vessels, and could prevent the rig from fouling the cockpit or helm, or injuring crew members during a dismasting, when the boom and sail are lowered in an emergency, and in the event of topping lift failure. Often a gallows is integrated with pipe stern davits, as in *Teresa*. I prefer to make the top from wood, with three leathered saddles for the boom to rest in. The wood gallows fits over the tops of the pipe stanchions by means of holes drilled about two-thirds of the way up; stainless-steel flathead machine screws are then drilled and tapped through the wood into the pipe from each side, and everything is bedded in liquid rubber compound.

The stanchion bases consist of pipe flanges threaded on or welded to the angle of the deck, and through-bolted into plywood backup blocks below deck. The bolt holes are epoxy-sealed prior to installation, and the flanges are bedded in rubber. Hardwood or phenolic blocks may be placed between the flange and deck to distribute load and protect the fabric and epoxy covering.

I use galvanized pipe and fittings to make up the gallows stanchions. After welding, the welds and surrounding areas are ground, sanded and cold-galvanized with ground zinc in a liquid base (such as Galvicon). The galvanized surfaces are then washed with white vinegar, primed with epoxy metal primer and polyurethane-painted. If the whole process is carefully done, the steel treated can be maintenance-free for many years.

Boom crutches are of two general types: a single support and a scissored double support. The former is often incorporated into a fife rail to support the boom of the next mast forward. The scissors type sets into two sock-

Photo 31-6. Booms with jaws can be raised with the halyard forward and set in a scissors crutch aft over which to hang a boom tent.

ets on deck or in a davit crossbar. The single type requires either guys to help keep it centered, or sometimes the sheet can be set up tightly enough to hold it steady. Another variation is the folding type incorporated into a gallows or coach roof, which folds up to support the boom in a higher position.

The crutch keeps the boom above head-bashing height on many vessels, and often simplifies rigging an awning. Booms with jaws can be raised forward to the same height as the crutch aft, and a boom tent can be employed over or just under the boom. (See Photo 31-6.)

DAVITS

Davits may be wood (solid or laminated) or metal pipe. Most yachts make better use of pipe davits of the type popular in the patent sterns of the Chesapeake Bay Bugeyes of the 19th century. Wood davits are usually fairly straight, employing a gentle S-curve, and are best used on a rather high stern, as they don't lift the tender very high. Thus they are limited to large vessels with high transoms or smaller vessels with flush-decked aft cabins. Examples of wood davits are found in Chapelle's *The American Fishing Schooners*,

in the notebook section previously mentioned.

I often incorporate pipe davits into a sheet/traveler and gallows, somewhat like the patent stern arrangement. Large-radius sweeps—90-degree curved pipe sections—can be purchased from any commercial electrical supplier, and these form the curved portion of the davits. Pipe may also be bent, but a hydraulic bender will be needed, and sometimes the galvanized zinc coating cracks in the process. Pipe diameter is usually 2-inch I.D. (inside diameter), having an outside diameter of nearly $2^1/_2$ inches. Long, straight pipe sections are welded to the sweeps or connected with a threaded sleeve. Compression posts of the same diameter pipe are welded to the undersides of the straight sections, and sections may be welded above this junction, leaning inboard somewhat, to support the gallows crossbar. Diagonal load supports of a smaller diameter pipe are welded from near the stanchion base to the underside of the davit arm as far out as possible without interfering with the tender when hauled up. Flat-stock tangs are welded onto the davit pipe ends, both to seal the pipe and to hang the blocks from (see Fig. 31-4). These may be stainless steel, which can be welded to mild steel using stainless-steel welding rod. Galvanized steel pipe flanges are welded to the davit bases (stanchions and sweeps) to match the deck angle, or they may be threaded on and mounted on fairing blocks of hardwood or phenolic block (better) tapered to match the deck angle and contour. Care should be taken to align the davits to each other and to the vessel.

In laying out or designing davits, I make the davit pipe angle slightly more steeply inclined than the deck sheer at the stern, so that it complements the vessel's sheer line. In plan view from above, I angle the davits inboard aft to somewhat follow the lines of the deck

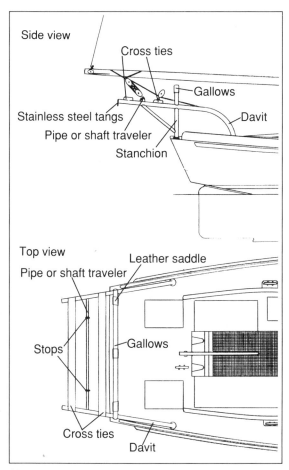

Side view

Cross ties

Gallows

Stainless steel tangs

Davit

Pipe or shaft traveler

Stanchion

Top view

Leather saddle

Pipe or shaft traveler

Gallows

Stops

Cross ties

Davit

Figure 31-4. Pipe stern davits (TERRAPIN 45).

as they approach the transom. In vessels with narrow sterns, the davits may extend parallel to each other to avoid being awkwardly close together at the tackles. I usually make the stanchions vertical in both planes, but lean them inboard several degrees above the davits when they extend up to a gallows. In some cases, I have made the stanchions perpendicular to the deck in the side view, particularly on vessels with a flat sheer line.

The wood crossmembers are bolted to the davit pipes with stainless-steel flat-head machine screws, drilled and tapped into the steel. If sheet turning blocks are to be used outboard of a traveler, or in a three-block arrangement for main or mizzen sheets, large shoulder eyebolts for the blocks are used to secure the crossbar, being bolted through the davit pipes. When supporting a sheet traveler or center block, the inner crossbar would normally be at least a 2-inch by 6-inch hardwood plank on vessels around 40 feet on deck, and the outer crossbar might be 2 inches by 5 inches of Douglas fir or yellow pine. Yellow pine or fir is also adequate for the inner crossbar, though I usually make it of oak, preferably white oak, for its shock-absorbing properties during accidental jibes. It is obvious that this sheeting arrangement can impose heavy loads, particularly shock loads, on the davit structure. All components must therefore be very strongly made, attached and bolted to the deck. All wood-to-steel connections are heavily bedded in liquid rubber. Large plywood backup blocks are located under the deck below the stanchion and sweep base flanges, which are through-bolted with the largest possible diameter stainless-steel flat-head machine screws (usually 3/8 inch or 1/2 inch). Fairing blocks between the flange and the deck help distribute the load, compensate for different rates of expansion and contraction and protect the deck, in addition to compensating for differing angles between the flange and the deck. Hardwood, usually teak, is adequate for this purpose, but needs maintenance and may eventually rot. Therefore it is much inferior to phenolic block, which may be purchased in 1/2-inch–thick sheets from commercial plastics suppliers, requires no maintenance (deterioration is almost nil), and is really the ultimate intermediate material for bedding load-bearing metal fittings to any deck material. Don't forget to epoxy-seal the holes through the deck.

After many jibes with *Teresa's* 24-foot–long main boom (three year's worth), there were no signs of fatigue or weakness in her davit/gallows/sheet structure. Indeed, the structure absorbs the shock of jibing with less deleterious effect than most other sheeting arrangements.

The gallows crossbar is made from a timber large enough to encapsulate the pipe stanchion tops as described previously in the discussion of gallows—usually around 3 inches by 5 inches (starting with a nominal 4 x 8). Use the deck beam template during layout to achieve crown parallel to the deck—the bottom may be straight if so desired. Holes are drilled with a hole saw for the pipes, which extend about two-thirds to three-quarters of the way up into the wood. Stainless-steel flat-head machine screws, drilled and countersunk through each face of the wood and tapped into the pipe, hold the gallows timber in place. The connections are heavily bedded in liquid rubber. It is essential that no water or air be allowed into the steel pipes anywhere in the structure. Saddles are cut into the gallows and leathered, as already mentioned.

The metal structures should have hot-dipped galvanized components, and are painted as described earlier in the discussion on gallows stanchions. The wood crossbars may be painted, varnished or oiled. My preference is the two-part Deks Olje system.

Galvanized steel cleats may be bolted or welded to the steel pipes wherever needed for the davit tackles or sheets.

Davits and gallows may also be made of stainless steel, aluminum, brass or bronze pipe, at much greater expense. When using aluminum, brass or bronze, order schedule 80 (thick-wall) pipe, since these materials are not as strong as steel. Aluminum should be carefully painted.

CLEATS AND CHOCKS

Many modern yachts have cleats and chocks that are inadequate both in size and mounting strength. I find 6 inches to be about the minimum size for deck, sheet and halyard cleats on a sailboat in the 25-foot to 35-foot size range. I prefer the Herreshoff-type cleat, fastened with four large screws or bolts through its double flange base. These may be cast bronze or hot-dipped galvanized steel, preferably not hollow, and tapered at each end. Deck cleats should be bolted through the deck into plywood backup blocks below deck. Holes should be epoxy-sealed, the backup block should be epoxy-painted on all sides before installation, and the cleat and bolts should be bedded in liquid rubber. A spacer block, preferably phenolic, placed between cleat and deck will protect the deck covering and distribute loading over a greater surface in addition to reducing the possibility of leaks. Regardless of the cleat material, I always use stainless-steel fasteners for strength and longevity.

I like to use open-type chocks on the rail or bulwark cap to fairlead dock lines to deck cleats, thereby avoiding chafe. Large bulwarks allow the use of chocks through them; these may be made of hardwood such as ironbark (New Zealand red eucalyptus) or lignum vitae, in the traditional diamond pattern. Another chock I like is the type that is let into the log rail or bulwark, usually of cast bronze and open in the top. These are often used in place of hawse pipes in smaller vessels and have integral face plates which are routed or chiseled for and finish flush with the bulwark or rail surfaces. They are fastened with large screws into the end grain of the bulwark cutout and sometimes also into the wood below. Chocks should be bedded in rubber compound or bedding compound such as fungicidal Dolfinite, and fastened with stainless-steel or bronze screws.

I have been purchasing most of my chocks and cleats from Chinese sources, who make them from American patterns in cast bronze, through suppliers such as A & B Industries in California.

WINCHES

I often feel that winches are vastly over-rated and overused, particularly on American sailing yachts. My personal preference is for a well-designed and laid out block and tackle, using winches only where they are really needed, usually for jib sheets and wire-rope jib halyards. I have never owned or used a self-tailing winch, although I can appreciate what they do.

For sheeting large jibs, I like the big, two-speed Barient winches. I find them to be beautifully engineered and manufactured, and they need very little maintenance. I would rather have one big, powerful Barient stainless-steel two-speed winch heavily mounted in the back of a cockpit to tend both port and starboard genoa sheets than a bunch of those cheap little aluminum or brass winches that are so awkward to use and peri-odically corrode to the point of failure. The big Barient can even be used to warp your vessel off mud banks and sandbars stern first. I like to keep one of those two-handed handles around for this purpose. The winch base should be through-bolted to a heavy, large plywood backup block below deck. A thick, strong base should be used between winch and deck, often made of stack-lami-nated plywood covered with fabric and ep-oxy, having a hardwood or phenolic cap on which the winch is mounted.

Wire halyard winches are a mixed bless-ing. There is no question about their ability to set up and maintain jib luff tension, but they tend to jam occasionally, particularly when the sail is being lowered, and the "fishhooks" that inevitably occur in the wire rope are rough on sails and human flesh.

Another application for winches on seri-ous cruising vessels is for slab or jiffy reefing, where small winches are placed on one or both sides of the boom far enough forward where they can be used on any point of sail. Barient #10s are great for this, if the reef tackle is no larger than 1/2 inch.

Locking handles are essential for safety; without them, a handle can easily fly loose, causing personal injury, damage to the vessel or loss overboard.

HANDRAILS AND HANDLES

Coach roof handrails today are almost al-ways manufactured from teak and imported at great expense. But they are really easy to make. I make mine from 1-inch hardwood stock, 2 inches or $2^{1}/_{4}$ inches high, with "feet" every 9 inches to 12 inches. I make the rail 1-inch square, then rout it into a round using a 1/2-inch quarterround bit. Handrails can be fastened from above, down into a coach roof beam preferably, or up from below into the feet, or some combination of both. On larger vessels, I usually make the rail size a little larger, $1^{1}/_{8}$ inches or $1^{1}/_{4}$ inches round, so its proportions better suit the vessel. Handrails should be well planned and placed where you need them. This often includes along the deck underside in flush-decked vessels, par-ticularly if there is a wide cabin sole; but they should not compromise headroom. An alter-native way to make handrails is by cutting the feet and rail separately: The feet are made from rectangular blocks with beveled sides, such that the base is wider than the top (which is the same width as the rail). The rail is routed or rounded everywhere except where it covers the feet; here it is left flat. The feet are usually attached with four screws from below, and the rails attached from above with two screws that need not pene-trate into the coach roof. All screws fastened from above should be countersunk and bunged using epoxy. Screws from below can be left exposed (it may be convenient to be able to tighten them at some point), or slightly countersunk and puttied over with a mixture of epoxy and titanium dioxide (white pigment). Handrails should be bedded in a liquid rubber compound or bedding compound. This kind of hand rail, properly made, is stronger than the first type.

Handles should be placed near companionways, doors, along wheel houses, near bunks and heads—wherever they are needed. Often handholds can be unobtru-

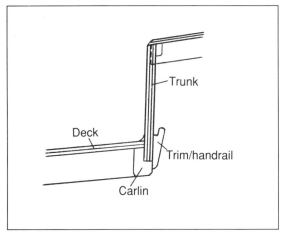

Figure 31-5. Trim incorporating handrail over trunk/deck/carlin joint.

Photo 31-7. Handholds cut into companionway hatch carlins make going up safe and easy.

sively incorporated into other structures. Countertop fiddles should be strongly made and attached and trim covering the deck/carlin/cabin trunk joint should be strong and firmly attached if they are to double as handrails. (See Fig. 31-5.) Holes cut into the higher portions of companionway ladders are very useful, as are holes cut into upper companionway hanging knees incorporated into sliding hatch carlins (see Photos 19-3, 31-7).

STEERING SYSTEMS

Other than tiller steering, there are three common systems using wheel steering: hydraulic, cable and quadrant, and mechanical (using a worm gear or rack and pinion).

Hydraulic systems consist of a wheel-driven pump which activates one or two pistons attached to a short tiller arm via copper tubing and rubber hoses. Such systems are expensive and often require many turns of the wheel to move the rudder through its full arc (usually about 90 degrees). Hydraulics are very convenient for installations where more than one steering station is required, where there is a long distance between helm and rudder, and where other systems are impractical to install. Consult a manufacturer to determine the components for each application.

Cable and quadrant systems are most common on older power boats. They are driven by the cable taking several turns around a drum on the wheel shaft. Cable springs are frequently incorporated to maintain cable tension and absorb shock. Turning blocks for the cable must be very strong, have good bearings and be firmly attached. The whole system must be carefully designed and laid out; if cables lead from quadrant or drum at the wrong angles, the system may not work. Consult a professional to help determine quadrant size, cable size, turning block location, and drum size; sensitivity (number of

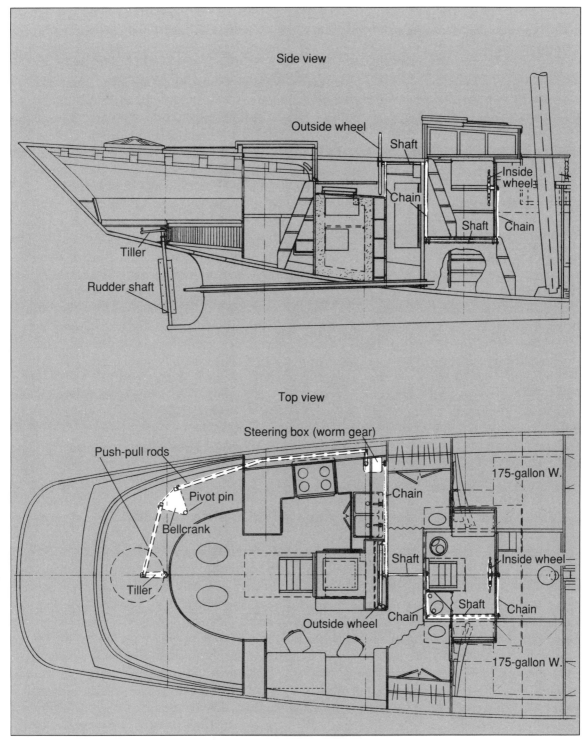

Figure 31-6. Mechanical steering system using push-pull rods, worm gear and shaft/sprocket/chain for multiple helms (EXUMA 68).

turns to swing the rudder through its total travel) is determined both by quadrant radius and drum size.

Most large American and Canadian sailing vessels, particularly those used in the fishing industry, have incorporated manufactured worm gears from companies such as Edson, Robinson and Lunenburg. These gears are mounted in a wheelbox on deck and are connected directly to the rudderhead. They are still available in a variety of sizes and types and work beautifully. Their limitation is location, as they are above the rudder.

I have built several steering systems using automotive steering boxes, usually from trucks or buses, though smaller vessels (under about 35 feet) can make use of automotive gears or rack-and-pinion systems. The box is very securely mounted, typically on a steel plate, which is in turn bolted to floor timbers, stringers or blocking mounted securely to the hull. The steering arm from the box is set up parallel to a short, heavily made tiller arm of the same length, and connected by a linkage, usually by means of large ball joints. This can also be an automotive item; often the linkage arm from the vehicle that supplied the box, complete with ball joints, can be cut and welded to the desired length.

The input shaft of the steering box is connected to a universal joint, which in turn is connected to a transfer shaft. This latter is mounted in Dodge bearings (pillar blocks) and leads to a point below the helm. Often there is more than one transfer shaft, connected by universal joints and carried in Dodge bearings, particularly in large vessels. Sprockets are placed on the ends of both the transfer shaft and the helm shaft, and these are connected by a heavy-duty chain (for example, 5/8-inch #40 for vessels under 50 feet). The helm shaft is also mounted in Dodge bearings. In some vessels, a bellcrank may also be incorporated in the system, to transmit the steering via a push-pull motion instead of rotation, particularly where there is insufficient room for the steering box near the rudderhead. In this case, the bellcrank is welded to a shaft, which is mounted in Dodge bearings, which in turn must be securely mounted to the hull. An example of this may be seen in Figure 31-6. Multiple helms are connected via chains, sprockets and jack-shafts, as shown in the example.

A system of this type is, as far as I am concerned, the ultimate in powerful, accurate sensitive steering. It costs less than a hydraulic system, and about the same as (or less than) a cable and quadrant system, assuming that some of the components are purchased from a junkyard. It has better feedback sensitivity than a hydraulic system, and more powerful feedback control than a cable and quadrant system. It also requires less maintenance and repair. Chains can be bronze, stainless steel or conventional steel motorcycle type. The first will need to be of larger size to compensate for the lower tensile strength of bronze; the latter two should be kept away from salt water and inspected and greased once or twice a year.

CABINET HARDWARE

Household-type cabinet hardware is usually made of plated or painted steel, and doesn't fare well in marine applications, particularly in galley, head and companionway locations where it is bound to contact salt water. However, solid brass hardware can often be purchased from conventional hardware suppliers, frequently at a lower price than from marine suppliers. But be careful that such hardware, particularly hinges and latches, doesn't have steel hinge pins or springs. Screws should be stainless steel, solid brass or bronze.

I purchase most of my cabinet hardware

from A & B Industries in Costa Mesa, Calif. They supply it in both brass and stainless steel, and for larger items, in bronze. Prices are reasonable and quality has been good.

The simpler hinges and latches are, the longer they seem to last. I have seen excellent hinges made entirely of hardwood or leather that have lasted many years. Primitive wooden turn-latches are effective and almost never fail. Avoid magnetic latches altogether, as well as household friction, spring and ball-type latches—they corrode and will fail when the cabinet contents are thrown against them when the vessel is heeled over and bouncing around in a seaway. External brass turn-latches, such as casement-window latches, work well, but should not be used where they can hook clothing or other gear. Piston latches are good, either the common sliding bolt type or flush-mounted, spring-loaded cabinet latches. The latter also tend to catch clothing if they have a pull-type handle. The kind with a round knob attached directly to the bolt are simpler; and ones you pull out

Photo 31-8. *Teresa*'s ABI hardware is spread out for inventory. Blocks have teak cheeks, stainless-steel shafts and beckets, and bronze sheaves and bearings, at a reasonable price.

before they slide are perhaps the best, if the springs are nonferrous.

Hatch and skylight hardware seems to be pretty standardized. I prefer the large cast-bronze hinges with removable pins, and piston-type skylight supports with knurled knobs. These come from many sources; I get mine from A & B Industries. Photo 31-7 shows A & B Industries' hardware for *Teresa*.

CHAPTER 32
RIGGING

Standing Rigging/ Running Rigging/ Splices and Knots/ Centerboard Tackle/ Flags/ Lifelines/ Davit Tackle/ Cathead Tackle/ Pinrails and Pins

STANDING RIGGING

Most wire rope used in standing rigging today is stainless steel of 1 x 19 construction. This type has eclipsed others because of its low stretch, which has become increasingly desirable in modern marconi rigs. It is too stiff (the individual strands are too large) to be spliced, and it tends to work-harden and fail more often than wire rope constructed of smaller strands. It must be used with terminal fittings, of which there are now many types, most of which are very expensive. Two types of compression fittings are popular: swaged terminals and Nicopress terminals, both of which are squeezed in place on the wire. Swaging requires a large press, capable of exerting thousands of pounds of pressure on the terminal fitting, which is typically stain-less steel. Nicopress fittings are made of a softer alloy and are compressed with a pow-erful hand tool analogous to a large crimping tool. Both types are more prone to failure than other fittings, and should, in my opinion, be totally avoided in standing rigging. Their best application is for lifelines and wire rope

halyard ends. The former can frequently employ swaged end terminals, and the latter can make good use of two Nicopress fittings in forming an eye around a thimble using 7 x 19 stainless steel wire rope. One problem of any squeezed-on fitting is that it also squeezes the wire rope, often causing work-hardening and failure.

Other common end fittings for 1 x 19 wire are CastLok fittings, which rely on epoxy resin, and several mechanical terminals, which employ a cone-shaped plug and a compression fitting. In both of these types, the very end of the wire rope is partially un-laid, and either the metal cone or epoxy in-serted inside the splayed end wires. These fittings are expensive, but can be reused. The CastLok fittings are heated with a torch to burn out the epoxy; the mechanical terminals are simply unscrewed.

There is one other terminal type which has all but disappeared from yacht use: This is the poured zinc fitting. It is usually a bail-type terminal with a hollow, conic socket for the wire rope end, which is partly unlaid after insertion and fixed in place by pouring molten zinc from a small crucible into the preheated socket. The fittings are hot-dip galvanized steel; the zinc must be pure "mil-spec" (military specification). These fittings can be purchased commercially, and industrial rigging shops use them. Their breaking strength is higher than that of most other fittings available on the market—very close to that of the wire rope with which they are employed. The poured zinc and plating protect both the stainless-steel wire rope and the steel bail and socket from corrosion. I have personally re-rigged vessels having terminals of this type that were 30 years old and in perfect condition; I reused the fittings. All that is needed is a gasoline blowtorch and a small cast-iron crucible. After the zinc is molten, the terminal fitting and wire ends are heated (taking care not to melt the zinc coating off the fitting), and the zinc carefully poured into the inverted socket. Rigging shops will make up your standing rigging for you for a fraction of the cost of any other end fitting I know of. Frankly, I do not understand why these fittings have fallen from general use in yachting, unless it is simply that they are not as pretty as the more contemporary fittings, even though these are vastly more expensive and more prone to failure in many cases. The only limitation I can think of is that they should not be immersed in salt water.

My own preference in standing rigging is 7 x 7 IWRC (internal wire rope core), either stainless steel or galvanized plow steel. This wire rope can be hand-spliced around a thimble, is more flexible and hence slightly stretchy and more forgiving than 1 x 19 construction, and less likely to fail due to work-hardening. Spliced end fittings are desirable because they have a breaking strength very near that of the wire rope, and can be made anywhere with little more than the thimble and some seizing wire and marlin. Tools consist of a splicing fid and a vise.

Because wire splicing is described in many other books, I will not describe it here, other than to say that the best splice to use is the Liverpool or marine splice. (See Photos 32-1 and 32-2.) Thimbles should be heavy duty, specified for wire rope, of a size equal to the wire plus marlin serving (that part of the wire which will lay up in the thimble is served

Photo 32-1. The portion of the wire rope that lays in the thimble is served with tarred marlin.

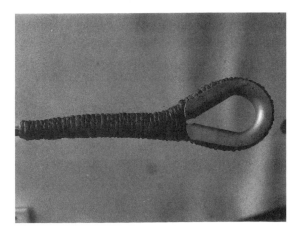

Photo 32-2. The finished Liverpool splice is seized with three-strand annealed stainless-steel seizing wire, and served with tarred marlin. Note the heavy-duty stainlesssteel thimble, which has no ears (tabs) at the ends. Shown here is 3/8-inch stainless-steel 7 x 7 IWRC wire rope spliced around a 1/2-inch stainless-steel thimble. The splice takes 30 minutes to make; the seizing and servings take about 10 minutes. Breaking strength is very nearly that of the wire rope, and materials costs are very low.

prior to splicing). For example, 3/8-inch wire rope will use 1/2-inch thimbles. The thimbles should have the largest radius possible, as this places less stress on the wire rope (a common place to find wire rope failure is at the bottom of an undersize thimble). A thimble intended for rope will be made of thinner metal than one intended for wire rope, and it may deform under standing rigging tensions. Rope thimbles may be identified by their "ears" (the ends come to a point at their junction); wire rope thimbles are rounded, and have no ears (see Photo 32-2).

It is ideal, but not essential, to have a rigging vise to make splices. I use a machinist's vise myself, but can get by with any vise or even none at all. In replacing rigging on vessels where it is not worthwhile to remove everything on a mast above a stay or shroud that loops around the mast, I have made splices in place while hanging in a bosun's chair.

CHAINPLATES

Chainplates have evolved to include several new variations, but the most common are usually stainless steel straps, with an eye at the top for a toggle, shackle or rigging screw jaw. They may be bolted to the outside of the hull in the traditional fashion, to the inside of the hull, which became popular in the first half of this century, or to a bulkhead or specially made structural unit beneath the deck and inboard of the rail. The latter has become popular with contemporary racing yachts, as it allows the headsails to be sheeted in flatter when beating to weather.

I believe in making the chainplates heavy, and of one-piece construction (there was a tendency some years ago to use a stack of thinner straps). I like stainless steel for chainplates because it is less prone to bleed rust

down the deck or topsides, provided it is polished and kept clean. Because the tools used in shaping and drilling stainless components are usually steel, molecules of steel left behind will instigate corrosion. Stainless fittings should therefore be electrochemically passivated (if possible) and polished just before installation, and thoroughly cleaned after installation (as the wrenches used may leave steel molecules behind). Small stainless or bronze wire-bristle brushes (they look like toothbrushes) are best for this. Use them with abrasive soap and water or metal cleaners intended for stainless steel. Avoid getting the cleaner on painted surfaces.

When bolting chainplates to cold-molded wood hulls, glue a plywood backup block with epoxy or a rubber bedding compound (such as 3M #5200 or Sikaflex) to the inside of the hull. This block should be nearly the thickness of the hull. Holes drilled in the hull should be epoxy-sealed, sleeved with PVC pipe, and chainplates and bolts should be bedded in rubber compound. It is important that the chainplates be installed at the correct angle with respect to the rigging (so that all tension is in line with the chainplate and bolts and not pulling off to the side). Where the chainplate protrudes above the sheer, bulwarks or deck, the head (top "free" portion) should be angled to the same direction of pull as that of the rigging. In most cases, chainplates should not place any load on bulwarks; in some cases they are blocked clear with channels, in some cases the bulwark and cap are grooved out for the chainplate. Exceptions involve unusually strong, reinforced bulwarks. Chainplates installed through the deck should have a rectangular piece of stock welded around them as a flange just above the deck level (prior to installation) to block water from finding its way down the hole through the deck from which the chainplate protrudes. Bed this flange in rubber compound and check it periodically, particularly after sailing the vessel hard, as the chainplates will work slightly, sometimes breaking the seal of the bedding. It is for this reason that I prefer traditional chainplates mounted outside the hull.

Chainplates should extend far enough below deck level to allow distribution of tensile forces to several large bolts at least several inches apart; this information is normally supplied by the designer. To give an idea of proportion, chainplate stock for a 40-foot cruising sailboat of moderate displacement might be 3/8 inch by 2 inches by 18 inches long, where 6 inches extends above the sheer across a 4-inch high bulwark, and 12 inches overlaps the hull. The chainplates should be bolted to the hull with four 1/2-inch stainless-steel bolts, the topmost two of which are installed through the sheer clamp and blocking. Large, heavy washers are installed inside the hull, or even a stainless-steel plate around 1/8 inch thick and extending from the bottom of the clamp to just below the lowest bolt. A 30-foot cruising sailboat might use 1/4-inch by 1½-inch by 15-inch chainplates bolted with four 3/8-inch bolts. Backup blocks are used below the sheer clamp only, and in both cases would be 3/4-inch plywood or phenolic block about 3 inches wide.

After the mast is stepped and chainplates installed, the standing rigging lengths are measured in place; these are never computed from plans, for the obvious reason that nothing comes out exactly as planned. Also, never assume that shrouds on both sides of a rig will be equal—they rarely are.

Temporary mast wedges are used to position the masts as accurately as possible. Someone must go aloft on a halyard with the bitter end of a long tape measure to measure for stays and shrouds. Very flexible masts, particularly if they are raked, may need temporary support from halyards to compensate for the weight of the person aloft. Measurements are taken from bearing point to bearing point: the actual contact points of the holes in chainplates and mast fittings. Stays or shrouds that loop the mast with spliced eyes are measured around the mast to the point where the wire splices back into itself, and the dimension of the loop is recorded. All lengths are recorded by the person measuring below.

To determine lengths of stays and shrouds, subtract shackles, toggles, rigging screws (turnbuckles) and any other intermediate hardware (such as insulators) from the total length measured. Rigging screws are measured in an almost open (or extended) position, as the wire will stretch when it is set up tight. Rigging is perhaps the only case where too short is better than too long. A shackle can always be added, but a finished wire rope that is too long is pretty hopeless, unless it has fittings that are easily changed.

Wire rope can be shortened or lengthened slightly by taking up or letting out turns (twists in the wire), but this should not be abused. Note that 7 x 19 wire is generally not suited for standing rigging as it is too stretchy and more vulnerable to corrosion than the two previously mentioned types; it is designed and made specifically as running rigging wire (winch cable, etc.).

Shackles used in standing rigging should be heavy duty. A rule of thumb for selecting size is that the shackle *bodies* should be one or two sizes up from the wire rope diameter. Thus, 7/16-inch or 1/2-inch shackles would be used with 3/8-inch wire rope. Shackle pin sizes vary somewhat; a 7/16-inch shackle should have a pin no smaller than 1/2 inch. Another rule of thumb is that all pins in standing rigging should be at least two sizes up from the wire rope diameter. Shackles should have threaded pins with eyes in their heads for seizing wire; all components of standing rigging should be seized so they cannot come apart.

Turnbuckles should be either twice the wire rope size, or one size under twice. Thus 3/4-inch or 5/8-inch turnbuckles would be used with 3/8-inch wire rope. Turnbuckle size is typically defined by thread diameter and take-up, or how much shorter the turnbuckles can be made from fully open to fully closed. Nine-inch take-up is adequate for most yacht applications. My preference in turnbuckles is the open-body type jaw and eye, made of galvanized steel. Bottle screw, or closed-body rigging screws, are more expensive, have finer threads (which are also shallower) and don't allow visual inspection of how much thread is inside the body. They are usually stainless steel or bronze, which I trust much less than galvanized steel. I use the jaw end of my turnbuckles to connect directly to the shroud or stay end, and the eye end is shackled to the chainplate; this is simply the most economical arrangement, as shackles are less expensive than toggles (the link often used between turnbuckle and chainplate). It is considered poor practice to attach a turnbuckle jaw directly to a chainplate because there is no provision for lateral motion in such a connection (it is less flexible in one plane—usually athwartships), and often the turnbuckle will fatigue and fail just above the jaw. After the entire rig has been tuned, "sailed-in and fine-tuned," it is desirable to sew canvas covers over the turnbuckles to keep spray off them as well as to keep their coating of grease or anti-seize compound off the sails, running rigging and sailors.

All threaded components in standing rigging should be assembled with an anti-seize compound, and, as stated before, be seized or moused with soft seizing wire to prevent anything from coming apart. Seizing wire should be stainless steel or Monel; I prefer an-

nealed, three-strand, stainless-steel wire. The cut ends of seizing wire should be covered or beat down so that they cannot cut sails or flesh, or catch on anything. In cases where jaw or shacklepins are fixed with cotter pins instead of being threaded, the cotter pins should be the largest size that will fit through the holes, and the ends should be folded back around the pin body in such a way that they cannot cut or chafe anything. Nut and bolt pins, as in jaws, should have a hole drilled in them and fitted with a cotter pin to prevent them coming loose. I prefer stainless-steel cotter pins over other metals, but because stainless becomes brittle (work-hardened) when flexed, these should be discarded after their removal and replaced with new ones.

RUNNING RIGGING

Lines used for running rigging are calculated at their maximum running length plus a little extra.

Halyards equal the total amount from sail head (with the sail down) to mast truck, down to the deck, plus enough to comfortably cleat off the end. If the halyard involves more than one part, the length from head to truck is multiplied by the number of parts in the tackle. I often figure my main and sometimes fore (or mizzen) halyards to be able to reach the surface of the water. They then can be used to lift objects out of tenders, and to heel the vessel over by securing to a swamped tender, submerged drum or immovable object such as a dock or deadhead. Except on very small craft, halyards should not use line smaller than 1/2 inch, because anything smaller is difficult to pull hard on.

Sheets are calculated with booms all the way out, plus enough to get several wraps on winches (if used) and cleat off comfortably. Heads'l sheets must be long enough to get around the mast or inner forestays, reach the clew of the largest jib when sheeted flat, and likewise be able to take several turns around a winch and be cleated off comfortably at the other end. Sheet size will vary with line load, but again, should not be less than 1/2 inch. I use 5/8-inch sheets for everything on vessels over 40 feet, except possibly stays'l sheets involving a three-or-more-part tackle. Vessels over 60 feet would typically use 3/4-inch sheets.

All sheets and halyards last longer if they are end-for-ended once in a while, so that chafe doesn't always affect the same places.

Topping lifts on many yachts are cleated off on the boom, an awkward arrangement I have never cared for. I splice two topping lifts around the boom near its end, lead them high aloft, then down to cleats or pinrails near the base of the mast, but far enough away that they won't slap against it. I splice smaller diameter line into the topping lifts (see the sail plans in the Appendix A) for lazyjacks; there are usually two such lines, which pass under the boom and are allowed to slide free, so that they yield as the sail pushes against them. With two topping lifts, there is very little chance of failure, and the boom can be used to lift heavier weights. When running, the lee side lift can be slacked way off so as not to deform the airfoil (this is rarely necessary). I also find it easier to peak the boom by dropping my weight down on the lift rather than pulling along the boom, which can be awkward and difficult or even dangerous in worst case scenarios (such as trying to secure a boom in heavy weather). The topping lifts should be long enough that there is still enough line left to cleat off the ends even with the boom-end on deck. On large vessels, the topping lifts may terminate at a block 12 feet or 14 feet above deck, through which is rove a second line terminated at its bitter end to the deck, coach roof or pinrail eye,

and whose working end constitutes a two-part purchase for the topping lift. I use 1/2-inch line for most topping lifts, and 3/8-inch line for lazyjacks on vessels between 30 feet and 50 feet.

Downhauls may be used on heads'ls as well as boomed sails. On boomed sails, they connect to either a gooseneck or jaws, to add luff tension, and usually consist of a two- or three-part tackle employing 3/8-inch or 1/2-inch line. When raising sail, the gooseneck or jaws should be lifted 6 inches or so higher than where they normally rest, providing room for stretch. The downhauls are usually shackled to an eyebolt at the mast base through the deck. When running and reaching, downhauls are slacked, especially when used with jaws. Jib downhauls are very handy used with heads'ls that don't have powerful halyard arrangements (tackle or winches). The jib may be raised on a single-part halyard, and then tensioned along the luff with the downhaul. This reduces the windage created by a several-part halyard aloft (as well as its cost, since the downhaul will be very short), and is much less expensive than a jib halyard winch.

The clew outhaul arrangement (also described in Chapter 30) I prefer best uses a shoulder eyebolt lagged or through-bolted into one side of the boom-end and a cheek block attached opposite it. The outhaul is spliced or tied (a stopper knot works well) to the eye, leads through the clew to the cheek block, and then runs forward to a cleat on the side or bottom of the boom near its forward end. This gives a two-part purchase, and works well on nearly any size vessel, though for large sails tension will have to be set up with the halyard slack and no wind in the sail. Because there is chafe and high tension at times, I rarely use line under 1/2 inch for outhauls except on vessels under 30 feet.

For cruising vessels, I rig a two- or three-part tackle under the boom (also described in Chapter 30), terminated somewhere near the aft end as a vang or preventer. The forward end of this tackle ends with a large hook shackled to the block becket. When not in use, this hook is inserted in an eyebolt under the forward end of the boom (usually the same one the downhaul uses) and the tackle is set up tightly under the boom. When in use, the hook is placed through a deck cleat, and the tackle set up as either vang or preventer, the end being cleated to the same cleat, thus preventing the hook from inadvertently disengaging should the tackle go slack. The aft end usually terminates in a block shackled to an eyebolt or sling (strop) around the boom. The line for the vang/preventer should be long enough to allow the boom to come fully amidships while being prevented as far forward as possible; this will allow the vessel to come into the wind from an accidental jibe without loosing the bitter end when the preventer is fully slackened. Line size is 3/8 inch to 1/2 inch. Nylon is best because stretch absorbs shock loads.

I set up reef outhauls the same as clew outhauls, using the same size line, with an eyebolt on one side of the boom and a cheek block opposite. I leave this tackle rove always, because I am used to reefing a lot, which simply means that I sail under a wide spectrum of wind conditions. The reef outhauls end at cleats on the side of the boom near its forward end, where they can always be worked. On large vessels, I also leave reef tack downhauls rove, preferring line to the hooks often seen today. The line for this starts on one side of the forward end of the boom, goes up through the reef tack grommet, and comes down the other side to either a small belaying pin in the jaws or to a cleat on the boom. When jaws are present, this line is rove through holes on each side, one through each jaw. The bitter end simply has a stopper knot; the hauling end leads from its hole to a cleat or pin. When a gooseneck is used, the bitter end is tied or shackled either to an eye in the gooseneck or in the mast, and the working end goes to a cleat on the opposite side near the base of the mast. The advantage of a reef tack downhaul is that the sail can be reefed on any point of sail without losing all halyard luff tension. This is a great help on any shorthanded cruising vessel and during a race.

Cruising and working vessels can make good use of downhauls rigged to the heads of sails, particularly jibs on bowsprits. These should go from the head of the sail through a block somewhere near the tack of the jib, and lead back to the vicinity of the jib halyard so the same person who releases the halyard can haul down the jib. This downhaul can be considerably smaller than the halyard, usually 3/8 inch or 1/2 inch on vessels over 40 feet. The downhaul should have one or two fairleads along the jib luff to keep it from blowing back and fouling when the jib halyard is slacked. The bitter end is usually permanently tied off so that the downhaul is taut when the jib is all the way up. Laced-on sails can also benefit from downhauls that lead from sail head down through the lacings to the boom gooseneck or jaws. This usually applies to marconi rigs only, as gaffs have enough weight to help bring the sail down, and gaff rigs have shorter luffs anyway.

SPLICES AND KNOTS

There are several excellent books available on splicing and knots; these are in the Suggested Reading List.

Three-strand line is quickly and easily spliced, and should become second nature—like tying a knot. I am not overly fond of braided line, as it tends to kink and form "assholes" more readily than three-strand line. It also costs a lot more and is more complicated to splice.

Splicing wire rope is a useful skill, but I think it is the kind of work that is more easily learned firsthand than from books. I took a sequence of photographs once to illustrate a magazine article I intended to write on making the Liverpool splice the way an elderly rigger taught it to me, and discovered that it took me almost seventy photos to show the different steps! I would be curious to know if anyone has ever learned to make good, fast Liverpool splices from a book.

The knots most useful initially to a sailor are the bowline, the slipped square or reef knot (a loop passed through the final tuck makes it easy to untie), the clove hitch, the stopper knot (figure eight), the tension knot or rolling hitch (used for tying a line off to itself while under tension), the trucker's hitch (among other names, wherein a loop is formed in the standing part of the line and used as a block to set up a two-part purchase), and the tugboat hitch (used for making fast anchor or towing lines to bitts or bollards so that they don't jam). These knots should be researched in a book or learned firsthand.

The lines made off either to cleats or belaying pins need not look like a spaghetti factory. The line should approach the far end of the cleat (or the bottom of the belaying pin), leaving the near end free (see Fig. 32-1), take a half-turn around the cleat passing under the near end, cross over the cleat and around the far end, and then turn a loop to lock over the near end in such a way that the line crosses the cleat again as it goes into the loop. The working end will lay up parallel to the first line that crossed over the cleat, forming a single figure eight. Belaying pins are made off in a similar manner, except that instead of making that first half-turn, you cross over. More turns than this are redundant and just clutter the cleat or pin. Now, when cleating off a sheet, *do not turn the loop*. Just cross over the cleat and pass under the near end and then take another half-turn around it. The reason for this is that sheets must be easily and quickly let go, and a lot of sheet tension and salt water can cause the loop to jam on the cleat, usually at the most embarrassing or even dangerous moment. Many sailors prefer not to turn loops when cleating off halyards also, though I have never had trouble getting a halyard uncleated. After several days beating to windward in rough weather with a single-part halyard that gets very tight, I might change my mind; the right decision varies with each boat or even each sail. Consistency is important, however.

CENTERBOARD TACKLE

Because it is always easier to pull with gravity than against it, the ideal centerboard tackle is the old kind that leads to a block aloft, either at the mast truck or hung on a fixed line from somewhere aloft to reduce the amount of line (and windage) hanging in the sky. Smaller vessels, 45 feet and under, can make do with a three-part purchase pulling up. A single block with becket is shackled to the centerboard eyebolt, and a single block is hung from somewhere just above the deck (the underside of the fife rail or an eyebolt in the mast, usually). The line goes from an eyesplice shackled to the centerboard block's becket, over the upper block sheave, under the lower block sheave, and up to a cleat or belaying pin. Assuming the board was ballasted correctly (so as to weigh very little when fully down but enough to *get* fully down), a small person in average health will be able to haul the board full-up with this tackle in several seconds. To give an example, one of my crew members, who weighs 95 pounds and stands 4 feet 10 inches tall, can bring *Teresa*'s 750-pound center-board fully up in about five seconds. Line size is 5/8 inch.

I dislike centerboard winches because they are so slow and awkward to use that the board is often jammed in the case with the winch cable all tangled up down one side before you even get many cranks on it. When maneuvering in shallow water, it is essential to be able to raise the board in several seconds, or at least keep up with the line as the board comes up during grounding. Also,

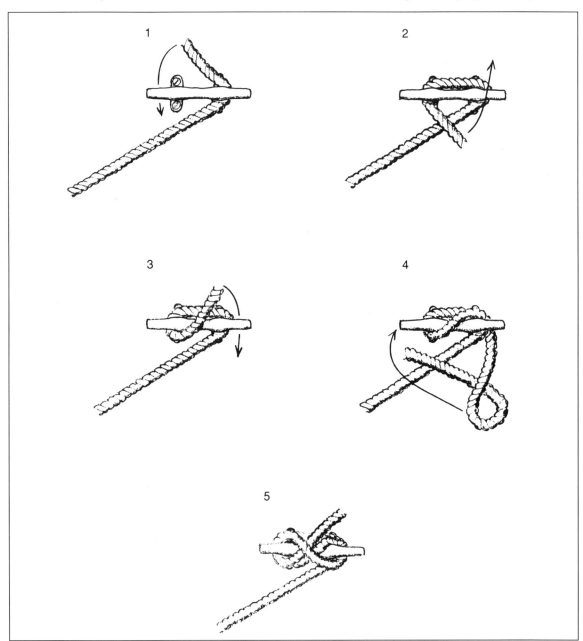

Figure 32-1. Cleating off.

large diameter line rarely gets caught between the board and the trunk; it usually stays on top of the board.

Many of the old schooners had a rigid steel rod hinged to the top of the centerboard, as some small craft have today. The lower block was shackled to the top of this rod, and hence never became immersed in salt water. When running aground, the skipper could see the rod move, and hence could judge the depth of the water.

One other means of raising large centerboards is with a two-speed self-tailing winch, such as a Barient 28, and either a single line directly from the board or a two-part tackle using a block shackled to the centerboard eye. With this second arrangement, the line starts at a fixed point above the centerboard block, leads through the block and up to the winch, usually over a cheek block above the board to convert the angle of pull from vertical to horizontal. This arrangement is useful where the board is controlled from the cockpit, as with single-handed vessels. The advantage over a cable winch is that the board can be raised and lowered more rapidly, and when running aground the line slack can be taken up by hand by pulling it in with one turn around the winch. The two speeds allow rapid pulling at first, and more powerful pulling as the weight of the board increases. Line diameter should be 5/8 inch.

FLAGS

Most modern yachts have only two flag halyards: one to fly the national flag, usually flown two-thirds of the way up the leech of the mains'l, and one from the starboard side masthead or spreaders to fly a courtesy flag of the host country. Blocks for these are often small bronze or galvanized-steel shell types, and 1/4-inch nylon is adequate for their halyards. Often the halyard ends are tied together to form a continuous loop, so the free end can never get away and run through the block. The national flag halyard is cleated off near the end of the boom, and the courtesy flag halyard is made off to the starboard side pinrail. A Q flag is flown on the courtesy flag halyard when entering a foreign country. This solid yellow flag requests "free pratique" (clearance), and signals customs and immigration officials that the vessel wishes to clear into the country. After clearing, the Q flag is taken down and the courtesy flag raised.

LIFELINES

Lifelines are typically wire rope, sometimes plastic coated, and rove through stanchions attached to the deck and often to bulwarks. The wire used is typically running rigging of 7 x 19 construction, though 7 x 7 is better because it doesn't break strands and form "fishhooks," which tear sails and flesh alike. End terminals are frequently swaged or "Nicopressed" on, though spliced ends may be used. Most cruising vessels have two lifelines, the second being halfway between the deck and the upper lifeline. Wire rope diameter varies from 1/8 inch to 1/4 inch. Vessels carrying children and pets frequently seize netting to the lifelines as well. Pelican hooks are often used to disconnect the lifelines between two stanchions amidships to simplify getting on and off the boat. Small turnbuckles are incorporated somewhere in each wire rope to adjust tension. Frequently the lifelines terminate forward at a pulpit, and sometimes aft at a pushpit. I usually run single lifelines from the stern davits forward to the upper end (usually the jaw) of the forestay turnbuckle and shackle it there because I cannot adjust to the ugly appearance of pulpits, and I believe in rigging a jib downhaul, which makes the pulpit unnecessary anyway. Another alternative is to terminate the forward ends at the tip of the bowsprit. On large vessels, I seize a net between the whisker stays below the bowsprit.

DAVIT TACKLE

Wooden davits can use two sheaves set in slots cut into their ends. Metal pipe davits generally have a tang to which a single or double block is shackled. A single block with a hook is used to lift the boat. For small yacht tenders, usually without motors, two single blocks are usually adequate for each davit, but for large vessels, such as inboard-powered yawl boats or big tenders with large outboard motors, more purchase will be necessary. Davit tackle should lead to a comfortable pulling position on deck, and be made off to a cleat, usually mounted on the davit. In most cases, the line should be 1/2 inch.

CATHEAD TACKLE

Catheads (described in Chapter 31) allow large anchors to be "catted," or hauled up via a block and tackle to deck level, clear of the hull. Their tackles consist of three or more parts, often incorporating sheaves set into slots in their ends when made of wood, and having a single or double block shackled to a tang when made of pipe. The other end of the tackle is a single or double block with a large hook shackled to its becket. A large ring is welded or seized at or near the crown of fisherman or plow anchors, and a rope strop is rove through holes in the crown plates of Danforth types; they are catted by swinging the hook into the ring or strop from the deck. After catting—hauling the anchor crown as high as possible—the anchor is brought over to the bulwark and firmly lashed in place. Chafe pads are usually installed at areas of contact. Most modern anchors are rather differently shaped from the fisherman that was

universally used a century ago, but large, heavy anchors, especially storm anchors, of any shape can still benefit from catheads on cruising vessels. Other benefits of catheads is that they bring the weight of large anchors several feet aft from the stemhead, plus keeping them off the deck and out of the way of feet, chain and line. Line size for most davit tackle would be 3/8 inch to 1/2 inch.

PINRAILS AND PINS

Pinrails are convenient on sailboats of all sizes except small craft. They are the easiest thing to make halyards off to, and allow them to be neatly coiled and hung. Another big advantage is that lines don't slap the mast. Vessels with masts stepped through coach roofs especially benefit from pinrails, as they eliminate having to climb up to handle rigging.

I make my pinrails from wood, usually Douglas fir, around $2^1/_2$ inches wide by $3^1/_2$ inches high for vessels between 40 feet and 60 feet. I notch each end to encapsulate the upper ends of the shroud turnbuckles (jaws), and nail copper caps (with felt under them) around the ends to hold them in place, although they can also be notched around the wire rope or turnbuckle threads and seized in

Photo 32-3. Oak belaying pins are rough-cut on the bandsaw prior to turning on the lathe to save time. Each finished pin takes less than one-half hour to make.

place. They must be stoutly made and firmly attached to the shrouds if halyards are to be made off to them, otherwise deck irons (hooks through-bolted into the deck) will be needed. With deck irons, the halyard is looped under the hook, and then made off to the pinrail, so that line tension pulls down instead of up. The deck irons are located close to the bulwarks, out of the way of feet. In some cases, large thumb cleats mounted inside the bulwarks perform this same function.

I make my belaying pins of oak, preferably white oak, 1 inch in diameter by 12 inches long, of traditional shape. I rough-cut them on a bandsaw so that the lathe won't have so much wood to remove (see Photo 32-3). The pins are finished to slightly under 1 inch so they fit in 1-inch holes drilled in the rails. Maximum diameter of the handles is around $1^3/_8$ inches.

For vessels below 40 feet, dimensions should decrease slightly, so that pins and rails don't look out of proportion. Similarly, very large vessels might have slightly larger rails, though pins rarely exceed 16 inches.

CHAPTER 33
SAILS, CANVASWORK AND UPHOLSTERY

Choosing a Sailmaker, Bending On and Sail Maintenance/ Canvaswork and Marlinspike Seamanship/ Upholstery

Cost-saving projects that an amateur boatbuilder can undertake include upholstery, lee cloths, awnings, sailcovers, mast boots, bimini tops, curtains, various covers and spray dodgers.

CHOOSING A SAILMAKER, BENDING ON AND SAIL MAINTENANCE

This is not the place to discuss how sails are designed and made; rather, it is my goal to provide some perspective on choosing the right sails, and, consequently, the right sailmaker, to equip your boat. I believe that sailmaking is best left to an experienced professional with a reputation for making high-quality sails for the kind of vessel you need to equip. It is best by far to employ local talent, since sails need repair, maintenance and finally replacement. A good, well-established local sailmaker will be there for you when you need him or her. This business of having

sails made in China is risky. If they don't set right or have flaws in size or hardware, what are you going to do with them? Send them back to China for alterations? I have seen reasonably good sails from several overseas firms, but I have also seen some awful mistakes, particularly where the sails are unusual. The same is true of having sails made more cheaply in a different part of the country. Most serious professional sailmakers like to be on your boat when the sails are raised the first time. They make a critical evaluation of their own work, how the sail shape looks, and even go out for a sail if possible; at least this has always been the case with Bob Henderson of Henderson Sails in San Diego, California, who has made many sails for me.

Different boats have vastly different requirements in sail shape, weight and materials. Sailmaking is, today, more than ever a blending of high technology, experience, and artistic and mechanical skills. Wherever you might try to save money on your boat, do not do it above deck. The spars, rig and sails may be simple, but they should not be cheap. Sails should be the best you can possibly afford. I would leave out the engine before buying cheap sails.

When new sails are bent on for the first time, a thorough evaluation of both sails and their related rigging should be made. The hanks, cars or lacing systems should be strong and move freely and easily. Downhauls should bring the sails down without fouling or jamming. Halyards should feel comfortable, winches should be the right size and speeds; chafe, slapping and fairleads should be examined. Topping lifts, lazy jacks, outhauls and reefing tackle should all be checked for ease of use, lack of chafe and fouling possibilities. Sheets should be large enough, blocks free and well placed and lead angles should be correct. Sail shape and set will require study, and the vessel will have to be sailed under a wide variety of conditions before final conclusions are made. Another consideration is sail shape after reefing; if you are clawing off a lee shore in a gale, you are going to want excellent windward performance from your reefed sails, and I promise you, if you sail a lot you will find yourself in this situation eventually. Finally, mast shape and the tune of standing rigging is also judged. There are almost always changes to be made; this should be expected.

CANVASWORK AND MARLINSPIKE SEAMANSHIP

Canvaswork and marlinspike seamanship may be undertaken by everyone on board. There are many good books and magazine articles on the subjects. Start a scrapbook of the ideas that you find most useful, and gradually teach yourself marlinspike seamanship, handwork for maintaining your sails, and all the related canvaswork skills that are part of life aboard. Assemble a stock of canvas, leather, sail needles, various kinds of thread and twine, a palm and several replacement grommets into a ditty bag or bosun's kit. (I keep a stock of 1/2-inch grommets with punch and iron to install them.) Emergency sail repairs often can best be made with sail tape and contact cement, so I always keep these useful albeit inelegant items in stores as well. A good bosun's chair is essential, along with a safe, comfortable halyard on which to go aloft (there should always be at least two halyards on each mast—in case you lose one and need to retrieve it). My own preference is a two-part block and tackle without a winch. It is safer, and you can haul yourself aloft if necessary. A pin seized across the D-rings or splices at the top of your chair allows you to cleat yourself off, making you independent of the deck. Make the halyard off to the pin with two figure eights. Your bosun's chair should have some provision (usually pockets or pouches) for carrying tools and gear aloft. Heavy, awkward tools can have lanyards tied to them to prevent accidents. A bucket tied just below your seat is handy, too.

Mast boots are put on upside down and sewn shut in place. Seize the boot base to a wooden ring around the mast on deck. Make a paper template first, as mast boots can be confusing, and make sure it fits with no wrinkles. Use a rubber compound between the mast and the boot, and seize it around the mast upside down and inside out after sewing up the seam (also inside out). Then pull the boot down, right side out, over the wooden ring (which should be painted first), and seize it around the ring. Carefully trim away any excess at the bottom. Then paint or seal the whole boot with soft paint or linseed oil and pine tar.

I have mentioned pine tar several times—it is handy stuff to have around. If you can't find it, try a sports store—it is also used on base-ball bats and rifle stocks.

Chafe points on sails are best protected with leather patches, which are sewn on by hand and replaced as they wear. Sailcovers are vital to sail maintenance: Sunlight (ultraviolet rays) kills most synthetics just as moisture (rot and mold spores) kills canvas. In sails, the thread goes first. Seams should be triple-stitched. The thread stands proud, hence it chafes and gets burnt rapidly by the sun. Dacron fabric exposed to intense sunlight eventually becomes so fragile that you can poke your finger through it. So make good sailcovers that are easy and fast to put on and take off, and use them.

Reef nettles should never have the ends melted (butane backspliced). Melted ends form little knives that cut nice neat arcs in your sails as they swing back and forth against them. Put whippings on the nettle ends, and cut the rest off with a sharp knife, leaving a nice, soft, fuzzy 1/4 inch beyond the whipping. For that matter, all line ends should be whipped, even those melted or cut with a hot-knife. Melted ends eventually come apart.

Lee cloths are canvas fences to keep crew in their berths during heavy weather. They run the length of the berth, or nearly so, are anchored under the mattress at the bottom (often by wrapping the bottom edge around a thin batten, which is fastened down with screws) and the top edge is sewn over a line, which is tied or clipped to stout hooks at bulkheads or the overhead.

Awnings, dodgers and bimini tops vary drastically with individual tastes and needs. They should be made strongly—triple-stitched and heavily reinforced at corners and chafe areas. Stainless-steel bimini top hoops frequently have thick-wall aluminum pipe inside both to reinforce curves and to prevent the pipe from folding during bending, espe-

cially when using a "hickey" bender. *Sarah*'s bimini provides standing headroom in the cockpit while allowing the boom to clear.

UPHOLSTERY

All I want to say about choosing foam is to avoid the soft stuff. It goes dead almost immediately, and when you sit or lie on it, you end up sore. I always use 4-inch firm or extra-firm foam. The green foam (HR-28) seems to be the best, but it's also the most expensive. Something to remember about interior upholstery is: Once it gets wet or even damp with salt water, it never dries out. Salt crystals absorb water from the atmosphere or any other source, and hold onto it. This results in clammy, uncomfortable cushions, and rapidly leads to mold, fungus and rotten foam. It also contributes to painful sores on the sitting ends of sailors. I recommend that a bucket of fresh water be kept on deck for rinsing salt off the crew before they come below, and clothing with salt should be left at the companionway. Foul-weather gear dripping with salt spray can be left in the cockpit or shaken out on deck and put in a wet locker. This may sound radical, but after you live on board for several years, if you are so fortunate, you will understand.

Use butcher or kraft paper to make patterns for upholstery. Push the paper into the corners of the area to be covered and mark it with a pencil. Foam for cushions is typically cut 1/2 inch oversize, so the covers don't wrinkle and crawl around the cushions (1/4 inch beyond each pencil line—don't forget bevels). The covering material is cut so the seams lie at the pencil lines. Edges (sides) are the height of the foam, and bevels are determined by how much larger the tops are than the bottoms for which the pattern was made. Zippers are centered in backs and sides. I use a razor-sharp fillet knife to cut foam; it will have to be sharpened after every three or four cuts because the foam dulls the blade rapidly, so keep a sharpening stone handy. For those so equipped, an electric carving knife does an admirable job of cutting foam.

Closed-cell foam is best for cockpit cushions, as it does not absorb water. I leave these cushions unupholstered, using large towels or terrycloth covers instead. Permanent covers get wet and soggy in rain and spray, provoking removal of the cushions during wet weather, which in turn leads to unnecessary discomfort. With the towels, you just remove them and sit on the bare foam, which is unaffected by water. As mentioned earlier, I like closed-cell cushions as man-overboard flotation devices, with certain qualifications. They are large and white, and in calm seas you can lie comfortably on them. But they would not keep the head of an unconscious person above water, and in rough seas, they would be hard to hang onto. In an actual emergency, I would throw both a life ring (or jacket) and a large cockpit cushion overboard. A person in the water should go for the ring first, and then the cushion. To a search vessel, the white cushion will be easier to spot at sea than a life jacket or ring.

CHAPTER 34
LAUNCHING AND TRIALS

Launching/ Engine Trials/ Sail Raising and Lowering Procedures/ Sail Shape and Trim/ Reefing/ Backing the Booms/ Kites and Light Air Sailing/ Using the Centerboard/ Preparing to Cruise

LAUNCHING

Launching is a great day in boatbuilding, regardless of the size of the vessel and whether the builder is a huge professional yard or a one-time amateur. There is just something unique about building a vessel, a thing that will float and move on the water, and contain the lives and perhaps livelihoods of people who venture into the capricious environment of the sea. Women and boats contain life; they nurture and protect us—no wonder we think of boats as female.

The launching of any boat is, therefore, a significant birth in the lives of her people. Launching a big boat you have built with your own hands and mind and resources is essentially a religious experience. Small wonder that religion gets involved, be it a priest's blessing or a flat-out pagan celebration. In the Lesser Antilles, after the village priest has gone, a lamb is slaughtered at the bow of a new boat, "so she be docile and go where you point her," a young bull is slaughtered at

the stern, "so she go with drive and courage," and a chicken is slaughtered on deck, the blood splattered around, "so she have plenty of food to eat, catch many fish, mon!" Then the cribbing supports are simultaneously chopped down, shorter and shorter at their bases, by a crew of men with machetes, until the boat lies on her side on logs, upon which she is rolled and dragged into the sea.

In the United States we do it a little differently. When I was a much younger man, building my own dream cruiser near the California coastal fishing village of Half Moon Bay, we built a trailer under my 23-ton cutter with old I-beams and ancient truck axles and any scrap metal we could beg, borrow or steal. The Village Boat Yard welded the thing together, and through an all-night, slow-motion parade we dragged the extravaganza through the village streets, lifting phone and electric cables above the deck with broom sticks, behind a huge Mack tractor. In the dawn, with coffee and food still coming from the local fisherman's eatery (Ketch Jo-Ann's—which relayed sandwiches and coffee to us all night), Karren vigorously smashed a bottle of champagne on her stem and gave her a name. Then the groaning cable winch of the *Mother Ducker*, the boatyard's rusted out army-surplus amphibious vehicle, backed by the Mack playing deadman, lowered *Fishers Hornpipe* slowly and carefully down the public launching ramp into the Pacific Ocean. And so began my life as a sailor.

These days we use cranes or travelifts to launch our boats, and the processes seem tame and controlled by comparison. Yet the occasional adventure still finds us: When we tried to move the 57-foot ketch *Lucayan* out of the dirt back-street Key Largo yard where her life started, she jammed, trailer and all, between trees and power poles at the last turn of the driveway, blocking the crane in. It was touch and go for a very tense hour while Gunky (the crane operator), performed several miracles of crane magic that would have soiled the pants of an OSHA inspector. But he got her out.

Good planning, attention to details, the correct equipment, and competent professionals are key elements in a successful launch. Take your time (allow for glitches when planning to meet tides or moving-permit requirements), and think everything through carefully before doing anything. Preparation is of key importance.

If your vessel has to be moved by truck, make sure you have the necessary permits and research the route carefully for potential problems involving zoning, turns, ditches or banks, mud or sand, and power and phone lines. Once when we moved a boat, the utilities company actually had to shut off power in the middle of the night and remove and replace power lines that we couldn't get under. Make sure that cranes and Travelifts are

rated for the weight they will be required to lift, that lifting is physically possible (as cranes boom out, their capacity decreases), that length, beam and draft needs will be provided for, and so on.

And regardless of your particular religious persuasion, don't neglect the ritual and ceremony of giving thanks for being able to launch a boat, don't forget to thank and reward all the people who made it possible, and don't forget to have a hell of a good party!

ENGINE TRIALS

As soon as a hull hits the water, regardless of whether it is brand new or at the end of a routine haulout, the first and immediate job is to inspect for leaks. The second thing, typically, is to start the engine. Assuming it starts and runs, make a thorough inspection of belts, hoses, connections, through hulls and seacocks, oil pressure, water temperature, pumps, exhaust system, controls, stuffing box, vibration, electrical systems, propeller thrust and so on.

During engine trials under way, check for engine operating temperatures under different loading conditions, and temperature of all components in the exhaust system after high-load extended running. Test propeller thrust under different conditions in both forward and reverse, influence of prop rotation and aperture on directional stability in both forward and reverse under a wide variety of wind and current conditions (this is extremely important), and maneuvering and turning abilities under the same wide spectrum of conditions (particularly with different depths of centerboard if your vessel has one). Check possible restrictions to exhaust flow while heeled sharply if your exhaust through hull can be submerged. Monitor temperatures and leak rates of your stuffing box at different engine speeds, rates of expansion and contraction of engine parts, and vibration under different load, speed and r.p.m. conditions.

After initial trials, the whole engine and related systems will require thorough examination and evaluation. There are almost always changes to be made. The stuffing box should be tightened or loosened as necessary (almost no dripping should occur when the engine is off; a slow, steady drip should be present whenever the shaft is turning). If the stuffing box gets extremely hot during extended running, it may be too tight or starved for cooling water, which comes in either through the Cutless bearing or a special inlet. I use shaft logs of large inside diameter because they contain a larger volume of water for cooling and eliminate the necessity of a separate water inlet.

It is very important to disconnect the shaft coupling at this point and carefully check engine alignment. Hulls tend to change shape slightly between being on the land and floating, and initial break-in running involves expansion and contraction never experienced by the engine and its components. Frequently you will find it necessary to adjust the engine alignment. Also check the shaft for straightness, and make sure the stuffing box is centered on the shaft log. Check the log hose and clamps.

If there is a bonding system, or corrosion monitors, grounds or deliberately isolated metal hull components, these should all be checked with a milli-voltmeter for differences in electrical potential. Electrolysis or a galvanic corrosion cell can cause severe damage.

All parts of the engine—block, heads, expansion tank, exhaust manifold, mounting of pumps and alternators, and heat exchangers—must be thoroughly inspected. Bolts should be retorqued as per the manufacturers' instructions.

Failure to be thorough about all of the above can result in problems, damage or systemic failures that may not become apparent until your safety and welfare depend on them.

A last item is leakage. All through the above processes, check constantly for engine and system leaks, including periodic examination of the exhaust for oil and fuel discharge. Please remember that we only have one environment, and it is both illegal and immoral to pollute it. Fuel and oil that end up in the bilges usually go through the bilge pump and end up in the sea. Install drip pans under problem areas, and dispose of their accumulations in such a manner that they don't harm our environment.

SAIL RAISING AND LOWERING PROCEDURES

Beyond what I talked about in the last two chapters, I have a few notes on procedure for those who are new to sailing. Sails raised near the bow of a boat blow her head off and run her first sideways, then downwind. Sails raised near the stern make her point up, first drift sideways, then accelerate upwind (especially if they are sheeted in). These phenomena have a profound effect on what the boat is going to do, both while she is still anchored or moored, and especially after the anchor breaks out or the mooring is cast off. So it is essential that you study your surroundings, wind conditions (is the wind gusty or flukey?) and current. With heads'ls up, most vessels will sail back and forth at anchor, but rarely sail past it. With mains'l up (or mizzen), she may do both.

Normal procedure is to raise sails from aft to forward, and to lower them from forward to aft. Sheets are usually left free with lots of slack, to keep the vessel from sailing over her anchor or mooring. Perhaps the hardest thing is to get off on the desired tack, particularly in a crowded or restricted anchorage. This takes planning, timing and practice, and still often doesn't work out every time. When raising sails while motoring under way, procedures may vary.

Often heads'ls are raised after the vessel is under way, frequently when she has room to round up and stall.

SAIL SHAPE AND TRIM

Working to weather, there should be little or no luffing in any sails. Frequently, where there are several sails involved that interact through slot effects and blanketing, sails are trimmed flatter further aft. Every individual vessel has its own sheeting points for varying conditions, beyond which oversheeting becomes inefficient and the vessel slows down. The careful use of vangs, usually on the mains'l, can flatten the whole foil of that sail, making it faster and more efficient; vangs can also stop luffing caused by an overlapping heads'l or fores'l sheeted flat. Weather helm, caused by an imbalance between hull/keel lateral plane and sail effort, forces the vessel to round up. This can often be alleviated by taking a reef in the aft-most sail, allowing the vessel to stand more "on her feet" (upright), with less compensatory rudder drag, and hence move faster. Both too much sail area aft and too much angle of heel will cause weather helm.

Off the wind, a general rule to keep in mind is that sails aft should be sheeted to the lee side (which may be subtle if the wind is nearly dead astern), and sails forward sheeted to windward. Because the sails are being used more to catch the wind than perform as airfoils, they should generally be sheeted out as far as possible until they are nearly perpen-

dicular to the apparent wind. The sails should not be flat (use no vangs), but should be round and full. Preventers hold the booms from falling back, jibing or oscillating up and down too wildly. Cat ketches and schooners with freestanding masts are delightful downwind because the fores'l can actually be let out with the boom forward of abeam, sometimes nearly on a beam reach, balancing the helm and letting the vessel steer herself (particularly in centerboard hulls with the board up). Photo 34-1 shows *Teresa* running wing and wing downwind on the Bahama Banks.

In many cases, the most powerful portion of a sail is the top third. If this portion luffs a lot, you are not getting maximum efficiency from the foil, and either a vang should be set up, or sometimes alterations may be needed to the sail, lacing lines, if used, or the mast shape. This latter involves springing the upper third or so of the mast aft, thereby flattening the sail by pulling the center of the luff forward in that portion of the sail. Don't, however, get drastic with this unless you know what you are doing.

Photo 34-1. *Teresa* is running wing and wing along the Bahama Banks behind the EXUMAs. Sail battens are 1-inch PVC pipe fitted with spruce inserts for the aft two-thirds of their length. Her freestanding masts allow her fores'l to be let out forward of the mast. With centerboard full-up, she can steer herself downwind at speeds over 10 knots.

REEFING

Reefing is virtually always done from aft forward, whether beating, reaching or running. It reduces weather helm and heel angle when beating or close reaching, and reduces yawing, rolling, broaching and oversteering when broad reaching and running. Other than in racing, it is usually prudent to reef early. In heavy or unpredictable weather, it is a comfort to know that your vessel is safe and under complete control, as well as balanced and efficient. Conversely, reefs are typically shaken out from forward aft. When necessary to take sail in, the outer heads'l usually comes off first, then the aftermost sail. A shortened rig for a cutter usually has a fully reefed main and stays'l; for a ketch, the same or a stays'l and reefed mizzen. A schooner will carry a fully reefed fores'l and stays'l. A cat schooner or cat ketch shortens to a fully reefed fores'l if reaching or running, or a fully reefed main (or mizzen) if close reaching. If the vessel must be driven, both sails are carried fully reefed.

Most vessels heave to under fully reefed main and backed storm jib or stays'l. Cat-rigged vessels will heave to under fully reefed aftermost sail sheeted flat and the helm trimmed to fall off. They can be made to "jog" (lie ahull) by sheeting in a fully reefed fores'l and putting the helm down to come about. They will ride nicely in the troughs this way, making good, slowly, a beam reach. Vessels with centerboards can raise them and "roll with the punches," often being more comfortable than keel hulls when riding out heavy weather; they also can run with the board full-up, without the terrible broaching tendencies of keel hulls, which tend to trip over their own feet. These are all compromises, however: Centerboard vessels beat ineffectively in a large seaway in gale conditions.

BACKING THE BOOMS

The technique of backing the booms is used to force a vessel's head around, either while getting oriented to come off a mooring or anchor, or when coming about and either stalled or in danger of stalling (becoming locked in irons). It is usually the aftermost boom that is backed to the side you want to turn to. This forces the vessel's head in that direction. But booms forward can be backed to push the bow off also, especially if the vessel's head is dead in the wind. In this case, the boom is pushed away from the direction you want the vessel's head to go. A logical extension of this is backing the heads'ls, the most common application being holding a jib sheet until the jib is backwinded, thereby pushing the bow through a tack. On two-masted rigs, booms can be backed in opposite directions to turn a boat more powerfully than by backing only one boom. The danger in this is that backing the booms tends to slow a vessel's motion, or even drive her backwards, such that when she falls off, she is either dead in the water or has no steerage, and will need to gather way before coming into control. This can make her vulnerable, particularly if she is sheeted flat on all sails, and is slow to accelerate. In gusty or shifting winds, often a vessel can be knocked down before she gathers way; hence the sheets should be eased or at least tended until the time of vulnerability has passed.

KITES AND LIGHT AIR SAILING

The art of sailing fills volumes, and handling light air sails is one of the longer subjects. All I want to talk about here is the kite, because it is a little known sail in the late 20th century. Basically a cousin to the gollywobbler and fisherman tops'l, the kite is set between masts of nearly equal height, and is basically a light air reaching sail. Peak and throat halyards are set up tightly when the wind is forward of the beam, as is the luff downhaul or tack. The sheet can lead to a snatch block on the end of the main (aftermost) boom, or to a block or cleat on deck far aft. The sail can often be sheeted very flat and even used close hauled on the wind. Off the wind the peak (or after) halyard and sheet are eased, and the sail balloons. On a broad reach, it tends to become blanketed by the mains'l until one or the other sail must come down. On a dead run it is useless, as it collapses on itself. However, on an extended broad reach, the sail is powerful and can be used to great advantage by taking the mains'l down. It is possible, especially with freestanding masts, to let the fores'l out to windward on a broad reach, running wing and wing; the fores'l will help keep the kite full of wind, and the two together act like a yankee jib and drifter or single-luff spinnaker being flown together on twin headstays. The four-sided kite is flown free-flying, and is usually raised by two people (one on each halyard), in the lee of the working sails, and taken down similarly. Tack downhaul and sheet are set up after the sail is flying. It is flown most effectively to the lee of the fores'l, although it will work on either side when tacking. When it is on the windward side of the fores'l, during tacking for example, it may be lowered without coming about by carefully sliding it down the fores'l and gathering it below the boom. Photos 34-2 and 34-3 show *Teresa* sailing her kite, on and off the wind, respectively.

Photo 34-2. The nylon kite can be sheeted in flat enough to beat to weather in very light air.

Photo 34-3. When the sheet and peak halyard are eased, the kite can be used to broad reach. The sheet is led to a snatch block at the end of the main boom when reaching.

USING THE CENTERBOARD

Vessels which have centerboards enjoy an entirely new dimension of sailing, as well as having access to places where keel vessels simply cannot go. Having owned, lived aboard and traveled in both deep-keeled and centerboard vessels, I doubt I will ever own a deep, fixed-keel vessel again. The only real advantage to deep, heavy keels involves beating to weather in rough open ocean conditions; centerboard vessels can do virtually everything else better, I firmly believe. Vulnerability in knockdowns is the other concern, and deserves consideration from the safety standpoint. Vessels which are not self-righting involve a calculated risk, which must be very seriously considered. My own feelings are that a family cruising vessel in the hands of other than highly skilled and highly experienced sailors (not just one sailor) should be self-righting. This is hard to achieve in extremely shoal-bodied hulls, and involves lead shoes in most but not all cases. Commodore Ralph Munroe's *Presto*-type vessels were self-righting with all inside ballast because of their deep, rounded, flat-bottom bodies (the EXUMA 36, whose lines are in the Appendix, shows this type of hull section). On the other hand, many shoal hulls have extremely high initial form stability, and can only be capsized by extremely bad judgment or a combination of very unfortunate circumstances.

When it comes to deciding between the two, the biggest factor is where you intend to sail. Living on the U.S. East Coast and sailing there and in the Bahamas would strongly indicate a centerboard vessel. Living on the U.S. West Coast and sailing up and down there, with possible trips to Hawaii and the South Pacific, would indicate a deep, full keel. There are also compromise hulls, having many different configurations of keel and centerboard. The problem is that you want a keel and low ballast to beat across an ocean windward passage, and then a centerboard once you get somewhere and want to explore and gunkhole. Like everything involving boats, the right compromise must be made. I think the hydraulic ram daggerboard with a delta wing ballast bulb deserves development. Then there are multihulls . . . but not if you want to take anything with you.

The first thing to learn about the centerboard is that steering changes dramatically when it is up or down. Many shoal hulls are difficult or impossible to turn around, particularly downwind with the board up—at best they will need a lot of room. Their long, straight keels give them excellent directional stability, hence they will go downwind well and easily with the board up. Going to weather, or maneuvering, the board must be part or all the way down, with response improving with depth. Because leeway is no problem off the wind, the board is hauled full-up. When beating, the sail drive vectors are largest athwartships, and the board is let fully down to diminish leeway, vital when beating. On a beam reach, the board is usually most of the way up, leaving a little down for steerage response.

In very shallow water, the board is a depth sounder, like it or not. For this reason it pays to have a good, tough stainless-steel shoe well fastened to its lower leading edge, under the point, and 6 inches or so up the trailing edge. You learn to feel the board touch, raise it slightly, and wait to feel it touch again. Usually you can hear it hit, but in soft mud you must develop a sense for the vessel slowing slightly. In this manner you can work into a shallow anchorage, across a flat or up a river, when you can't see the bottom. As the board touches, it is raised a foot or so, each time, until you have what you feel is the thinnest depth you are willing to navigate. Then when the board touches, you either back off completely or look for another passage.

Similarly, the board can be used to break a vessel's speed when moving slowly and under low power (short-sailed, as with only the last part of one sail up while coasting into an anchorage, in extremely light air, or under power at idle speed or coasting in neutral). The board will also hold the vessel in one place when not under sail, power, or in strong wind or current, such as in a canal waiting for a bridge to open or by a beach. This literally involves "parking" the boat in shallow water with the board down. It works particularly well in reverse. I have often put *Teresa*'s bow gently on a beach and dropped her board, even under sail, leaving the sails

Photo 34-4. Centerboard vessels can be parked in fair conditions by dropping the centerboard in shallow water. Here *Teresa* rests on a beach on Paradise Island, Bahamas, while the crew takes a sunbath and a swim.

luffing with sheets free. I've done this to drop off or pick up passengers (they can get on and off without getting their feet wet!), look for shells briefly or wait for a bridge to open. You must, of course, be aware of the tide, never park on a lee shore, and never leave the vessel untended. Photo 34-4 shows *Teresa* parked on the beach at Paradise Island in the Bahamas.

Another extension of deliberate grounding involves close maneuvering in extremely shallow water, where there is not sufficient depth to let down enough board to obtain necessary steerage. In this instance, the board is dropped until it hits, with someone standing by the tackle, and the vessel is literally steered by pivoting the stern with the rudder about the axis of the board, carving its way into whatever bottom is present—hopefully sand or soft mud. This works extremely well, providing excellent maneuverability, but is hard on the board over any bottom besides mud. It is a tactic to use judiciously.

One inevitable consequence of all these centerboard shenanigans is that some day the centerboard is likely to be forced into its slot while no one is there taking up on the tackle,

resulting in rolling one or more of the tackle parts between trunk and board. Normally the tackle will just fold up on top of the board (I design mine to do so), but in the rare instance where it doesn't, you are in deep trouble. The board can neither be raised nor lowered, and if you are aground, which is extremely likely at that point, the tide will probably be ebbing (this is a centerboarder's addendum to Murphy's Law). Here's what you do: If the sails are up, take them down. Make off the main (or mizzen in ketches) halyard to the centerboard tackle, and haul like hell, being ready to sit down hard when she lets go. Or you can run the centerboard tackle through a snatch block hung on something that won't break, tag it to another line, (use bowlines so you can untie them later) and run it back to your biggest winch, or to the windlass.

To remove a centerboard with the vessel afloat, first remove the trunk plug (or plugs), and tie a line to the forward lifting eye, if there is one. If not, sling a line beneath the keel about 3 feet aft of the front of the board while the board is fully up, and set up tightly, the ends being made off to cleats so they can be slacked gradually. The pin, hopefully above water or outside in the keel, is loosened or prepared to be pulled as the case may be. Slowly lower the board by its tackle until enough weight is on the sling so that the pin can be removed. With a forward eye, follow the same procedure, or lead the line from the eye to a winch or tackle, which is used to lift enough weight so that the pin can be pulled. The board is then lowered gently by slacking the tackle and either the sling or forward eye line until it clears the keel slot. Lines are then made to the eyes beneath the boat (you can use the pinhole forward), the tackle shackle and forward eye line are removed, and the board may be dragged on its side by the new lines to a beach, dock or the side of the vessel. Taken alongside, it may be brought to shallow water or a facility for lifting it onshore, or in some instances, it is lifted by halyards and repaired on deck, or shifted from deck to a dock with the halyards. For vessels like *Sarah* or *Teresa*, these procedures would present no problem, but will probably never have to be used.

PREPARING TO CRUISE

This topic could obviously be another book, so I'm just going to mention a few things. Hang nets for produce. Put together a really good first-aid and medical chest with the help of a doctor. Take classes in advanced first aid and learn cardiopulmonary resuscitation. Assemble an incredible tool kit, along with a really thorough store of spare parts. Read about and study sailing, cruising and the places you want to visit. Learn the language! It's not that hard (in most cases), and

Photo 34-5. *Sarah* in Fort Pierce Inlet during sail trials.

you'll be glad you did. Practice sailing your boat in every conceivable situation and condition. Make sure your crew can sail the boat without you. Practice man-overboard drills. Forget about time, money and schedules. Don't bring pets (well... maybe a cat or a parrot, if it grew up on the boat). Learn to dive (at least advanced snorkling). And go!

APPENDIX A

DESIGNS AND ADAPTATIONS

These 10 designs demonstrate the wide variety of hull types that can be built using cold-molded methods. With the exceptions of the TERRAPIN schooners, all the hulls are of triple-laminate construction. Most of them incorporate laminated plywood topsides, except for the first and last examples, which carry the triple-laminate method up to the sheer.

The designs are adaptations, replicas, or inspirations from traditional 19th century American working vessels and yachts. Only the BLUE WATER 40 is a strictly contemporary type—being an IOR-type racer/cruiser. All 10 designs are my originals, and are in no way exact copies of the types from which they were adapted. Only the PILOT schooner 45 is an adaptation of a single specific hull (Isaac Webb's 1833 schooner-yacht *Dream*), and the lines shown here take into consideration the long evolution of hull design that has followed the early 19th century.

In essence, I have tried to combine the best of all worlds in my designs, integrating mod-

ern marine architecture and construction technology with the highly refined wisdom, experience, survivalism, and sheer beauty of the traditional vessels that served as my models.

DESIGN COMMENTARIES

Figure A-1. ISLES OF SHOALS 28

Howard I. Chapelle describes the Isles of Shoals' boats in *American Small Sailing Craft*. These small double-ended fishing boats were launched from the beaches of New Hampshire, and were used for fishing around the offshore Isles of Shoals. After the Civil War, a hotel built on one of the islands stimulated the boats to become larger (25 to 30 feet), and the vessels were used to transport guests. The originals were enlarged Hampton boats of lapstrake construction with planked keels of moderate draft.

The model shown here has slightly softened bilges, to accomodate double-diagonal planking using 1/4-inch by 6-inch plywood

Figure A-1. ISLES OF SHOALS 28

L.O.D.	28'4"
L.O.A.	30'
L.W.L.	27'9"
BEAM	9'4"
DRAFT	3'3"
SAIL AREA	465 sq. ft.
DISPLACEMENT	11,300 lbs. (5.65 U.S. tons)
BALLAST	4,500 lbs.

RIG

Gaff rigged cat schooner with overlapping foresail.

POWER

Small diesel if desired. Vessel originally rowed from two or more stations; can be sculled also.

TYPE

Double ended coastal fishing and cargo vessel. Very seaworthy open boat—the model is a close cousin to the Block Island Cowhorn.

ACCOMMODATIONS

These vessels were usually open boats, but can be decked with self-bailing cockpit and trunk cabin between the masts to become an extremely seaworthy all-weather/all-oceans pocket cruiser for an adventurous couple.

CONSTRUCTION

Cold-molded wood/epoxy/fabric: Hull—double diagonal 1/4" ply planks over 5/8" tongue and groove fir or yellow pine. All exterior surfaces and bilges covered with epoxy impregnated Xynole-polyester cloth and painted with linear polyurethane.

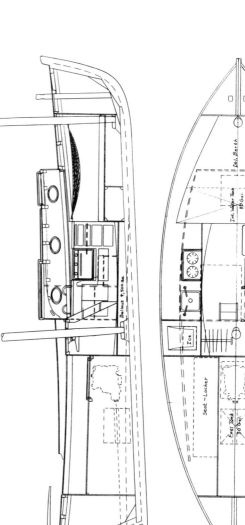

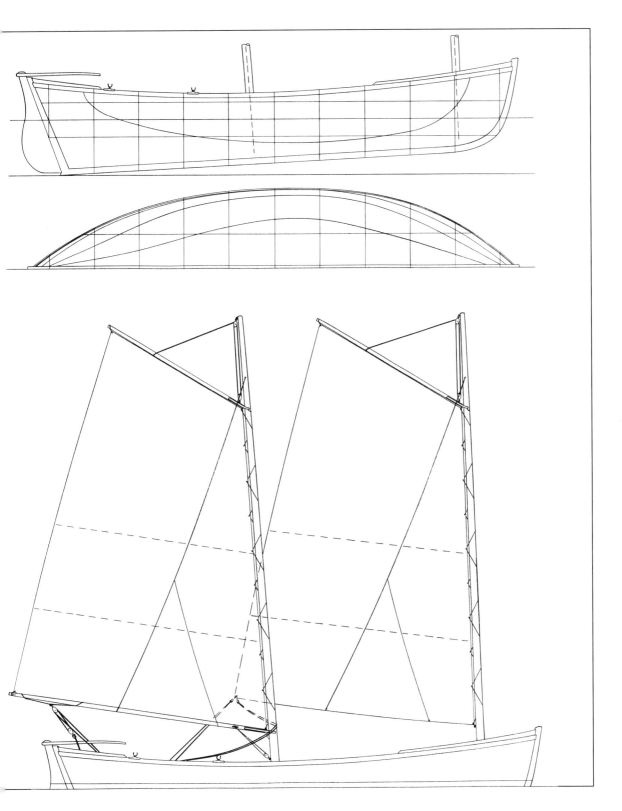

over a fore-and-aft layer of 5/8-inch by 3¼-inch tongue-and-groove stock. The hull ends are slightly finer than those of the original models, and the center of buoyancy has been shifted slightly farther aft in keeping with modern theories.

I have drawn the lines for an open boat, as the originals had little or no decking, and included an interior plan for a decked version with a cabin and small inboard diesel under a large cockpit. This "pocket-cruiser" version constitutes an extremely seaworthy small boat for an adventurous couple to take sailing in all seasons.

Figure A-2. EXUMA 36

The EXUMA 36 is based on Commodore Ralph Munroe's *Presto*. The design is for a canoe-type centerboard hull incorporating laminated plywood in the topsides. A "false" chine log, or longitudinal stringer, joins the hull bottom to the topsides, but there is no angular joint as in the other EXUMA series hulls shown here. The log is essentially a fastening plane—a full-length butt-block—to which the different thickness bottom and topsides planking are attached.

Commodore Munroe was one of the early settlers of Biscayne Bay, Florida and introduced several innovative boat types to the area. The original *Presto*, though light and very shallow of draft, demonstrated excellent seaworthiness and versatility in all weather conditions. The EXUMA 36 design stations are very similar to the original's, but the design lacks the *Presto*'s long stern overhang. Munroe's later designs had shorter sterns, so I feel justified in this modification.

Figure A-3. EXUMA 44

The EXUMA 44 *Teresa* was designed to be the smallest of a particular hull type (which originated with the EXUMA 52 *Sarah*) that would have full standing headroom. The hull

Figure A-2. EXUMA 36

L.O.A.	36'11"
L.O.D.	36'0"
L. EXT.	42'1" with bowsprit; 44'4" with davits
L.W.L.	30'5"
BEAM	10'6"
DRAFT	2'6" board up, 6'3" board down (internal ballast)
	3'3" board up, 7'2" board down (external ballast)
DISPLACEMENT	14,500 lbs.
BALLAST	5,000 lbs. lead

TYPE

Shoal bodied centerboard cruiser based on Commodore Munroe's *Presto*.

POWER

Twin 9.9, 4-cycle outboards in wells or inboard 2-cylinder diesel.

SAIL AREA

Cutter—831 sq. ft. working.

ACCOMMODATIONS

The layout shown for the cutter rigged version is for a live-aboard couple with occasional guests (sleeps four). The ketch and cat-ketch with divided cabins sleep two in a private aft cabin and two forward in the main cabin. Other layouts are available on a custom basis.

CONSTRUCTION

Cold-molded wood/epoxy/fabric: Bottom—double diagonal marine ply planks (1/4" x 6") over 5/8" tongue and groove planking laid fore and aft. Sides—double laminated 1/4" marine ply. Decks—double impregnated Xynole-polyester cloth finished with linear polyurethane paint systems. Spars—mast(s) hollow hexagonal laminated Douglas fir/epoxy, booms solid Douglas fir. Interior—painted ply trimmed with varnished hardwoods.

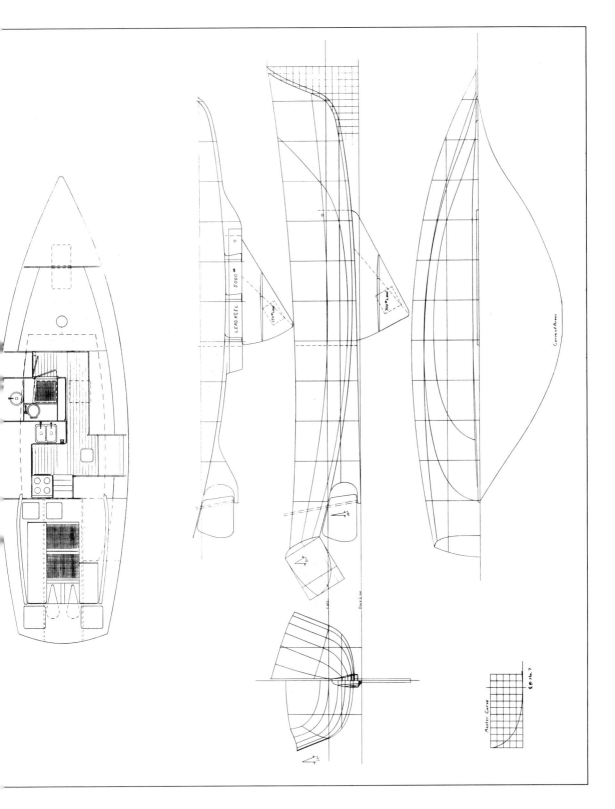

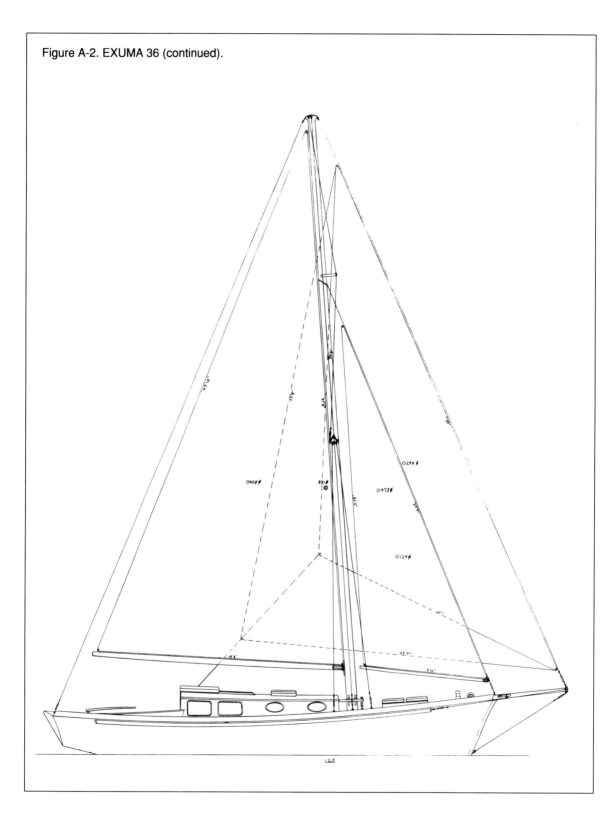

Figure A-2. EXUMA 36 (continued).

Figure A-3. EXUMA 44 *Teresa*

L.O.A.	43'9"
L.W.L.	40'
BEAM	12'
DRAFT	2'8" board up, 6'1" board down
SAIL AREA	856 sq. ft. working, 1,520 sq. ft. max.
DISPLACEMENT	22,000 lbs.

BALLAST

7,000 lbs. lead, internal, boxed.

TYPE

Shoal draft centerboard schooner.

POWER

Twin 9.9 h.p. Yamaha 4-cycle outboards in wells.

RIG

Florida sharpie cat schooner. Fully battened sails. Self-tending rig. Other rigs available.

ACCOMMODATIONS

Twin cabins separated by watertight bulkheads. Layout shown for live-aboard family with guests, sleeping six. Other layouts available on request.

CONSTRUCTION

Cold-molded Douglas fir: Bottom—tongue and groove planking laid fore and aft covered with double diagonal marine ply planking, finished thickness 1 1/2". Sides—laminated marine ply, 7/8" thick. Decks—laminated marine ply over sawn deck beams. Covering system—epoxy impregnated Xynole-polyester fabric painted with epoxy primers and linear polyurethane finish coats. Spars—hollow laminated free standing Douglas fir masts: solid Douglas fir booms with leathered oak jaws, finished bright. Bulwarks—stack laminated Douglas fir. Interior—as requested, usually exotic hardwoods finished bright.

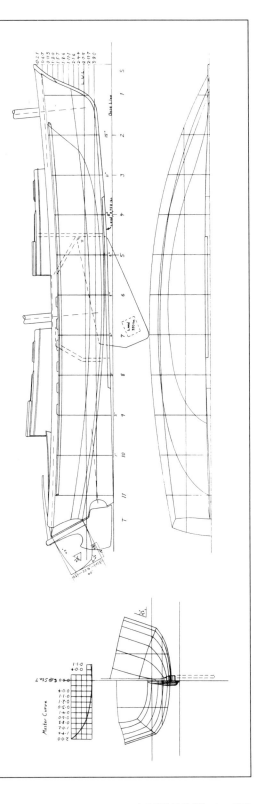

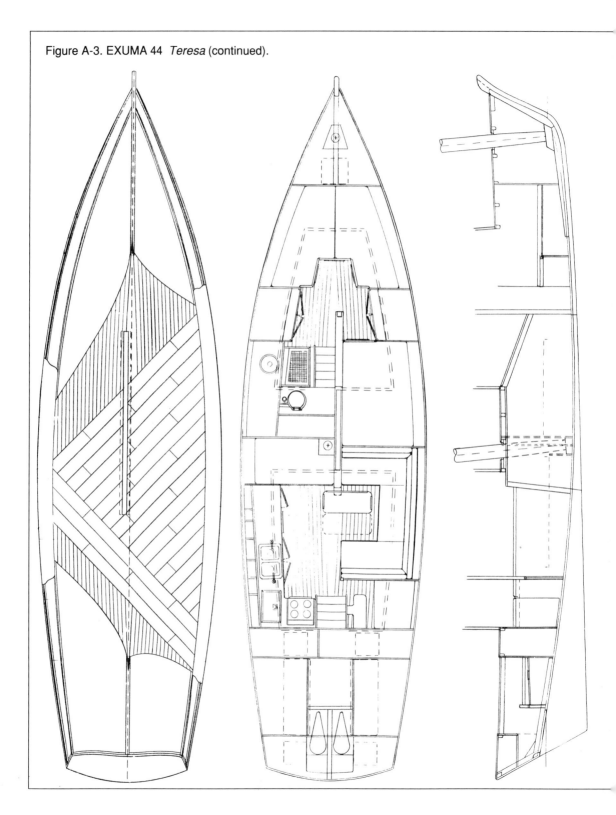

Figure A-3. EXUMA 44 *Teresa* (continued).

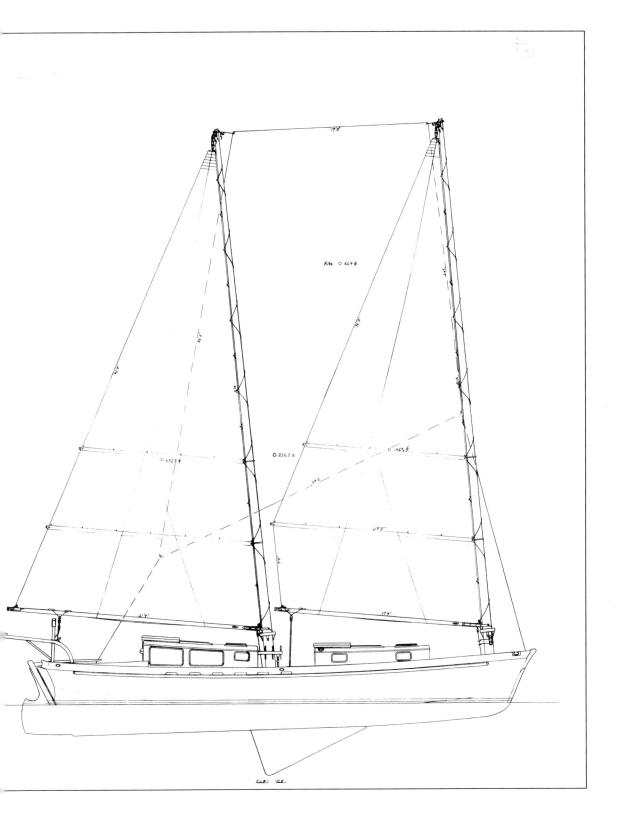

Kite ○ 664 ∮

is a combination of Chesapeake Bay bugeye, batteau, and Munroe boat, having many properties of Commodore Munroe's later designs *Wabun* and *Utilis*. The chine, at which the triple-laminated bottom is joined to the laminated plywood topsides, is gently rounded to avoid the appearance common to hard-chine hulls. The arced bottom and conic stern sections in the topsides combine with the deck crown to create an elliptical, curved transom.

At 22,000 pounds, *Teresa* is not a light vessel—she is of moderate displacement and stands up well to her 50-foot-tall cat-schooner rig. The hull is fast, stiff, and powerful, capable of frequently exceeding her hull speed of 8.5 knots. In a passage from Bimini to Miami during a mild "norther" of 15 to 18 knots, *Teresa* averaged 9.5 knots, running wing and wing downwind, steering herself for most of the passage. Never in my sailing experience have I seen this performance in any other monohulled yacht. The hull surfs easily and controllably in seas as large as eight feet without broaching tendencies. I have run *Teresa* through inlets in breaking seas at peak speeds over 15 knots with no threat of a sea overtaking her buoyant stern, which gently lifts the dinghy in the stern davits from harm's way, allowing the sea to roll under and along each side of the hull. My only criticism of the hull is that it pounds uncomfortably when driving the vessel to weather in large head seas (five feet and larger). She does, however, lie ahull very comfortably, making good a little less than a beam reach while riding in the troughs. She is capable of clawing her way off a lee shore in rough weather, though the ride may be uncomfortable. With internal ballast alone, the hull is not self-righting; with an external 3,000-pound lead shoe, it is.

Figure A-4. EXUMA 52

The EXUMA Series of shoal-draft cruising

Figure A-4. EXUMA 52 *Sarah*	
LENGTH EXTREME	63'2"
L.O.A.	52'6"
L.O.D.	51'
L.W.L.	45'
BEAM	13'
DRAFT	2'9" centerboard up, 6'9" centerboard down
SAIL AREA	1,200 sq. ft.
DISPLACEMENT	28,155 lbs.

BALLAST

8,000 lbs. lead, internal, boxed. Additional to trim.

RIG

Florida sharpie schooner with forestay, triatic, and running backstays. Fully battened sails. Self-tending.

TYPE

Shoal draft centerboard schooner.

POWER

Twin 9.9 h.p. Yamaha 4-cycle outboards in wells.

ACCOMMODATIONS

Layout shown for live-aboard family with two children and occasional guests. Other layouts, including commercial, available on request.

CONSTRUCTION

Cold-molded Douglas fir: Bottom—double diagonal marine ply planking over tongue and groove planking laid fore and aft, finished thickness 2". Sides—laminated marine ply, 1" thick. Decks—laminated marine ply over sawn deck beams. Covering system—epoxy impregnated Xynole-Polyester fabric painted with epoxy primers and linear-polyurethane finish coats. Spars—hollow laminated free-standing Douglas fir masts; solid Douglas fir booms with leathered oak jaws. Bulwarks—stack laminated Douglas fir. Interior—as requested by client; usually exotic hardwoods.

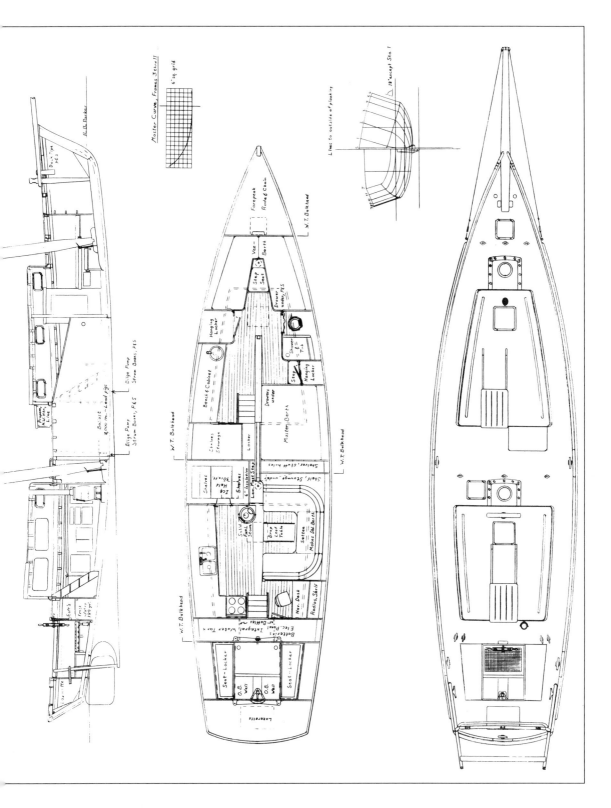

Figure A-4. EXUMA 52 *Sarah* (continued).

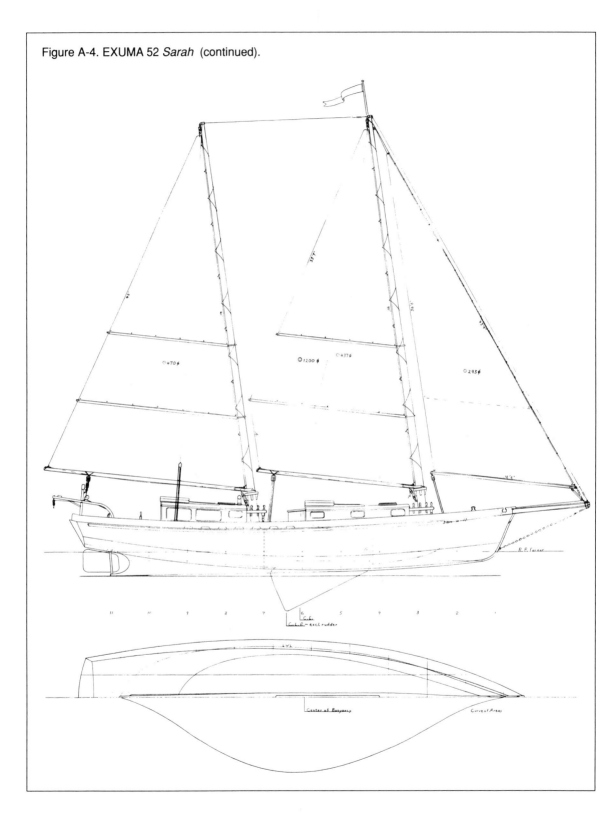

boats originated with this design in 1984. It started with a friend who wanted a simple cruiser, economical to build and maintain but large enough to live aboard comfortably, for the Bahamas and Florida Keys. After working with some sharpie concepts, we both concluded that the vessel should be modeled after Commodore Ralph Munroe's remarkable vessels and should have some features common to the Chesapeake Bay bugeyes. The vessel that evolved is 52 feet 6 inches on deck, has a 13-foot beam, and draws a mere 2 feet 9 inches, giving her access to cruising grounds about which most big sailboats can't even dream. In a world with increasingly crowded anchorages and ever more expensive marina slips, her ability to "get away" is invaluable.

A simple schooner rig with fully battened sails was chosen for low cost and ease of handling by a husband-wife team with two small children. Reefing is traditional slab style, and the reef points are above the battens, substantially reducing the number of nettles needed. The hollow laminated Douglas fir masts are free-standing except for the forestays. Running backstays from the mainmast truck provide extra jib luff tension but are terminated far enough forward on deck to allow short tacking without letting them go; thus the vessel is completely self-tending. The powerful balanced rudder turns her quickly, yet the long, straight skeg keel provides her with excellent tracking capabilities. She will steer herself to weather, and with her big centerboard all the way up, can steer herself wing and wing running downwind.

Divided trunk cabins provide privacy, circular living areas (the design makes better use of space than a walk-through arrangement, which loses living space to wasted cabin sole), and enable tankage and ballast to be placed in the hull's deepest part, which is also closest to its center. Free-standing masts

the size of *Sarah*'s must have partners at the deck rather than a coach roof, which simply could not be made strong enough to take the athwartships loads. A watertight bulkhead between the cabins has a gasketed hatch to allow emergency access between cabins, or just to let adults, active in the aft cabin, listen in on children asleep forward. *Sarah* has five full bulkheads, all of which can be made watertight, providing great safety. Either cabin can be flooded to the waterline without preventing sailing the vessel to safety.

Because *Sarah*'s hull is nearly flat along the centerline and her construction has no internal structure, the inside of the hull can serve as the cabin sole. This allows a much lower cabin profile, increased headroom, less weight and windage in the hull and cabin trunks above the waterline, and simpler interior construction at greater savings in labor and materials than otherwise possible. After building and sailing several vessels with this feature, I am convinced that the "walk-on hull" is the main selling point in shoal-draft hulls which allow its incorporation.

In sail trials, *Sarah* has proved to be a fast, powerful, weatherly sailing machine. She has fulfilled our expectations, and outsails all the vessels she has encountered under informal conditions. Capable of speeds exceeding 10 knots, she steers herself both to windward and wing-and-wing off the wind.

Figure A-5. TERRAPIN 34

To give credit where credit is due, this design is based on, or inspired by, Harry Sucher's wonderful drawings for a TERRAPIN schooner in his book *Simplified Boatbuilding*. The type was a sharpie turtle fisherman used in the Florida Keys in the late 19th century.

This renewed version came about in response to the quest for an extreme shoal draft, very low cost, day charter bareboat for

Figure A-5. TERRAPIN 34 schooner

L.O.D.	34'3"
L.W.L.	30'8"
L.O.A.	40'6"
BEAMS	10'0"
DRAFT	2'3"
SAIL AREA	600 sq. ft.
DISPLACEMENT	12,896 lbs. (both hull models).
BALLAST	4,000 lbs. lead in boxes.
HEAD ROOM	4'7"
RIG	Gaff schooner
POWER	Outboard in well or inboard diesel.
TYPE	Turtle fisherman adapted as yacht.

ACCOMMODATIONS

Layout shown sleeps 6 in large, comfortable berths. Vessel intended for protected water and coastal cruising; the batteau hull model is more seaworthy than the sharpie.

CONSTRUCTION

Quick-molded: Epoxy/fabric covered laminated plywood. Bottom—double diagonal 5/8" x 12" x 8' plywood planking over longitudinal stringers and partial backbone. Sides and deck—5/8" plywood. Spars—solid Douglas fir. Interior—painted plywood trimmed with hardwoods.

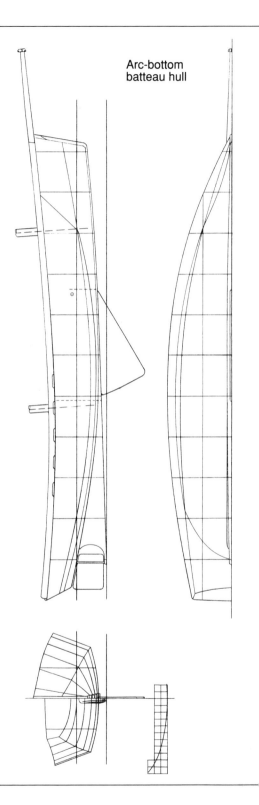

Arc-bottom batteau hull

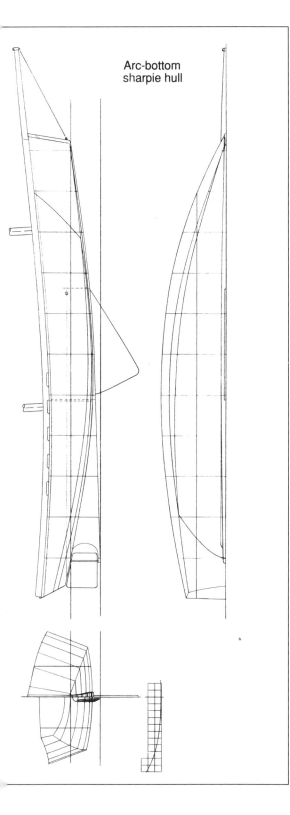
Arc-bottom
sharpie hull

the Indian River area of Florida's east coast.

Two hulls are available in Quick-molded construction: a radius bottom sharpie and a radius bottom V-bow batteau. The sharpie would be cheaper and easier to build by a small margin, and a little faster off the wind than the batteau, which would be more weatherly, seaworthy, and comfortable in a seaway.

The boat is designed to be built almost entirely of southern yellow pine form-ply, which is very inexpensive, made with waterproof glue, and has two "B" faces ("footballs" are rare). The oil coating used to provide release from concrete is compatible with epoxy resin.

The rig is traditional. Spars can be made rapidly and easily from Douglas fir stock available in many commercial lumberyards (30-foot 6 x 6s). The gaff rig is the best for this hull form because it gives lots of drive down low, and presents maximum sail area to the wind when running wing and wing. The hulls will surf off the wind beyond hull speed.

I doubt that more boat can be obtained for the money. Materials costs, including sails, outboard motor and simple interior furniture, are around $20,000 as of early 1989. Total costs, including labor and materials, are approximately $60,000 for a complete sail-away TERRAPIN 34.

Figure A-6. BLUE WATER 40

This design is obviously in a different category from the rest. I conceived the boat for a friend who is skipper of a New York 40 IOR (International Offshore Racer) boat. The faceted, flat-bottom section, IOR hulls lend themselves beautifully to my cold-molded construction methods. The delta-wing fin keel is supported inside the hull by welded stainless steel I-beam floor timbers. The open stern provides a swim/dive platform out-

Figure A-5. TERRAPIN 34 schooner (continued).

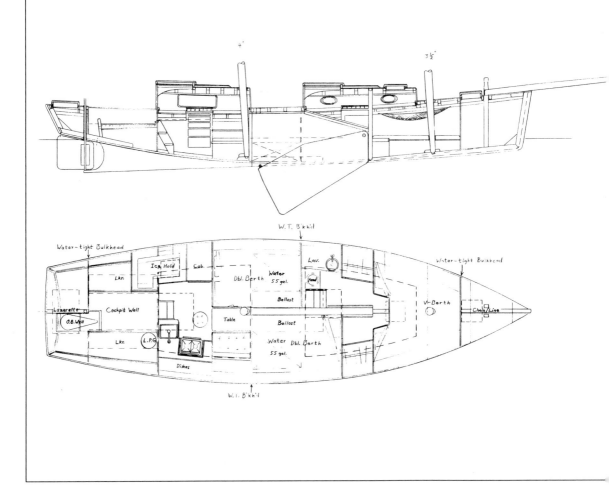

board of the recessed transom. The cockpit is generous and T-shaped to allow a large wheel aft. The chart table over the foot of the master berth is close to the cockpit and seating consists of padded knee and buttock supports, allowing the navigator comfort and stability with the torso free to move with the vessel's motion.

Figure A-7. SCOW SCHOONER 44

Scow schooners have fascinated me since the 1970s when I lived and sailed on San Francisco Bay. Their traditional flat and V-bottom hulls lend themselves perfectly to arc-bottom cold-molded construction. Again, by using a "walk-on" hull for the cabin sole, you get lower profile, simplified construction, and more internal volume.

The scow shown can serve as a yacht, charter boat, or cargo carrier. The raised deck aft provides a large, open main cabin. Cargo hold capacity is 10 U.S. tons at 500 cubic feet, assuming no permanent ballast is used. If it were used as a yacht or passenger carrier, the

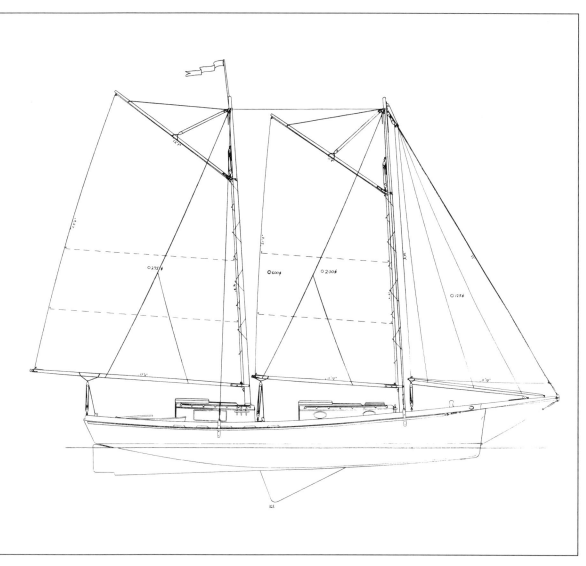

scow would need to carry 10,000 pounds of lead.

Figure A-8. PILOT SCHOONER 45

I have loved this hull ever since I first found the original's lines in Chapelle's *Yacht Designing and Planning*. This particular design represents as incredible a yacht as could be had in any age. She is large, comfortable, seaworthy, and of moderate draft for her size. Her rig is based upon the Chesapeake Bay pilot schooners, which were sailed home single-handed from the offshore Atlantic in all weather after discharging their pilots. These schooners had to be simple and practical but also fast and weatherly to compete in their trade.

Note: There are, at present, seven vessels in the EXUMA Series, ranging from 28 to 68 feet; two vessels in the TERRAPIN schooner series; three vessels in the PILOT schooner series, ranging from 37 to 55 feet, and three double-ended vessels similar to the Isles of Shoals boat, ranging from 28 to 42 feet.

Figure A-6. BLUE WATER 40

L.O.A.	40'4"
L.W.L.	35'3"
BEAM	12'0"
DRAFT	6'0"
SAIL AREA	1,073 sq. ft.
DISPLACEMENT	19,526 lbs.
BALLAST	7,000 lb. fixed keel, lead, additional to trim.
RIG	Cutter or sloop. Fully battened mains'l.
POWER	Inboard diesel, 30-50 h.p.; Vee drive.
TYPE	Offshore racer/cruiser.

ACCOMMODATIONS

Layout shown for live-aboard couple with children, crew, or guests. Other layouts available.

CONSTRUCTION

Cold-molded Douglas fir: Bottom—double diagonal 1/4" marine ply planking over 3/4" tongue and groove planking laid fore and aft. Sides—laminated 3/8" marine ply (2). Decks—marine ply over and under foam core. Covering system—epoxy impregnated Xynole-polyester fabric painted with epoxy primers and linear polyurethane finish coats. Spars—aluminum or hollow laminated Douglas fir; triple panel rig. Interior—painted ply trimmed with exotic hardwoods.

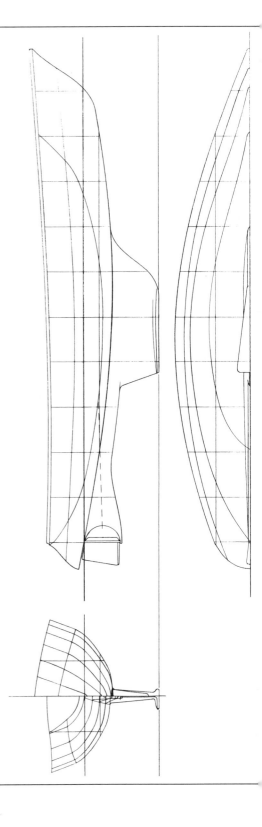

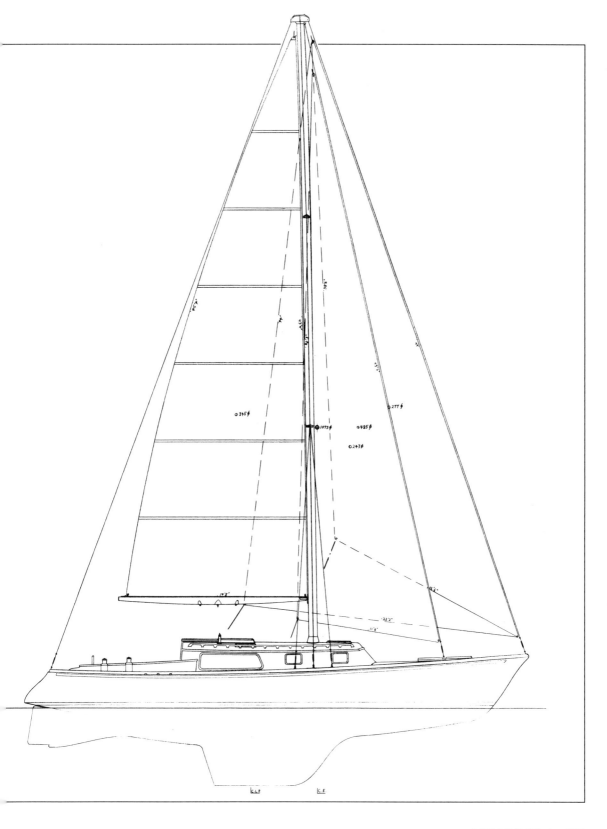

Figure A-6. BLUE WATER 40 (continued).

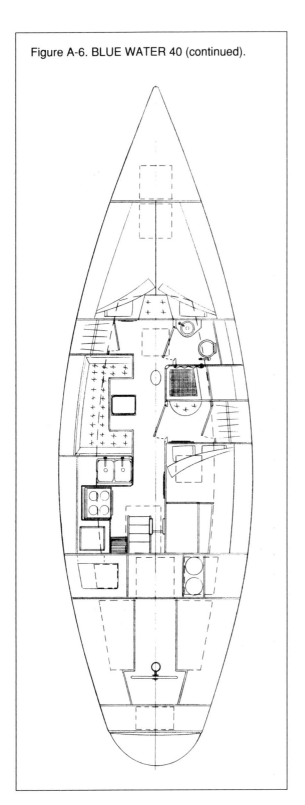

From top left, counterclockwise as follows:
(1) The TERRAPIN 34 Tomfoolery cooking along at 8 knots on a reach. (2) Tomfoolery prior to launch. (3) Teresa's mainmast and fiferail (EXUMA 44). (4) A slide-out cutting board above a bank of galley drawers. (5) Teresa's navigation station and electric panel.
(6) Teresa's main salon and fold-out table.

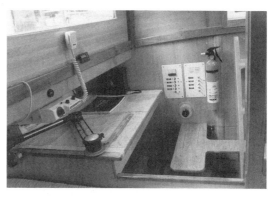

Figure A-7. SCOW SCHOONER 44

L.O.D.	44'0"
L.W.L.	42'3"
L.O.A.	50'9"
L. EXT.	61'0"
BEAM	14'0"
DRAFT	2'9"
SAIL AREA	1,143 sq. ft.
DISPLACEMENT	44,531 lbs., laden for cruising trim. 36,000 lbs., light sailing trim with ballast.
BALLAST	10,000 lbs. for yacht use; none for cargo use.
CARGO CAPACITY	10 U.S. tons; 500 cu. ft.
RIG	Gaff schooner.
POWER	Inboard diesel 50 h.p.

TYPE

Cruising yacht/cargo carrier/passenger carrier.

ACCOMMODATIONS

Layout shown sleeps 3 in aft cabin (two in double) and 4 in double berths in fo'c'sle.

CONSTRUCTION

Cold-molded Douglas fir and marine plywood covered with epoxy impregnated Xynole-polyester cloth. Masts hollow hexagonal laminated Douglas fir; booms and gaffs solid Douglas fir. Rig designed to be easily dropped (masts in tabernacles) for river and canal work (bridges). Finished hull thickness: 2 1/8". No frames or floors are used. Yellow pine can be used in place of fir, including ply, which can be yellow pine form-ply.

OPTIONS

Other layouts, cabins, deck arrangements including twin houses or continuous trunk cabin available on request. For cargo carrier diesel would be located under cockpit sole utilizing Vee-drive and tankage aft. For cruising yacht, diesel would utilize a hydraulic pump and motor and would be located in hold, as would tankage, generator, tools, and cruising gear. Hold can also be fitted with pipe berths. Complete plans, including construction drawings and sequential photographs, can be purchased for $500. Vessels can be purchased at any stage of construction from bare hull to sail-away.

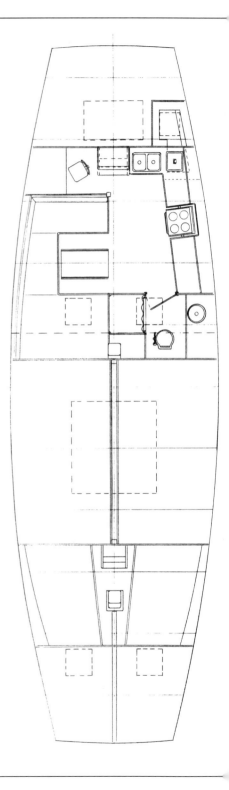

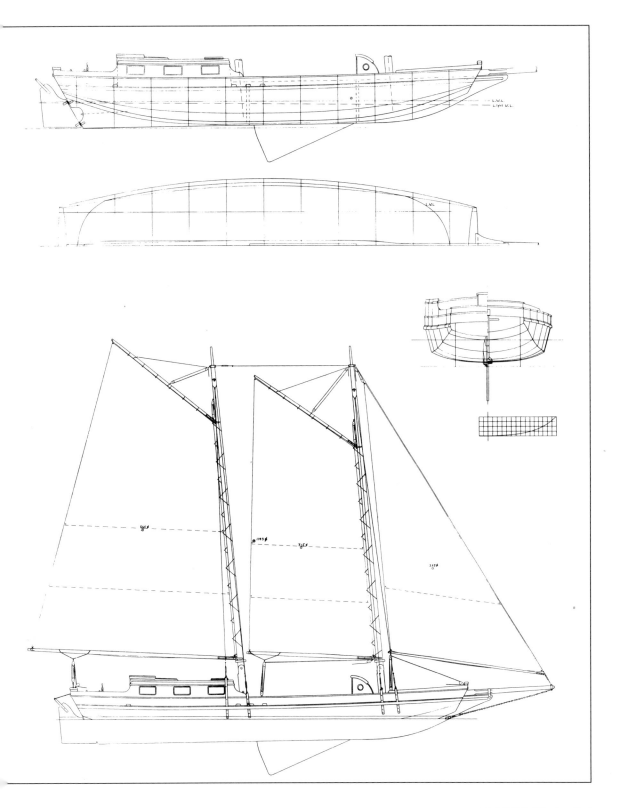

Figure A-8. PILOT 45 schooner

L.O.A.	46'4"
L.O.D.	44'
L. EXT.	69'4"
L.W.L.	41'1"
BEAM	13'10"
DISPLACEMENT	34,300 lbs. (17.15 U.S. tons).
BALLAST	14,000 lbs., lead.

TYPE

Full keel pilot schooner yacht based on Isaac Webb's Dream (1833).

POWER

Four-cylinder diesel, 50 to 80 h.p., under bridge deck.

RIG

Free-standing gaff rigged schooner with overlapping fores'l, self-tending jib, and fisherman tops'l. Jib is set flying; luff tension is provided by downhaul. Jib is lowered by luffing up, releasing halyard and downhaul, and stuffing the sail and club-foot into the fore-hatch.

SAIL AREA

1,265 working/1,670 total square feet.

ACCOMMODATIONS

Interior shown sleeps 8 to 10. Master cabin is aft, with navigation station. Both cabins have a head and shower. This is a comfortable, luxurious vessel for her size, capable of extended ocean cruising anywhere in the world. Water capacity is 220 gallons. Fuel capacity is 40 gallons.

CONSTRUCTION

Cold-molded wood/epoxy/fabric: Hull—double diagonal 3/8" marine ply planks over 3/4" tongue and groove lumber. Inside Kevlar covered below the water; outside Xynole-polyester covered. Decks—double laminated 3/8" ply over sawn beams, Xynole-polyester covered. Teak overlays are glue-laminated without fasteners. Masts are hollow hexagonal free-standing Douglas fir: booms and gaffs are solid Douglas fir. Interior—painted plywood trimmed with varnished hardwoods.

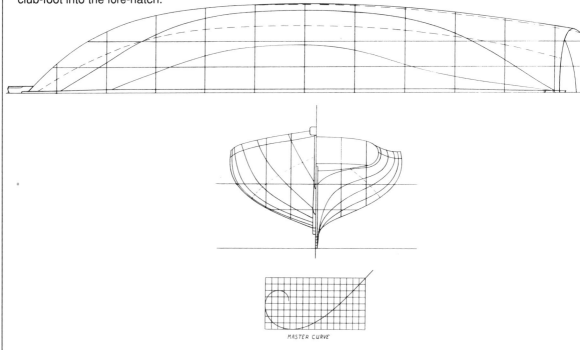

MASTER CURVE

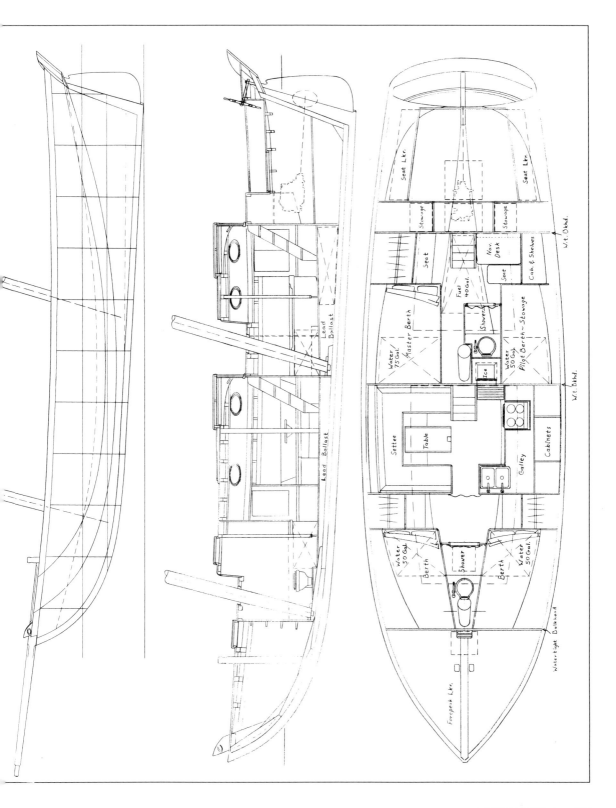

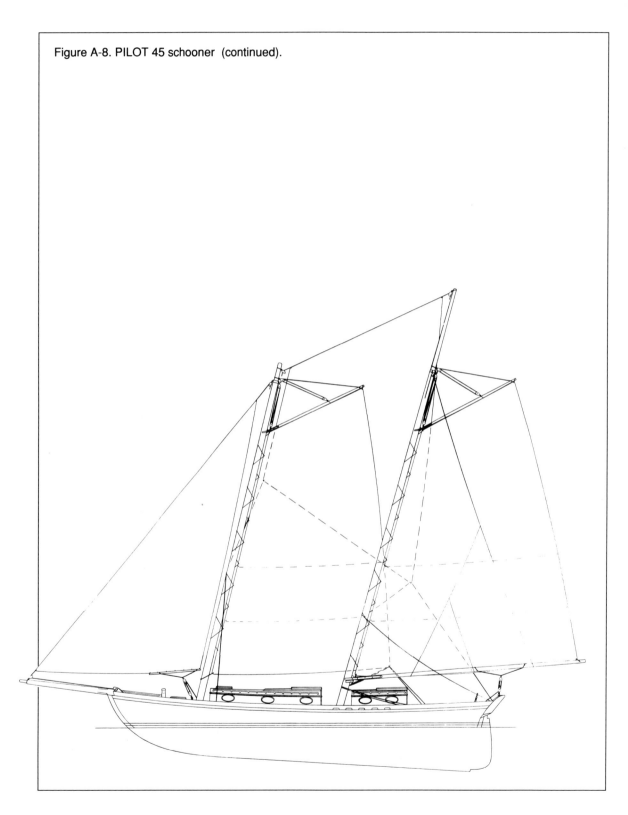

APPENDIX B

THE TEMPORARY BUILDING

Everyone has a version of a temporary building; mine is very simple. The dimensional parameters are the size of the boat and of locally available poly tarps. When luck is with you, the hardware store carries tan tarps up to 20 by 40 feet. More often you'll have to settle for blue tarps that are 20 by 24 feet—sometimes even smaller.

I like my boat sheds to be one and one-half to two times the boat's beam if possible—wider if I plan to keep tools in the shed. The shed roof is usually 19 feet wide and 5 to 10 feet longer than the hull. If you can't get tarps long enough to cover the frame—poly tarps' finished sizes are 6 to 12 inches smaller than the "cut" sizes in which they are sold—use as many tarps as you need, overlapping them several feet.

I build simple gable frames out of 2 x 4s and place the frames about eight feet apart. I join the frames along the top with a 2 x 4 ridge pole and at the rafter ends with 2 x 4 face boards. Two-by-four studs support the gables.

Photo B-1. Make gable frames from 2 x 4s and place them about eight feet apart.

Photo B-2. Use a 2 x 4 ridge pole to join frames along the top.

Photo B-3. Two-by-four face boards join the frames at the rafter ends.

Photo B-4. Fasten poly tarps to the frame with lath that is pneumatically stapled over the perimeters.

I join the rafters with plywood gussets which I either glue (using yellow carpenter's glue, aliphatic resin) and staple or nail on both sides. The rafter heads are separated by the ridge pole, and the gussets are fastened just below the pole so as to support it.

I make the studs about seven feet high, which is just high enough so that a tall man can carry a sheet of plywood under the edge of the roof without having to bend his knees. (Similar practicality calls for gable peaks to be high enough that boatbuilders can walk on the boat's deck without having to stoop.) I gusset the studs to the rafters at or near their ends. Then I dig shallow holes for the studs and pour about one-half to one cubic foot of concrete around the foot of each one. At this

stage, I position the tarps and fasten them with lath pneumatically stapled over their perimeters.

In southern Florida weather conditions allow us a great deal more freedom than anywhere in the United States, except southern California, Hawaii, and Puerto Rico. We can work outdoors year-round in 70- to 85-degree temperatures with very little rain. Hence I make my buildings open on all sides, occasionally hanging tarps to windward during showers. The resulting air circulation is ideal for work in sawdust and epoxy fumes, which are virtually innocuous in the open air, and the natural light is best for any work.

My work crew and I use two buildings during boat construction—one for the shop and one for the boat. The shop measures 19 feet by 23 feet and the boathouse is 19 feet by 40 feet or longer. Gable frames are added or subtracted as needed.

The shop has two workbenches, one along each side; the woodworking bench is 4 feet by 8 feet and the paint/epoxy bench is 3 feet by 8 feet. At one end of the shop are the table saw and planer, staggered so as not to interfere with each other. At the other end is the tool trailer, which can be locked (security is not a problem here however). We store lumber above the woodworking bench and plywood behind the bench or in unit stacks outside under tarps. Fasteners and clamps are stored under the bench. We store paints under the paint/epoxy bench and keep trays, roller frames, covers, brushes and related supplies on a shelf above the bench. Epoxy is stored on a drum rack or low shelf near the paint bench. We have about 10 saw horses with staging and plywood tables, which we can set up when and where needed. These we often place downwind from other work areas, particularly when we will be generating sawdust or fumes. The whole area is kept clean, orderly and as simple as possible.

APPENDIX C

TIME AND MATERIALS LABOR SHEETS FOR *TERESA* (EXUMA 44)—1985

Materials and Costs

$ 4,770 . . . Solid lumber

$ 3,015 . . . Plywood

$ 8,000 . . . Fasteners, hardware, Xynole-polyester cloth, electrical and plumbing
                        supplies, metal stock, ground tackle, line, blocks, miscellaneous
                        parts and fittings

$ 3,380 . . . Epoxy resin, paint, varnish, oil, application systems and supplies

$ 3,055 . . . Motors, fuel tanks, batteries

$ 3,560 . . . Sails (3)

$ 1,230 . . . Upholstery, fabric, foam (including closed-cell cockpit cushions)

$ 300 . . . Stove, propane tanks, fittings

$ 7,000 . . . Rent, utilities, property maintenance, temporary buildings, building
                        repairs, refuse removal

$ 4,500 . . . Tools (in addition to $30,000 worth of existing tools), tool repair and
                        maintenance, fuel and vehicle maintenance, miscellaneous

$ 1,000 . . . Telephone expenses (for ordering materials)

$ 55,000 . . . Total labor—four workers at $20/hr, $10/hr, $5/hr, and $5/hr—
                        for a total time of 5,500 hours

$ 5,250 . . . Interest on borrowed/invested money

$100,060 . . . Total costs

Times for *Teresa*'s Construction Stages (Four-Person Crew)

Activity	Time Weeks	(Days)	(Hours)
Hull; lofting and site preparation to turning over	7	43	1,376
Hull interior, bulkheads, deck and deck substructure to completion, ice hold, outboard well construction, centerboard trunk	6	37	1,184
Interior furniture, ballast boxes and ballast, centerboard, rudder, cockpit, water tanks, metal work and fittings, hatches	4	26	940
Cabin trunks, coach roofs, skylights, portlights, bulwarks, rubrails	3	18	576
Masts, booms, fife rails, rigging	2	13	416
Paint, varnish and oil work (two-stage system), miscellaneous finish work	3	18	576
Electrical, plumbing, light fixtures, pumps, related work	2	12	384
Total labor time	**27**	**167**	**5,452**

APPENDIX D

SUPPLIERS

The following suppliers are listed by material categories—epoxy; fabrics and upholstery; fasteners; hardware (including propellers); lumber; rope, rigging, and equipment; tarps; tools. The list is by no means definitive; it includes suppliers I have used and some better known ones that are located outside my area. You can find many other sources by reading the advertisements in boating and boatbuilding magazines such as *Small Boat Journal* and *WoodenBoat.*

Epoxy

Chem Tech, 4669 Lander Road, Chagrin Falls, OH 44022; (216) 248-0770

Defender Industries, 255 Main Street, P.O. Box 820, New Rochelle, NY 10801; (914) 632-3001

E-Bond, 501 NE 33 Street, Ft. Lauderdale, FL 33334; (305) 566-6555

Gougeon Brothers, P.O. Box X908, Bay City, MI 48707; street location: 100 Patterson Ave., Bay City, MI; (517) 684-7286

LBI, Inc., 973 North Road (Route 117), Groton, CT 06340; (203) 446-8058 or (800) 231-6537

MRP, 736 NW 8th Ave., Ft. Lauderdale, FL 33311; (305) 462-1155

System Three Resins, P.O. Box 70436, Seattle, WA 98107; (206) 782-7976

Fabrics and Upholstery

Defender Industries—listed under "Epoxy"—sole source for Xynole-polyester fabric

LBI, Inc.—listed under "Epoxy"

Fasteners

Chesapeake Marine Fasteners, P.O. Box 6521, Annapolis, MD 21401; (301) 268-8973 or (800) 526-0658

Jamestown Distributors, 28 Narragansett

Avenue, Jamestown, RI 02835; (401) 423-2520 or (800) 423-0030 (outside RI)

Miami Discount Tool & Hardware, 10890 Quail Roost Drive, Miami, FL 33157; (305) 235-1553

Parker Merrick, 245 SW 32 Street, Ft. Lauderdale, FL 33335; (305) 761-1677 or (800) 432-3700 (Florida only)

Hardware Supplies

A & B Industries, 415 Tamal Plaza, Corte Madera, CA; (800) 422-1301

Boat Yard Equipment, Inc., P.O. Box 749, Hainesport, NJ 08036; (609) 261-0550 (answering service number)

Brass Works Division, P.O. Box 606, Ft. Lauderdale, FL 33302; (305) 467-2515

Corona Brushes Inc., 5065 Savaresa Circle, Tampa, FL 33614; (813) 885-2525

Jamestown Distributors—listed under "Fasteners"

LBI, Inc.—listed under "Epoxy"

Lunenburg Foundry & Engineering, Ltd., P.O. Box 1240, Lunenburg, Nova Scotia, Canada B0J 2C0; (902) 634-8827

Marine Equipment Mart, 3568 SE Dixie Highway, Stuart, FL 33997; (407) 286-5900

P.Y.I., Max-Prop, 6309 Seaview Ave. NW, Seattle, WA 98107; (206) 784-4468; propellers

Miami Discount Tool & Hardware—listed under "Fasteners"

Sailorman, 350 East State Road 84, Ft. Lauderdale, FL 33316; (305) 522-6717; new and used marine equipment.

Shell Lumber & Hardware, 2733 SW 27 Avenue, Coconut Grove, FL 33133; (305) 856-6401

United Marine, 1400 NW 159 Street, Miami, FL 33169; (305) 620-4111 or (800) 432-8575; KGS, South & Phillips.

West Marine Products, P. O. Box 1020, Watsonville, CA 95077; street location: 500 West Ridge Drive, Watsonville; 408-728-2700; (800) 538-0775 (outside CA)

Lumber

Atlantic Lumber, 6805 NW 25 Street, Miami, FL 33122; (305) 871-7103

Boulter Plywood Corporation, 24 Broadway, Somerville, MA 02145; (617) 666-1340

Dixie Ply, 3561 NW 54 Street, Miami, FL 33142; (305) 633-8141/525-7515 or (800) 432-9767 (Florida only)

Dantzler Lumber, 1451 SE 9 Court, Hialeah, FL 33010; (305) 887-7373

Georgia Pacific Lumber, 3201 NW 110 Street, Miami, FL 33168; (305) 688-6603

Harbor Sales Company, 1400 Russell Street, Baltimore, MD 21230; (301) 727-0106

Hardwoods, Inc., 760 NW 72 Street, Miami, FL 33150; (305) 836-3381

Hudson Marine Plywood Company, P.O. Box 1184, 30244 County Road 12, Elkhart, IN 46515; (219) 262-3666

Maurice Condon Lumber, 260 Ferris Avenue, White Plains, NY 10603; (914) 946-4111

Shell Lumber & Hardware—listed under "Hardware Supplies"

Paint

Coast Auto Paint & Supply, 1200 Bell Avenue, Ft. Pierce, FL 34982; (407) 465-4031

Jamestown Distributors—listed under "Fasteners"

LBI, Inc.—listed under "Epoxy"

Sherwin-Williams, Commercial Branch, 805 NW 5 Avenue, Ft. Lauderdale, FL 33311; (305) 940-8824

United Marine—listed under "Hardware Supplies"

Rope, Rigging, and Equipment

Atlantic & Gulf Fishing Supply, 7000 NW 74th Avenue, Miami, FL 33166; (800) 432-3888 (Florida only), (800) 327-6167 (rest of U.S.A.); rope, chain, net, gloves, foul weather gear.

Boat Yard Equipment Co., Inc.—listed under "Fasteners"

Edison International, 460 Industrial Park Road, New Bedford, MA 02745; (508) 995-9711

Jamestown Distributors—listed under "Fasteners"

Lunenburg Foundry & Engineering, Ltd.—listed under "Hardware Supplies"

Miami Cordage, 3890 NW 132 Street, Opa Locka, FL 33054; (305) 769-1111 or (800) 432-7707 (Florida only)

New Found Metals, Inc., 240 Airport Road, Port Townsend, WA 98368; (206) 385-3315 (answering machine)

United Marine—listed under "Hardware Supplies"

West Marine Products—listed under "Hardware Supplies"

Tarps

Jamestown Distributors—listed under "Fasteners"

Poly-Steel Shelters, 1209 E. Ocean Blvd., Stuart, FL 34996; (407) 287-9294

Tools

Boat Yard Equipment, Inc.—listed under "Fasteners"

Garret Wade Co., Inc., 161 6th Avenue, New York, NY 10013; (212) 807-1155

Jamestown Distributors—listed under "Fasteners"

LBI, Inc.—listed under "Epoxy"

Woodcraft Supply Corporation, 41 Atlantic Avenue, Box 4000, Woburn, MA 01888; (617) 935-5860

Woodworkers Supply, Inc., 5604 Alameda Place NE, Albuquerque, NM 87113; (505) 821-0500

APPENDIX E

REPAIRING COLD-MOLDED BOATS

Cold-molded boats are simple and economical to repair and maintain, particularly when compared with other types of construction. Tools and materials for cold-molding can usually be found in most boatyards and can be carried on board long-range cruising or commercial vessels intending to travel to remote areas.

Repairs for cold-molded boats can use a greater variety of materials than those for steel, aluminum, ferrocement, and fiberglass boats. Even wooden, plank-on-frame hulls have specific wood requirements, which often make repairs complicated and expensive. By contrast, almost any wood can be used to repair a cold-molded hull without compromising its integrity or requiring a repair that must be corrected later.

Epoxy requirements are the method's major challenge. Many types and brands of epoxy may be used in repair work, however other resins do not substitute well. For example, plastic resins and urea-formaldehyde glues used in wood lamination do not have the gap-filling or user-friendly qualities of epoxy, nor can they be used in conjunction with fabric coverings. Obviously, the owner of a cold-molded boat must carry epoxy and related supplies when cruising. (Epoxy resins, catalysts, and reducers are toxic and corrosive chemicals so thought and planning should go into their storage on board.)

Carry some of the fabric used to protect the hull and decks. Even though it is inexpensive, it could be difficult to find in some ports and it is easy to store on board.

A basic hand tool kit, augmented by four power tools (and electricity to run them), can repair extensive damage on virtually all cold-molded hulls. The router is the most useful power tool; it is by far the fastest and easiest to use, although other tools can perform its work. Another really helpful tool is the low-speed body grinder with a softpad. The final two power tools—the circular saw and the drill motor—tend to be in most collections anyway.

Types of Damage

Damage to cold-molded hulls falls into one of five categories: planking damage; internal structural damage; surface damage; deck problems, and rot.

Planking damage is usually caused by severe or prolonged grounding on rock or coral, collision, explosion, fire, or lightning. In a vessel damaged at sea, the first step is to assess the extent of the damage and make an emergency repair. This may consist of stuffing a mattress in the hole, covering the damaged area from outside with a tarp or sail, or nailing a plywood patch over the hole. If the vessel is in adverse circumstances or the crew is injured, things get complicated. My own experiences and opinions have made me a strong believer in self-reliance and survivalism, therefore I carry emergency supplies and make sure my crew knows where they are and how to use them.

Emergency supplies should always include an assortment of scrap plywood in a variety of sizes from doorskin pieces smaller than a square foot to 1/4-inch and 3/8-inch plywood pieces as large as 2 feet by 4 feet.

Most hull damage must be repaired from the outside, so keep diving gear handy. Unappealing as it may sound, jumping in the water during a storm at sea to nail a patch on your hull after a collision beats losing your boat. With a safety harness and lots of adrenalin, the job can be done, even at night. Nighttime repairs will require an underwater light and probably someone to hold it for you (often from on deck). Carry a sharp diving knife and tie a lanyard between the hammer handle and your wrist. If possible, maneuver the boat so the damage is on the lee side, and go overboard on that side. If under sail, heave to or lie a-hull first, making as little headway as possible. A vessel with at least a riding sail is easier to work on than one pitching and rolling in a seaway. Attach a lifeline as far forward of the work area as possible, and have someone on deck tend to your needs, if feasible.

After a quick exploratory dive to determine the size of the patch needed (measure with your arm), prepare a patch by presetting nails around the plywood perimeter about every two inches and apply a liberal coat of tar or bedding compound. Get in the water and have someone hand the patch to you (this way you'll be less likely to lose it). If the hull has a lot of curve, try to nail the corner over the most curve first, and work the patch into place by driving the nails alternately along the two edges coming out of the corner; don't nail around the perimeter in one direction. You will be surprised how much compound curve can be worked into a plywood panel. After the emergency patch is in place, you must void the hull of water and check for leaking.

This information is not theoretical; I have performed this repair myself to the 44-foot cat schooner *Teresa*. Fortunately I wasn't at sea, it was during daylight, and the water was flat, calm, and warm. However, more than once I have been in the water at sea, at night, during violent squalls, when it was cold. Perhaps the only positive revelation is that you can be surprisingly more comfortable in the water than on deck, at least physically. I would rate the task of nailing on a large patch underwater as approximately equal to that of freeing a badly fouled propeller; they both take 5 or 10 dives using snorkle gear.

Photo E-1 shows the hole in Teresa's hull bottom, and Photo E-2 shows the plywood patch I nailed on underwater. The repair took about five minutes, after the patch was prepared. My patch on *Teresa* didn't leak one drop and could have remained in place for months before making a proper repair.

The hole was caused by lightning, one of the few things capable of putting a hole

Photo E-1. A lightning strike made this hole in *Teresa*'s hull.

Photo E-2. The author made an emergency repair using a plywood patch.

through a heavily built cold-molded hull. (*Teresa*'s bottom is a triple-lamination 1½ inches thick, consisting of an inner layer of 5/8-inch tongue-and-groove Douglas fir covered by two opposing diagonal layers of 3/8-inch marine plywood.) The lightning traveled down the mast wiring to the batteries, through the batteries and the battery boxes, and then through the hull. Nothing in line above the batteries was damaged; everything below was destroyed in a direct path to the water. Had the ground wires led to the water and a ground plate, there would have been no damage. Later I installed a 12-inch diameter copper plate beneath each mast and grounded a #6 copper wire to each through a 5/16-inch bronze carriage bolt. This simple protection system was within hours of completion at the time of the lightning strike and would have been finished during the next haulout.

Repairing damage at or above the waterline is similar and, of course, easier to do. A sail or tarp can substitute for plywood in some cases, by coating it with tar (roof cement) and tacking, stapling or even tying it in place. Water pressure will help hold fabric over a hole in the hull once it is positioned and the wrinkles are smoothed out.

The time to assess damage and make a

Photo E-3. The proper patching begins with cutting out the hole. The text give a detailed explanation of this process.

final repair plan is after the vessel has been hauled out and any emergency patches removed. In general, the hull's repair should be similar to its construction—i.e., planking should be of the same dimensions and lie in the same direction as that which it replaces.

The repair to *Teresa*'s hull was simple. Photo E-3 shows the cut-out hole ready to be patched. The inner plank layer was cut out parallel and perpendicular to the grain. The ends (perpendicular cuts) were made right to the edges of the bulkheads that defined the battery compartment. Instead of putting numerous tongue-and-groove planks in the inner layer, I was able to simply install a short length of 5/8-inch by 12-inch Douglas fir plank. Although the hull had compound curves in this area, they were so slight that I was able to deform the plank to the desired curve by gently applying pressure from inside with a hydraulic jack. I installed temporary posts and wedges alongside the jack in case it lost pressure during the repair (it didn't). The total required deformation was less than 1/4 inch I also installed cleats between the inner plank layer and both adjacent bulkheads, to insure that the patch could never be pushed into the hull (this was probably unnecessary; but it was so easy to do that it couldn't hurt, and there was not enough room to cut scarfs). The intermediate and outer layers were installed together, immediately after the first layer was in place. Both of these layers consisted of single pieces of 3/8-inch marine plywood. All layers were prefit, predrilled for screws, and ready to be installed simultaneously. Predrilling is always a good idea; it keeps epoxy off your twist drills and bits. I use Fuller bits for drilling holes, and I install the screws with a hardened slot-head bit in a half-inch, variable-speed, reversing drill motor.

After the patch cured, I feathered the cloth covering back four to six inches and laid on a new skin of epoxy-impregnated Xynole-polyester cloth (see Photo E-4). The discoloration around the perimeter of the patch is a fairing compound made from epoxy and microballoons. After sanding the area smooth with a bodygrinder and softpad, I applied a coat of Sherwin-Williams Tile-Clad II Hi-Bild epoxy primer (matching the original), followed by three coats of bottom paint. When I removed my bracing and jack inside the hull, I detected perhaps 1/32 inch of "spring back." From outside, the repaired area conforms perfectly to the shape of the hull, and after three years no one has any idea that there was ever a large ugly hole in the hull. Even

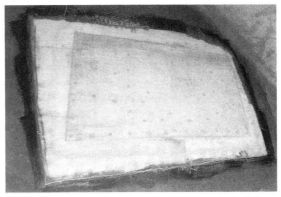

Photo E-4. A new skin of epoxy-impregnated cloth covers the patch. The discoloration around the perimeter is a fairing compound made of epoxy and microballoons.

the sharpest surveyor may never know, simply because the repair is as good as the original. The repair took four days, including the painting; but the labor time during the last two of those days was only two hours each.

Whenever repairing surface damage, grind away all of the paint before laminating new material in place. Epoxy and primers will not stick to bottom paint. Clean all surfaces by removing dust with compressed air or a tack rag and by wiping with a clean rag moistened with acetone or toluene. Paint layers should be similar to existing ones, particularly below the waterline. I use epoxy high-build primers (see above) and high-copper vinyl-type bottom paints such as Interlux Super Vinyl-Lux antifouling paint. Above the waterline, paint systems will depend on whether the topsides have been covered with fabric and epoxy. If they have, I prefer to use linear polyurethane primers and finishes such as Awlgrip, Imron or Sherwin-Williams Polane H.S. My second choice is high-gloss industrial or marine enamel applied over a high-build primer such as Z-Spar Hi-Hide Enamel Undercoat. Uncovered wood topsides should be treated in an entirely different manner, as wood expands, contracts and flexes to a much larger degree than epoxy-impregnated cloth. Dobber, the old-timer who taught me how to really paint, said "use a hard paint on a hard surface and a soft paint on a soft surface." I have found that most modern paint systems fare poorly when applied to wood; they crack, blister, peel, delaminate and cannot be sanded to a feathered edge when touching up or repainting. As a result I prefer heavy oil-based enamels such as Dutch Boy's porch and floor enamel. I thin the first coat (when applying to bare wood) about 10 percent with mineral spirits, thicken the next two or three coats with talc to make a sanding primer, and finish up with two coats of full-strength enamel with a little Floods Penetrol added to help the paint flow. When two people are available, I have one person apply the paint with a 3/8-inch nap, nine-inch roller (best quality available); the other person follows immediately with a large soft bristle brush or sponge brush smoothing the paint out. Do this on a cool, cloudy day or in the shade.

Rot is less prevalent in cold-molded construction than in conventional boatbuilding, but it does occur. The most common locations are in trunk cabins (particularly around windows and portlights), bulwark caps and bulwarks, mast partners and masts (especially under spreader fittings), deck beams and decks (around fastened deck hardware and in teak-overlaid decks), and along bilge stringers. Repair procedures are similar to those for conventional boats in most cases. Epoxy, as wonderful as it is, cannot be thought of as a panacea for all rot problems. I have seen and repaired rot damage that was completely encased in epoxy except for one fresh-water and air entry point—usually a screw or bolt hole. For this reason I recommend drilling all bolt holes oversize and carefully epoxy sealing the inside of the hole or sleeving it with PVC pipe that is epoxy-glued in place.

Repair damage around windows and port-lights by replacing damaged wood using epoxy glue, thoroughly sealing all wood edges with epoxy (use extra coats on end-grain), and applying bedding compound liberally to all mating surfaces (not just one). Take care not to trap air voids during installation, and use bedding compound on the screws before insertion.

After repairing damage to bulwarks and caps, seal the mating surfaces of these wood components with epoxy, varnish, or paint. Apply bedding compound to both mating surfaces and fasteners. Epoxy the bungs in place, taking care to align their grain to that of the cap.

Deck and mast hardware often shift under the high loads imposed on them, allowing water to get past bedding compound. One solution is to mount hardware on phenolic blocks and sleeve all bolt holes with PVC pipe epoxied in place. The hardware, blocking and through-bolts should all be well bedded in a synthetic rubber bedding compound such as 3M #5200 or Sikaflex. The most common rot problem area is the teak-overlaid deck. As the teak wears thin, the bungs become loose and water travels down the fasteners. The deck layer beneath, be it plywood or diagonal-planking, and the deck beams also eventually rot. Solutions are difficult, expensive, and often ineffective since the problem is built-in and self-perpetuating. I usually recommend removing the teak overlay to facilitate thorough repairs to the deck layer beneath. If the boat owner still wants a teak deck, I recommend covering the deck first with epoxy-impregnated Xynole-polyester fabric, then installing a new teak overlay using no fasteners (see Chapter 14). Holes drilled through the deck for hardware should be sealed or sleeved as described above. Screws that must penetrate both the overlay and deck beneath (such as for fastening bulwarks or toerails) should be coated with bedding compound. The flexible qualities of epoxy-impregnated Xynole-polyester decrease the likelihood of leaking because the holes in the cloth will tend to seal around the fasteners.

Rot in bilge stringers is caused by fresh water being trapped above them; early cold-molded powerboats in particular have this problem. It is aggravated by the absence of limber holes, plugged limber holes, and poor paint systems. My solutions include drilling large limber holes at the low points along the stringers (big enough to stick your finger through), sistering the stringers or scarfing in new segments, epoxy-sealing and thoroughly painting all woodwork (be thorough in the limber holes).

It is my own conviction, after years of repairing boats built of all materials, that well-designed, built and maintained cold-molded wooden boats are by far the best all-around boats ever devised. They are lower in maintenance and damage is generally easier and faster to repair than for other hull materials.

APPENDIX F

FABRIC COVERINGS FOR COLD-MOLDED BOATS

The rapidly evolving technologies used by the marine industry have provided builders of cold-molded wooden boats with a whole new spectrum of fabrics for covering, reinforcing and laminating—both for new construction and repairs.

Fiberglass has been, and remains, the most widely used fabric. But new combinations of laminates, beyond the industry standard mat, woven roving and cloths, have come on the market. Examples of these are combination chopped strand and roving, unidirectional sewn fabric, bi-ply roving and mat, and extremely light sheathing layers such as Veilmat (10 mils thick) and Ultrathin (3/4-ounce "angel hair"), as well as the new multidirectional weaves. The addition of carbon fiber compensates for fiberglass' lack of high-tensile strength.

Kevlar has become a popular high-strength reinforcing and laminating material. It is often applied to the inside of cold-molded and plywood hulls. Bill Knowles, a Stewart, Florida, builder of custom sportfishing boats, once told me that during a turning-over accident he saw a cable carve into a cold-molded hull and stop dead when it hit the Kevlar that had been applied to the hull's inside.

For outside skin protective covering systems, polypropylene, Dynel (acrylic), and Xynole-polyester have become the popular alternatives to glass. And none of them make the builder itch! All three are more flexible than fiberglass cloth, and have higher tensile strength per unit weight and better abrasion resistance. Impregnated with epoxy, they are not as stiff as glass and therefore not as brittle. When compared with fiberglass, all three of the aforementioned "wet out" more rapidly and thoroughly, and have higher peel strength from wood and better impact resistance. They are also more expensive; however, since they weigh less than glass for finished thickness and comparative strengths, they may cost slightly less in application.

Polypropylene and Dynel commonly are available in 4-ounce weights; Xynole-polyester in 4.2-ounce weight. Polypropylene and Xynole-polyester come in 60-inch widths; Dynel comes in a 63-inch width.

When resin-saturated, these lightweight cloths bulk up to the thickness of 8- to 10-ounce glass cloth. Polypropylene is the lightest of the three and has a tendency to "float" during resin saturation, a characteristic that makes overhead work difficult. All three fabrics tend to get a little fuzzy during grinding, hence it pays to work neatly to minimize the need for grinding.

My favorite fabric covering has become Xynole-polyester. It conforms to shapes that have severe compound curves, loses its fuzziness after a fresh coat of resin (following the first grinding or feathering) and is simply user-friendly. Three coats of epoxy resin applied with 3/8-inch nap rollers saturate the cloth. Two coats seal it thoroughly but leave a deep texture that has good non-skid properties and the attractive look of traditional canvas deck covering.

Fairing can be done with epoxy resin and various combinations of the common thixogens Cabosil, microballoons and talc. Each thixogen makes special demands: Cabosil has the least sag but is the hardest to sand; microballoons are expensive, and talc must be kept very dry.

The best paint systems for use with fabric coverings are two-part polyurethanes—such as Awlgrip, Imron and Polane HS—over epoxy, or polyurethane primers.

An excellent poor man's alternative to the three fabrics already discussed and a good covering material for plywood decks, houses and coachroofs is Yellowjacket, a polypropylene-coated lightweight glass cloth. It can be used with Arabol—a latex rubber lagging compound—and painted with rubber, epoxy or even oil-base house paints such as urethane reinforced porch and floor enamel. Yellowjacket can also be used with epoxy.

Please note that no thin layer of cloth and epoxy applied over a conventional planked boat will be strong enough to withstand the working of a planked hull or deck in a seaway. A planked hull first needs splines glued between the planks; then it must be sheathed either with diagonal wood planking or with several layers of reasonably heavy cloth bonded with epoxy prior to a final "skin" coat.

Most of the products described in this appendix are available from your local industrial suppliers, however Xynole-polyester fabric may be hard to find. I know it is available from Defender Industries, which is listed in Appendix D. Yellowjacket and Arabol can be purchased from Doc Freeman's (999 North Northlake Way, Seattle, WA 98103; (206) 633-1500).

SUGGESTED READING LIST

Although some of these books are out-of-print, they may be available through your library or from a used/out-of-print book dealer, who specializes in boating books.

Adrift by Tristan Jones. New York: Avon Books, 1983. (I recommend all of Jones's books.)

After Fifty Thousand Miles by Hal Roth. New York: W. W. Norton & Co., Inc., 1977.

The American Fishing Schooners: 1825-1935 by Howard I. Chapelle. New York: W. W. Norton & Co., Inc., 1973.

American Sailing Craft by Howard I. Chapelle. New York: Bonanza Books, 1936.

American Small Sailing Craft by Howard I. Chapelle. New York: W. W. Norton & Co., Inc., 1951.

Boatbuilding by Howard I. Chapelle. New York: W. W. Norton & Co., Inc., 1941.

The Boat That Wouldn't Float by Farley Mowatt. New York: Bantam Books, Inc., 1981. (I recommend all of Mowatt's books.)

The Commodore's Story by Ralph Munroe Middleton and Vincent Gilpin. New York: Washburn, 1930 and reprinted by The Historical Association of Southern Florida, 1966.

The Encyclopedia of Knots and Fancy Rope Work by Raoul Graumont and John Hensel. New York: Cornell Maritime, 1952.

Gaff Rig by John Leather. Camden, ME: International Marine Publishing Co., 1989.

The Good Little Ship by Vincent Gilpin. Newtown Square, PA: Harrowood Books, reprint of 1952 edition.

Gougeon Brothers on Boat Construction: Wood and WEST System Materials by Gougeon Bros., Inc. Bay City, MI: Gougeon Bros., Inc., 1985.

The History of American Sailing Ships by Howard I. Chapelle. New York: Bonanza Books, 1935.

John G. Alden and His Yacht Designs by Robert Carrick and Richard Henderson. Camden, ME: International Marine Publishing Co., 1983.

Modern Wooden Yacht Construction by John Guzzwell. Camden, ME: International Marine Publishing Co., 1979.

The National Watercraft Collection by Howard I. Chapelle. Washington, DC: Smithsonian Institute Press and Camden, ME: International Marine Publishing Co., 1966.

Oceanography and Seamanship by William G. Van Dorn. New York: Dodd, Mead & Co., 1974.

The Ocean Sailing Yacht, Volumes I and II, by Donald M. Street, Jr. New York: W. W. Norton & Co., Inc., 1973 and 1979.

Pete Culler's Boats: The Complete Design Catalog by John Burke. Camden, ME: International Marine Publishing Co., 1984.

The Rigger's Apprentice by Brion Toss. Camden, ME: International Marine Publishing Co., 1985.

Sailing Yacht Design by Douglas Phillips-Birt. London: Adlard Coles Ltd., 1976.

The Search for Speed Under Sail: 1700-1855 by Howard I. Chapelle. New York: W. W. Norton & Co., Inc., 1967.

Sensible Cruising Designs by L. Francis Herreshoff. Camden, ME: International Marine Publishing Co., 1973.

Skene's Elements of Yacht Design, revised by Francis F. Kinney. New York: Dodd, Mead & Co., 1981.

Skiffs and Schooners by R. D. Culler. Camden, ME: International Marine Publishing Co., 1974 and Ann Arbor, MI: Books on Demand UMI, no date.

Yacht Designing and Planning by Howard I. Chapelle (revised edition). New York: W. W. Norton & Co., Inc., 1971.

INDEX